Peer-to-Peer File Sharing and Secondary Liability in Copyright Law

Peer-to-Peer File Sharing and Secondary Liability in Copyright Law

Edited by

Alain Strowel

Professor, Facultés Universitaires Saint-Louis, Brussels and University of Liège, Avocat, Belgium

Edward Elgar

Cheltenham, UK • Northampton, MA, USA

Published by
Edward Elgar Publishing Limited
The Lypiatts
15 Lansdown Road
Cheltenham
Glos GL50 2JA
UK

Edward Elgar Publishing, Inc.
William Pratt House
9 Dewey Court
Northampton
Massachusetts 01060
USA

A catalogue record for this book
is available from the British Library

Library of Congress Control Number: 2009922756

PEFC
PEFC/16-33-111
CATG-PEFC-052
www.pefc.org

ISBN 978 1 84720 562 9

Typeset by Cambrian Typesetters, Camberley, Surrey
Printed and bound in Great Britain by the MPG Books Group

Contents

Contributors

Graeme W. Austin is the J. Byron McCormick Professor of Law at the University of Arizona. He holds a J.S.D. and LL.M. from Columbia University and is a graduate of Victoria University of Wellington. Born in New Zealand, where he practiced commercial law and was a senior lecturer at the University of Auckland, his work focuses on cross-border intellectual property issues. He recently served as advisor to the American Law Institute Project on Intellectual Property, Principles Governing Jurisdiction, Choice of Law, and Judgments in Transnational Disputes, and is co-author of *International Intellectual Property: Law and Policy* (2nd ed.). He also teaches regularly as a visiting professor at the University of Melbourne, Australia.

Robert Clark is an Associate Professor of Law at the School of Law, University College Dublin. Since 1992, he has been the Irish national representative in the European Commission Copyright Experts Group and is a member of the Irish government's Internet Advisory Board and the Patent Office Users Council. He is the founder and chair of the Irish ALAI group (1996). Since 1999, Robert has been employed as a consultant to the leading Irish law firm Arthur Cox where he specialises in intellectual property and information technology law. He is the co-author (with Shane Smyth) of *Intellectual Property Law in Ireland*, now in its second edition, and is the author of *Irish Copyright and Design Law*, both of which are currently published by Tottel.

Graeme B. Dinwoodie is Professor of Law, Associate Dean, and Director of the Program in Intellectual Property Law at Chicago-Kent College of Law. He also holds a Chair in Intellectual Property Law at Queen Mary College, University of London. Professor Dinwoodie has authored numerous articles on intellectual property law. He holds a First Class Honours LL.B. degree from the University of Glasgow, an LL.M. from Harvard Law School, where he was a John F. Kennedy Scholar, and a J.S.D. from Columbia Law School, where he was a Burton Fellow. He was elected to membership in the American Law Institute in 2003.

Allen N. Dixon is a lawyer who has represented the intellectual property interests of the technology and traditional content industries in various capacities for more than 20 years. He has served in General Counsel and Assistant General Counsel positions in Asia, the US and Europe. As European counsel and partner at Covington & Burling, he was the senior legal advocate of the business software sector on intellectual property matters in Europe in the late 1990s, acting as counsel to the Business Software Alliance and individual software companies. From 2000 to 2005 he was General Counsel and Executive Director of the international recording industry association IFPI. Since 2005, he has been the principal and managing director of International Intellectual Property & Technology Consulting.

Jane C. Ginsburg is the Morton L. Janklow Professor of Literary and Artistic Property Law at Columbia University School of Law, and Co-Director of its Kernochan Center for Law, Media and the Arts. With Professor Sam Ricketson, she is the co-author of *International Copyright and Neighbouring Rights: The Berne Convention and Beyond* (Oxford University Press, 2006). Other books include *Foundations of Intellectual Property* (Foundation Press, 2004) with Professor Robert P. Merges, and *Intellectual Property Stories* (Foundation Press, 2005) with Professor Rochelle Dreyfuss. With Professor Dreyfuss and Professor François Dessemontet, she is also a co-reporter for the American Law Institute Project on Intellectual Property: Principles Governing Jurisdiction, Choice of Law and Judgments in Transnational Disputes.

Vicky Hanley is a UK associate in the Brussels office of Covington & Burling LLP. Her practice involves legislative advocacy and advising on policy-making and legislative processes. Miss Hanley has recently advised leading multinational companies on regulatory issues in areas including intellectual property and telecommunications, including the current review of the electronic communications regulatory framework. She is also an Edmund Davies Scholar of The Honourable Society of Gray's Inn (2002) and a member of the European Bar Group. Recent publications include 'Last-ditch attempt to improve the EU patent system' in the *Journal of Intellectual Property Law & Practice* (September 2007), which she co-authored with Alain Strowel.

Alexander Peukert is Associate Professor of Civil Law, Commercial Law and Intellectual Property Law at the Johann-Wolfgang-Goethe University Frankfurt/Main, Cluster of Excellence 'The Formation of Normative Orders'. He graduated in law (1998) and earned his doctorate in law (1999) from the University of Freiburg. After his second state examination (2001), he worked at a law firm in Berlin, specializing in IP and media law. From 2002 to 2008, he was a senior research fellow at the Max Planck Institute for

Intellectual Property, Competition and Tax Law in Munich. In 2008, he obtained his postdoctoral lecture qualification from the University of Munich.

Jerome H. Reichman is the Bunyan S. Womble Professor of Law at Duke Law School. He has written and lectured widely on the diverse aspects of intellectual property law, including comparative and international intellectual property, and the connection between intellectual property and international trade laws. In collaboration with Keith Maskus, he recently published *International Public Goods and Transfer of Technology Under a Globalized Intellectual Property Regime* (Cambridge Press, 2005). He is a consultant to numerous intergovernmental and nongovernmental organizations, a member of the Board of Editors for the *Journal of International Economic Law*, and also of the Scientific Advisory Board of *il Diritto di Autore* (Rome).

Pamela Samuelson is the Richard M. Sherman '74 Distinguished Professor of Law and Information at the University of California at Berkeley, a Director of the Berkeley Center for Law & Technology and an advisor to the Samuelson High Technology Law & Public Policy Clinic at Boalt Hall. She is a Fellow of the Association for Computing Machinery (ACM), a Contributing Editor of *Communications of the ACM*, a past Fellow of the John D. & Catherine T. MacArthur Foundation, and an Honorary Professor of the University of Amsterdam.

Michael Schlesinger is Of Counsel to Greenberg Traurig. His practice focuses on intellectual property with an emphasis in international copyright law and trademark law. Mr Schlesinger represents the International Intellectual Property Alliance (IIPA) in worldwide copyright legislation and enforcement reform efforts, as well as government affairs and trade-related aspects of intellectual property rights. His regional focus is on Asia, the Middle East and Africa. He works with governments on implementing emerging standards of IP protection, as well as compliance with international intellectual property and trade agreements.

Alain Strowel is a professor at the Saint-Louis University in Brussels, the University of Liège and the Catholic University of Brussels-Leuven, where he teaches copyright, design law and media law. A member of the Brussels Bar since 1988, he graduated in law (1983) and obtained a Ph. D. in law (1992) from the University of Louvain-la-Neuve. Prior to joining the US firm Covington & Burling in 2001, where he concentrates on the IP issues in relation to IT, he worked in the Brussels IP section of the Dutch firm NautaDutilh. He has authored numerous articles and several books, including *Droit d'auteur* *et copyright* (LGDJ and Bruylant, 1993) and *Droit d'auteur et numérique: logiciels, bases de données, multimédia* (Bruylant, 2001) with Estelle Derclaye. He has also edited various books including *Of Authors and Origins* (Clarendon Press, 1994) with Brad Sherman, and *Droit d'auteur et liberté d'expression* (Larcier, 2006) with Fr. Tulkens.

Table of cases

Introduction: peer-to-peer file sharing and secondary liability in copyright law

Alain Strowel[1]

Every book has a history. This book originates in a 2005 Brussels conference discussing the impact of peer-to-peer technology on the future of copyright law.[2] Peer-to-peer technology, as further explained below, allows people to exchange information over the Internet via many equal or 'peer' machines linked across a network, rather than on a central server. From a copyright point of view, the main controversy surrounding peer-to-peer networks is whether providers of peer-to-peer technology and services can be liable when users infringe copyright through their networks. This issue has been hotly debated in legal circles and in the press, especially in 2005, when the US Supreme Court issued its highly anticipated decision in the controversial case *MGM Studios, Inc. v Grokster Ltd.*[3] In this decision, the Supreme Court held that the two popular file-sharing networks, Grokster and Streamcast (dba Morpheus), were indeed liable for 'actively inducing' the end-users' acts of infringement. As will be explained, the liability for inducement is one form of secondary liability for copyright infringement.

Peer-to-peer (or P2P) file sharing and secondary liability are the central themes in this collection of essays on copyright. Both topics are closely linked. 'Secondary' (or derived) liability presupposes a primary infringer. In peer-to-peer networks, the primary infringers, those who upload copyrighted files without authorization, are numerous and difficult to reach, and going after them poses many legal and practical issues. Copyright owners thus prefer to direct their legal actions against those who allow or promote direct infringements, for instance, those who operate the peer-to-peer networks or develop

1 The author would like to thank Marisa Kakoulas, Esq. who was tremendously helpful in the preparation and editing of this collection of essays.

2 During this conference organised by the Centre for Intellectual Property and Innovation of the Facultés Universitaires Saint-Louis, Professors Terry Fisher (Harvard Law School), Jane Ginsburg (Columbia Law School) and Bernt Hugenholtz (University of Amsterdam) discussed the influence of peer-to-peer technology with a panel of stakeholders.

3 125 S. Ct. 2764 (2005).

the technical means (in particular the software) to make primary infringements online possible. The development of peer-to-peer networks over the Internet has, therefore, brought the issue of secondary liability to the forefront.

FROM PEER-TO-PEER TECHNOLOGY…

Peer-to-peer technology is quite well known in copyright circles, but at the same time, the variety of applications covered by this broad term is largely ignored. Napster was one of the first P2P networks to become widely known at the end of the 1990s; however, it works quite differently than Grokster or Kazaa, which had their moments of fame in the early 2000s. In general terms, peer-to-peer technology is a decentralized system of computers that are able to interact with each other without the intervention of servers. The computers are linked across a network and act as equal peer nodes, allowing them to share information with each other directly; thus, the computers in the network can act as both server and client. There lies the main difference between Napster-like systems and those like Grokster or Kazaa. While Napster, for example, based its file-sharing services on a centralized indexing system (using a proprietary network protocol), P2P networks like Grokster or Kazaa use a decentralized process called the 'FastTrack', which assigns indexing functions to computers connected in the network, called 'supernodes', when needed. Virtually any computer in the network can be a supernode.

Alexander Peukert best describes the hopes and fears of these P2P networks in his original essay *A Bipolar Copyright System for the Digital Network Environment* (an abbreviated version of this text can be found later in this collection):

> Peer-to-peer networks provide architecture for stable, cheap and global sharing of any digitized information, be it music, movies, software, writings or other data. The end-to-end or peer-to-peer architecture makes it possible for thousands of terabytes to rush through P2P networks every month without anybody having to invest in and provide for a centralized server.[4] The technology features characteristics that prompt great hopes for the advent of the global knowledge community. However, it also terrifies copyright owners to definitely lose control over their works, which for the user of these networks actually seem to be 'free as the air to common use'.

In more current developments in P2P technologies, however, these fears are largely being addressed by working with rights holders and government agen-

---

4 See *MGM Studios, Inc. v Grokster Ltd.*, 125 S. Ct. 2764, 2770 (2005). See 'Streaming Media', *Wired*, June 2004, 148–149 for a discussion on the growth of P2P traffic over the last few years and the content shared.

cies. For example, BitTorrent, a P2P communication protocol that uses trackers and metafiles to coordinate file distribution, has had its share of legal controversy (although no significant case law yet), but in recent years has worked with media companies and organizations to reduce illegal use of its protocol. In 2005, BitTorrent Inc. signed an agreement with the Motion Picture Association of America (MPAA) to collaborate on stopping Internet piracy; specifically, BitTorrent agreed to remove all links to unlicensed copies of movies owned by the seven MPAA studio members. Other ways to reconcile the use of this promising technology with the possibility to protect and remunerate copyright holders are explored.

Despite such progress, copyright infringement online remains ubiquitous, triggering particularly important and fascinating legal discourse extending beyond that of direct infringement to the liability of third parties.

. . . TO SECONDARY LIABILITY IN COPYRIGHT LAW

Although this book is focused on peer-to-peer file sharing, it also addresses other situations and technologies likely to trigger secondary copyright liability, in particular, the situation of Internet intermediaries, such as hosting or access providers, and technologies, such as (dedicated) search engines or hyperlinking. Secondary liability rules are flexible and include doctrines applying to many different circumstances. For instance, in January 2008, the press announced that the Warner Music Group was suing the company Seeqpod, which offers both a search engine and an online music player, for 'direct, contributory and vicarious infringement' of the record label's music.[5] Seeqpod users can search through a virtual 'library' of more than eight million songs hosted in different locations, and then stream those they like (no downloading is involved). Such streaming, Seeqpod claims, is protected 'fair use' under US copyright law.

Contributory and vicarious infringements, discussed by various contributors in this book, are just two forms of secondary liability that US copyright law distinguishes. However, other doctrines and approaches to secondary liability exist, and a number of these contributors offer compelling insight into the way alternative doctrines of secondary liability apply in other countries, for instance, in Europe and Asia.

---

[5] See Antony Bruno, 'WMG Sues Music Search Site Seeqpod', Billboard.biz, 23 Jan. 2008.

AN OVERVIEW OF LEGAL DOCTRINES AND CASE LAW ON SECONDARY LIABILITY

In a contribution entitled 'Liability of Users and Third Parties for Copyright Infringement on the Internet', Allen N. Dixon, an intellectual property and technology consultant with extensive experience in the software and music industry, offers a very comprehensive overview of the international developments on the different rules that extend copyright liability to those who encourage, assist or benefit from the infringements committed by the primary infringers. Secondary liability applies to the 'brick-and-mortar' jukebox and music hall operators, copy shops and other purchasing agents on the market. On the Internet, intermediaries also exist, contrary to what is sometimes believed: hosting and access providers, search engines and other providers of information location tools, such as links, are only some among the many intermediaries that help the information sought to be identified by and conveyed to the users. Allen Dixon's paper really sets the scene for any discussion on secondary copyright liability by thoroughly defining the various actors in the Internet chain and by carefully distinguishing the various sources and theories that have been used in different countries to address this liability. While US law uses the rubrics 'contributory liability' and 'vicarious liability', along with the more recently developed principle of 'inducement liability', other common law countries (in particular, the UK and Australia) rely on the notion of 'authorisation' enshrined in statutes deriving from the UK Copyright Acts. For civil law countries, Allen Dixon rightly stresses the role played by the general tort rule (*responsabilité civile* in France and Belgium) from which a duty of care (*zorvuldigheidsnorm* in the Netherlands) can be derived, or the liability that allows some injunctive relief, but no damages (such as the German doctrine of *Störerhaftung*).

Similarly, Michael Schlesinger, Of Counsel to the law firm of Greenberg Traurig LLP in Washington, DC, provides an overview of the most recent case law on peer-to-peer, with a special focus on Asia. Michael Schlesinger's paper is more focused on primary liability; it starts with an analysis of the 'umbrella solution' enshrined in the WIPO Treaties, that is, the 'making available right'. A crucial part of a P2P transaction involves the acts of the uploader who makes available a copyrighted file on the P2P network, but P2P file sharing also involves the acts committed on the receiving end by the downloader (in particular, the reproduction of the file on his or her system). The 1996 WIPO Treaties created a new right covering interactive transmissions: the making available right of Art. 8 of the World Copyright Treaty. This right is supposed to cover the acts of the uploader who makes the file available online. When transposing this right in their national system, member states retain some room to manoeuvre: the US relied upon the distribution right to cover the delivery of protected files through online transmissions; in Europe, distribution is limited to tangible copies and cannot apply to online acts of dissemination. Regarding online transmissions, the 2001 EC Directive on Copyright in the Information Society has thus opted for an autonomous 'communication to the public right', which includes the 'making available right'.

A string of recent US cases discussing whether the making available right is included in the distribution right provided by the US Copyright Act is later discussed by Michael Schlesinger. His contribution ends with an extensive review of the case law from Asia, including Hong Kong, China, Taiwan and Japan; the summaries and comments on those Asian decisions is particularly useful for those of us who do not have easy access to this case law.

SECONDARY COPYRIGHT LIABILITY AND HYPERLINKING

Further analysing the seminal case decisions cited by Allen Dixon, other contributors raise additional situations triggering secondary liability. For one, the case law on the liability for linking is analyzed by Vicky Hanley, an associate with Covington & Burling LLP, and the editor of this collection, Alain Strowel, who is a professor at the Facultés Universitaires Saint-Louis, Brussels and Of Counsel with Covington & Burling LLP. As hyperlinking is a widely used tool, essential to the functioning of the web as well as multi-faceted (one can distinguish standard links from deep links, frames and embedded links), many cases have made their way before courts internationally, and the various legal solutions addressing secondary liability have been applied. Hyperlinking clearly engages the responsibility of the link provider in some instances (such as when the provider knowingly endorses the illicit materials to which s/he links), but other intermediaries have also been targeted in actions based on liability for hyperlinking, in cases where responsibility is not so clear. For instance, some hosting providers were specifically directed to take down links posted by their clients on pages hosted on their servers. More importantly, the issue of liability for dedicated search engines, which retrieve lists of links, or for content aggregators relying on the collection of links, have been involved in cases that have helped draw the line between 'dangerous (online) liaisons' and the 'good relationship' that Internet sites and intermediaries should have.

THE LEADING P2P CASES AND THEIR LEGAL CONSEQUENCES

Various contributions explore in detail how the rules of secondary liability have been applied to P2P in some national laws.

In a contribution called 'Copyright Control v Compensation: The Prospects for Exclusive Rights after *Grokster* and *Kazaa*', Jane Ginsburg, the Morton L. Janklow Professor of Literary and Artistic Property at the Columbia University School of Law, offers a thorough analysis of the criteria applied by US and Australian courts in delineating secondary liability for copyright infringement. Her review of the key US decisions, including *Sony*,[6] *Napster*,[7] and *Grokster*,[8] elucidates the reasoning of US judges in dealing with third-party infringements and in distinguishing between contributory liability, vicarious liability and inducement liability. Also, Jane Ginsburg's presentation of Australian case law shows that similar outcomes can be reached through different means: the decision in the leading Australian case, *Kazaa*,[9] offers striking resemblance to the *Grokster's* analysis. However, while the US approach is grounded in the common law, the Australian view relies on a provision of the Australian Copyright Act that renders the 'authorisation' of infringement a direct violation of the statute. After Kazaa, a P2P business that deliberately foregoes control that it could have exercised had it designed its service differently may be found to have 'authorized' the ensuing infringements, and therefore, may be held liable.

Professor Graeme Austin, the J. Byron McCormick Professor of Law at the University of Arizona, further explores the international character of the emerging law on P2P networks in the same common law jurisdictions, Australia and the United States. Graeme Austin's starting point is that while the law applicable to P2P networks may still be tethered within domestic borders, its application to P2P results in a 'de facto' export of the national rules on secondary copyright liability.

Indeed, the rulings on P2P tend not to distinguish infringements (or 'acts of authorization' in the case of Australian law) that occur *in* or *outside* the country where the copyright infringement case is brought. The remedies sometimes imposed (for example, a filter in the Australian *Kazaa* case) also potentially affect *all* users of the P2P system, including those located abroad. The extraterritorial reach of the leading P2P decisions, such as *Kazaa*, means that a 'de facto' export of liability theories is occurring although most intellectual property laws, and particularly the US case law (for example, the 2007 *Microsoft v AT&T* decision of the US Supreme Court) analysed by Graeme Austin later on, are based on a territoriality principle that prohibits the extension of domestic law to conduct in foreign territories. Graeme Austin believes

---

6 *Sony Corp. of American v Universal City Studios*, 464 U.S. 417 (1984).

7 *A&M Records, Inc. v Napster, Inc.*, 239 F.3d 1004 (9th Cir. 2001).

8 *MGM Studios, Inc. v Grokster Ltd.*, 125 S. Ct. 2764 (2005).

9 *Universal Music Australia Pty Ltd. v Sharman License Holdings Ltd.*, (2005) FCA 1242.

that a strict view on territoriality – which would require domestic courts where the primary acts of infringements occur to take responsibility – could make the legal analysis largely unmanageable. In addition, Graeme Austin considers the impact of public international law norms (the Berne Convention) on private international law and on the conflict of law issue; if those international norms are taken seriously, Graeme Austin argues, courts imposing liability for indirect infringement should not be impeded by the fact that their decisions might have extraterritorial effects.

COPYRIGHT IN THE AGE OF P2P: TOWARDS A 'COMPENSATION WITHOUT CONTROL' MODEL?

Peer-to-peer software and other information location tools enabled by the digital revolution have made copyright appear somewhat out-dated to some observers. A few contributions of this book explore, beyond peer-to-peer technology, the ways copyright could eventually be reshaped to respond to this new environment.

Proposing a forward-looking analysis of the P2P phenomenon and its impact on copyright is Alexander Peukert, an Asssociate Professor of Civil Law, Commercial Law and Intellectual Property Law at the Johann-Wolfgang Goethe University Frankfurt/Main. In his paper 'A Bipolar Copyright System for the Digital Network Environment', he reviews proposals made by various commentators[10] that non-commercial file sharing should be considered lawful, while copyright owners would be compensated indirectly through a voluntary collective licensing scheme, a levy (or non-voluntary licence) or a tax system. Those alternative proposals rely on the premise that efficient control of the use of P2P networks is not possible without banning the technology altogether or, at least, without severe encroachments on privacy and other drawbacks associated with systematic monitoring of the Internet. Alexander Peukert's paper first analyses the compatibility of those alternatives with the international obligations deriving from the Berne Convention, the TRIPS Agreement and the WIPO Copyright Treaty, in particular with the three-step-test establishing the distinction between exclusivity and non-voluntary licences.

---

[10] Most advocates of those alternative solutions, for example, Terry Fisher, Neil Netanel, Aric Jacover, Jessica Litman, Mark Lemley and Anthony Reese, are US-based academics. It is in France, however, that the solution of a non-voluntary licence ('the licence globale') was at some point seriously considered by the legislature during the Parliamentary discussions leading to the adoption of the 2006 French Copyright Act.

Beyond reviewing the shortcomings of those alternative proposals, Peukert's contribution advocates the adoption of a new copyright model for the digital online environment, which he calls the 'bipolar copyright system'. The bipolar copyright system allows the right holder to choose freely between exclusive exploitation (possibly with the aid of DRMs) and participation in the levy/tax system as regards non-commercial file sharing. In Peukert's complex model, the choice between an individual licence or a levy/remuneration can be made at the time of the works' first publication, but to switch-over from one system to the other one is still possible later.[11]

Peukert's view that copyright exclusivity should not rule cyberspace is not shared by all commentators. On the contrary, the case law on P2P has, in the words of Professor Jane Ginsburg, 'taken some of the wind out of the sails of proposals to substitute a P2P levy scheme for authors' exclusive rights'. Compensation through levies (or compensation without control) is not an easy substitute for the control offered by the authors' exclusive rights: copyright practitioners and collecting societies in continental Europe who have experienced the wealth of issues raised by levies, such as the difficulty of collection, are ready to accept this evidence, while US academics are more easily tempted by a system that looks attractive from a distance, but whose implementation is prone to generating difficulties and litigation.

ONLINE COPYRIGHT AND THE EVOLVING LIABILITY OF INTERMEDIARIES

Other contributors do not challenge the exclusive right model, but rather its use by rights owners against primary infringers. Robert Clark, professor at the University College, Dublin, is sceptical about the increased use of criminal law by the music industry in fighting uploaders. In his chapter 'Sharing Out Online Liability: Sharing Files, Sharing Risks and Targeting ISPs', he considers that such a development is not a proportionate response to the mass infringements on P2P networks, especially when civil law remedies are available. However, the use of civil remedies is sometimes directly impeded by data protection rules – as shown by his review of decisions on discovery of subscribers' data held in various jurisdictions (Ireland, Netherlands, Spain, UK, etc.). According to Robert Clark, liability decisions in Canada, Ireland and the UK – which are helpfully compared with the US and Autralian deci-

[11] Although Peukert's paper emphasises some issues linked with a levy system, a thorough discussion about the merits and drawbacks of levies is well beyond the scope of the present volume.

sions discussed elsewhere in the book – show a trend towards a system of 'sharing risks' for 'sharing files': most decisions explore the possibility of allocating both the risk and liability in a much more horizontal way than the early stages of the debate on file sharing could have possibly anticipated. Robert Clark's chapter, in essence, focuses on the online liability of Internet Service Providers and on the interpretation of the 'safe harbour' provisions of the 2000 EC Electronic Commerce Directive. His review of recent case law, including the Belgian *Scarlet* case on access provider liability for P2P file sharing, points towards a possible weakening of ISP immunity in Europe. At the very least, the case law partly supports the legislative attempts to have ISPs more directly involved through the use of filtering systems at different levels. Technological tools, and their imposition by law, now move towards the centre of the debate on secondary liability and P2P.

The issue of technological measures of protection and the link with ISP liability is also central in the comprehensive and forward-looking contribution jointly prepared by Jerome H. Reichman, the Bunyan S. Womble Professor of Law at Duke Law School; Graeme B. Dinwoodie, Professor of Law at Chicago-Kent College of Law; and Pamela Samuelson, the Richard M. Sherman Distinguished Professor of Law at Boalt Hall School of Law. In 'A Reverse Notice and Takedown Regime To Enable Public Interest Uses of Technically Protected Copyrighted Works', those authors plead in favour of a more balanced system for protecting copy or access control technologies, usually embedded in, or complemented by, digital rights management systems (DRMs). Technological measures and DRMs are, in theory, a possible solution to limit mass infringement online – but their effective implementation by rights owners and their acceptance by the public, at least in the field of music, seems quite remote and improbable. That said, the three authors of this chapter are primarily concerned with the law on technological measures as it should be designed. Interestingly, their proposal to adjust the anti-circumvention rules relies on the checks and balances embedded in the ISP safe harbour rules. They argue that the notice and takedown procedure first developed through common law adjudication about ISP liability for wrongful acts of users, then incorporated in the US Digital Millenium Copyright Act, offers a good balance that is still missing in the anti-circumvention rules adopted in the US and in the EU. They advocate, therefore, what they call a 'reverse notice and takedown' process, that is, a process where users give notice of their desire to make public interest uses of technically protected copyrighted works, and content owners would have the responsibility of taking down the works or enabling their lawful use. In Europe, this 'reverse notice and takedown' process would possibly effectuate the obligation that EU Member States have to ensure that users are able to enjoy some copyright exceptions (Art. 6(4) of the 2001 EC Directive on Copyright in the Information Society).

THE RECENT LEGISLATIVE DEVELOPMENTS AFFECTING ONLINE INTERMEDIARIES: THE OLIVENNES AGREEMENT IN FRANCE AND BEYOND

P2P file sharing and other online technologies such as hyperlinks and search engines remain a core concern for copyright owners, especially for the music and film industries. Developments since 2007 have shown increased attention to the role of online intermediaries, particularly access providers, in fighting online piracy.

For instance, in France, an agreement between various stakeholders (the music and film companies on one side, the ISPs on the other side) was concluded on 23 November 2007, following a study conducted by Mr Denis Olivennes. The so-called 'Olivennes Agreement' is part of a new 'government-led crackdown on copyright violation by users of P2P file sharing services'.[12] Under this new initiative, ISPs should cooperate more effectively with copyright holders to deter high-volume users of P2P sites. The draft law adopted by the French Council of Ministers on 18 June 2008 seeks to codify the Olivennes Agreement. It will be submitted to Parliament for adoption in the Spring of 2009. One of the main contributions of this legislative development is the creation of a new independent copyright enforcement authority (the High Authority). It appears that fighting mass copyright infringement through the standard court system is not fully adequate: the judicial procedure is generally slow and costly; the remedies are relatively inadequate; and the processing and disclosure of personal data is not usually allowed in relation to civil proceedings, making it difficult to establish such infringements in the first instance. These are just some of the reasons justifying the development of an alternative solution to the standard court system. The magnitude of copyright infringement through P2P and new online platforms (such as user-generated sites or online auction sites) probably requires new authorities and new remedies, at least if one intends to tackle direct infringements by Internet users. This does not necessarily mean that stronger remedies are needed, at least initially; in a sense, the new draft law in France proposes a quite moderate approach in the so-called 'graduated response', which prescribes a sequence of measures to be applied to repeat infringers.[13] To circumvent the

---

[12] Lawrence J. Speer, 'France Launches Innovative Crackdown on P2P Downloads, ISPs Will Participate', *Online News of the Bureau of National Affairs*, 26 November 2007.

[13] The High Authority will first issue warnings to end-users. In case of repeated infringement, the High Authority can propose a one to three months Internet access suspension to the subscriber as a settlement measure. In case the subscriber refuses this proposed settlement and new infringements are committed within one year of the warn-

issue of data protection, special rules are also defined in the draft, that allow certain designated private parties to collect personal data and transmit it to the High Authority for processing.

Other developments at the EU level (such as the European Commission's consultation and the January 2008 Communication on 'Creative Content Online in the Single Market') and at the national level (such as the February 2008 UK Green Paper entitled 'Creative Britain: New Talents for the New Economy') all point towards the creation of a new framework for addressing mass copyright infringement on the Internet and the increasing role to be played by intermediaries.

We will see whether the new French approach to tackling online copyright infringements, should it be incorporated into law, will succeed. The coming months will be decisive in that regard. Even if such a system is integrated into the French legal arsenal, it is doubtful that many other (European) countries will follow this example in the mid-term. However, it is clear that the role of ISPs in fighting online infringements will continue to be hotly debated.

Although legislative changes could potentially redefine the way online infringement is addressed, the standard rules on secondary liability as applied by the courts in civil proceedings for copyright infringement will remain the preferred way to combat P2P and other mass copyright infringement. Thus, an overview of the main doctrines and issues of secondary copyright liability remains a valuable tool.

---

ing letter, the High Authority may order the suspension of access for a period of three months to one year.

1. Liability of users and third parties for copyright infringements on the Internet: overview of international developments

Allen N. Dixon*

OVERVIEW

Civil and criminal law have never limited liability only to the person who personally commits a tort or criminal offence. In every country, a range of different rules extend such liability in some cases to others who *encourage, assist or benefit from* another person's tort or crime.

Copyright is no different. From music hall and boot sale operators, to copy shops, to various service and product providers on the Internet, those who are linked to the direct copyright infringements of others may find themselves subject to liability for those infringements in some circumstances.

This chapter reviews recent international developments in the area of user and third-party liability, particularly regarding the Internet and so-called file sharing. It tries to make sense of the labels variously applied to these activities and examines the holdings of various cases. Finally, it summarises the general principles that courts and legislators are using to evaluate different types of third-party activity in determining copyright liability.

A NOT-SO-FARFETCHED SCENARIO

A new taxi service *GetawayQuick* drives members of the public to the destinations they choose. Unlike most car services, however, the business model of this one is to become the car service of choice among bank robbers. Because of its inside knowledge, and the speed and nondescript nature of its cars, this

* The author acknowledges the kind research assistance of St. John's University law sudents Nicholas Madonia and Edward McNamara.

service is particularly good at getting bank robbers to the banks and doing a quick getaway.

Ninety percent or more of its work is bank jobs. In theory, the service could drive customers to estate-agent offices, blind dates, or free-speech rallies among Chinese dissidents, but no one has actually proved that any jobs of that sort have ever happened. The drivers take the robbers to the bank, wait outside during the stick-up, carry the robbers with the loot away – to other jobs if they like – and make money in the process. The service is so efficient that huge numbers of people have decided to get into the bank robbing game, and the cab service's business is booming. Advertisers are queuing up to sell things to their customers.

When arrested for aiding and abetting multiple bank robberies, the taxi company is shocked. 'Our drivers never pulled a gun on anyone, or touched the money,' they say. 'We had no idea what was going on in all those banks – these people may have been visiting friends or engaging in perfectly legitimate bank transactions. If they happen to come out with money, they're not *stealing* it, they're just *sharing* it. As a matter of fact, banks are greedy institutions that deserve what they get. They charge way too much in fees and interest, and have been entirely too slow in adopting Internet banking, which would have been a lot more secure. This arrest is just a continuation of outdated police practices, which violate our right to drive, and chill the development of new and exciting taxi service models.'

Meanwhile, the national taxi association and the major automobile manufacturers – while not threatened with such prosecutions themselves – have gone to the legislature *en masse* to be sure they are not prosecuted for bank robberies. Friends of these industries in the legislature are regaled with nightmare scenarios about the dangers to them of prosecuting *GetawayQuick*. *GetawayQuick* itself organises its *nouveau riche* customers to stage sit-ins and write to their representatives. The legislature 'clarifies' the common law of aiding and abetting to deal with a few specific cab services and manufacturing activities. *GetawayQuick* changes its business slightly to make sure it is not caught by the new legislation.[1]

DEFINITIONS

Given that this area is replete with catchwords that different people use differently, it may be useful to define a few terms before examining what the courts and legislators have been doing in this area.

1 This scenario is entirely fictional and satirical. Any resemblance to real persons or events is entirely coincidental.

'User'. This term is used here to mean the person who engages in an act of infringement – the person who makes a reproduction, adaptation, performance, communication or distribution in violation of the copyright or related-rights owner's rights.

'Third party'. This term means the person who has not engaged in an act of infringement, but who is somehow connected with it. There are a range of activity-related words (for example, 'intermediary', 'service provider') and qualitative terms (for example, 'accomplice', 'contributor', 'inciter') regularly used for such third parties and their activities.

'Intermediary'. An 'intermediary' is one type of third party. The term is commonly applied to telecommunications companies that provide, at a minimum, Internet access and connectivity between two or more individuals.

'Service provider'. In common parlance, this can mean anyone providing any kind of service, whether Internet-based or otherwise – any of whom might become involved as third parties in infringement. The US Digital Millennium Copyright Act applies this term for some purposes to Internet access providers, and for other purposes to all types of providers of services on-line.[2] The EU E-Commerce Directive opted for a broader definition, covering all providers of 'information society services'.[3] These and other similar laws grant liability exemptions to a defined set of 'service providers', not typically on the basis of their status but with respect to specifically defined activities that meet specific conditions.

'Internet'. This is the publicly accessible telecommunications network of interconnected computers and networks that operate on the basis of 'packet switching' technology and standard protocols such as IP (Internet protocol), HTTP (hypertext transfer protocol) and the like. Approximately 1.5 billion people world-wide use the Internet.[4]

'File sharing'. File sharing is the making available of files from a user's own computer for copying and transmission to other users over the Internet,

---

[2] 17 U.S.C. § 512(k): '(A) As used in subsection (a), the term "service provider" means an entity offering the transmission, routing, or providing of connections for digital online communications, between or among points specified by a user, of material of the user's choosing, without modification to the content of the material as sent or received. (B) As used in this section, other than subsection (a), the term "service provider" means a provider of online services or network access, or the operator of facilities therefor, and includes an entity described in subparagraph (A).' http://www.copyright.gov/title17/92chap5.html.

[3] Arts. 2(a)–(b), Directive 2000/31/EC of the European Parliament and of the Council of 8 June 2000 on certain legal aspects of information society services, in particular electronic commerce, in the Internal Market ('E-commerce Directive'), O.J. L 178 (17 July 2000), at 1–16, http://europa.eu.int/eur-lex/lex/LexUriServ/LexUriServdo?uri=CELEX:32000L0031:EN:HTML.

[4] http://www.Internetworldstats.com/stats.htm.

and the receipt of files made available this way. File sharing thus involves *uploading* as well as *downloading*. File sharing takes place in networks of users. Third parties have developed the file-sharing services and technologies required to connect users and enable them to carry out such transmission and copying activities in the third party's particular 'peer-to-peer' (P2P) network.[5]

COMMON LAW AND CIVIL LAW RULES

The law in the area of third-party liability derives from a number of sources – statutory rules specific to the copyright area, case law developments in copyright, and more general common law or civil law legal rules.

US: Common Law Copyright and Tort Principles

The US law on third-party liability for copyright infringement traditionally uses the rubrics *contributory liability* and *vicarious liability* as applied in a long line of case law in the copyright area, and more recently the principle of *inducement* liability.

- **Contributory liability** arises where a third party with *knowledge* of the infringing activity, induces, causes or *materially contributes* to the infringing conduct of another.[6] The *Sony* Betamax case[7] of 1984 found that intent to cause infringement could not be presumed or imputed solely from the design or distribution of a product capable of substantial lawful use, which the third party knows is in fact used for infringement.[8]
- **Vicarious liability** is imposed where a third party *controls* the infringer's actions and receives a *financial benefit* from the infringement.[9]
- **Inducement liability** has been recently reinvigorated by the US Supreme Court in the *Grokster*[10] case, which found that a third party

[5] To speed up searches, these services and technologies typically create indexes of users on-line and files on offer. Such indexes can be maintained by the service or technology provider ('centralised indexing'), but sometimes are pushed down to the users' own computers ('decentralised indexing').

[6] *Gershwin Publishing Corp. v Columbia Artists Management, Inc.*, 443 F.2d 1159, 1162 (2d Cir. 1971).

[7] *Sony Corp. of America v Universal City Studios, Inc.*, 464 U. S. 417 (1984).

[8] This summary of the *Sony* holding was set forth in the Supreme Court's decision in *Grokster, infra* n. 10, at 16, 17.

[9] *Shapiro, Bernstein & Co. v H.L. Green Co.*, 316 F.2d 304, 306 (2d Cir. 1963).

[10] *Metro-Goldwyn-Mayer Studios Inc., v Grokster, Ltd.*, No. 04-480, at 1 (S. Ct.

> who distributes a device with the *object of promoting its use to infringe copyright*, as shown by clear expression or other affirmative steps to foster infringement, is liable for the users' resulting acts of infringement.[11]

Commonwealth Countries: Statutory and Common Law 'Authorisation', 'Vicarious Liability', 'Joint Tortfeasor' and Incitement Rules

In Commonwealth countries, third-party copyright liability has sprung from the notion of 'authorisation' – now enshrined in statutory law and interpreted more broadly than its strict meaning – as well as from other common law tort and criminal law principles.

---

27 Jun. 2005), http://www.supremecourtus.gov/opinions/04pdf/04-480.pdf. The Kazaa and Grokster defendants settled this litigation following the Supreme Court decision. RIAA, Press Release: Music Industry Announces Grokster Settlement (7 Nov 2005), http://www.riaa.com/newsitem.php?news_year_filter=&resultpage=16&id=81648953-2457-2877-94B4-D28C93625445; RIAA, Press Release: Kazaa Settles with Record Industry and Goes Legitimate (27 Jul. 2006), http://www.riaa.com/newsitem.php?id=46A7DBAB-CEFA-B6D5-F81A-BBB34C2A2581. Streamcast continued to challenge the plaintiffs' case, including the need and scope of any potential filtering remedies. *See* Plaintiff's Opposition to Defendant Streamcast Networks Inc.'s Request for Additional Discovery, *MGM Studios Inc. v Grokster Ltd.*, No. CV 01-08541 (C.D. Cal. Filed 16 Apr. 2007).

[11] The US courts are continuing to explore the limits and the interplay of the various bases for third party copyright liability in the wake of the *Grokster* decision. *See Perfect 10, Inc. v CCBill LLC,* No. 04-57143 (9th Cir. 31 May 2007) (amended opinion) (reviewing ISP liability limitations); *Perfect 10, Inc. v Visa International Service Ass'n,* No. 05-15170 (9th Cir., 3 Jul. 2007) (payment processing providers made no 'material contribution' to infringement and were not vicariously or contributorily liable); *Perfect 10, Inc. v Amazom.com, Inc.*, No. 06-55405 (9th Cir., 16 May 2007) (search engine linking to full-sized infringing photographs on other sites not vicariously liable but could be contributorily liable 'if it "has *actual* knowledge that *specific* infringing material is available using its system," *Napster,* 239 F.3d at 1022, and can "take simple measures to prevent further damage" to copyrighted works, *Netcom,* 907 F. Supp. At 1375, yet continues to provide access to infringing works'); *Viacom International Inc. v YouTube Inc.,* Civ Action No. 07 CV 2103 (S.D.N.Y. filed 13 Mar. 2007) (lawsuit against operator of user-uploaded content site for alleged direct, inducement, contributory and vicarious liability), http://news.justia.com/cases/viacom-youtube/337988/1/0.pdf.

Various rights owners brought lawsuits against Bertelsmann in its role as *investor* in the original Napster service. Without admitting any liability, Bertelsmann has paid more than $200M to settle the suits against Bertelsmann – $110M to Warner Music, $60M to Universal Music, and a reported $44.5M to EMI. Warner Music Corp., SEC Form 10-Q, para. 16 (8 May 2007), http://www.sec.gov/Archives/edgar/data/1319161/000119312507105272/d10q.htm; *EMI, Bertelsmann settle Napster suit,* Financial Times (26 March 2007); Bertelsmann, Press Release: *Bertelsmann remains on track in first quarter* (15 May 2007), http://www.bertelsmann.com/bertelsmann_corp/wms41//customers/bmir/pdf/Q1_2007_e.pdf.

- **'Authorisation' theory.** Under both statutory[12] and common law[13] principles in the UK and other Commonwealth countries, it has long been unlawful to 'authorise' another person to infringe copyright. 'Authorisation' has not just been interpreted literally, that is, purporting to grant a licence to use copyrighted material. It has been used to cover a broader range of activities that the third party may 'sanction, approve or countenance',[14] 'permit' or even treat with 'inactivity' or 'indifference'.[15] For example, juke box providers, bandstand owners, purchasing agents and similar third parties have been held liable for 'authorising' the infringement of others.[16] In *CBS Records v Amstrad*,[17] by contrast, the House of Lords held that equipment manufacturers and distributors that marketed and sold cassette duplication equipment merely 'facilitated' or gave users the 'power' to infringe – which did not rise to the level of 'authorisation', given that users determined whether and what they were going to copy, the devices could be used for lawful as well as unlawful purposes, the suppliers had given warning that some copying required permission which they had no authority to give, and the suppliers had no control over use of the equipment after the sale.
- **Australian three-part test for authorisation.** In the Copyright (Digital Agenda) Act that Australia adopted in 2000, the offence of 'authorisation' was spelled out more specifically to reflect Australian case law, including the *Moorhouse* case.[18] In *Moorhouse,* a three-judge panel of the Federal Court found that a university library that offered coin-operated photocopiers and implemented inadequate supervision and warnings against a user's copyright infringement was liable for 'authorising'

---

12 See for example, UK Copyright Act 1911, s. 1(2) (copyright includes the sole right 'to authorise any such acts as aforesaid.'); UK Copyright Act 1956, s. 1(1) (copyright means the exclusive right 'to authorise other persons to do' certain acts in relation to that work; UK Copyright Designs Patents Act 1988 ss. 16(2), 16(3)(b) (copyright is infringed by a person who 'authorised another to do' any of the acts restricted by the copyright, whether 'directly or indirectly')

13 *Falcon v Famous Players Film Co.* [1926] 2 KB 474.

14 Id. at 491.

15 *Adelaide Corp. v Australasian Performing Right Ass'n Ltd.,* (1928) 40 CLR 481 (High Ct. Australia).

16 See generally *Copinger and Skone-James on Copyright*, 15th ed., para. 7-133, at 451–453 (2005). Laddie, Prescott & Vitoria (2000), *The Modern Law of Copyrights and Designs*, 3rd ed., §§ 39.16, at 1773–5.

17 *CBS Songs Ltd. v Amstrad Consumer Electronics Plc* [1988] AC 1013, [1988] All E.R. 484.

18 *University of New South Wales v Moorhouse,* [1975] HCA 26; (1975) 133 CLR 1 (High Ct. Australia, 1 Aug. 1975), http://www.austlii.edu.au/cgi-bin/disp.pl/au/cases/cth/HCA/1975/26.html.

that infringement.[19] Section 36(1A) of the Australian Copyright Act now sets forth three factors to be 'taken into account' in a determination of authorisation: *control*, *relationship*, and *due care*.[20]

- **Vicarious liability.** Under general common law principles, an employer can be held vicariously liable for *employees' or agents'* infringements done under the *employer's authority*.[21]
- **Joint tortfeasor liability.** Similar common law principles hold a third party liable if he or she is engaged in a '*common design*' with someone who commits or authorises an *infringement in pursuance of that design*.[22]
- **Criminal law accomplice liability.** Although rarely applied in practice, the common law rules on criminal accomplice liability can be applied to a third party who *knowingly incites* ('solicits, encourages, pressurises, threatens or endeavours to persuade'), or *aids*, *abets*, *counsels* or *procures* another to commit a criminal copyright offence.[23]

Civil Law Jurisdictions

- **Knowing assistance.** In civil law countries, third parties generally can be held liable under either civil or criminal law where they *knowingly assist* in the copyright infringements of another.[24]

---

19 Id.

20 Sec. 36(1A), Australia Copyright Act 1968, as amended, provides as follows: 'In determining, for the purposes of subsection (1), whether or not a person has authorised the doing in Australia of any act comprised in the copyright in a work, without the licence of the owner of the copyright, the matters that must be taken into account include the following:

(a) the extent (if any) of the person's power to prevent the doing of the act concerned;

(b) the nature of any relationship existing between the person and the person who did the act concerned;

(c) whether the person took any reasonable steps to prevent or avoid the doing of the act, including whether the person complied with any relevant industry codes of practice.

21 See for example, *Performing Right Society Ltd. v Mitchell and Booker, Ltd* [1924] KB 762.

22 *In The Koursk* [1924] All ER Rep 168, at 175, cited with approval in *Amstrad, supra* n. 17.

23 See generally Garnett, Rayner James and Davies (1999), *Copinger & Skone James on Copyright,* ss. 23–24, at 1099–1100 (14th ed.).

24 See for example, *TONO v Bruvik,* Civil Case No. 2004/822 (S. Ct. Norway, 27 January 2005) (defendant found liable for users' unlawful Internet communications of music files via hyperlinks on defendant's site, where defendant 'deliberately assisted' such uploading, acted with intent, advertised 'Download as much as you

- **Duty of care to avoid damage.** Civil law countries also tend to impose, under a general legal '*duty of care*', an obligation to act reasonably to prevent harm to others. The duty required typically depends on the facts and circumstances. An *illegal act* by someone is necessary (the user's infringement itself is usually sufficient), and some level of *knowledge* on the part of the third party is typically required for liability to attach. Courts often look at *economic benefit* to the third party and engage in *cost-benefit analysis* (cost of harm, cost of avoidance, magnitude of harm) in determining the duty of care, the existence of any violation of that duty, and any remedy therefor.[25]
- **Injunctive relief against third parties.** Civil law typically allows prospective injunctions against persons involved in someone else's tort, even if those third parties did not have prior knowledge of the wrong-doing. The German doctrine of *Störerhaftung*, for example, allows injunctions against third parties engaging in affirmative acts that cause a 'disturbance', even though damages will not be imposed against such parties without proof of knowledge.[26] Along these lines, the EU's 2001 Copyright Directive requires that national law make injunctions available to rights owners against intermediaries whose services are used to infringe copyright, even if the intermediaries themselves are not liable for the infringement.[27]

APPLICATION AND LIMITATIONS OF COPYRIGHT LIABILITY TO ON-LINE ACTIVITIES

User Liability

With the advent of Internet and other on-line services, the question arose as to how traditional copyright rules would apply to a range of on-line activities. The initial question of the early- and mid-1990s was whether and how

---

wish', and 'was undoubtedly aware' that users were uploading without consent. See generally Sterling, *World Copyright Law,* ss. 13.08–13.09 (London: Sweet & Maxwell 1998) ('the general rule is that one is liable for *consciously bringing about* or *assisting* in the bringing about of infringements by other persons. Liability in this area is frequently (but not exclusively) linked to questions of *knowledge*' (emphasis added)).

25 See generally Koelman & Hugenholtz, *Online Service Provider Liability for Copyright Infringement,* WIPO Workshop on Service Provider Liability (9–10 December 1999).

26 See Hartwig (November 2004), *Online auctioneers must work harder in Germany,* Managing Intellectual Property (describing doctrine of the Rolex/Ricardo.de case).

27 *See infra* n. 75 and accompanying text.

copyright applied to *user* activities in the first instance. Copies now are stored, transmitted and used electronically – sometimes even temporarily. Could the copyright concepts of reproduction and distribution, traditionally applied to articles in tangible form, be interpreted to cover computer and on-line storage, transmission or usage?

The international community in the WIPO Copyright Treaties[28] of 1996 answered this question with a resounding *Yes*. Copyright does cover storage in digital form.[29] Copyright also covers not just Internet transmissions but the very act of 'making available' copyrighted material for access on the Internet.[30]

Thus, with rare exceptions,[31] courts far and wide have found users liable for posting and transmitting copyright material on the Internet without authorisation, including over file-sharing services.[32] This result has been reached

---

28 WIPO Copyright Treaty (WCT) (Geneva, 20 December 1996); WIPO Performances and Phonograms Treaty (WPPT) (Geneva, 20 December 1996).

29 'The reproduction right, as set out in Article 9 of the Berne Convention, and the exceptions permitted thereunder, fully apply in the digital environment, in particular to the use of works in digital form. It is understood that the storage of a protected work in digital form in an electronic medium constitutes a reproduction within the meaning of Article 9 of the Berne Convention.' Agreed Statements Concerning Article 1(4) of WCT; see also Agreed Statements Concerning Articles 7, 11 and 16 of the WPPT.

30 Art. 8, WCT; Arts. 10, 14, WPPT.

31 Reasons for Order and Order, *BMG Canada Inc. v Doe,* 2004 FC 488 (Canada Fed. Ct. 31 March 04) (uploading and downloading not a copyright offence), *reversed and aff'd in part,* 2000 FCA 193 (Canada Ct. App. 19 May 2005); *SCPP v Anthony G.,* No. 0504090091 (Tribunal de Grande Instance de Paris, 8 December 2005) (private copy exception excuses P2P reproduction and transmission), *reversed, Anthony G./SCPP* (Cour d'appel de Paris, 27 April 2007) (user fined and ordered to pay damages and costs); www.legalis.net/jurisprudence-decision.php3?id_article =1954.

32 Courts have issued judgments against music 'file-sharers' in many countries, including Denmark, France, Finland, Germany, Italy, UK. Examples of judgments include *Polydor Ltd v Brown,* No. HC 05C02035, [2005] EWHC 3191 (Ch) (UK High Ct. Chancery Division, 18 November 2005) ('Connecting a computer to the Internet which is running P2P software and in which music files . . . are placed in a shared directory falls within this infringing act. This is a primary act of copyright infringement and it does not matter whether the person knows or has reason to believe that what they are doing is an infringement.'). See also Order in Interlocutory Injunction Proceedings, No. 308 O 58/06 (Civ Chamber 8, Hamburg Landgericht, 25 January 2006); Order in Interlocutory Injunction Proceedings, No. 28 O 634/05 (Köln Landgericht, 23 November 2005); Judgement, No. 95 Ds 1653 Js 15556/04 (57/04) (Kottbus D. Ct., 24 May 2004); Judgement, No. 461 Cs 509 Js 1607/02 (Fürth D. Ct., 29 March 2004) (offering of recordings for downloading violates reproduction and/or 'making available' rights) Most of these cases have been settled following compensation payments averaging several thousand US dollars. See IFPI, *Breakdown of legal cases against*

under copyright rules in place both before and after implementation of the WIPO Treaties, on the basis that the copyright or neighbouring rights owner's reproduction right, communication right and/or 'making available' right has been violated. As of November 2007, for example, the recording industry had brought over 80,000 cases against users in 20 countries for making recorded music available without authorisation on file-sharing services.[33]

Third-Party Liability

1. Statutory exemptions for Internet service providers

Questions of third-party liability for Internet activities have come up in both legislative and litigation contexts. Major telecommunications companies made an initial pre-emptive push for specific statutory exceptions to the general third-party liability rules for certain Internet-related telecommunications activities. These 'Internet service provider' liability rules have been implemented with a fair amount of consistency throughout the world:

- ***'mere provision of physical facilities'*** as such does not make a telecommunications provider liable for someone else's communication of copyrighted material;[34]
- ***'mere conduit'*** providers of Internet access, real-time routing between third parties, caching and similar transient and intermediate storage en route, are exempt from damages if their users infringe;[35] and
- ***'hosting'*** providers whose systems are used indefinitely by users to store infringing material, are exempt from damages so long as they remove or block infringements when they know or reasonably should have been aware of them.[36]

---

illegal file-sharing (15 November 2005), http://www.ifpi.org/content/section_news/20051115h.html.

[33] Source: IFPI. See IFPI Press Release, *Polish music industry continues legal actions against illegal file-sharing* (20 April 2007), http://www.ifpi.org/content/section_news/20070420.html.

[34] Agreed Statements Concerning Article 8, WCT, *supra* n. 28 ('It is understood that the mere provision of physical facilities for enabling or making a communication does not in itself amount to communication within the meaning of this Treaty or the Berne Convention.').

[35] 17 U.S.C., *supra* n. 2, § 512(a)–(b) (mere conduit, caching exemptions); E-Commerce Directive, *supra* n. 3, Arts. 12–13 (same); Arts. 20-21, Regulations on the Protection of the Right of Communication Through Information Networks, (China) State Council Order No. 468 ('China Internet Regulations') (16 May 2006) (same).

[36] 17 U.S.C., *supra* n. 2, § 512(c) (hosting exemption); E-Commerce Directive, *supra* n. 3, Art. 14 (same); China Internet Regulations, *supra* n. 35, Art. 22.

A range of due-care requirements (such as effective user policies, or prompt take-down upon notice), and other particular requirements or limitations, are sometimes included in these statutory exemptions. While other types of on-line services, particularly file-sharing services, have tried to take advantage of such exemptions,[37] and some service providers have attempted to stretch the ordinary meaning of words like 'temporary' reproduction and 'caching' to include more permanent and less passive activities,[38] courts have been fairly consistent in applying these exemptions to the ordinary telecommunications functions for which they were initially designed.[39]

2. Third-party liability for 'links' sites

The first major area to be litigated in many countries involved dial-up bulletin boards or Internet-based databases or websites. These caused very little trouble for the courts in determining that such sites were either directly infringing or unlawfully assisting in users' on-line infringements.

The area of liability for hyperlinks or 'links' to infringing files produced a surprising number of cases, however, as defendants who hosted or made Internet hyperlinks available have tried to find distinctions between communicating the infringing material and communicating a link to infringing material – that is, their main argument was that the linking itself was not illegal. Internet service providers in some countries also tried to avoid taking down links to infringing material on the same basis.

Courts have tended to treat hyperlinks to infringing copyright material under a theory of assisting an infringement,[40] or even as a matter of direct

---

[37] See e.g., *A&M Records, Inc. v Napster, Inc.*, 114 F. Supp. 2d 896, at 919 n.24 (denying summary judgment to Napster under § 512(a)), aff'd, 239 F.3d 1004; *Universal Music Australia Pty Ltd v Sharman License Holdings Ltd* [2005] FCA 1242 (5 September 2005) (denying Sharman defence under sec 112E of the Australian Copyright Act, which provides that 'A person (including a carrier or carriage service provider) who provides facilities for making, or facilitating the making of, a communication is not taken to have authorised any infringement of copyright in an audio-visual item merely because another person uses the facilities so provided to do something the right to do which is included in the copyright.').

[38] For example, *Ellison v Robertson*, 189 F. Supp.2d 1051 (C.D. Cal., 2002), rev'd in part, 357 F. 3d 1072 (9th Cir. 2004) (14-day storage of newsgroups is 'transitory').

[39] See, for example, *Cooper v Universal Music Australia Pty. Ltd., infra* n.42, [2006] FCAFC 187, which found that an ISP that was aware of the intensive use and copyright problems of a links site on its service, that gave free web hosting to the site, and that took no steps to prevent the site's infringement, could not rely on a 'mere facility' exception to liability.

[40] For example, *TONO v Bruvik*, Civil Case No. 2004/822 (S. Ct. Norway, 27 Jan. 2005); *Perfect 10, Inc. v Amazom.com, Inc., supra* n.11 (no vicarious liability, no contributory liability '*solely* because the design of its search engine facilitates such

infringement.[41] In the case of so-called 'deep links' in particular, courts have rarely found difficulty in finding infringement under some theory because these hyperlinks function in the same way in commencing the transmission and copying of an infringing file regardless of whether the file is located on the link provider's own computer or that of another person.

The Australian case of *Universal Music Pty. Ltd. v Cooper*,[42] provides a good example. The defendant website owner was held liable for 'authorising' user infringement by knowingly designing and organising a large links site in a manner that enabled and facilitated illegal downloading by users and illegal uploading by other sites. The court found that Cooper 'exhibited a degree of indifference from which permission ought to be inferred', by failing to control his site and remove links to infringing files.[43]

Similarly, a Chinese court has found Yahoo! China (owned by the entity Alibaba) liable for 'assisting infringement' and ordered it to pay damages and to remove links to infringing music files in its MP3 search engine as well as its Music Box site, which offered users a storage space for such links. The court found no direct infringement on the part of Yahoo! China and ruled that providing a searching or linking service would not bring liability if the service disconnected the links to an infringing work, performance or phonogram after receiving notice from the rights owner. However, such a service would be 'jointly liable for infringement if it is aware of or ought to know that the linked work, performance or phonogram product constitutes an infringement' and failed to remove the link.[44]

---

infringement', but contributory liability could be imposed if Google 'had knowledge that infringing Perfect 10 images were available using its search engine, could take simple measures to prevent further damage to Perfect 10's copyrighted works, and failed to take such steps'). See generally Dixon, *Internet Copyright Litigation: Non-US Developments,* World E-Commerce & IP Report, June 2003, at 5, 6.

41 *IFPI Belgium v Beckers,* A.R.K. No. 99/594/C (Antwerp Law Courts, 21 December 1999), aff'd, *Beckers v IFPI Belgium,* No. 2000/RK/27 (First Chamber, Court of Appeal, Antwerp, 26 June 2001); *KODA, NCB, Dansk Artist Forbund, Dansk Musiker Forbund & IFPI Denmark,* Case Nos. VL. B-1943-99 and VL. B-2089-99 (High Ct. of Justice, Western Div, 20 April 2001).

42 [2005] FCA 971 (Fed. Ct. Australia, 17 Jul. 2005), aff'd, *Cooper v Universal Music Australia Pty. Ltd.* [2006] FCAFC 187 (Fed. Ct. Full Court Appeal, 18 December 2006).

43 Id., paras. 77–88.

44 *Go East Entertainment Co. Ltd. v Beijing Alibaba Information and Technology Co. Ltd.,* Civ No. (2007) 02627 Er Zhong Min Chu Zi (Beijing No. 2 Intermediate People's Court, 24 April 2007), aff'd, 2007 Gaomingzhongzi No. 1191 (Beijing Higher People's Court, 20 December 2007). *Cf. Gold Label Entertainment Ltd. v Beijing Baidu Network Information Scien-tech Co., Ltd.,* Civ No. (2005) 7965 Yi Zhong Min Chu Zi (Beijing No. 1 Intermediate People's Court, 17 November 2006) (automated MP3 search engine not liable for an injunction or damages where copyright owners had not sent adequate notices of infringements), aff'd on appeal.

In some cases, courts have found that operating or hosting an unauthorised links site is a breach of the general duty of due care owed to the rights owner. In *Stichting BREIN v Techno Design 'Internet Programming' BV*,[45] the Dutch appeals court found that operating an MP3 search engine by which a site created and made available links to unauthorised music files, constituted 'tortious' activity towards the owners of copyright and neighbouring rights in such music. The court found that every download of an unauthorised file (even for private purposes) also involved a communication that was unauthorised. The court imposed a duty of care based on the fact that the 'lion's share' of MP3 files on the Internet were unauthorised, most users were searching for unauthorised files, and the defendant knew of and profited from its linking to such unauthorised communications.

3. The liability of file-sharing services

The most hotly litigated area in the field of third-party liability for on-line infringements involves, of course, file sharing. Beginning with the US lawsuit against Napster in 1999, there now have been a range of cases not only in the US but also spanning the Netherlands, Japan, Korea, Taiwan and most notably Australia, which together have begun to build up a picture of how and why file-sharing services can be held liable for users' infringements:

- **Netherlands: *Kazaa v Buma/Stemra*.**[46] In 'summary proceedings' involving a licensing dispute between peer-to-peer service Kazaa and the Netherlands authors' collecting society Buma/Stemra, the society counterclaimed that Kazaa was violating its member's copyrights. The Amsterdam District Court found on 29 November 2001 that Kazaa breached copyright law by giving users the opportunity to download music files by means of its computer program and network without a licence, and ordered Kazaa to take such measures as to render impossible any communication and copying of the Buma/Stemra repertoire. The Appellate Court of Amsterdam reversed the District Court's decision on 28 March 2002. The court relied almost exclusively on a last-minute affidavit of a Professor Ir. E. Huizer, who opined that Kazaa could not control the exchange of infringing files and that its software had uses other than to infringe copyright. Due to the nature and appeal

---

[45] Docket No. 1157/04 (Ct. App. Amsterdam, 5th Civ Div, 15 June 2006), overruling *Techno Design 'Internet Programming' BV v BREIN,* No. 85489/HA ZA 02-992 (D. Ct. Haarlem, 12 May 2004).

[46] No. KG 01/2264 OdC (Amsterdam Ct. of Justice, 29 November 2001), reversed, *Kazaa v Buma/Stemra,* No. 1370/01 (Amsterdam Ct. of Appeal, 28 March 2002), aff'd, No. C02/186HR (Netherlands S. Ct. 19 December 2003).

process for 'summary proceedings', facts contradictory to those presented by Prof. Huizer were not considered by the Appellate Court (but could have been considered subsequently in any substantive proceedings). This decision was upheld on 19 December 2003 by the Netherlands Supreme Court. Given that the factual record could not be challenged in the Supreme Court, the Supreme Court issued a procedurally focused ruling saying that the Court of Appeals was not wrong given the facts before it.[47]

- **Japan:** ***Nippon Columbia Co., Ltd et al. v Yugen Kaisha Nippon MMO.***[48] Japan MMO operated a peer-to-peer service used by approximately 42,000 persons, who made available about 80,000 files at any one time. Like Napster, Japan MMO created an index of files available for download, and users transmitted and copied files directly to each other. The court found, both at the preliminary injunction and 'interlocutory judgement' stage, that Japan MMO and its principal Michio Matsuda were themselves 'making transmittable' the files on users' computers, in violation of Japanese copyright law. Japan MMO was enjoined from offering the service on 9 April 2002, and was found liable on the merits on 29 January 2003. On 17 December 2003 the Tokyo District Court ordered peer-to-peer service Japan MMO to pay compensation of ¥ 36.89 million (US$ 335,000) in total, plus late payment charges, to RIAJ members and affiliates for infringing their 'making transmittable' right.
- **Korea:** ***Soribada (Asia Media Inc. et al. v Yang et al.).*** Several civil cases and one criminal case have examined various incarnations of the Soribada file-sharing service, largely finding Soribada liable for assisting copyright infringement and subject to civil damages and injunctions as well as criminal liability. The operators of the original Soribada service (Soribada 1), which offered 'centralised' file sharing of unauthorised music files, were indicted by the Korean prosecutor in August 2001 and sued civilly by Korean record companies in February 2002.

---

[47] *BUMA/STEMRA v Kazaa BV,* No. C02/186HR (Netherlands S. Ct. 19 December 2003).

[48] 2002 (Wa) Case No. 4249 (Tokyo District Court, 29th Civil Division, interlocutory judgement 29 January 2003, damages decision 17 December 2003). See RIAJ Press Release, *Court decided Japan MMO, a file-sharing service company, for illegality; Interlocutory judgment by the Tokyo District Court,* http://www.riaj.com/e/news/20030129.html (29 January 2003); RIAJ Press Release, *File-sharing service company was ordered to pay 37 million Japanese yen; Tokyo District Court decided the damages* (17 December 2003), http://www.riaj.com/e/whatsnew/20031217.html.

The criminal case initially failed,[49] but in July 2002 the civil court found Soribada liable because it knew or ought to have known of the infringements taking place on its service. The court issued an injunction requiring the peer-to-peer service to stop letting users download the plaintiffs' recordings, and to stop operating the service on the Korean Data Centre's servers.[50] This decision was upheld on appeal,[51] and Soribada 1 shut. (In January 2005, the court also awarded the music publishers' society KOMCA about 19 million Won (US$ 18,000) for Soribada's secondary infringement of KOMCA members' reproduction and transmission rights in about 5,000 songs.)

Soribada reopened in 2004 as a decentralised file-sharing service (Soribada 2), which was improved and expanded into what became known as Soribada 3. On 29 August 2005, the Seoul Central District Court again ordered Soribada to suspend operation of its service and distribution of the service's software on the basis that the defendants:

- *knew* that the service was used for infringement;
- *had a level of involvement in management and control,* in particular through a log-in function, a points system for 'sharing', and creation and distribution of the software;
- *failed to filter* infringing files even though they could have done so; and
- *made significant profits* through banner advertising and the sale of the service. [52]

---

49 The criminal case was dismissed on 15 May 2003 on the ground that the charges did not adequately specify how Soribada aided and abetted copyright infringement. The prosecutor appealed this dismissal to the High Court. On 12 January 2005 the High Court rejected the criminal appeal, finding that Soribada had not been given adequate notice of specific infringements and therefore could not be found aiding and abetting a crime. *In re Yang and Yang,* Docket 2003 No. 4296 (Seoul D. Ct., Crim. Ct. No. 5, 12 January 2005). The Supreme Court overturned this High Court decision, finding that if the developers could expect infringements to occur in their P2P system, they abetted users' infringements if they did not stop them. Case 2005 Do 872 (Korea S. Ct. 14 December 2007).

50 *Asia Media Inc. v Yang*, No. 2002KAHAP77 (Suwon D. Court, Seongnam Branch, First Civ Dep't, 9 July 2002).

51 *Sinchon Music Co., Ltd. v Yang,* Docket No. 2003 Na 21140 (Seoul High Ct., Civ Ct. No. 4, 12 January 2005), aff'd, 2005 Da 11626 (Korea S. Ct. 25 January 2007).

52 *Korean Assn. of Phonogram Producers v Soribada Inc.,* Docket No. 2004 Ka Hap 3491 (Seoul D. Ct., Civ Ct. No. 50, 29 August 2005). See *Court Blocks Free File-Sharing Services,* Korea Times (31 August 2005), http://search.hankooki.com/times/times_view.php?term=soribada++&path=hankooki3/times/lpage/nation/200508/kt2005083117362711960.htm&media=kt.

The Korean record companies and Soribada settled the case in February 2006, with Soribada agreeing to pay 8.5 billion Won in compensation (US$ 8.7 million). Following the settlement, Soribada opened a new centralised P2P service (Soribada 5) which purported to use filtering technologies to prevent infringement of the record companies' rights. A preliminary injunction sought by the record companies against this service initially failed in August 2006, based on Soribada's defence that stopping infringements would be 'technically impossible'. The High Court found on appeal, however, that Soribada had not used requisite best efforts in filtering out infringing files.[53] The parties have since entered into a new settlement, and Soribada opened an authorised subscription P2P service.

- **China Taipei (Taiwan): *EzPeer*.**[54] Subscription file-sharing service EzPeer was indicted for aiding and abetting infringement, and sued for civil copyright infringement. EzPeer was a centralised peer-to-peer service in Taiwan that charged users for 'file sharing' of music, film and software files. IFPI Taiwan secured a civil injunction on 11 December 2003 requiring EzPeer to remove 105 infringing Chinese repertoire tracks from its service. The Shih-Lin District Court dismissed the criminal case against EzPeer principals on 30 June 2005, finding among other things that the defendants did not have the requisite criminal intent or knowledge to be deemed accessories to users' crimes. Several individuals also were indicted, found guilty and sentenced for illegally reproducing MP3 files from the EzPeer and Kuro services. IFPI and EzPeer reached a civil settlement in June 2006. EzPeer shut down its unauthorised file-sharing service, and set up a licensed and digital rights management protected service called EzPeer+.[55]
- **China Taipei (Taiwan): *Kuro*.**[56] In December 2003, subscription file-sharing service Kuro was indicted for aiding and abetting infringement; civil infringement proceedings were also brought. Kuro was a centralised peer-to-peer service in Taiwan that charged users for file sharing music files. Kuro's CEO and President (brothers Chen), and the Chen brothers' father (deemed a 'legally responsible' person) were indicted on 1 December 2003 for aiding and abetting unauthorised

[53] No. 2006 Kahap/535 (Seoul D. Ct. 22 August 2006), rev'd, No. 2006/a 1535 (Seoul H. Ct. 10 October 2007).

[54] *Global Digital Technology Co., Ltd.*, 2002 Zhen Zi No. 10786 and No. 4559 (Shih-Lin (Taiwan) Dist. Ct. 30 June 2005).

[55] G. Kennedy & S. Doyle, *Pacific Rim News*, 23 Computer L. & Sec. Rep. 152–153 (2007).

[56] *Fashion Now Ltd.*, 92 Suit No. 2146 (Taipei (Taiwan) Dist. Ct.).

reproduction of sound recordings. On 9 September 2005, the Taipei district court found that the service operators jointly (with users) infringed the record companies' copyrights, having provided users the means of illegal reproduction, 'obviously foreseen' and known of users' infringing acts, 'shared' acts of searching and downloading with users, promoted the software and services for such purposes, and earned subscription fees from the service. As such, the service operators had criminal intent, and the requisite association of mind and participating acts with its users.[57] On the civil side, IFPI Taiwan secured an injunction requiring Kuro to remove 105 infringing tracks from its service on 2 April 2004. The parties reached a settlement in September 2006, by which Kuro agreed to close its P2P service, stop distributing its software and pay a substantial sum in damages.[58]

- **Australia: *Universal Music Australia Pty Ltd v Sharman License Holdings Ltd.***[59] Following an extensive 'dawn raid' on 6 February 2004, Australian record companies brought infringement proceedings against 10 companies and individuals related to the Kazaa peer-to-peer service. The case alleged that these parties were engaged in the promotion, facilitation and authorisation of the illegal copying of music through the use of Kazaa's software and service in Australia. The liability hearing took place from 29 November to 17 December 2004. On 5 September 2005, the federal court found six of the respondents liable for 'authorising' user infringement, on the basis of several findings:

  - *provision and maintenance of the means ('facilities')* for infringement;
  - *knowledge* of infringements (the defendants had 'long known' that the system was 'widely used' for sharing copyright files);
  - *encouraging infringement* through positive acts such as web-site messages and a 'Join the Revolution' marketing campaign;
  - *the 'primary', 'major' or 'predominant' use* of the system was for the sharing of copyright-infringing material;

57 *Press Release re Kuro Case,* Taipei District Court (9 September 2005); Press Release, Taiwan Intellectual Property Office, *On September 9, the Taipei District Court convicted Kuro and one of its subscription members* (9 September 2005), http://www.tipo.gov.tw/eng/press/ne20050909.asp. The Taiwan High Court upheld this judgement in July 2008.

58 IFPI, Press Release: *Taiwan's Kuro in substantial settlement with recording industry* (14 September 2006), http://www.ifpi.org/content/section_news/20060914.html.

59 [2005] FCA 1242 (5 September 2005), http://www.austlii.edu.au/au/cases/cth/federal_ct/2005/1242.html.

- *financial interest* of the defendants in maximising infringement (for there to be 'ever increasing' file-sharing and users);
- *failure to take steps to prevent or curtail infringement* (warnings were inadequate, filtering was possible but not implemented).

The defendants found liable were ordered to stop authorising infringement, which would be met by implementing a filter for infringing music tracks; to pay 90 per cent of the plaintiffs' costs; and to come back to court for a damages hearing. The parties settled the litigation in July 2006, with the defendants paying a reported US$100 million in settlement damages to record company claimants and agreeing to filter their service.[60]

- **Netherlands: *Stichting BREIN v Leaseweb BV.***[61] The defendant ISP was hosting a customer (Everlasting) that operated a 'BitTorrent' site, a recent hybrid of links and file sharing by which Torrent files point users to particular content files and 'tracker' sites coordinate the simultaneous uploading and downloading of those files between numerous users of the BitTorrent software. Without deciding at the preliminary injunction stage whether the customer's site violated copyright, the court found that 'Everlasting structurally facilitates the infringement of copyrights and neighbouring rights and ... (the holder of) Everlasting must be aware of this. Everlasting's conduct therefore is unlawful, because it is contrary to the principle of due care that must be observed *vis-à-vis* those entitled to copyrights.'[62]

---

[60] *Kazaa to pay record groups $100m*, Financial Times (27 July 2006); IFPI, Press Release: *KAZAA settles with record industry and goes legitimate* (27 July 2006), http://www.ifpi.org/content/section_resources/piracy-report-current.html.

[61] No. 369220 / KG ZA 07-850 AB/MV (D. Ct. Amsterdam, Civ Sector, 21 June 2007), aff'd, LJN: BD 6223, Amsterdam Court, 106.007.074/01KG (Amsterdam Ct. App. 3 July 2008).

[62] Id., para. 5.4. *Accord, Stichting BREIN v KPN*, No. 276747 / KG ZA 06-1417, para. 4.4 (Hague Ct., 5 January 2007):

> [The BitTorrent site operator is] 'facilitating structural infringements of copyrights and neighbouring rights. In light of the nature of the files alone, it cannot be otherwise than that the Website Owner is aware of this. It is furthermore relevant that income is being generated by means of the website because – before being able to download torrents – a user is required to pay a certain amount. In these circumstances it must be concluded for the present that the Website Owner's actions are wrongful, not because the Website Owner is infringing the copyrights or neighbouring rights vested in the rightful owners, but because its actions conflict with the due care that must be observed towards the rightful owners.'

4. Third-party injunctions

Another development in this area has been the willingness of courts internationally to issue orders against Internet service providers and other third parties to put a stop to infringers' Internet activities. Thus for example, German courts have held Internet account holders responsible for copyright infringements claimed to be conducted by others using their accounts,[63] enjoined an auction site to cut off offers that infringe trademark,[64] enjoined an eDonkey file-sharing server operator from allowing the making available of infringing music files from his server,[65] and enjoined payment-system providers from conducting transactions on behalf of an infringing website.[66]

In the same vein, French courts have ordered ISPs to cut off more than 100 subscribers' Internet accounts found to be involved in unauthorised file sharing.[67] The Danish Supreme Court ordered service provider TDC, the country's largest telecommunications provider, to terminate the Internet connections of two individuals on the TDC service that were offering infringing music files from FTP servers.[68] And in the Netherlands *Leaseweb* case, the court ordered the ISP to disclose the customer's identification and remove his BitTorrent site from its service.[69]

5. Filtering or blocking

Courts increasingly have proved willing to grant injunctions that include a requirement that a service provider filter or block infringing files or other

---

[63] Order in Interlocutory Injunction Proceedings, No. 308 O 58/06 (Civ. Chamber 8, Hamburg Landgericht, 25 January 2006) ('he is the owner of the Internet connection . . . and no fault is necessary for the restraining order demand'); Order in Interlocutory Injunction Proceedings, No. 308 O 41/06 (Civ. Chamber 8, Hamburg Landgericht, 18 January 2006) ('when he makes his Internet connection available to his underage son, he …has the duty .. to stop illegal conduct').

[64] *Montres Rolex v Ricardo,* I ZR 304/01 (Germany Supreme Civil Ct. (BGH), 11 March 2004).

[65] *Universal Music GmbH v Rac*, No. 308 O 273/07 (Hamburg D. Ct., Civ. Div. No. 8, 24 April 2007).

[66] Judgement, No. 27 O 836/04 (Berlin Regional Ct., 23 November 2004).

[67] See IFPI, *Breakdown of legal cases against illegal file-sharing*, http://www.ifpi.org/site-content/press/20060404a.html.

[68] *TDC v IFPI,* No. 40/2005 (Denmark S. Ct., 10 Febuary 2006) (failure to impose such an injunction would violate Art. 8(3) of the EU Copyright Directive); *Danish Court Tells ISPs To Cut Pirates' Connections,* Billboard.Biz (15 February 2006), http://www.billboard.biz/bb/biz/newsroom/legal_management/article_display.jsp?vnu_content_id=1002033151.

[69] *Stichting BREIN v Leaseweb BV, supra* n. 60, paras. 7.1–7.2; accord, *Stichting BREIN v KPN, supra* n. 61, para. 4.15 (ISP would breach its *own* duty of care by not disconnecting the customer's BitTorrent site).

activities as a remedy for infringements found – whether or not the service itself is deemed to be a primary infringer or a third party liable for its users' infringements.

In the *Napster*[70] and *Sharman*[71] cases, in which the courts found service providers liable for promoting or authorising their users' infringements, the courts had no difficulty in imposing a filtering obligation on the service as a *remedy* for the infringement. (Remember that failure to filter itself may be evidence, albeit not conclusive evidence, of the service's liability in the first place.[72])

Likewise, in *IFPI Danmark v Tele2 A/S*,[73] a Danish court issued a targeted injunction requiring an ISP to block access to the Russia-based music download service *allofmp3.com*. The court found that not only was the Russian site offering music files to the ISP's Danish customers without authorisation, but the ISP itself was infringing the plaintiffs' copyright by transmitting those files.

---

70 *Napster, supra* n. 37, 239 F.3d at 1027: 'Napster has both the ability to use its search function to identify infringing musical recordings and the right to bar participation of users who engage in the transmission of infringing files....Napster ... bears the burden of policing the system within the limits of the system.'

71 Order para. 5, *Universal Music Australia Pty. Ltd. v Sharman License Holdings Ltd, supra* n. 59:

> '5. Continuation of the Kazaa Internet file-sharing system (including the provision of software programs to new users) shall not be regarded as a contravention of order 4 if that system is first modified pursuant to a protocol, to be agreed between the infringing respondents and the applicants or to be approved by the Court, that ensures either of the following situations:
> (i): that:
> (a) the software program received by all new users of the Kazaa file-sharing system contains non-optional key-word filter technology that excludes from the displayed blue file search results all works identified (by titles, composers' or performers' names or otherwise) in such lists of their copyright works as may be provided, and periodically updated, by any of the applicants; and
> (b) all future versions of the Kazaa file-sharing system contain the said non-optional key-word filter technology; and
> (c) maximum pressure is placed on existing users, by the use of dialogue boxes on the Kazaa website, to upgrade their existing Kazaa software program to a new version of the program containing the said non-optional key-word filter technology; or
> (ii) that the TopSearch component of the Kazaa system will provide, in answer to a request for a work identified in any such list, search results that are limited to licensed works and warnings against copyright infringement and that will exclude provision of a copy of any such identified work.'

72 See e.g., *Grokster, supra* n. 10; *Sharman, supra* n. 58.

73 Case No. FI-15124/2006 (Copenhagen City Ct., 25 October 2006).

US copyright law,[74] EU copyright directives[75] and many countries' general law in principle also would permit an injunction requiring a service provider to filter or block infringing material or activities of sites or users on its system, even *without* a finding that the service provider itself was liable for the infringement.

While injunctions covering particular sites or users would be the expected norm in this area as well, the recent Belgian case *SABAM v SA Scarlet*[76] illustrates the extent to which one court was willing to go in requiring a service provider to implement broad filtering of Internet traffic. The Belgian music publishers' collecting society SABAM sought and obtained an injunction requiring the ISP Scarlet (previously known as Tiscali) to prevent its customers from the unauthorised sending or receiving via peer-to-peer applications of any electronic files containing musical works represented by SABAM. The court's expert witness had analysed various technical filtering systems, which the Court found could provide effective measures to recognise and prevent up to 90 per cent of such copyright infringements at the ISP level (a finding that the ISP has challenged on appeal).

In its ruling the court found that such filtering could recognise 90 per cent of the illegal music files exchanged on the Internet, and could be scaled up to deal with Scarlet's large volume of Internet traffic. The court rejected Scarlet's objections about future encrypted files as remote and speculative, about cost

---

[74] 17 U.S.C. § 512(j) (permitting injunctions requiring even 'mere conduit' ISPs to block account access or foreign sites even though the ISP is not liable for damages).

[75] Art. 8(3), Directive 2001/29/EC of the European Parliament and of the Council of 22 May 2001 on the harmonisation of certain aspects of copyright and related rights in the information society, Official Journal L 167/10, 22/06/2001 P. 0010–0019 ('EU Copyright Directive'):

> 'Member States shall ensure that rightholders are in a position to apply for an injunction against intermediaries whose services are used by a third party to infringe a copyright or related right.'

E-Commerce Directive, *supra* n. 3, recital 40:

> '[S]ervice providers have a duty to act, under certain circumstances, with a view to preventing or stopping illegal activities....the provisions of this Directive relating to liability should not preclude the development and effective operation, by the different interested parties, of technical systems of protection and identification and of technical surveillance instruments made possible by digital technology within the limits laid down by Directives 95/46/EC and 97/66/EC.'

Id. recital 45:

> 'The limitations of the liability of intermediary service providers established in this Directive do not affect the possibility of injunctions of different kinds; such injunctions can in particular consist of orders by courts or administrative authorities requiring the termination or prevention of any infringement, including the removal of illegal information or the disabling of access to it.'

[76] No. 04/8975 A of the General Roll (D. Ct. Brussels 28 June 2007).

concerns (0.50 per user per month) as ultimately payable by the users of the service and not excessive, and about possible 'false positives' as insufficient reason not to issue the injunction.

The court's analysis in *SABAM* makes clear that the normal issues relevant to any injunction – such as its efficacy, technical feasibility, and economic reasonableness – will be equally relevant to any specific requirement to filter. The court also found that such an injunction did not impose a general monitoring requirement, did not impose liability on the service provider or eviscerate its general exemption from liability, and did not violate privacy laws.

LEGISLATIVE TRENDS

Some proposed legislation to deal with third-party copyright liability generally, or peer-to-peer activities specifically, have started to appear after a fairly long gap that followed the development of the original ISP liability-limitation rules in the late 1990s.

- **US.** The 2004 US 'Induce Act' proposal[77] was subject to intense criticism and went nowhere, as did calls to change contributory-liability rules in the US following the *Grokster* decision.
- **European Union.** The European Commission's 2005 and 2006 proposals for a criminal-enforcement directive for intellectual property included a provision to criminalise 'attempting, aiding or abetting and inciting' infringements 'on a commercial scale'[78] – a fairly standard accomplice-liability provision.
- **France.** The French legislature enacted amendments to the copyright law in 2006 that appear to be directed specifically at publishers of file-sharing software. The law imposes a fine of 300,000 and three years imprisonment on those who provide software 'obviously intended to

[77] S. 2560 (22 June 2004), http://thomas.loc.gov/cgi-bin/query/z?c108:S.2560.

[78] Amended proposal for a Directive of the European Parliament and of the Council on criminal measures aimed at ensuring the enforcement of intellectual property rights, No. 2005/0127 (COD), COM (2006) 168 final (26 April 2006). The European Parliament has recommended that this be amended to read as follows: 'Member States shall ensure that all intentional infringements of an intellectual property right on a commercial scale, *and aiding* or abetting and inciting *the actual infringement*, are treated as criminal offences.' Position of the European Parliament adopted at first reading on 25 April 2007 with a view to the adoption of Directive 2007/.../EC of the European Parliament and of the Council on criminal measures aimed at ensuring the enforcement of intellectual property rights. This proposed directive is still under consideration.

make available to the public unauthorised works or protected objects'.[79] The law also allows the court to order 'any measures necessary' to protect the copyright, so long as such measures 'conform to the state of the art' and do not affect 'the essential characteristics or the initial destination of the software'.[80] Much remains unclear about the meaning of these amendments and how they will be applied.

- **Korea.** The 2006 Copyright Act of Korea contains a provision requiring certain 'special types' of 'on-line service providers' (those that 'mainly enable people to transmit literary works among themselves using computers' – a reference to peer-to-peer services) to take 'necessary measures such as blocking illegal transmission' of covered works when requested by the right holder.[81] A June 2007 presidential decree specifies the notice requirements for such requests, and defines 'necessary measures' as technical measures for identifying and filtering infringing content and sending warning notices with respect thereto.[82] The Ministry of Culture and Tourism's July 2007 notification defines the covered 'special types' of on-line services as including P2P service or program providers who receive payment or other commercial benefit, who give their users such a benefit or convenience, or who provide a program 'purported mainly' for searching and transmitting works stored in an individual or company's computer.[83]
- **Taiwan**. Taiwan's Legislative Yuan passed an amendment to its Copyright Law in June 2007 making it illegal to provide software or other technology that enables the transmission or reproduction of copyrighted works 'with the intention' to facilitate unauthorised transmission

---

79 Code de la propriété intellectuelle (France), Art. 335-2-1, http://www.celog.fr/cpi/lv3_tt3.htm#c5.

80 Id., Art. L. 336-1.

81 Korea Copyright Act, art. 104:

'Article 104 (Duty of online service providers of special types, etc.)

(1) Online service providers that mainly enable people to transmit literary works, etc. among themselves using computers, etc. (hereinafter 'online service providers of special types') shall take necessary measures such as blocking illegal transmission of said literary works, etc. when requested by the right holder. In this case, matters regarding requests by right holders and necessary measures shall be determined by a Presidential Decree.

(2) The Minister of Culture and Tourism may specify and notify the scope of special types of online service providers as defined under Paragraph 1.'

82 Proposed Amendment to the Enforcement Decree of the Copyright Act, Presidential Decree No. 20135 (Korea) (29 June 2007).

83 Ministry of Culture and Tourism (Korea), Public Notification No. 2007-24 (6 July 2007).

or reproduction. Such intention can be found where the provider advertises or takes 'other positive measures to abet, induce, procure or persuade the public' to infringe.[84]

SOLUTIONS?

Factors for Future Cases

Lawyers in the US and Commonwealth and civil law jurisdictions have prided themselves on knowing and applying discrete rubrics and doctrines for finding third parties liable for users' infringements, but it is increasingly apparent that:

- these doctrines overlap;
- particular tests such as 'authorisation' are being interpreted more broadly and even differently than their literal meaning;
- courts are applying a broader set of considerations in determining third-party liability regardless of the rubric chosen; and
- these trends can be seen in all three types of legal traditions, with similar results.

In the US, for example, the pre-*Grokster* debate was whether the doctrine of contributory liability applied where the third party file-sharing service arguably *knew about*, *intentionally facilitated, promoted* and *benefitted from* user infringements, but had tried to put himself beyond any real-time *control* of user activities, and could articulate at least theoretical non-infringing *uses* of his service.[85] The defendants argued that the element of control (or at least

---

[84] Art. 87(7), Taiwan Copyright Act (promulgated 11 July 2007):
'Provision of computer programs or other technologies that enable the public to publicly transmit or reproduce copyrighted works, with the intent to facilitate the public, via the Internet, to publicly transmit or reproduce other's works without approval or authorization of the economic rights holder, thus infringing on the economic rights of others and thereby gaining profits.
Person engages in the activity as described in Subparagraph 7 of the preceding paragraph, shall be deemed with the intent as referred to in that subparagraph shall the said person advertise or take other positive measures to abet, induce, procure or persuade the public to utilize a computer program or other technology to infringe on the economic rights of others.'

[85] The district court noted that the defendants in the *Grokster* case 'may have intentionally structured their businesses to avoid secondary liability for copyright infringement, while benefiting financially from the illicit draw of their wares.' *Metro-*

file-by-file, post facto control) of the contributory liability doctrine was not met. They also argued that *any* non-infringing use would also defeat a finding of liability under the *Sony* doctrine.

Nevertheless, not a single member of the Supreme Court would let Grokster off. Appealing to older formulations of third-party liability rules that included 'inducing' infringement,[86] the court found that a third party could be found liable if he *promoted* infringement. That promotion need not be subjective or overt – it could be proved from more than one objective activity of *communication (soliciting infringing users), failure to prevent or curtail infringement (that is, to filter),* or *profiting* from the infringement. In such circumstances, actual or potential *lawful use*, even if substantial, was no defence.

In the Commonwealth, commentators likewise have agonised over the boundaries of the doctrine of 'authorising' infringement,[87] probably unnecessarily. For one thing, 'authorising' infringement is not, as we have seen, the exclusive rubric under which third parties can be held liable for users' infringements. Doctrines of joint tortfeasorship, inciting, aiding and abetting and the like have equal footing to authorisation as bases for third-party liability, and as the commentators note, liability can be and sometimes is founded on more than one theory.[88]

Moreover, courts in the Commonwealth have rarely taken the word 'authorisation' literally. As a practical matter, doing so would make the offence nearly meaningless. It is rare to find a major infringer that has overtly told users to do something illegal – any sensible third party would not be caught dead doing so. Courts therefore have interpreted the term 'authorisation' more broadly to include activities with similar intent or effect – 'countenancing', 'counselling', 'aiding', 'controlling', 'inducing', and even 'inactivity or indifference' to a degree from which authorisation, promotion or permission may be inferred.

Goldwyn-Mayer Studios Inc., v Grokster, Ltd., 259 F. Supp. 2d 1029, 1037 (C.D. Cal 2003), aff'd, 380 F.3d 1154 (9th Cir. 2004), rev'd, No. 04-480, at 1 (S. Ct. 27 June 2005).

[86] E.g. *Kalem Co. v Harper Brothers*, 222 U.S. 55, 62-63 (S. Ct. 1911) (defendant that 'not only expected but invoked [infringing use] by advertisement' was liable for infringement 'on principles recognised in every part of the law.')

[87] E.g. Laddie, Prescott and Vitoria, *The Modern Law of Copyrights and Designs*, 3rd ed., London: Butterworths 2000. §§ 39.14, at 1772 ('the breadth of this [authorisation] tort is unclear, and some of the cases, mostly concerned with copyright, are hard to reconcile with one another').

[88] Id. § 39.18, at 1777 ('in a number of cases in which a defendant has been found guilty of authorising infringement he could have been held to have committed infringement either vicariously or as a joint tortfeasor').

Elements of 'knowledge' are likewise interpreted broadly. Third parties put in the dock seem surprisingly ignorant about users' infringements, however rampant or blatant. Courts thus have interpreted elements of knowledge to include situations where the third party 'should have known' of the infringement or the likely effects of the third party's actions.

In civil law countries, the results are similar. It was not at all surprising that the Dutch district court found Kazaa to be liable for users' infringements – in the court's mind Kazaa owed a *duty of care* not to assist users in such widespread illegal activity and could be ordered to stop doing so. It was only when the Court of Appeals got Professor Huizer's opinion – that Kazaa was unable to *control* the unlawful exchange of infringing files purportedly because it was impossible to recognise which files contained copyrighted material (assertions that Buma/Stemra inexplicably did not refute) – that liability was dismissed.[89]

Consistent Application of Common Elements

What seems to have emerged is that regardless of the particular law, liability rubric, technology or activity involved in a case, courts consider evidence on a common set of elements in determining whether a third party is sufficiently connected with infringement to be deemed culpable himself. These elements are principally the following:

- ***Relationship*** of the third party with the user. Sometimes expressed in terms of 'control' or 'causation', this element relates to the actual or potential influence that the third party has over the user himself.
- ***Extent*** of the third party's involvement. This looks at the connection between the third party and the user activity that constitutes infringement. This may involve the third party promoting the infringement ('sanctioning', 'countenancing', 'causing'); participating in preparatory, auxiliary or subsequent acts; providing the 'means' of infringement; or maintaining ongoing contact with the infringer, such as through the provision of services.
- ***Knowledge*** of infringing activities. As in other areas of law, knowledge that copyright infringement is illegal is not required, but complete ignorance as to an infringer's activity is not likely to raise third-party liability. Actual, real-time knowledge of individual acts of infringement is not required; knowledge will be imputed where the third-party 'should have known' the likely behaviour of the user.

[89] Declaration of Professor Dr. Ir. E. Huizer (18 February 2002), *Kazaa v Buma/Stemra, supra* n. 46.

- ***Intention*** of the third party. It is typically relevant whether a third party intended that one or more users engage in behaviour that infringes copyright. Given that third parties in the dock never admit this was their intention, courts can determine intention on the basis of oral and behavioural evidence that encourages infringement, even including inactivity or indifference of such a nature that a certain desired result may be inferred.
- ***Extent*** of infringement and lawful activities. This element evaluates whether there is 'substantial non-infringing use', or a primary use for infringement. The greater the proportion of infringing activity vis-à-vis legal activity that flows from a third-party's acts, the more likely courts will be to find third-party liability.[90]
- ***Financial or other benefit*** of third party. The more that a third party profits from user infringement, particularly if the third-party's business model depends on infringement or is not viable in the absence of infringement, the more likely liability will attach.
- ***Ability to prevent or deter*** infringement. If the very nature of a third party's activity or technology (for example, a stand-alone cassette or video recorder) is such that the third party in fact cannot prevent infringement, courts have been unlikely to find liability absent other countervailing factors. Courts have recognised, however, that in situations like library copying or file-sharing services, the third party may in fact have the ability – either beforehand, as user infringements happen, or even afterwards – to prevent or deter those infringements.
- ***Due care*** of third party. The element of due care – already a common feature of civil law jurisprudence – has also begun to appear in US and Commonwealth legislation and cases. Internet service providers must implement certain responsible practices to benefit from liability exemptions in the US.[91] Failing to implement filtering technology[92] or blind-

[90] The actual level of non-infringing use is a determination of fact which at times defendants have even sought to adjust artificially during litigation. See, e.g., *Stichting BREIN v Leaseweb*, *supra* n. 61, para. 2.5:

> On 14 May 2007, the following was posted on Everlasting:
>
> 'Hello everybody, This afternoon I was called by the provider of the server. He told me that he had been warned by BREIN about our site. At that time, this man was having a meeting with the company's lawyer…The lawyer recommended that I upload some personal files, such as some nice photographs you once made or recipes etc, as long as they are NOT copyright protected….'

[91] See 17 U.S.C., *supra* n. 2, § 512(i) (policies against infringement, accommodation of standard technical protections).

[92] *Grokster*, *supra* n. 10; *Sharman*, *supra* n. 59.

ing oneself to infringement[93] have also been condemned as failures of due care.

- ***Cost-benefit analysis.*** Legislators and courts have seemed unwilling to impose liability on technology providers, service providers and other third parties where the benefit of preventing or deterring copyright infringement is outweighed by technologically infeasible or economically unreasonable requirements such as third party.[94]

Application of this multi-factor analysis to the leading cases is instructive:

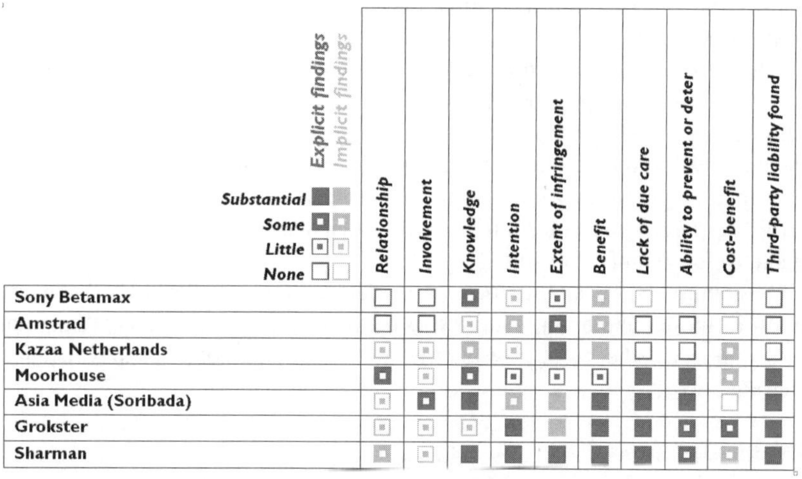

Figure 1.1 Factors in court decisions

It seems clear from these cases that no one factor itself will impute liability, but the strong presence of two or more accumulated elements ties a third party more closely to the infringement in ways that courts may find sufficient to

93 E.g. *In re Aimster Copyright Litigation*, 334 F.3d 643 (2d. Cir. 2003).

94 E.g. 17 U.S.C.§ 512(i)(2)(C) (service providers must accommodate certain technical protections that 'do not impose substantial costs on service providers or substantial burdens on their systems or networks'); *In re Aimster Litigation*, *supra* n. 92 ('if the infringing uses are substantial then to avoid liability as a contributory infringer the provider of the service must show that it would have been disproportionately costly for him to eliminate or at least reduce substantially the infringing uses').

impose liability on the third party. For example, 'merely' describing in a magazine how to copy music illegally and asking 'Why buy spend $10 on the latest David Bowie album when you can tape it?' may indicate intention to assist or promote infringement, but without any further evidence of some relationship with the user, financial benefit or further involvement with any particular copying, making such a publication may not result in liability.[95]

Releasing a generic product or service like a cassette duplicator or VCR that has primarily or substantial non-infringing uses, where there is no further involvement with the users, no express or implied promotion of infringement, and no benefit that can be tied directly or indirectly to the infringement, has not resulted in third-party liability to the manufacturers, even where these third parties knew or should have known that users would engage in infringement from time to time.[96]

On the other hand, even though a particular peer-to-peer service might be used for non-infringing purposes, where it was mostly used by users for infringement, and the third party had actual or imputed knowledge of user infringement, promoted the service for such purposes, got a financial benefit and engaged in an on-going connection with users, with inadequate (or no) efforts to prevent or reduce infringement, such a third party will likely be held liable for users' infringements.[97]

Regardless of the liability theory articulated, therefore, it is likely that many or all of these factors will continue to be the elements that courts will weigh in deciding whether to impute liability to third parties for activities like 'file sharing'.

Defunct Defences

In the area of litigation against peer-to-peer services, it appears that several of the defences commonly raised by such services are on their way to extinction. These are the following:

- ***The Frankenstein defence:*** 'I've created a monster that has gone on the rampage and now I can't control it.' This type of defence has been effectively rejected in the *Aimster* and *Sharman* litigation.
- ***The Einstein defence:*** 'This system is so complicated that the court and even I, the service operator, cannot understand it.' This was also rejected in the *Sharman* litigation.

---

95 See *RCA Corp. v John Fairfax and Sons Ltd.*, [1981] 1 NSWLR 251 (Australia).

96 *Sony, supra* n. 7; *Amstrad, supra* n. 17.

97 *Grokster, supra* n. 10; *Sharman, supra* n. 59.

- ***The Land-of-Far-Far-Away defence:*** 'This system was created in Holland, Denmark and Estonia, is run out of Vanuatu, and operates all over the world. Nothing you do can stop it.' The judge in the *Sharman* litigation had no problem in issuing a judgement against the service in his own country.
- ***The Scintilla defence:*** 'This service is (well, perhaps, could be) used for matchmaking, real estate listings and political communication among Chinese dissidents. So you can't touch the massive infringement.' This defence was rejected both in *Grokster* and *Sharman.*
- ***The Wink-Wink defence:*** 'We did tell users that the service was '100 per cent legal' but also told them they really shouldn't violate copyright, know what I mean, know what I mean?' The judges in *Soribada* and *Sharman* rejected this defence as well.

Getting Beyond the Myths to the Facts

All of this points to a final theme that runs through the international litigation in this area: solid, evidentiary proof is crucial. There is so much mythology, unsubstantiated rhetoric, and unexamined assumption floating around in areas like file sharing, that detailed and possibly expensive proof of the underlying facts will make or break any case in this area.

In the Dutch *Kazaa* case, for example, an unchallenged academic opinion that Kazaa could not control infringements[98] was enough to defeat Buma/Stemra's motion for summary judgement on the issue of third-party liability. Detailed courtroom evidence in the recording industry's case against *Sharman* in Australia, which involved the same underlying Kazaa file-sharing system, proved the opposite – the system could have been designed to control infringing activities, and could even be altered after-the-fact with a filter to do so. On the basis of this and other detailed evidence submitted on the issues described above, the record companies won their case in Australia against Sharman.

CONCLUSION

The area of third-party liability with respect to Internet activities like file sharing seem to have gone through a phase of 'de-mythologising'. In the US, Commonwealth and civil law jurisdictions, judges seem to be having little trouble in applying long-standing legal doctrines of third-party liability in a

98 See *supra* n. 89 and accompanying text.

technology-neutral way. A common set of elements is in play wherever these cases arise. None of these elements on its own typically results in liability, but as more elements are proved in a particular case, culpability may be found. And, as ever, truth is only what can be proved in the courtroom – an axiom that is as true in the area of third-party copyright liability as in any other area of the law.

2. Legal issues in peer-to-peer file sharing, focusing on the making available right

Michael Schlesinger*

The Internet must not become a high-tech Wild West, a lawless zone where outlaws can pillage works with abandon or, worse, trade in them in total impunity.

– Nicolas Sarkozy, President of France

I think the failure of ISPs to engage in the fight against piracy, to date, has been the single biggest failure in the digital music market.

– Paul McGuinness,[1] manager, U2

OVERVIEW

Peer-to-peer file sharing has had a profound effect on the copyright industries in recent years, especially the music industry, creating legal questions surrounding liability for illegal distribution of copyright materials online. Indeed, in many countries, existing exclusive rights under copyright, or slightly modified rights, comprise all the chief activities undertaken in the course of a P2P transaction – largely through implementation of the interactive 'making available'

* Michael Schlesinger is Of Counsel to the law firm of Greenberg Traurig LLP in Washington, DC. Mr. Schlesinger also serves as Professorial Lecturer in Law at George Washington University School of Law and is a Lecturer at the Munich Intellectual Property Law Center (MIPLC). He represents the International Intellectual Property Alliance (IIPA). The views expressed in this chapter are solely those of the author, and are not necessarily endorsed by Greenberg Traurig LLP, GWU School of Law, MIPLC, or the IIPA. Mr. Schlesinger can be reached at SchlesingerM@gtlaw.com.

1 One more quote could be added to these, that of John F. Smith, President, International Federation of Musicians (FIM): 'ISPs are the gatekeepers of the Internet – they have the technical means and the moral responsibility to play an important role in protecting copyrighted content on their networks and to ensure that performers receive fair remuneration for the sale and use of their work on those networks.'

right. The touchstone of this interactive right, as supported by case law in most countries, is that a work can be made available to others in a manner such that they *may* access it from a time and place chosen by them, and nothing more (that is, even if the specificity of the onward transmission is not proven). The future for copyright industries depends on the continued robustness of such exclusive rights in the digital environment, preservation or confirmation of secondary liability for copyright infringements online, and the continued or increasing cooperation of service providers.

P2P FILE SHARING: IS IT TOO LATE TO SAVE THE MUSIC INDUSTRY?

In IFPI's *Digital Music Report 2008*,[2] the international record industry's group reported that 'music sales via online and mobile channels have risen from zero to an estimated US$2.9 billion [representing a roughly 40 per cent increase on 2006 (US$2.1 billion)] – 15 per cent of industry sales – over the last five years, making music more digitally advanced than any entertainment sector except games.'[3] However, that report also indicated that '[t]ens of billions of illegal files were swapped in 2007,' and '[t]he ratio of unlicensed tracks downloaded to legal tracks sold is about 20 to 1.' In addition, third-party studies show that illegal file sharing results in less legitimate copyright products purchased,[4] an assertion supported by the following fact: the growth rate of around 40 per cent in digital sales of music did not offset the sharp fall in music CD sales globally, meaning that the overall market for 2007 declined compared with 2006.

It's a complicated picture – one in which more than 500 legitimate digital music services worldwide offer over 6 million tracks, with legal music downloads up 40 per cent; yet up to 80 per cent of ISP traffic still comprises distribution of copyright-infringing files. Expansion of broadband, particularly in developing markets like China, Southeast Asia and Latin America, is driving an increase in unauthorized file sharing on P2P networks. The first spectres of large-scale mobile telephone music piracy have emerged in countries like

---

2 *Digital Music Report 2008*, 24 January 2008, at http://www.ifpi.org/content/section_resources/dmr2008.html.

3 In the world's biggest digital music market, the US, online and mobile sales now account for 30 per cent of all revenues, according to IFPI.

4 Id. (reporting that 'Italy's Luigi Einaudi Foundation in 2007 found that 30 per cent of peer-to-peer users bought fewer CDs and DVDs, while only 6 per cent said they bought more CDs,' and 'In Australia, research undertaken for ARIA (February 2007) shows that 57 per cent of P2P downloaders rarely or never purchase the music they download – pointing to straight substitution of legitimate sales').

Japan (with more than one third of all mobile users admitting to regular illegal downloading on mobile networks) and in Southeast Asia, where mobile technologies are ubiquitous, but legal services remain sparse.

In Europe, illegal file sharing of copyright materials has proliferated in recent years; however, where good cooperation in enforcing copyright exists, the rate of Internet users regularly sharing files illegally has remained relatively low. Contrast that with countries that have little or no enforcement in the online space, like in the Netherlands and Spain, and the rates of illegal file sharing are greater: 28 per cent and 35 per cent, respectively, of Internet users regularly engage in illegal file sharing.

THE P2P LEGAL ENVIRONMENT: IMPLEMENTING THE 'MAKING AVAILABLE' RIGHT

While one aspect of P2P file sharing will always involve reproduction on the receiving end, the crucial part is the sender making available the work or object of related rights. Thus, unquestionably, one of the most important results of the adoption of the World Intellectual Property Organization (WIPO) Copyright Treaty (WCT) and the WIPO Performances and Phonograms Treaty (WPPT) was the recognition of an exclusive right to 'make available' protected works or objects of related rights in an interactive context. The drafters achieved this through the adoption of an exclusive 'communication to the public' right, including an exclusive 'making available' right in Article 8 of the WCT,[5] and an exclusive 'making available' right in Articles 10 and 14 of the WPPT (as to performers and producers of phonograms, respectively).[6] Simply put, these rights ensure that authors of copyright works and related rights holders can authorise or prohibit transmissions of their creative products, whether they be transmissions over the Internet, including transmissions over P2P networks, or (increasingly) over mobile devices.

More specifically, the drafters recognized that right holders must have the following exclusive right:

---

5 WIPO Copyright Treaty, S. Treaty Doc. No. 105-17 (1997); 36 ILM 65 (1997) (entry into force March 6, 2002), at http://www.wipo.int/treaties/en/ip/wct/pdf/trtdocs_wo033.pdf (WCT), Art. 8 ('Right of Communication to the Public').

6 WIPO Performances and Phonograms Treaty, S. Treaty Doc. No. 105-17, 36 ILM 76 (1997) (entry into force May 20, 2002), at http://www.wipo.int/clea/docs_new/pdf/en/wo/wo034en.pdf (WPPT), Arts. 10 ('Right of Making Available of Fixed Performances') and 14 ('Right of Making Available of Phonograms').

> making available to the public of their works [performances/ phonograms] in such a way that members of the public may access these works [performances/phonograms] from a place and at a time individually chosen by them.[7]

The adoption of such rights in the WCT and WPPT importantly sought to close gaps in coverage in the existing conventions and treaties (either as to certain acts or as to certain subject matter), as no right in the existing treaties adequately or completely dealt with the transmission of works and objects of related rights through the Internet or other similar digital interactive networks. Two essential theories for the type of new exclusive right to be granted emerged at the 1996 Diplomatic Conference: one seeking to fit digital and interactive transmissions within existing notions of distribution, and another seeking to fit such transmissions within existing notions of communication to the public. Neither a 'distribution' model nor a 'communication' model seemed entirely satisfying (or acceptable) to the delegates at the 1996 Diplomatic Conference because of the nature of digital transmissions; for example, the transmission from one computer to another does not result in the transfer of property or possession (because the 'source' copy remains in the possession of the sender), but by the same token, such a transmission does not resemble a traditional non-demand broadcast (because of the interactive nature of making available).

What emerged was a flexible approach owing to the differences in national legislations and approaches at the time, an approach Dr. Mihály Ficsor has dubbed the 'umbrella solution'. As long as the act of making works, sound recordings and performances available interactively is covered by one or more exclusive rights, national legislatures could have considerable flexibility in labeling or characterizing the exclusive rights involved.[8] Thus, while the WCT and WPPT do not require that the so-called 'distribution' right extend beyond the distribution of tangible copies, the umbrella solution does permit signatories to implement the 'communication to the public'/ 'making available' right by applying the exclusive distribution right in a country's law to electronic transmissions of works, sound recordings, and performances fixed in sound recordings. Most countries, however, have opted for adapting other existing rights, most commonly the 'communication to the public' right, to ensure that interactive transmissions are covered. As to related rights, most countries have

---

7 WCT Art. 8; WPPT Arts. 10 and 14.

8 The 'making available' right is characterized in what Dr. Ficsor calls a 'neutral, legal-characterization-free description of interactive transmissions . . . [that is] included in Article 8 [of the WCT] in the following way: making available to the public of . . . works in such a way that members of the public may access these works from a place and at a time individually chosen by them.' Mihály Ficsor (2002), *The Law of Copyright and the Internet* (Oxford University Press) at C8.06.

added a standalone 'making available' right or have subsumed the interactive right within a concept of 'communication' or sometimes 'broadcast'.

In any case, what is clear about this interactive right is that a work (or phonogram/performance in the case of the WPPT) can be made available to others in a manner such that they *may* access it from a time and place chosen by them, and nothing more. The onward distribution or communication may be shown (for example, to discern damages), but need not be because, owing to its interactive quality, the act of making available a work only consists of 'making the work accessible to the public … in which case, the members of the public still have to cause the system to make it actually available to them'.[9] In other words, it should not depend on the public to cause the system to further communicate the work for the right to be invoked, as long as the work has been made available in such a way as it *is capable of being accessed.* Most of the jurisprudence recognizes this essential element of the right of making available.[10]

US and EU Implementation Compared

The US concluded that a 'distribution' approach more closely approximates the real market impact of on-demand, and other online transactions, in which the recipient of the transmission often ends up with a copy of a work that he or she did not have before. Thus, it relied upon the distribution right to cover distributions/transmissions beyond physical distribution of tangible copies.[11] When deciding whether US law needed to be amended to implement the 'making available' right, the drafters (and those advising them) determined it need not because 'making available' as defined in the WCT (and WPPT) was adequately covered by the broad reading of the distribution right in conjunction with the reproduction right (which would protect against someone making an illegal copy when uploading it to a server or when an end-user downloads it), and other rights under US law.[12]

---

9 World Intellectual Property Organization, *Guide to the Copyright and Related Rights Treaties Administered by WIPO and Glossary of Copyright and Related Rights Terms*, WIPO Pub. No. 891(E) (2003), CT-8.6, at 208.

10 For example, in the United States, the Supreme Court held in *New York Times Co. v Tasini*, 533 US 483, 488 (2001), that notwithstanding absence of proof that individual copies of plaintiffs' articles on defendant's database were transferred to users of the database, 'it is clear' that the defendants 'distribute copies' of the plaintiffs' articles merely by making them available for download. *Id.* at 498, 505. The Court rejected the defence that there was no distribution under US law by the defendants since it was the database subscribers who were responsible for the downloading.

11 See, e.g., *Playboy Enterprises, Inc. v Frena*, 839 F. Supp. 1552 (M.D. Fla. 1993).

12 The Register of Copyright and the United States Congress concluded that

Unlike the US, the EU opted for a 'communication to the public'.[13] At the time these standards were adopted, there was little question that making available works (including objects of related rights) in such a way that anyone can access them at their own time and place, including P2P uploads or downloads, would be covered. It would have been absurd, for example, for the United States to leave a gap in coverage for any acts of 'making available' as defined under the WCT and WPPT because at that very moment it was amending its

§ 106(3) covered the 'making available' right, such that no amendment to the US Copyright Act was necessary. Letter from Marybeth Peters to Rep. Howard L. Berman (25 September 2002), reprinted in *Piracy of Intellectual Property on Peer-to-Peer Networks: Hearing Before the Subcomm. on Courts, the Internet, and Intellectual Property of the House Comm. on the Judiciary*, 107th Cong. 2nd Sess. 114–15 (2002) ('[M]aking [a work] available for other users of a peer to peer network to download . . . constitutes an infringement of the exclusive distribution right, as well of the reproduction right.') ('As you are aware, in implementing the new WIPO Copyright Treaty (WCT) and WIPO Performances and Phonograms Treaty (WPPT) in the Digital Millennium Copyright Act, Congress determined that it was not necessary to add any additional rights to Section 106 of the Copyright Act in order to implement the "making available" right under Article 8 of the WCT.').

[13] See Council Directive 2001/29/EC of 22 May 2001 On the Harmonisation of Certain Aspects of Copyright and Related Rights in the Information Society, 2001 O.J. (L 167/10), Art. 3. See also Mihály Ficsor, *The Right of Communication to the Public and the Making Available Right* (on file with author). Article 3(1) of the 'Directive 2001/29/EC of the European Parliament and of the Council of May 22, 2001, on the harmonisation of certain aspects of copyright and related rights in the information society', in a way, is only a slightly adapted version of Article 8 of the WCT as it reads as follows: 'Member States shall provide authors with the exclusive right to authorise or prohibit any communication to the public of their works, by wire or wireless means, including the making available to the public of their works in such a way that members of the public may access them from a place and at a time individually chosen by them.' The recitals concerning this provision clarify that it includes two elements. Recital (23) refers to the need for harmonizing the provisions on communication to the public in general: 'This Directive should harmonise further the author's right of communication to the public. This right should be understood in a broad sense covering all communication to the public not present at the place where the communication originates. This right should cover any such transmission or retransmission of a work to the public by wire or wireless means, including broadcasting. This right should not cover any other acts.' Recital (25) addresses the issue of on-demand transmissions in respect of copyright: 'The legal uncertainty regarding the nature and the level of protection of acts of on-demand transmission of copyright works and subject-matter protected by related rights over networks should be overcome by providing for harmonised protection at [the] Community level. It should be made clear that all rightholders recognised by this Directive should have an exclusive right to make available to the public copyright works or any other subject matter by way of interactive on-demand transmissions. Such interactive on-demand transmissions are characterised by the fact that members of the public may access them from a place and at a time individually chosen by them.'

law to implement the two treaties and was in the process of negotiating Free Trade Agreements (for example with Singapore) that expressly included the requirement to provide authors and right holders with an exclusive right to make available works (and objects of related rights).

Global Implementation of Article 8 of the WCT and Articles 10, 14, and 15 of the WPPT

Globally, the number of implementations has grown markedly in the past several years, whether they be by changes to domestic legislation (or proposed changes), by commitments through bilateral agreements (most notably through Free Trade Agreements entered into between several countries and the United States), by interpretation, and by self-implementation (that is, through accession to the treaties as 'superior' law). As of April 2008, at least 96 countries/territories have, committed to have, or are in the process of legislating to add, interactive rights of 'communication to the public'/'making available' or provide such rights by interpretation. Of those 96 countries/territories, 77 provide WPPT-compatible 'making available' rights for producers of sound recordings and/or performers, or had draft legislation providing such rights.[14] There are several others that have broad interpretations consistent with the treaties or that implement the treaties provisions through self-execution (for example, Ghana, Guinea).

Anecdotal Implementation Data (keying on Asia)

Anecdotally, there seem to be four different implementation scenarios:

- Countries that provide fully or near fully treaties-compatible rights as to works and objects of related rights (examples are Australia and in Asia include Brunei Darussalam, Cambodia, Hong Kong,[15] Japan, Malaysia, Papua New Guinea, Singapore, and Taiwan).[16]

---

14 Draft legislation: Oman (legislation awaits signature by the Sultan), Swaziland, the Philippines, Thailand, Macedonia (Former Yugoslav Republic of), and Kuwait have draft legislation that, if enacted, would provide an interactive 'making available' to the public right. India's 2006 HRD draft would provide such a right. FTAs: Panama (once FTA goes into force) and Colombia (if approved) would be obligated to provide 'making available' rights as to works and objects of related rights.

15 Hong Kong begins with the concept of distribution (similar to the US) but also includes express language that largely mirrors the treaties. Copyright Ordinance Section 26 (Cap 528) (2001). Section 26 of the Ordinance provides as to works (including sound recordings):

- Countries that provide WCT-compatible rights but not WPPT-compatible rights, or vice versa (only Nepal from Asia falls into this latter category), or for which implementation of either is problematic or in question in some way (examples in Asia are Indonesia, the Philippines, Republic of Korea, Samoa, Sri Lanka, and Vietnam).
- Countries that provide broad exclusive rights for works and/or objects of related rights (for example, 'communication to the public' and 'broadcast' rights) but no express interactive 'making available' right (examples are New Zealand and in Asia include Bangladesh, Bhutan, Fiji, Mongolia, Pakistan, and Thailand).
- Countries that provide no comparable rights to those in Article 8 of the WCT and Articles 10/14/15 of the WPPT (examples in Asia include Laos and Myanmar).

Implementation of Related Rights under the WPPT: Incomplete Solutions for the 'Making Available' Right

One problematic aspect in implementing the 'communication to the public'/'making available' right in the new digital environment is the treatment of related rights. Some countries have incompletely or improperly defined the scope of the right, marring their implementation of the WPPT with respect to related rights.[17] Other countries have simply failed to implement the

---

(1) The making available of copies of the work to the public is an act restricted by copyright in every description of copyright work.
(2) References in this Part to the making available of copies of a work to the public are to the making available of copies of the work, by wire or wireless means, in such a way that members of the public in Hong Kong or elsewhere may access the work from a place and at a time individually chosen by them (such as the making available of copies of works through the service commonly known as the Internet).
(3) References in this Part to the making available of copies of a work to the public include the making available of the original.
(4) The mere provision of physical facilities for enabling the making available of copies of works to the public does not of itself constitute an act of making available of copies of works to the public. The provision for performers is essentially the same.

[16] Taiwan has taken the approach of creating a new 'public transmission' right to satisfy the WIPO treaties. Taiwan Copyright Law, Art. 3(10). Taiwan's approach appears to adopt the broad 'communication to the public' approach, but given the various exclusive rights in Taiwan's draft law that together provide treaties-compatible coverage, it can be said that Taiwan's approach may be closest to Dr. Ficsor's 'umbrella solution', and may be an indicator that the notion of an 'umbrella solution' remains viable.

[17] For example, some African countries that have implemented provide broad exclusivity for communications to the public (including 'making available') for works

WPPT at all.[18] For example, while Indonesia's prompt ratification of the WCT (the first country in the world to ratify the WCT, on 5 June 1997) set an excellent example, its 2002 Copyright Law failed to implement an interactive and exclusive 'making available' right as to sound recording producers and performers. Indonesia has since joined the WPPT in 2005, but is yet to draft implementing regulations for the WPPT.

Indonesia is not alone in its failure to properly implement the WPPT. Part of some countries' reluctance to act with respect to related rights may be a reflection of the uncertain outcome at the 1996 Diplomatic Conference, specifically, the inability of the delegations to completely resolve all the issues related to rights to be afforded to producers of phonograms and performers in the networked (for example, Internet) environment. Specifically, the delegates at the Conference adopted an agreed statement in connection with Article 15 of the WPPT. It reads as follows:

> It is understood that Article 15 does not represent a complete resolution of the level of rights of broadcasting and communication to the public that should be enjoyed by performers and phonogram producers in the digital age. Delegations were unable to achieve consensus on differing proposals for aspects of exclusivity to be provided in certain circumstances or for rights to be provided without the possibility of reservations, and have therefore left the issue to future resolution.

This agreed statement reflects the discussions and negotiations about the so-called 'near-on-demand' forms of broadcasting and communication to the public by cable, such as subscription services. In respect of such services, the demand of rights owners seems to be quite justified that, at least a right to remuneration should be granted, but in cases where such services most seriously conflict with a normal exploitation of the rights in phonograms, an exclusive right should be considered.[19] What is clear is that the 'making avail-

---

but provide an incomplete approach to related rights, affording exclusivity only with regard to 'making available' for producers of sound recordings and performers, and creating a right to a single remuneration for 'other' communications to the public and broadcasts. See, e.g., Botswana, Copyright and Neighbouring Rights Act (2000) (A. 19), § 26(1); Tanzania, The Copyright and Neighbouring Rights Act, No. 6 (1999), § 33; Burkina Faso, Law No. 032-99/AN Law for the Protection of Literary and Artistic Property (1999), § 79.

18 While beyond the scope of this chapter, another area in which implementation strategies differ, but in which mistakes can be very costly to the system and leave countries out of compliance, is in the area of exceptions and limitations on the rights granted in the WCT and WPPT with respect to communications to the public and the 'making available' of works or objects of related rights.

19 An example of existing legislation trying to respond to such a demand may be found in §§ 106(6), 114(a) and 114(d) to (j) of the US Copyright Act.

able' right in Article 14 is to be considered a starting point for countries' implementation approaches, not an end point. It would be unfortunate to stifle new ways of distributing copyright materials in these countries, including subscription services, interactive or on-demand services, or near-on-demand services, by enacting only a making available right as to phonograms, without considering levels of exclusivity that ought to be granted to right holders in such cases.[20]

RECENT P2P CASES WITH A FOCUS ON 'MAKING AVAILABLE'

Over the past several years, there has been steady growth in the number of cases and the number of jurisdictions in which courts have been asked to grapple with infringement issues involving the 'communication to the public' and 'making available' of works and other objects of protection, including over P2P networks.

The following sections are a brief but non-exhaustive survey (in alphabetical order) of the variety of recent cases and trends in several jurisdictions.

Australia

In *Universal Music Australia Pty Ltd v Sharman License Holdings Ltd*,[21] the Federal Court of Australia (Judge Wilcox) held several defendants associated with Sharman Networks liable for 'authoris[ing] ... making a copy [and] communicating ... to the public' various sound recordings using the Kazaa peer-to-peer file-sharing network, all arising out of the distribution of the Kazaa P2P file-sharing software to end-users.[22] The Statement of Claim

---

20 Express rights for record producers and performers in the online environment (as for other right holders) can provide economic rationales for investment in the creation of recorded music (and other subject matter). In an environment increasingly dominated by digital transmissions rather than product delivery, and by an increasing variety of methods of distribution, it is important to address the level of exclusivity to be afforded over interactive transmissions of recordings and performances – uses that are fast becoming the central economic uses of recordings and performances.

21 *Universal Music Australia Pty Ltd v Sharman License Holdings Ltd* [2005] FCA 1242 (5 September 2005).

22 The court noted three factors supporting a finding of secondary (authorization) liability: (1) defendants' knowledge that the system was being 'widely used for the sharing of copyright files'; (2) failure to take 'any action to implement' ... 'technical measures (keyword filtering and gold file flood filtering) that would enable the respondents to curtail – although probably not totally to prevent – the sharing of copy-

specifically included references to 'making available', the actionable claim being that of 'authorising' the making available as follows: 'authorising Kazaa users to make available online, or electronically transmit, to the public MP3 or other digital music files constituting copies of the whole or a substantial part of the relevant sound recordings.' In describing the infringing activity of the defendants, the court noted, '[t]here is no evidence as to the identity of the particular Kazaa user or users who made available for sharing, or downloaded from another user, each of the Defined Recordings. However, somebody must have done so. Witnesses for the applicants gave uncontested evidence of *being able to* download each of these sound recordings as blue files' (para. 415) [emphasis added].

In *Cooper v Universal Music Australia Pty Ltd*,[23] the Federal Court of

---

right files'; and (3) encouraging infringement, for example, by including 'on the Kazaa website exhortations to users to increase their file sharing and a webpage headed "Join the Revolution" that criticises record companies for opposing peer-to-peer file sharing.' The remedy included defendants being 'restrained, by themselves, their servants or agents, from authorising Kazaa users to do in Australia any of the infringing acts, in relation to any sound recording of which any of the applicants is the copyright owner, without the licence of the relevant copyright owner.' However, the court was willing to allow the continuation of the service if the new versions of the software impose filtering (non-optional key-word filter technology). More specifically, the defendants were given a choice to continue operating the website if one of the two situations could be confirmed:

(i) that

(a) the software program received by all new users of the Kazaa file-sharing system contains non-optional key-word filter technology that excludes from the displayed blue file search results all works identified (by titles, composers' or performers' names or otherwise) in such lists of their copyright works as may be provided, and periodically updated, by any of the applicants; and

(b) all future versions of the Kazaa file-sharing system contain the said non-optional key-word filter technology; and

(c) maximum pressure is placed on existing users, by the use of dialogue boxes on the Kazaa website, to upgrade their existing Kazaa software program to a new version of the program containing the said non-optional key-word filter technology; or

(ii) that the TopSearch component of the Kazaa system will provide, in answer to a request for a work identified in any such list, search results that are limited to licensed works and warnings against copyright infringement and that will exclude provision of a copy of any such identified work.

NOTE: On 5 December 2005, the Federal Court of Australia ceased downloads of Kazaa in Australia after Sharman Networks failed to modify their software by the December 5 deadline. Users with an Australian IP address were greeted with the message 'Important Notice: The download of the Kazaa Media Desktop by users in Australia is not permitted' when visiting the Kazaa website. Sharman planned to appeal the Australian decision, but ultimately settled the case as part of its global settlement with the record labels and studios in the United States.

[23] *Cooper v Universal Music Australia Pty Ltd*, FCAFC 187 (18 December 2006).

Australia found the proprietor of a website MP3s4free.net (Cooper), the website host (the ISP),[24] and a director liable for authorising infringement by knowingly allowing others to place on his website hyperlinks to infringing material and encouraging website users to access infringing files via the links. Regarding the making available right, the court found that '[a] recording is communicated within the meaning of § 85(1)(c) if it is made available online or electronically transmitted (§ 10).'[25] In this case, the website in question provided 'deep links' to infringing files located at remote third parties' IP addresses. Because of this, the court characterized the activity as providing 'ready access' to the files, but nonetheless stopped short of concluding that the defendants themselves had 'communicated' the files.[26] Rather, it was the third parties who had communicated (by uploading and making the files available for download). In order to find the defendants' liable, the court looked to the Copyright Act and found that the defendants were liable for 'authorising' [§ 110] infringement taking place between third parties.[27] In the lower court decision, Judge Tamberlin noted that 'communicate' under the Australian law points to 'both limbs of the definition of communicate, namely, to make available on-line and to electronically transmit the subject matter.'[28]

---

[24] The Court also rejected the possibility that the Australia-US Free Trade Agreement safe harbour scheme could apply to the ISP, holding that the amendments do not apply retrospectively, and that even if they did, the ISP would not have been able to rely on the safe harbour provisions because it received a financial benefit from the infringements (in the form of free advertising on the website) and failed to take action against the owner of the site despite having knowledge of the infringements.

[25] In the lower court decision, Judge Tamberlin discussed the meaning of 'make available online' citing the Australia law, which almost exactly mirrors the WCT definition.

[26] Another argument, that Cooper had infringed copyright by 'exposing for sale or by way of trade' infringing music files on his website, was also rejected.

[27] One interesting and perhaps important note as to international copyright law principles involves the posture of the Australian court in *Cooper* as to extraterritorial acts of infringement, that is, infringing acts outside of Australia but linked to on Cooper's website. Section 101(1) of the Australian law provides that 'copyright is infringed by a person who, not being the owner of the copyright and without the licence of the copyright owner, authorises another person to do *in Australia* an infringing act.' At least in the *Cooper* case, the location of the third parties either 'making available' or 'electronically transmitting' the works or sound recordings is not made clear, and there seems to be some question open as to whether the mere authorization in Australia of acts occurring outside Australia can constitute infringement of s. 101(1). Contrast this possibility with the clear holding in the US case of *Subafilms, Ltd. v MGM-PatheCommunications Co.*, 24 F.3d 1088 (9th Cir.) (*en banc*), *cert. denied,* 513 US 1001 (1994), in which the US court held that the mere authorization of an infringing act occurring outside the United States is not actionable in the US.

[28] Judge Tamberlin also held that the remote websites had infringed as they had 'made available … the recordings,' not the one providing the deep link.

Canada

In *BMG Canada Inc. v John Doe (F.C.)*,[29] the Federal Court of Canada denied issuing a court order to turn over records of P2P file sharers partly on the ground that the plaintiffs (record companies) had failed to make out a *prima facie* case of copyright infringement. Plaintiffs alleged that defendants installed a peer-to-peer application on their computers, copied files to 'shared directories', used ISP services to connect their computers to the Internet, ran the peer-to-peer application while on the Internet, and made files in the shared directories available for copying, transmission and distribution to millions of users of the peer-to-peer service. Specifically regarding the 'making available' right, the court held that there was 'no evidence that the alleged infringers either distributed or authorized the reproduction of sound recordings ... [a]ll they did was place personal copies into shared directories accessible by other computer users.' The Federal Court cited the judgement of the Supreme Court of Canada in *CCH Canadian Ltd. v Law Society of Upper Canada*[30] for the proposition that 'the provision of facilities that allow copying does not amount to authorizing infringement.' Interestingly, the court focuses on the missing 'authorisation' from which liability could have been found, noting, '[h]ow is what was done here different from a library placing a photocopier in a room

---

29 *BMG Canada Inc. v John Doe (F.C.)*, 2004 FC 488 (CanLII).

30 *CCH Canadian Ltd. v Law Society of Upper Canada*, [2004] 1 S.C.R. 339, 2004 SCC 13. In *CCH*, plaintiffs sued the Law Society over its Great Library at Osgoode Hall in Toronto, a reference and research library with one of the largest collections of legal materials in Canada. The Great Library provided a request-based photocopy service for Law Society members, the judiciary and other authorized researchers. Under this 'custom photocopy service,' legal materials were reproduced by Great Library staff and delivered in person, by mail or by facsimile transmission to requesters. The Law Society also maintained self-service photocopiers in the Great Library for use by its patrons. CCH specifically attacked the provision of a photocopy machine for 'self-service' photocopying of copyright materials. The Supreme Court of Canada, in its holding, defined the contours of secondary liability, noting, '[w]hile authorization can be inferred from acts that are less than direct and positive, a person does not authorize infringement by authorizing the mere use of equipment that could be used to infringe copyright.' More specifically, the court held that a library 'does not authorize copyright infringement by maintaining a photocopier ... and posting a notice warning that it will not be responsible for any copies made in infringement of copyright.' (The court also noted that '[c]ourts should presume that a person who authorizes an activity does so only so far as it is in accordance with the law,' and that '[t]his presumption may be rebutted if it is shown that a certain relationship or degree of control existed between the alleged authorizer and the persons who committed the copyright infringement,' but noting that in this case, there was no evidence that the Society exhibited 'sufficient control' over the library patrons to conclude that the Society 'sanctioned, approved or countenanced the infringement').

full of copyrighted material? In either case the element of authorization is missing.' The court noted that the WIPO Treaties had not been implemented in Canada, and that an unlawful 'distribution' would not be found 'absent a positive act by the owner of the shared directory, such as sending copies or advertising the material's availability for copying'.

Hong Kong

The Hong Kong 'BitTorrent' case is also instructive as to how courts are dealing with the P2P phenomenon as well as the 'making available' issue.[31] On 18 May 2007, the Hong Kong Court of Final Appeal affirmed the conviction of Chan Nai-Ming for 'attempted distribution'[32] of illegal copies of copyrighted works. In this case, Mr Chan was accused of having 'seeded' copyright files to be shared using the 'BitTorrent' file sharing protocol – a P2P file sharing system by which small pieces of files are shared among a group (a 'swarm'), which can distribute files more quickly and efficiently the more people join the 'swarm.' One of the key points of discussion (both at the trial court level and on appeal) regarding the 'making available' right was whether there was any distribution, or any possibility of a distribution, as all Mr Chan allegedly did was 'seed' the files so that they could be downloaded using the BitTorrent method of file sharing.[33] The Court had no trouble holding that uploading files through the 'seeding' process and making them available for others to download constitutes 'distribution' under the Hong Kong SAR Copyright Ordinance.[34] Specifically, Mr Justice Rubeiro PJ said the following:

> Distribution in its ordinary meaning, is clearly capable of encompassing a process in which the distributor first takes necessary steps to make the item available and the recipient then takes steps of his own to obtain it. A simple example involves distribution of soft drinks or other consumer items by means of coin-operated vending machines.

---

31 *HKSAR v Chan Nai-Ming*, FACC 0003/2007, 18 May 2007.

32 Hong Kong prosecutors had initially indicted Mr Chan on a count of unlawful 'distribution' but amended the count to 'attempted distribution' to dispense with additional evidentiary burdens.

33 Indeed, Chan's defence was that 'seeding' the files on Torrent was not 'distribution' under s. 118 of the Hong Kong Copyright Ordinance, but rather, a way sharing the files.

34 One of the key defence points was that, while the statute provided for civil remedies for 'making available' as defined in s. 26 of the Ordinance, for criminal liability to attach, the prosecutor needed to show 'distribution', which is nowhere defined in the Ordinance (and is not therefore defined to subsume the concept of 'making available').

Japan

In what is known as the 'File Rogue' case, *JASRAC (Japanese Society for Rights of Authors, Composers and Publishers) v MMO Japan Ltd.*,[35] the Tokyo District Court found MMO Japan Ltd. and its representative Michihito Matsuda, who administered the peer-to-peer file-sharing service called 'File Rogue,' liable for copyright infringement of the rights of 'making copyrighted works transmittable' and 'public transmission of copyrighted works'.[36] One of the issues the court considered was whether a sender who stores an MP3 file in a share folder on his or her PC and connects to the defendant's server infringes the plaintiff's right of 'making copyrighted works transmittable'. The court held that 'the defendant's service provides its users with *an opportunity* to exchange MP3 files, which are reproductions of commercially available recordings (CDs)' [emphasis added]. More specifically, the court said, 'as far as the exchange of MP3 files is concerned, the defendant's service, in effect, *enables* its users to freely send and receive MP3 files.' [emphasis added].[37]

Korea

Korea's seminal P2P cases involve the various iterations of the Soribada P2P

---

35 *JASRAC v MMO Japan* (Tokyo District Court, 29 January 2003), H17.3.31, Tokyo Dist. Ct. No. 16 Ne 446 http://www.jasrac.or.jp/ejhp/release/2003/0129.html (English-language summary) (awarding preliminary injunction against distribution of FileRogue file-sharing program).

36 The case was continued to determine the scope of the injunction and the amount of damages to be paid. In a provisional injunction applied by JASRAC in 2002, the Tokyo District Court ordered MMO Japan not to allow the transmission of musical works administered by JASRAC.

37 Another P2P case in Japan worthy of note involved the file-sharing service called 'Winny'. The Winny software was developed by Mr Isamu Kaneko to allow for anonymous peer-to-peer file sharing. The anonymous system was styled after another program called 'Freenet' which purported to protect user identities to promote freedom of speech, but Winny was advertised on an Internet bulletin board well known for propagating copyright infringement on the Internet. The bulletin board, 2channel, has been cited in numerous press reports as a haven for copyright infringing activities. On 27 November 2003, police raided the home of Kaneko, known to 'Winny' users as 'Mr 47', and shut down his Internet home page. On the same day, in separate raids, police arrested two men for illegally distributing the Universal Studios film 'A Beautiful Mind' and for illegally distributing game software via 'Winny.' On 13 December 2006, the Kyoto District Court found Kaneko guilty of aiding and abetting the infringement of Japan's Copyright Law. See Motion Picture Association, *Japanese File-Sharing System Developer Guilty Of Abetting Copyright Infringement*, 13 December 2006 (Press Rel.).

service and are instructive as to how 'communication to the public' rights and 'making available' rights have become vital for right holders in practice. In the case involving Soribada 3,[38] an injunction was issued in 2005, among other relief, ordering the founders of the Soribada P2P system to cease allowing users of Soribada 3 to upload or download illegal MP3 files of the right holders. The key relevant issue in the case was whether the 'transmission' right is infringed by merely making available unauthorized copies of files in a shared folder. The court found that 'making an MP3 file available for downloading by other users after storing it on a shared folder requires only interfacing to the network receiving IP addresses, etc. ... thus, no separate transmission is necessary'.[39] In a key legal holding regarding the making available right, the court found that 'providing copyright material for use through wire communication for receipt or use by other users who interface to the network of the Soribada server anytime, anywhere ... [falls] under the infringement of the transmission right under s. 1, Article 91 of the Copyright Act.'[40] Another key holding was as follows:

> MP3 files ... saved to their own download folders or those ... stored themselves in the download folder shall be [deemed] stored in the shared folder ... for immediate downloading by other Soribada users. This is tantamount to providing copyright material for use through wire communication for receipt or use by other users who interface to the network of the Soribada Service anytime, anywhere; thus falling under the infringement of the transmission right of the Petitioner.

The founders of Soribada have since settled with many right holders and launched Soribada 5 in July 2006 as a purportedly legitimate service charging a monthly fee (currently 4,000 Won, or almost US$4), utilizing audio fingerprint technology to identify tracks and technology to filter out unlicensed

---

38 See *Korean Association of Phonographic Producers v Soribada Co., Ltd.*, Case No. 2001 Kahab 3491, Seoul Cent. Dist. Ct., 50th Civ Div., 29 August 2005 (Soribada 3). The *Soribada* services (Soribada 1–5) have changed over time, each becoming less centralized than the one before it. In *Soribada 1*, the defendants were found contributorily liable for the infringements of their third party customers; the service they provided was a website in which thousands of songs were indexed and hyperlinked to IP addresses at which the various files could be downloaded. See *Korean Association of Phonographic Producers v Soribada Co., Ltd.*, Case No. 2002 Kahab 77, Suwon Dist. Ct., 9 July 2002, aff'd Seongwan [sp] Branch Ct. (14 February 2003), aff'd in part, Seoul High Court (12 June 2005), Case No. 2003 11a2 1140 (Soribada 1). In *Soribada 2*, the defendants removed the hyperlinks to the IP addresses, but still retained an index on the site (resembling the architecture and business model which was struck down as illegal in the US *Napster* litigation).

39 *Soribada 3*, at § 1(a)(2)(a).

40 *Id.* at § 2(b)(2)(b).

tracks.[41] In June 2007, the Korean government enacted amendments to the Copyright Act of Korea, including mandating filtering for any 'special type of online service providers,'[42] defined to include services like Soribada.[43]

People's Republic of China

The making available right (codified in Article 10(12) and 41 as to sound recordings of the Copyright Law of the People's Republic of China (2001)) has not been prominent in the seminal Internet infringement cases in China. Nonetheless, the cases are worthy of note as they may be said to set the stage for how judges will deal with such cases in the future. In January 2007, the International Federation of Phonographic Industries (IFPI) filed 11 separate claims for an injunction and damages against the Chinese Internet search engine Yahoo! China, on behalf of local and international record companies, after the search engine walked away from talks regarding its making available of copyrighted songs for download without permission from record companies. Specifically, Yahoo! China, through its MP3 search page, offers a music delivery service that induces and facilitates users to search for individual MP3 music tracks, and then download and/or play them for free without ever leaving the website. On 24 April 2007, Beijing's No. 2 Intermediate Court ruled that the search engine was responsible for the copyright violations because it enabled web surfers to find the illegal music.[44] Similar to *Cooper*, the court

---

[41] As of January 2008, Soribada was reportedly the second largest music service provider in Korea with 700,000 paying subscribers. See *Soribada*, at http://en.wikipedia.org/wiki/Soribada. Soribada claims to have licensing deals with almost all local labels, with the exception of Seoul Records, which is owned by SK Telecom, Soribada's main rival in the online space. Among foreign labels, Soribada says it has a deal with Universal Music and that it is about to close deals with Sony BMG, EMI and Warner Music. See Mark Russell, *Soribada Gets OK For Legal P2P Service*, 13 March 2008, at http://www.billboard.biz/bbbiz/content_display/industry/e3i276690244f41c8186be5e51e3a031b19.

[42] The new Section 104(1) provides specifically,

'An online service provider whose service involves peer-to-peer use between different people's computers, for which the main purpose is the transmission of works (hereinafter referred to as "a special type of online service providers"), shall, at the request of relevant right holders, be required to take technical measures, including those to block illegal transmissions. In this case, the necessary measures to be taken at the request of relevant right holders shall be determined by the details of a Presidential Decree.'

[43] Ministry of Culture and Tourism Public Notification No. 2007-24.

[44] See *Statement from John Kennedy, Chairman and Chief Executive of IFPI, on today's Yahoo! China ruling*, 24 April 2007, at http://www.ifpi.org/content/section_news/20070424a.html.

had no problem finding Yahoo! China liable for linking to illegal downloads of copyrighted music,[45] and the company was ordered to pay a fine of 200,000 Yuan and remove the links. On 20 December 2007, the Beijing High Court upheld the lower court's decision.[46] Yahoo! China failed to comply and faced legal action again in February 2008 to enforce the December court order. The Yahoo! China case was decided under the 2006 *Regulations on the Protection of the Right of Communication through Information Networks* (1 July 2006) ('2006 Internet Regulations').

The Yahoo! China case stands in contrast with litigation brought by record companies against the major Chinese search engine Baidu in 2005 under the Copyright Law – prior to the 2006 Internet Regulations. In November 2006, the Beijing Intermediate People's Court found no liability for copyright infringement, holding the search engine's deep links 'did not constitute an infringement [by Baidu] as all the music was downloaded from web servers of third parties.'[47] The record companies appealed but the Beijing High Court upheld the lower court's decision on 20 December 2007 (the same date as the decision affirming the Intermediate Court's decision holding *Yahoo! China* liable). However, as the Baidu decision was based on the state of the law prior to the issuance of the 2006 Internet Regulations, on 4 February 2008, record industry groups filed new civil suits against Baidu and also Sohu/Sogou for their music deep linking services. A similar case brought by Hangzhou-headquartered online music service 5fad was likewise unsuccessful.[48]

---

[45] Mike Rosen Molina, *China court rules Yahoo! China violated copyright by linking to filesharing sites*, 24 April 2007, at http://jurist.law.pitt.edu/paperchase/2007/04/china-court-rules-yahoo-china-violated.php.

[46] However, the Yahoo injunction only extended to a few songs and the resulting damages were extremely low. Chinese officials responsible for drafting the *Regulations on the Protection of the Right of Communication through Information Networks* ('Internet Regulations') that became effective on 1 July 2006 have stated that under Article 23 of those regulations, ISPs are liable for deep linking.

[47] See *Baidu off the hook in copyright infringement case*, 20 November 2006, at http://digitalmusic.weblogsinc.com/ 2006/11/20/baidu-off-the-hook-in-copyright-infringement-case/.

[48] See Gareth Powell, *5fad loses copyright case against Baidu*, China Economic Review, 13 January 2007, at http://www.chinaeconomicreview.com/it/2007/01/13/5fad-loses-copyright-case- against-baidu/. More deeplinking and Internet-based infringement cases are sure to follow. For example, on 3 February 2008, Xunlei, one of China's largest download service providers, lost a piracy suit and was ordered to pay 150,000 Yuan (US$20,833) compensation to Shanghai Youdu Broadband Technology Co. (Youdu), according to the Pudong District People's Court. Youdu, a content provider for broadband users, paid 600,000 Yuan to get rights to 'Confession of Pain,' a blockbuster film starring Tony Leung and Takeshi Kaneshiro, from the copyright owner on 28 December 2006, six days after it debuted. Youdu was allowed to provide

Taiwan

As with China, the seminal cases in Taiwan involve P2P file-sharing programs aiding and abetting users to download illegally, but the courts in these cases did not directly address the 'making available' right. On 9 September 2005, the Taipei District Court convicted three executives of Kuro, Taiwan's largest file-sharing service, for criminal copyright infringement.[49] The court spokesman indicated, 'Kuro had violated copyright law in offering its members programs to download MP3 music.' The service was run as a commercial subscription business, with an estimated 500,000 registered users in Taiwan and mainland China, causing enormous losses to the music industry in both places.[50] The court found that Kuro ran advertisements that had encouraged members, who

a download service one month after the film's debut, according to the agreement. Youdu planned to charge 2 Yuan a download. However, a download link for the film appeared on Xunlei's website (www.xunlei.com) in early January 2007. By 4 January 2007, the film had been downloaded 520,869 times. In defense at court, Xunlei's attorney claimed his client provided only a third-party link for the film and did not violate Youdu's rights. The court said Xunlei objectively participated and helped the third-party website to disseminate the pirated film and promoted the film on its website. There are reportedly seven or more 'MP3 search engines' that offer 'deep links' to thousands of infringing song files and derive advertising revenue from doing so (accounting for the majority of online piracy in China) and over a dozen Chinese-based P2P services engaging in file sharing activities, including Muper, Kugoo, Xunlei and eMule.

[49] Sentences ranged from two to three years in jail and fines for criminal copyright infringement. In addition, one of Kuro's 500,000 paying members was sentenced to four months imprisonment for making 900 songs available for upload.

[50] In a subsequent development, the Taiwan International Federation of the Phonographic Industry and Kuro reached a settlement on 14 September 2006, whereby Kuro agreed to discontinue its file-sharing function by 15 October 2006, and would cease distribution of P2P software, as well as pay NT$300 million (approx. US$9 million) in damages to record businesses. Kuro has approximately five million members in China and Taiwan. Without obtaining distribution rights, Kuro collected a monthly fee from its members for use of P2P software for illegal file sharing; it was the largest website of its kind in Taiwan, and caused enormous financial damage to rights holders. In August 2003, IFPI Taiwan filed for a preliminary injunction against Kuro, prohibiting the illegal file sharing of the 105 songs owned by member rights holders; then, on 4 December of the same year, the Taipei District Prosecutors Office brought charges against Kuro for copyright infringement and commenced public prosecution. See, e.g., *Taiwan's Kuro in substantial settlement with recording industry*, 16 September 2006, at http://www.ifpi.org/content/section_news/20060914.html. The Kuro case contrasted with an earlier case in which Shihlin District Court found Weber Wu, president of EzPeer, a P2P file-sharing service, not guilty of criminal copyright infringement. See Jessie Ho, *Ezpeer found not guilty in landmark copyright verdict*, Taipei Times Online, 1 July 2005, at http://www.taipeitimes.com/News/front/archives/2005/07/01/2003261705.

paid a monthly fee of NT$99, to swap copyrighted music files via its site, and therefore held that Kuro was a party to infringement of the Copyright Law.[51]

United States

The Congressional drafters in the United States (and those advising them) did not deem it necessary to amend US law (specifically, § 106(3)) to explicitly include the 'making available' language from the WCT/WPPT, and advisors have since confirmed the existence of a 'making available' right under US law.[52]

The early Internet and P2P cases did not key on the making available right as there were either clear violations of the reproduction right (*MP3.com*) or, with the main targets in those cases being services (for example, *Napster*, *Grokster*), alleged facilitating infringement by third parties. As can noted below, 'making available' was presumed to be an infringement in *Napster*, and, in *Grokster*, the Supreme Court at least implied that making files available constitutes distribution.

In more recent cases involving recording company suits against individuals for illegal P2P file sharing, defence counsel – facing clear-cut cases against their clients for unlawful reproductions – have waged some spirited defences against the recording companies, claiming that US law does not in fact provide a 'making available' right, at least not without proof of an onward distribution. The decisions on this claim have cut both ways.

---

[51] See *Taiwanese Criminal P2P Convictions Set the Example*, 11 September 2005, at http://constitutionalcode.blogspot.com/2005/09/taiwanese-criminal-p2p-convictions-set.html. The Kuro case stands in contrast with the earlier District Court ruling in a criminal action against Weber Wu, owner of the P2P site EzPeer. On 1 July 2005, the Taipei District Court found EzPeer not guilty of 'engag[ing] in reproducing or publicly distributing works of copyright holders.' More recently, EzPeer and Kuro reportedly jointly launched a legal music site, called Kuro, in mainland China. See http://www.billboard.biz/bbbiz/content_display/industry/e3i4666d48f49725610e21ab472aba9283d.

[52] Register of Copyrights, Marybeth Peters, in a letter to Congressional hearings on piracy of intellectual property on peer-to-peer networks, said, 'making [a work] available for other users of [a] peer to peer network to download ... constitutes an infringement of the exclusive distribution right, as well as the reproduction right.' Letter from Marybeth Peters, Register of Copyrights, to Rep. Howard Berman, from the 28th Dist. of Cal. (25 September 2002), reprinted in *Piracy of Intellectual Property on Peer-to-Peer Networks, Hearing Before the Subcommittee on Courts, the Internet, and Intellectual Property of the House Committee on the Judiciary*, 107th Cong., 2nd Sess. 114–115 (2002).

The early cases: *MP3.com* through *Grokster*

- *UMG Recordings, Inc. v MP3.com, Inc.*, 92 F. Supp. 2d 349 (S.D.N.Y. 2000): This was not a P2P case but was one of the first instances of a copyright infringement claim against an Internet service offering music to users. The MyMP3.com service allowed users to listen to songs from the MP3.com website by loading their legally purchased CDs into their computers to be recognized by the site. MP3.com in turn uploaded (reproduced) thousands of albums/songs to its server to be accessed by such users. US District Judge Jed S. Rakoff said, '[t]he complex marvels of cyber spatial communication may create difficult legal issues; but not in this case. Defendant's infringement of plaintiff's copyrights is clear.' In finding direct infringement, the Court held that 'although defendant seeks to portray its service as the functional equivalent of storing its subscribers' CDs, in actuality defendant is re-playing for the subscribers converted versions of the recordings it copied, without authorization, from plaintiffs' copyrighted CDs.'
- *A&M Records, Inc. v Napster, Inc.*, 239 F.3d 1004 (9th Cir. 2001): This was the first major case in the United States to address the application of the copyright laws to P2P file sharing. The Napster file-sharing software allowed users to: (1) make MP3 music files stored on individual computer hard drives available for copying by other Napster users; (2) search for MP3 music files stored on other users' computers; and (3) transfer exact copies of the contents of other users' MP3 files from one computer to another via the Internet. The Ninth Circuit ruled that Napster could be held liable for contributory infringement (assuming it had knowledge, for example, through notification by a right holder) and/or vicariously liable (as it could control the activities of infringers using the Napster service) for infringement of 'at least two of the copyright holders' exclusive rights: the rights of reproduction, § 106(1); and distribution, § 106(3).'[53]
- *MGM Studios, Inc. v Grokster, Ltd.*, 545 US 913 (2005): Now the seminal P2P case in the United States, the Supreme Court held unanimously that 'one who distributes a device with the object of promoting its use to infringe copyright, as shown by clear expression or other affirmative

---

[53] To the question of how the secondary liability standards in the US were applied in the case, in the Opinion affirming the Appeal from the Motion to Modify the Preliminary Injunction against Napster, Judge Beezer of the Ninth Circuit affirmed the modified preliminary injunction, obligating Napster 'to remove any user file from the system's music index if Napster has reasonable knowledge that the file contains plaintiffs' copyrighted works. Plaintiffs, in turn, must give Napster notice of specific infringing files.'

> steps taken to foster infringement, is liable for the resulting acts of infringement by third parties.' In other words, file-sharing companies (in this case, Grokster and Streamcast) can be held liable for inducing infringement when they distribute a product 'with the object of promoting its use to infringe copyright, as shown by clear expression or other affirmative steps taken to foster infringement.' In this case, the Grokster software (and the StreamCast software) allowed users to swap files without having any information go through Grokster's (or StreamCast's) computers. It did this by assigning 'root supernodes' responsible for acting as the hubs for distribution of music from peer to peer.

Not much has been written about the *MGM v Grokster* litigation in the United States in the context of the making available right, but it is worthy of note. Specifically, in describing the infringement claims, the Court expressly said that the users of the Grokster and Streamcast service 'reproduced *and distributed* copyrighted works in violation of the US Copyright Act' [emphasis added]. Later in the opinion, the Court focuses on what files were 'available' on the networks for download. The Court used the term 'distribution' regardless of the fact that the peer-to-peer system described did not involve anything more than users opening up their folders for sharing, that is, 'making available' the files, without onward distribution.

The issue of 'making available' in recent US cases

As noted, the Congressional drafters in the United States did not deem it necessary in 1998 to amend US law to explicitly include the 'making available' language from the WCT/WPPT. The legislative history of the 1976 Copyright Act suggests that the drafters contemplated that an 'offer to distribute' would suffice for liability under § 106(3) of the Act and that no copy need change hands in order for the distribution right to be invoked under US law. Some evidence for this is in the Legislative History of the 1976 Act in which drafters referred to the right of 'publication' and 'distribution' in synonymous terms. The definition of 'publication' in § 101 not only subsumes the right of 'distribution' but also includes the 'offer to distribute' works.

Until recently, the minimal case law in the United States regarding the making available of copyright materials supports the interpretation of the 'distribution' right as including the right to 'offer to distribute' or rather to prohibit the unauthorized offering to distribute copyright materials. One case in point is *Hotaling v Church of Jesus Christ of Latter-Day Saints*,[54] in which

---

[54] *Hotaling v Church of Jesus Christ of Latter-Day Saints* 118 F.3d 199 (4th Cir. 1997).

the 4th Circuit found that placing unauthorized copies of books and an index of them for users to check out from a library constitutes an infringement of the distribution right under § 106(3) of the US Copyright Act.

Of even more persuasive effect is the Supreme Court's decision in *New York Times Co. v Tasini*, 533 US 483, 488 (2001), which held that, notwithstanding absence of proof that individual copies of plaintiffs' articles on defendant's database were transferred to users of the database, 'it is clear' that the defendants 'distribute copies' of the plaintiffs' articles merely by making them available for download.[55] The Court rejected the defence that there was no distribution under US law by the defendants as it was the database subscribers who were responsible for the downloading.[56]

Despite such legal precedents, defendants' lawyers have waged strong defences in ongoing cases involving individual P2P file sharers brought by the record companies, claiming that US law does not in fact provide a 'making available' right, at least not without proof of an onward distribution. The cases cut both ways: some courts have found that the distribution right under § 106(3) of the US Copyright Act encompasses the act of making copyrighted materials available for electronic distribution on a peer-to-peer network, regardless of whether actual distribution has been shown; other courts have decided that a § 106(3) claim cannot stand on the grounds that plaintiffs have failed to show an onward distribution.

The following is a small sample of cases in which a 'making available' right or its equivalent was found in US law:

- *Elektra Entertainment Group Inc. et al v Barker*, Case No. 7:05-cv-07340-KMK (S.D.N.Y.) (Opinion and Order, 31 March 2008). In an Order denying defendant's motion to dismiss for failure to state a claim, Judge Kenneth Karas agreed that distribution under § 106(3) is essentially synonymous with 'publication', noting 'it is unsurprising that courts faced with similar allegations as in this Complaint have looked to the definition of the word "publication" in 17 USC § 101 to construe the definition of the word "distribute" in § 106(3)'. The court held that 'the offer[] to distribute copies or phonorecords to a group of persons for purposes of further distribution, public performance, or public display,'

55 *Id.* at 498, 505. ('[w]e further conclude that the Print Publishers infringed the Authors' copyrights by authorizing the Electronic Publishers to place the Articles in the Databases.')

56 Thomas D. Sydnor II, *Thomas and Tasini: Did the Making-Available Debate End Before It Began?*, Progress and Freedom Foundation, Progress Snapshot, Release 4.13, June 2008 (e-mail publication) (pointing out that 'plaintiffs asserted that their copyrights were infringed when their articles were "placed in" these databases').

17 USC. § 101, can violate the distribution right of s. 106(3). The judge specifically equated distribution with publication but said that the plaintiff needed to re-allege the claim using the proper wording.

- *Motown Record Co. v Theresa DePietro*, Civ. No. 04-CV-2246, 2007 US Dist LEXIS 11626 (E.D. Pa.16 February 2007), at 7.[57] In this case involving a downloader using the Kazaa software, Judge Cynthia Rufe of the Eastern District of Pennsylvania stated, '[a] plaintiff claiming infringement of the exclusive distribution right can establish infringement by proof of actual distribution or by proof of offers to distribute, that is proof that the defendant "made available" the copyrighted work.[38]' Footnote 38 continues, '[w]hile neither the United States Supreme Court nor the Third Circuit has confirmed a copyright holder's exclusive right to make the work available, the Court is convinced that 17 USC § 106 encompasses such a right based on its reading of the statute, the important decision in *A&M Records, Inc. v Napster, Inc.*, 239 F.3d 1004 (9th Circuit 2001), and the opinion offered by the Register of Copyrights, Marybeth Peters, in a letter to Congressional hearings on piracy of intellectual property on peer-to-peer networks ('[M]aking [a work] available for other users of [a] peer to peer network to download ... constitutes an infringement of the exclusive distribution right, as well as the reproduction right').'
- *Atlantic Recording Corp. v Anderson*, No. H-06-3578, 2008 WL 2316551 (S.D. Tex. 2008): Summary judgment was granted for plaintiffs, as defendant placed songs into a shared folder to be distributed. The court found that distribution has been equated with publication which includes 'the offering to distribute copies or phonorecords to a group of persons for purposes of further distribution...,' and 'making copyrighted works available for download via a peer-to-peer network contemplates *further distribution*, and thus constitutes a violation of the copyright owner's exclusive *distribution* right....'

The following is a small sample of cases in which a 'making available' right or its equivalent was not found without a showing that there was an onward distribution (although *London-Sire v Does* paves the way for a 'deemed' distribution theory to succeed; that is, that there can be a reasonable inference drawn from the facts in a plaintiff's favour such that the reasonable fact-finder may infer a distribution actually took place):

---

[57] The procedural posture is denial of plaintiff's motion for summary judgment due to defendant's claim that she was 'misidentified' as the infringer and owing to alleged destruction of evidence by the defendant.

- *London-Sire Records, Inc., v Does*, No. 04cv12434-NG, 542 F. Supp. 2d 153 (D. Mass 2008) (Denial of Motion to Quash): In denying a motion to quash a subpoena (for identification information about 'Doe' defendants allegedly infringing copyright), the District Court in Massachusetts ruled that 'publication' and 'distribution' are distinct under US law, and therefore, 'the defendants cannot be liable for violating the plaintiffs' distribution right unless a distribution actually occurred.' The court then denied the motion to dismiss, noting that there may be a 'deemed' distribution:

  > But that does not mean that the plaintiffs' pleadings and evidence are insufficient. The Court can draw from the Complaint and the current record a reasonable inference in the plaintiffs' favor – that where the defendant has completed all the necessary steps for a public distribution, a reasonable fact-finder may infer that the distribution actually took place.

- In another case, *Atlantic Recording Corp. v Brennan*, Civil No. 3:07cv232 (JBA), 2008 US Dist. LEXIS 23801 (D. Conn. 13 February 2008), the court denied plaintiff's motion for a default judgment, finding the following:

  > without actual distribution of copies ... there is no violation [of] the distribution right.' 4 William F. Patry, Patry on Copyright § 13:9 (2007); see also id. N. 10 (collecting cases); *Perfect 10, Inc. v Amazon.com,* Inc., 508 F.3d 1146, 1162 (9th Cir. 2007) (affirming the district court's finding 'that distribution requires an "actual dissemination" of a copy').

In the most recent case, *Capitol Records Inc., v Thomas* (D. Minn. 2008), Civil File No. 06-1497 (MJD/RLE) (Memorandum of Law & Order of September 24, 2008), District of Minnesota Chief Judge Michael Davis ordered a new trial, overturning a 4 October 2007 federal jury award of $220,000 in damages to plaintiffs caused by defendant Thomas's downloading 1,702 songs through the Kazaa network (though only 24 were at issue in the case and subject to statutory damages). The new trial was ordered since it was unclear whether jurors found liability based on Jury Instruction Number 15 ('[t]he act of making copyrighted sound recordings available for electronic distribution on a peer-to-peer network, without license from the copyright owners, violates the copyright owners' exclusive right of distribution, regardless of whether actual distribution has been shown') or based on the actual infringement (either reproduction or circumstantial evidence of 'actual dissemination' which the defendant carried out and which was completed when MediaSentry [the firm hired by right holders to collect evidence of infringement] downloaded the files). Judge Davis 'implores' Congress to enact a legislative fix (which it should be noted could be done by adding 'or offer to distribute' after 'distribute to adequately cover' 'making available'), but Judge Davis also called the initial damage award 'unprecedented and oppressive.'

Two aspects of the Judge's Memorandum are worthy of note and will be helpful to right holders, notwithstanding the overall effect of the decision, which is to muddy the legal waters as to the existence of a 'making available' right per se in the United States. First, Judge Davis indicated that 'direct proof of actual dissemination is not required by the Copyright Act. Plaintiffs are free to employ circumstantial evidence to attempt to prove actual dissemination.' Thus, proof that the defendant merely made available files, along with evidence that someone actually downloaded them, or can be deemed to have downloaded them, may suffice for liability. However, the judge failed to define what kind of 'circumstantial evidence' will suffice. Second, Judge Davis held that 'distribution to MediaSentry can form the basis of an infringement claim.'

THE WAY FORWARD

The legislative record (80+ countries adopting an interactive 'making available' right in some form) and the case law in most countries demonstrates that an interactive 'making available' right is viewed as a critical part of establishing a healthy legal framework for copyright on the Internet. The hallmark of this right is that copyright owners should be able to authorize or prohibit acts along the chain of a communication, including the uploading, the making available (without more), and the onward communication of their materials in the online space. In the cases in Asia, courts have had little problem finding infringement when one makes available without authorization copyright content. In essence, making copyright materials available, without more, is akin to taking the steps necessary to facilitate infringement by others, and is an act in itself made subject to copyright liability, whether direct liability or secondary liability (such as in the *Cooper* case in Australia). North America seems to be struggling a bit more with the concept of the act of merely making available copyright content as a cognizable infringement, but even there, there is persuasive and powerful precedent, not only in copyright cases, but in other cases dealing with distribution, that no physical object need change hands in order for there to be a distribution.[58] Members of the European Union have universally implemented the interactive making available right into their laws.

[58] See, e.g., *United States v Shaffer*, 472 3d 1219 (10th Cir. 2007) (placing child pornography in a shared folder, and nothing more, constitutes 'distribution' under 18 USC § 2252A, and there is no requirement to show an actual download).

Indeed, with the damage caused by illegal file sharing to date, the future for copyright industries, and the music industry which has borne the brunt of illegal file sharing most acutely thus far, will depend on the preservation of long-standing legal principles of copyright liability in the online space, including against P2P infringements and unauthorized acts of making available. The further elaboration in case law (or statute if necessary) of secondary liability principles (or the development of such principles where none exist or where they remain under-developed) will likewise be crucial to healthy development of copyright protection online.[59]

In addition, there can be little doubt that increasing cooperation of service providers will be crucial to preserving a legal Internet market. President Sarkozy's 22 November 2007 announcement of the 'Olivennes Report' seemed to hold some promise for a new day of cooperation and compromise between service providers and copyright owner interests.[60] Under the plan, ISPs agreed that they would monitor what their customers are doing and pass on information about persistent pirates to a new independent body in France, with those identified getting a warning and then being threatened with either having their Internet access cut off or suspended if they do not stop illegal file sharing. In exchange, right holders agreed to do more – specifically, film-makers agreed to speed up the transfer of movies to DVD and music firms pledged to support DRM-free tracks on music stores. The Gowers Report in Britain[61] and the Renfors Report in Sweden[62] both have also recommended to government that

---

59 See Dixon, *Liability of Users and Third Parties for Copyright Infringements on the Internet: Overview of International Developments*.

60 Industries have recently noted some progress in cooperation among governments and in courts in Sweden, Belgium, the UK, the US and Asia.

61 *Gowers Review of Intellectual Property*, December 2006 (HM Treasury on behalf of the Controller of Her Majesty's Stationery Office), at http://www.hm-treasury.gov.uk/media/6/E/pbr06_gowers_report_755. Specifically, Recommendation 39 provides,

> Observe the industry agreement of protocols for sharing data between ISPs and rights holders to remove and disbar users engaged in 'piracy'. If this has not proved operationally successful by the end of 2007, Government should consider whether to legislate.

62 The report, by Swedish Justice Department investigator Cecilia Renfors, proposes a change in Swedish law so that ISPs would be obliged to take action to terminate the contracts of certain users who repeatedly use their connection to infringe copyright. This obligation could be enforced in court by right holders. According to the Swedish Ministry of Justice,

> It is proposed that the law be amended so that Internet Service Providers can be ordered, under penalty of a fine, to take action such as terminating the contract of a subscriber to prevent continued infringement using the Internet Service Provider's services.

ISPs should disconnect persistent infringers, by voluntary agreement if possible or legislation if not. A recent Belgian court ruling in the *SABAM v Tiscali*[63] case concluded ISPs should address mass copyright infringement and that they had the means to do so.

However, on 10 April 2008, the European Parliament[64] sent a message to France that its brokered deal was unacceptable. Specifically, para. 23 of the European Parliament resolution of 10 April 2008 on cultural industries in Europe states in relevant part, '[t]he European Parliament … calls on the Commission and the Member States, to avoid adopting measures conflicting with civil liberties and human rights and with the principles of proportionality, effectiveness and dissuasiveness, such as the interruption of Internet access.' So, we are at an impasse in Europe. Meanwhile, digital sales are weak in France due to high levels of unauthorised file sharing – which prompted the Sarkozy plan for action against piracy by ISPs. With high levels of unauthorized file sharing in other parts of Europe, it is perhaps surprising to see those elsewhere battling the French on this point of preserving the Internet for legal trade in cultural products. Yet, all agree that ISPs are the gatekeepers of the Internet, and as such, the question of how vital a role they must play in curbing copyright abuse will remain a vital question for years to come.

The report entitled 'Music and Film on the Internet – Threat or Opportunity?' was produced in response to a request from Sweden's Justice Minister. See *IFPI welcomes Swedish report calling on ISPs to tackle copyright Infringement*, 5 September 2007, at http://www.ifpi.org/content/section_news/20070905.html.

63 *SABAM v Tiscali*, No. 04/8975 A of the General Roll (D. Ct. Brussels 28 June 2007).

64 European Parliament Resolution of 10 April 2008 on cultural industries in Europe (2007/2153(INI)). para. 23 states in relevant part, 'The European Parliament … calls on the Commission and the Member States, to avoid adopting measures conflicting with civil liberties and human rights and with the principles of proportionality, effectiveness and dissuasiveness, such as the interruption of Internet access.'

3. Secondary liability for copyright infringement with regard to hyperlinks

Alain Strowel and Vicky Hanley

Without hyperlinks,[1] the World Wide Web would not be so compelling. Hyperlinks are, in a way, the threads with which the Web is spun. Instead of users getting tangled in information overload, they find what they are looking for by following links for further reference. Without these links, and without the search engines based on hyperlinking, the information posted online would lose much of its value as it would not be easy to find.

Despite their clear utility, hyperlinks can raise legal liability issues in certain circumstances. For instance, infringements to personality rights exist if the links have been intentionally posted to refer to content that prejudices a person's reputation, or certain types of links may raise unfair competition concerns or result in trademark infringement; similarly, copyright violations can arise if hyperlinks are clearly made to promote the dissemination of infringing files. It is this latter issue – (secondary) liability for copyright infringement involving hyperlinks – into which this chapter delves.

We will begin our discussion in Part I on the dual character of hyperlinks as a technique and as a form or expression that can nevertheless be limited by the law, followed in Part II by a summary of the forms of (copyright) liability that hyperlinking can entail. Parts III and IV then discuss current case law on copyright liability for linking. Finally, we will conclude with a discussion on how some links that trigger liability may in fact constitute 'dangerous liaisons' and how a few precautions should be taken to maintain 'good relations' online.[2]

[1] Also referred to, more simply, as 'links.' This chapter is based on, and updates, various contributions that A. Strowel devoted to the issue of linking liability, in particular, the joint article written with N. Ide, 'Liability With Regard to Hyperlinks', in *Columbia – VLA Journal of Law & the Arts*, vol. 24, no. 4, Summer 2001, pp. 403–48. Particular thanks to Nicolas Ide for allowing some sections of the 2001 article to be reused in the present chapter.

[2] For an analysis of the precautions to be taken at the contractual and/or technical level, see Alain Strowel (1998), 'Liaisons dangereuses et bonnes relations sur I'lnternet – A propos des hyperliens', *Auteurs & Medias* 296.

THE DUAL CHARACTER OF LINKING AS A TECHNIQUE AND A FORM OF EXPRESSION

The Various Techniques for Linking

In the broad sense, a 'hypertext link' covers two different things: one relating to the hidden and the other to the visible aspect of the link. In the technical sense of the term, a hyperlink is the HTML (HyperText Markup Language[3]) instruction that tells the browser to go to another document (external link) or another part of the same document (internal link). In its customary sense, the term hyperlink refers to the visible part of the link, the word(s) or image(s) used to inform visitors of the web page that they can follow a link.[4] The visible part of the link is called a 'pointer.' Pointers usually take the form of underlined words (usually in a different color from the one used for the main text). Sometimes they are represented by a still or moving image, such as a logo, thumbnail reproduction, pushbutton, etc. In the following pages, the words 'hyperlink' or 'pointer' will refer to the visible part of the link ('the HTML code' will refer to the hidden part of the link).

The function of a hyperlink is to transfer the visitor to another hypertext document such as a web page, a specific part of a web page or a picture. This function can be activated automatically, as is the case with embedded links,[5] or by clicking on the pointer. When clicking on a pointer, one is transported to a document located elsewhere online, with its own URL address.[6]

The techniques used for linking (that is, the type of HTML code) can be classified into four widely recognized categories: surface linking, deep linking, framing, and inlining or embedded linking. Surface linking uses an external link to transfer the user from the web page of one site ('the linking site') to the homepage of another site ('the linked site'), which is displayed on the user's screen in its original form, cleansed of any reference to the linking site (it is sometimes described as an HREF link).[7]

---

3 Hyper-Text Markup Language of HTML is the predominant markup language for web pages that offers means to describe the structure of text-based information in a document by denoting certain text as links, headings, paragraphs, lists, and so on (see HTML entry in Wikipedia.com).

4 However, it could be the URL address or domain name of the page to which the hyperlink refers.

5 See Part I on the types of hyperlinks.

6 A URL, or Uniform Resource Locator, is a string of characters used to represent a resource available on the Internet; on the web, it typically starts with 'http'.

7 The basic HTML command used is: <A HREF="URL of the page providing the link"> Hypertext Link</A>.

Unlike a surface link that connects the user to the linked site's homepage, a deep link connects the user to an interior page of the site, that is, any web page other than the homepage. An HTML command makes it also possible to present the content of a linked site's web page inside the frame of the linking site; in other words, the frame of the linking site will replace the frame of the linked site on the user's screen. With this type of link, the title of the page (above the toolbar) and the address of the linking site (in the address box) are not replaced by the title and address of the linked site. Therefore, even if users usually realize that they are browsing the content of another site, the browser does not display (solely) the URL of the linked-to site. With inlining or embedded links (also referred to as a 'dynamic' or 'automatic' links), an element (such as an image, a graphic, a logo, etc.) from another web page (belonging to the same or another site) can be inserted into a web page without leaving the page of the linking site. As an image (or any other embedded element) is an independent part of a web page, it has its own URL address, namely the place on the server where the image has been stored in digital form. This instruction takes the form of an HTML command giving the image's URL address.[8] The fact that the link is activated automatically by the browser gives surfers the impression that they are viewing an image from the web page that they are browsing while the image actually comes from another web page.[9] Thus, an embedded link enables a site operator to insert images without having to copy them. Indeed, the image is not reproduced at any time on the server hosting the linking site. The image is only reproduced (in a lasting form) on the server on which the originating site is stored and (in a temporary form) on the screen of the surfer visiting the page containing the embedded link. This technique saves space on the server hosting the page containing the embedded link.

It is not only linking techniques that can have an impact on third party liability. Other distinctions between hyperlinks (which overlap in part those that have just been presented) should be considered such as where the linked page is located,[10] whether the link must be activated by the Internet user, and the extent to which the origin of the linked material is visible.

---

8 The basic HTML command used to find the image on the server is <IMG SRC="URL of the GIF or PEG file">. For example, if one wants to include a picture of a Coca-Cola bottle on a page, all one has to do is include the command <IMG SRC="http://www.cocacola.com/images/bottle1.gif"> in the web page's HTML code. Such use of protected images – such as the Coca Cola bottle – are submitted to rights holders consent.

9 Even more so as the URL address of the site from which the image originates will not be displayed in the space where the URL address of the page opened is usually displayed (or where the URL address to which the user wants to go is entered).

10 Is it an 'Intra-page' hyperlink, that is, a link that refers to a URL address situated on the same web page as the linking one; an 'Internal' hyperlink, which refers to

The presence of any function automatically prompted by activating a link should also be considered. For example, links promoting an automatic download can lead to inferences of the link provider's intent.[11]

Linking as a Form of Expression

Linking is not only a technique, it has an expressive value. The person placing the links will consider the quantity and position of the links, the reasons for placing the links, the impact of these references on the reading and comprehension of the text, etc. All these variables show how incorporating links in a (online) document contributes to the manifestation of a personal thinking and to a lively (online) marketplace for ideas. Some court decisions, for example, the DeCSS case analysed below, have indeed recognized that links are a protected expression.

Linking, as a form of expression, should in principle remain free from interference. This results from the various provisions protecting freedom of expression, such as Article 10 of the European Convention on Human Rights ('ECHR').[12] However, in certain cases, the use of links can infringe the 'rights of others' to quote the terms used in Art. 10(2) ECHR, which allows for restrictions to the freedom of expression that are (1) 'prescribed by law' (2) 'necessary in a democratic society' and (3) 'in the interests' of a 'legitimate end' or 'for the protection of the rights of others'. The rights of others/third parties include copyright, as well as personality rights, trademark or unfair competition. Obligations prescribed by copyright law can justify some restrictions to the way hyperlinks are made if such limitations are 'necessary' to protect copyright. In practice, the condition of necessity requires an analysis of the proportionality of the restriction. Links that unnecessarily refer to illicit content, such as files infringing copyright, can thus be enjoined.

---

a URL address situated on a different web page from the linking one, but on the same web site; or an 'External' hyperlink, which refers to the URL address of another web site?

[11] See discussion of *KODA, NCB, Dansk Artist Forbund, Dansk Musiker Forbund & IFPI Denmark,* Case Nos. V.L. B-1943-99 and V.L. B-2089-99 (High Ct. of Justice, Western Div., 20 April 2001) *infra.*

[12] Article Art. 10 ECHR: 'Everyone has the right to freedom of expression. This right shall include freedom to hold opinions and to receive and impart information and ideas without interference by public authority'.

THE TWO TYPES OF COPYRIGHT LIABILITY FOR LINKING: DIRECT AND INDIRECT COPYRIGHT INFRINGEMENT

Direct copyright infringement requires that acts committed by the defendant in a civil action fall within the scope of copyright protection. For a direct infringement to exist, it is necessary to establish the following: (1) the existence of a protected work; (2) infringing use, such as a reproduction, a distribution or a communication to the public, and (3) the absence of any exceptions. We will see that some cases on hyperlinking mainly involve these three issues. In particular, cases where the pointer is a protected element raise direct liability issues. Various Web 2.0 services , such as aggregators of online news through linking (for example, Google.News), can also commit acts falling under copyright and be involved in direct copyright infringement.

It is also clear from case law that the providers of links (those posting the links on a webpage or responsible for the placement of the links on a page) can be held liable when the hyperlinks point to materials infringing copyright. Secondary liability for copyright infringement can apply in this case.

However, secondary liability can also apply to operators other than the providers of hyperlinks. The use of hyperlinks raises the delicate problem of the liability of online intermediaries, such as the providers hosting the pages with the links or the providers of information location tools such as search engines or other aggregators of hyperlinks.

The later analysis of the case law shows that the question of the link provider's complicity in the illegal act committed by the operator of the linked site is still controversial and depends on various factual circumstances, such as the knowledge of the link provider that infringing material is posted on the linked site.

A fortiori the same can be said about the liability of the hosting provider in the event of unlawful linking by its client. Indeed, to accept the liability of the hosting ISP, it would be necessary to prove that it is the 'accomplice of an accomplice'. In other words, the host could only incur liability if two other persons have already been found liable: the operator of the site containing the illegal content would have to be guilty of violating a statutory provision and the link provider's complicity in the violation would have to be established. To claim the liability of the host provider of the site containing the links is certainly not the most direct path as the injured party could take action, in principle, against the host provider of the site on which the illegal content is posted.

The liability of other intermediaries such as search engines or aggregators of links raises other issues as shown below by the case law. Pure search functionalities will, in principle, more easily escape liability than services, which also format the retrieved information and add value to the simple links. This is illustrated by the difference between Google's search engine service (automatic search and ranking of links based on a computer algorithm, PageRank) and the Google.News service (retrieval and organization of online news that comes closer to publishing).

The law in the area of third-party liability derives from a number of sources: statutory rules specific to the copyright area, case law developments in copyright, and more general common law or civil law legal rules. A clear distinction can be made between the principles followed under US case law and those applicable in civil law jurisdictions. In the US, third-party liability for copyright infringement generally falls under one of three heads: (1) contributory liability; (2) vicarious liability and (3) inducement liability.[13] These different grounds will be analysed below. In a civil law setting, the relevant concepts are: (1) knowing assistance, self explanatorily where a third party knowingly assists in the copyright infringements of another; and (2) breach of a duty of care, which necessitates an illegal act and third-party knowledge and takes into consideration any economic benefit to the third party and its magnitude relative to any costs.

Regarding liability for copyright infringement in relation to linking, three possible types of situations can be distinguished: cases where the infringement relates to the use of the pointer (or a collection thereof), cases where the infringement results from the linking technique or process used, and cases where the infringement is caused by the content of the linked site. While the first two types of cases can raise direct copyright liability (see below), the third type of case only involves secondary copyright liability (see p. 88).

CASES INVOLVING DIRECT COPYRIGHT LIABILITY

Infringements Relating to the Pointers

The pointers as copyrighted elements

In most cases, the pointers used for linking reproduce the address of the web site to which the link leads. In principle, these addresses do not include copyrighted elements. They are pure facts that, as such, are unprotected. Accordingly, the reproduction of a URL (http) address in the form of a pointer does not require any authorization.

In exceptional cases, however, the pointer may be made up of elements that enjoy copyright protection, such as headlines. While a UK court has addressed this issue in an early case involving two competing newspapers launching

---

13 See the contributions of A. Dixon Chapter 1 and J. Ginsburg Chapter 4 in the present volume.

online services, a recent Belgian case dealing with the same issue of the use of headlines for linking involves a group of newspapers opposing a news aggregating service, a typical Web 2.0 service.

Shetland Times v Wills[14] In this Scottish case, the defendant, Dr Jonathan Wills, ran an online news service called the *Shetland News,* which provided links to the site of the *Shetland Times.* The *Shetland News* reproduced on its web site the headlines of stories published in the print version of the *Shetland Times* and on the latter newspaper's web site. The plaintiff's web site was not financed by advertising, but the defendant's site carried advertising banners.[15] Users who visited the defendant's site could click on the headlines, copied verbatim from the *Shetland Times,* and then find themselves on the *Shetland Times'* site, at the page on which the story was posted.

The newspaper brought an action for an interim injunction for copyright infringement, alleging in particular an infringement of copyright in the headlines. In his order of 24 October 1996, the judge hearing the case held that it was probable that certain headlines – particularly the long ones consisting of eight words or more – enjoyed copyright protection as literary works and that consequently there was *prima facie* illegal copying.[16] In weighing the opposing interests, the judge stressed that it was essential for the plaintiff that its web site should be accessible only through its homepage.

The case did not end there. On 11 November 1997, the first day of the trial hearing, the parties came to a settlement under which the *Shetland News* was allowed to link to *Shetland Times* stories using the headlines as pointers subject to certain conditions:

- The link had to be acknowledged by the legend '*A Shetland Times* Story' placed underneath the headline used as pointer;
- The *Shetland Times*' logo had to be featured on a button adjacent to the pointer; and
- The legend and the button had to be hypertext links to the title page of the *Shetland Times'* site.

This case confirms the principle that 'web-linking' is authorized in principle unless the linking is done in a manner that is prejudicial to the owner of the linked to site.[17]

---

[14] *Shetland Times Ltd v Jonathan Wills and Another* 1997 SLT 669 (24 October 1996).

[15] This fact is important in terms of unfair competition.

[16] Within the meaning of s. 17 of the 1988 Copyright, Designs and Patents Act.

[17] To this effect, see also V. Marsland (1998), 'Shetland Times Web-linking Litigation Settles on First Day Trial', 13 *Computer L. Ass'n Bull* 30.

Copiepresse v Google In 2006, an association of Belgian newspapers sued Google for copyright infringement before the Brussels Court, claiming that the Google.News service, which aggregates and indexes various online published articles, infringes the newspapers' copyrights on (1) the headlines and (2) the first lines of the articles as those elements (as well as the deep hyperlinks to the linked-to pages) are reproduced on Google.News web pages. The headlines are used as pointers to the complete articles accessible on the newspaper web site; thus, clicking on the headlines automatically leads the user to the web site of the publisher of the article. In first instance, the Brussels Court considered that the headlines, as well as the first sentences of articles, are phrased with special care so as to attract the attention of the reader and that they could well be protected by copyright because their form of expression, which often involves word play, is usually original.[18] The Court recognized that not all the news article headlines can be considered original: some of them in fact appear to be purely descriptive and do not therefore show the distinctive stamp of their author, for example, 'Deserts threatened by global warming', 'The King visits Sweden'; nevertheless, others appear original like 'Monaco – between casino and stratego', and 'Music: it makes school cool'.

Further, courts in Belgium or France have been more willing to find copyright infringement for copying headlines than granting copyright protection for one (book) title (with some rare exceptions such as for '*Les Liaisons dangereuses*' in a well-known case[19]), especially when there is a massive and repetitive reproduction of those headlines.

Regarding the copying of the first lines of the articles, which are the 'hook' sentences, the Court found that it is very possible that they show the original stamp of the author and are, thus, protected as well.

The Court then had to check whether a copyright exception could apply. None of the possible exceptions were applicable. In particular, the standard quotation exception requires that the incorporated text is used to illustrate a proposition, but in the case of Google.News, the extracts of news articles are automatically indexed, placed next to one another and classified. The exception for reporting of the news – quotation for informational purposes – was also held not applicable as no commentary on the news is to be found on Google.News, which is limited to reproducing extracts of articles grouped thematically. Also, for the news reporting exception to apply, the protected works can only be incidental to the report and not its principle subject. The rationale of the news reporting exception – that the rapidity with which the

---

[18] See *Copiepresse v Google Inc.*, Trib. 1st Instance Brussels, 13 Febr. 2007 [2007] E.C.D.R. 5 at 125.

[19] Court of Appeal Paris, 4 April 1960, JCP G, 1960, II, 11659; Dalloz, 1960, 535, Note H. Desbois.

information has to be reported does not enable the prior consent of the author to be sought – is not present in this case as Google could obtain the agreement of the publishers of the indexed web sites in advance.

Google's argument based on the protection of freedom of expression (Art. 10 ECHR) was also rightly rejected by the Brussels Court who considered that the freedom to receive and to communicate information can be limited in order to protect copyright, and that the restriction prescribed by the copyright law was appropriate and proportionate in this case. Also, the Court points out that the system put in place by Google.News does not involve any human element as Google does not employ any chief editor to select the articles put on the Google.News page. Rather, the service is based on the automatic indexing by the GoogleBot robot of the press articles made available on the Internet. The Court seems to consider that freedom of expression has no real bearing in such context.

The plaintiff thus obtained an injunction against Google that has forced Google to refrain from indexing the articles of Copiepresse members. As an appeal is pending while a settlement is still under negotiation to eventually determine a fair remuneration for this reproduction, access to the articles has been allowed by Copiepresse members, who saw a sharp decline in consultation once their online pages were cut off from Google.News service. Copyright is used here to ensure compensation is paid for the investment made in creating the protected content.

Where images or other visual material (logos, etc.) are used as pointers, they may well enjoy copyright protection, and thus, the hyperlinks may infringe copyright. This was the issue with which the visual search engine Arriba was confronted. As pointers, Arriba used reduced versions of images, 'thumbnails', corresponding to the word entered in the search.[20] As the case also involves the issue of the linking technique, it will be addressed below.

A collection of unprotected hyperlinks (pointers)

The taking of a directory or collection of links comprising of non-protected elements, such as http addresses, could raise legal issues as well. While an http address on its own cannot enjoy copyright protection,[21] a list of web addresses

---

20 *Kelly v Arriba Soft Corp.*, 77 F. Supp. 2d 1116 (C.D. Cal. 1999). For further discussion of this case, see *infra* 'infringements involving the use of pointers and linking techniques' at p. 84.

21 Some elements of such an address can however be registered as trademarks (for example, a trademark can protect 'amazon.com', not only the second level domain name 'amazon'), but using those protected signs as pointers to the official web site of the trademark owner cannot be considered as objectionable trademark use under the EC trademark rules.

that is drawn up either in a reasoned manner (the case of directories that select sites or links from spontaneous registrations by site operators) or automatically (the case of search engines) may, on the other hand, be eligible for protection. To consider this question, it is interesting to compare a set of hyperlinks to an index, or bibliography. In an index, the establishment of a link between one entry and other words, which may themselves be used as entries in the index, cannot as such be appropriated by copyright. What is involved here is an association and thus a non-copyrightable idea.[22] Each link represents a piece of information that may have value in its own right but does not achieve the required level of expression to be protected as a work.

By contrast, an index considered as a whole may be eligible for protection as a compilation in that the selection of the words reproduced in it, but not their arrangement as it is alphabetical as a rule, may be the result of an original creative effort or, in order to use the established expression, may constitute the indexer's own intellectual creation. All those who have had the pleasure of compiling an index know that this work requires creative choices. In the same way, a compilation of hypertext links may enjoy copyright protection, but it will necessarily be limited in scope as it will concern the whole, or a substantial part of it, but not a particular hyperlink (element). A list of hyperlinks that requires some substantial investment for collecting, verifying or presenting them could potentially enjoy the *sui generis* protection conferred by the EC Directive 96/9 on the legal protection of databases.

Infringements Involving Linking Techniques and Processes

Apart from the cases involving copyrighted pointers, the different linking techniques identified above do not give rise to unlawful reproductions or communication of works, and no direct copyright infringement is involved. Indeed, the person creating a link never reproduces the linked document. This principle has been confirmed in various decisions. As one court put it: 'hyperlinking does not itself involve a violation of the Copyright Act . . . since no copying is involved'.[23]

The only copies made are the temporary ones on the screen of the surfer who activates the link, but those copies arguably are exempted from copy-

---

[22] If one reasons in terms of US law, one could say that what is involved is a 'discovery' (of a conceptual link) which, under s. 102(b) of the Copyright Act, is excluded from the scope of copyright protection. See also *Feist Publ'ns, Inc. v Rural Tel. Serv. v Co.*, 499 US 340, 356 (1991) (copyright protection does not extend to facts, which can be equated with 'discoveries').

[23] *Ticketmaster Corp. v Tickets.com, Inc.*, 54 USP.Q.2d (BNA) 1344 (C.D, Cal. 2000). See also *IFPI v T. Olsson*, and *the Copyright Board of Canada* discussed *infra*.

right.[24] In the case of an embedded link, the situation is the same, except that it is not the surfer, but the browser alone, that activates the link.

Framing and other contextual links

Things are a bit more complex in the case of framing. Indeed, under US law, the question of whether the *assembly* of (copyrighted) components of the linked site within the frame of the site of the provider of the link constitutes a new work – either a 'derivative work'[25] or a 'compilation'[26] – is a matter of debate. It is also a matter of fact that goes beyond the present contribution.

Another question is whether the provision of a hyperlink, particularly in the form of framing, is not equivalent to an act of communication to the public within the meaning of Article 8 of the WIPO Copyright Treaty of 20 December 1996, namely: 'the making available to the public of works in such a way that members of the public may access these works from a place and at a time individually chosen by them'.

We do not think this to be the case. As the work is already available to the entire Internet community at the linked site's web address, linking cannot be held as a new act of making available to the public. The link does not extend the work's audience: surfers who access the work by activating the link can also consult the page directly, as long as they know its URL. Concluding that there is a new communication to the public does not seem justified and would cause considerable difficulties in terms of copyright management.

Framing raises other issues in countries with robust moral rights that protect in particular the interest of the author to have the work's integrity protected. Some changes in the way the author's content is presented within the frame and the advertisement of the linking site might affect its moral interests and might be objected to in some countries.

It is possible to imagine situations in which the mere change of context between the linking site and the linked one could infringe the moral right to

---

[24] In Europe, these temporary copies for browsing purposes are exempt from the reproduction right under Art. 5(1) of the EC Directive 2001/29 on the harmonization of certain aspects of copyright and related rights in the information society.

[25] This claim was made by the plaintiff in a case involving framing. Without deciding on this matter, the judge nevertheless considered in his order on the defendants' motion to dismiss that such classification was not out of the question. *Futuredontics, Inc. v Applied Anagramics, Inc.*, 45 U.SP.Q.2d (BNA) 2005, 1998 US Dist. LEXIS 2265 (C.D. Cal. 1998), available at http://eon.law.harvard.edu/property/metatags/1998futu.html (accessible on 28 March 2009).

[26] This was argued by the plaintiff in *Imax Corp. v Showmax Inc.,* 2000 A.C.W.S.J. LEXIS 47376 (Fed. Ct. Jan. 18, 2000) (Can.), available at http://www.fja.gc.ca/fc/2000/ori/2000fc25888.html. The The court granted an injunction against the defendant, however, without taking a stand on this question.

the integrity of the work. Various courts throughout Europe have already ruled that certain electronic uses that have the effect of severing the link between a newspaper article and the newspaper to which it belongs could be detrimental to the journalist's personal and moral interests; the same reasoning could be applied to framing, which isolates content from its graphic and ideological online environment.

If we take a hypothetical case similar to *Shetland Times*,[27] allowing the journalists' articles to be accessed from a linking site that does not share the same ideology as the newspaper to which the link pointed might eventually justify an action based on the journalists' moral rights. In Belgium, the ruling of the Brussels Court of Appeal in a case involving a central database (*Central Station*) that was offering an online clipping service with all the articles published in Belgium on selected topics went quite far in granting journalists a right to be published within a specific context. According to the Court:

> [I]t is true that a journalist writes for a readership as wide as possible, but within the context of the newspaper or magazine that publishes his contributions ("his" newspaper or "his" magazine); and his article features with those of his colleagues who work, under the same editor, for the same values, in the same publication.[28]

The Court added that compiling several 'articles reflecting different leanings in a single collection', as in the case of the *Central Station* database, is a 'change of perspective from that of informing the readership of a single newspaper, and that having authorized distribution *intuitu personae* on a medium that reflects well-defined leanings does not imply that authorization has been given for distribution on the Internet.' The changes resulting from the link, for example, a frame, or from the context, for example, advertising banners and pop-ups, will be taken into account to assess whether the personal interests of the author have been hurt.[29] On top of the copyright argument relying on

---

27 Presented *supra*.

28 Brussels Court of Appeals, Oct. *28*, 1997, *Auteurs & Médias*, 1997, p. 383 (authors' translation). See also the special issue of the *Columbia-VLA Journal of the Law & Arts*: 'Symposium on Electronic Rights in International Perspective', 22 Colum.-VLA J.L. & Arts 127 (1998), and particularly Jane Ginsburg, 'Electronic Rights in Belgium and France; *General Association of Professional Journalists of Belgium v Central Station'* (Brussels Court of First Instance, 16 October 1996; Brussels Court of Appeals, 28 October 1997), *Union of French Journalists v SDV Plurimedia* (Strasbourg Court of Grand Instance, 3 February 1998)', 22 Colum.-VLA J.L. & Arts 161 (1998).

29 In the same way, a model's personality right allows the model to oppose his/her photographs being made available in a prejudicial context. See Landgericht München I, 7 October 2004, 7 O 18165/03 (Playboy-Fotos) (possibility to oppose links and advertising banners associating the photos of a naked Playboy model with pornography).

moral rights, other claims based on other bodies of law (unfair competition, passing-off, etc.) could be raised to oppose framing or other contextual changes, but those arguments are well beyond the scope of the present contribution.

Embedded links

One must also be more cautious when dealing with embedded links. Indeed, in such cases, visitors do not realize that they are consulting a document that, in fact, comes from another site. At any rate, visitors are given the impression that it is the provider of the embedded hyperlink who is communicating the work to the public. It is easier to hold the provider of an embedded link liable for contributory infringement insofar as he or she quite clearly 'endorses' the linked content that is virtually an integral part of his or her own site through the effect of the embedded link. These issues have already been debated in a case brought before the Copyright Board of Canada.

The Tariff 22 case before the Copyright Board of Canada and the Supreme Court of Canada In the Tariff 22 case, the Society of Composers, Authors and Music Publishers of Canada (SOCAN) filed a proposed tariff for the public performance of musical works through a telecommunications network for approval by the Copyright Board as part of an administrative procedure that is a feature of the Canadian copyright system. This tariff covers primarily Internet transmissions of musical works. Following a period of consultation, the board determined, in an initial decision of 27 October 1999, which activities on the Internet constitute acts that are subject to the payment of royalties.[30] When considering acts of communication to the public, the board made an interesting distinction between embedded links, which can be likened to acts of communication to the public, and other types of links, which do not imply any communication to the public:

> The person that creates an embedded hyperlink to a work authorizes its communication. The person that merely supplies a link which must be activated by the user does not.
>
> ....
>
> In itself, the creation of hyperlinks does not involve a communication to the public of any works contained at the linked sites. In their simplest form, hyperlinks represent an electronic directory of addresses.

---

[30] *Public Performance of Musical Works, Copyright Board of Canada*, 27 October 27, 1999, available at http://www.cb-cda.gc.ca/decisions/m27101999-b.pdf. This case went up to the Supreme Court of Canada (*Society of Composers, Authors and Music Publishers of Canada v Canadian Assn. of Internet Providers*, 2004 SCC 45, [2004] 2 SCR 427).

> However, the content provider who includes into a Web page an automatic link that effects the transmission of a musical work to the recipient without the need for further action by the end user holds itself out as responsible for the material at the linked sites and, therefore, authorizes its communication. This will be true even in the absence of a business relationship with the owner of the linked sites. By creating such automatic hyperlinks, the site owner makes itself 'a party in interest to the [communication] by warranting the right to [communicate]'.[31,32]

Thus, some form of 'authorization' is arguably involved in the case of embedded links, which results in the possibility of holding the provider of an automatic link as indirectly liable for copyright infringement under Canadian law (and under other laws based on the UK-originated concept of 'authorization').[33]

Infringements Involving the use of Pointers and Linking Techniques

Other copyright cases on linking combine the issues resulting from the use of protected elements as pointers and those generated by the type of links. Direct copyright liability is involved here, and the main issue is the application or non-application of copyright exceptions, as shown in the US *Kelly v Arriba* case where the scope of the 'fair use' exemption is the core of the debate.

Kelly v Arriba[34] In this case, the visual search engine 'Arriba' (currently available at www.ditto.com) enabled users to search for images on the Internet on whatever words the user entered. The results of the search were presented as reduced 'thumbnail' pictures. These reduced photographs also served as hyperlinks. By clicking on a 'thumbnail', the image (located on a third party's web site) was extracted from the original site and presented to the user in a new window, in its original size and with a few 'attributes', including the URL address of the site from which it originated. This URL address also served as a hyperlink to the page containing the image. Thus, the page of the site from which the image originated was not presented to the user.[35]

---

31 *Muzak Corp. v Composers, Authors and Publishers Assoc.* (Canada), [1953] 2. SCR 182, at 189.

32 *Public Performance of Musical Works, Copyright Board of Canada*, 27 October 1999, at 27, 48. The distinction between automatic links and user-activated links seems to be shared by the Supreme Court of Canada (see *Society of Composers, Authors and Music Publishers of Canada v Canadian Assn. of Internet Providers*, 2004 SCC 45, [2004] 2 SCR 427 at § 25).

33 See the contributions of G. Austin Chapter 5, A. Dixon Chapter 1, and J. Ginsburg Chapter 4 in the present volume for further developments on the 'authorization' approach for secondary copyright liability.

34 *Kelly v Arriba Soft Corp.*, 77F. Supp. 2d 1116 (C.D. Cal. 1999).

35 In a later version of its search engine, Arriba made a change so that two

The plaintiff, a photographer with his own site who had at least 35 photographs indexed by Arriba, objected to Arriba's use of his works on copyright grounds. It should be noted that Arriba did not dispute the allegation that it reproduced and displayed the plaintiff's photographs. In its defence, Arriba relied on the 'fair use' exception.[36] In his discussion, the judge found that several factors weighed in favour of fair use. First, Arriba's use of the photographs was considered as 'transformative' in nature, a factor identified by the Supreme Court to define 'fair use' in case of parody:[37]

> Defendant's use is very different from the use for which the images were originally created. Plaintiff's photographs are artistic works used for illustrative purposes. Defendant's visual search engine is designed to catalog and improve access to images on the Internet. The character of the thumbnail index is not esthetic, but functional; its purpose is not to be artistic, but to be comprehensive.[38]

While we somewhat doubt that the 'transformative' nature of the use, as defined by the Supreme Court, is present in the Arriba case we will not delve further as the issue goes beyond the scope of this chapter.

Second, the judge was sympathetic to Arriba's argument that the hyperlinks produced by its search engine increased the number of visits to the photographer's site, implying that economic harm[39] was not established.[40]

As to the amount and substantiality of the portion of the original work used, which in this case was all of it but in reduced, thumbnail format, the judge held that this practice seemed reasonably justified with regard to the engine's indexing purpose, but that, in the case of the display of the photographs in their original size in a new window, this practice was not necessary for the search engine's purpose of information retrieval.[41]

---

windows appeared when the 'thumbnail' was activated, one containing the image and attributes (as before) and the other containing the web page from which the image originated. This was viewed as a point in Arriba's favour when the judge was assessing the fair use factors. Id. at 1120 n.8.

36 Section 107 of the US Copyright Act requires a consideration of four factors for assessing 'fair use':

'(1) the purpose and character of the use, including whether such use is of a commercial nature or is for nonprofit educational purposes;
(2) the nature of the copyrighted work;
(3) the amount and substantiality of the portion used in relation to the copyrighted work as a whole; and
(4) the effect of the use upon the potential market for or value of the copyrighted work.'

37 See *Campbell v Acuff-Rose Music, Inc.*, 510 US 569 (1994).

38 *Kelly,* 77 F. Supp. 2d at 1119.

39 The fourth factor to be considered in determining whether there is 'fair use' under s. 107 of the US Copyright Act.

40 Id. at 1120–21.

41 Id. at 1120.

In the final balance of interests, the judge concluded that the various factors referred to above weighed in favour of fair use. The judge stressed the decisive importance of search engines for the Internet in ultimately authorizing Arriba's use of the photographs:

> The first and fourth factors (character of use and lack of market harm) weigh in favor of a fair use finding because of the established importance of search engines and the 'transformative' nature of using reduced versions of images to organize and provide access to them. Plaintiff's images were swept along with two million others available on the Internet, as part of Defendant's efforts to provide its users with a better way to find images on the Internet. Defendant's purposes were and are inherently transformative [...].[42]

In 2002, the Ninth Circuit affirmed this decision in part and reversed it in part.[43] The Court held that the defendant's actions in copying the photographs to create the thumbnail images were not infringing because they were deemed to be a fair use of the copyright works. The smaller, lower resolution thumbnail images were found to fulfil a different function from the plaintiff's original images. The copies were merely used to facilitate access to the images by cataloguing them in response to search results. In addition, their reduced resolution would prevent them being used effectively for the same artistic purpose as the originals, as any enlargement would result in a loss of the images' clarity. The Court went further than the District Court, holding that the display of the full-size version of the images when a thumbnail was clicked, however, was held to be an infringement of the plaintiff's exclusive right to publicly display the copyright work.[44] It should be noted that the image displayed was imported directly from the plaintiff's site and the defendant did not copy the images. The Court held that this public display of the full-size images was not a fair use because the defendant's use of the images was not for a different purpose than the plaintiff's use of them and the defendant's use of the images was likely to divert web users away from the plaintiff's site, thereby damaging the plaintiff's market for sales and licensing of the images.

In 2003, the same Court also affirmed the original finding that the defendant's copying of the plaintiff's photographs to create and retrieve the thumbnail images was a non-infringing fair use.[45] However, the Court avoided resolving the issue of whether the embedded linking to and framing of the full-size images hosted by third-party web sites was infringing. Instead, the

---

[42] Id. at 1121.

[43] *Kelly v Arriba Soft Corporation* 280 F 3d 934 (9th Cir, 2002), withdrawn 9th Cir 3 July 2003.

[44] Section 106 of the US Copyright Act.

[45] *Kelly v Arriba Soft Corp* 336 F 3d 811 (9th Cir, 2003).

District Court's opinion on this point was reversed as it was held to have made an *ultra vires* ruling.

The Courts finding that search engines' reproduction of images for use as thumbnails is fair use under the Copyright Act was upheld by the same Ninth Circuit Appeal Court in the later *Perfect 10 v Google* case,[46] a case that will be further reviewed below under the indirect liability heading. The District Court of California had originally ruled that the fair use defence did not apply to Google's use of thumbnail images it created, as these thumbnail images could be downloaded for use with a cell phone in direct competition with a similar service provided by Perfect 10. On appeal, the decision to vacate the District Court's original ruling relied heavily on the fact that there was no evidence to support the use of Google's thumbnails for cell phone downloads.[47]

Other cases involving linking to photographs A German First Instance Court also considered that offering links consisting of thumbnail reproductions of art works does not trigger copyright liability when the creator of those works has consented to their online reproduction.[48] To reach this conclusion, however, the decision relied on a completely different reasoning: the Court held that, by making available the thumbnails, the defendant Google had violated the communication to the public and the reproduction right belonging to the creator; contrary to the decision in *Kelly v Arriba*, no exception was discussed by the Court to exempt this use from copyright liability. Rather, the Court considered that an implied consent to such use could be derived from the fact the artist had first released the photographs on her web site. The works were broadly available at no cost and her web site did not use any metadata (such as 'robottxt'), thus, indicating she consented to the use of thumbnails.

The issue of implied consent is regularly discussed in cases involving search engines and Google in particular. In the Belgian case *Copiepresse v Google* (see above), the argument was also made against the copies of the press articles made on the Google cache pages. The press publishers in particular complained about the online availability of protected articles, through cache copies, that were no longer available on the publishers' web pages. By indexing those pages and storing them as cache copies, Google was offering free access to articles for which the readers should in principle pay. According to the publishing model adopted, the articles are removed from the online web

---

46 *Perfect 10, Inc. v Amazom.com, Inc.*, No. 06-55405 (9th Cir., 16 May 2007).

47 See *infra* for a discussion of the Court's ruling in relation to Google's liability for secondary infringement.

48 LG Erfurt, 15 March 2007 – 3 O 1108/05, MMR 2007 Heft 6 p. 393 (*Thumbnails bei Google*).

site a few days after their placement and are then only accessible subject to payment. Google's practice was bypassing the business model used by those publishers. In such a case, the argument that some form of implied consent results from the fact no metadata is used by the publisher to prohibit the automatic indexing and the cache copies has some validity.

In addition to the infringement of copyright subsiding in a photographic image, the provision of links to photographs can fall foul of privacy rights. The defence of 'implied consent' was also applied by the District Court for the District of South Carolina when considering the infringement of privacy rights in the context of a hyperlink to a photograph on a publicly accessible web site. In October 2007, the Court held:

> a person who places a photograph on the Internet precisely intends to forsake and renounce all privacy rights to such imagery, particularly under circumstances...where [the subject] did not employ protective measures or devices that would have controlled access to the Web page or the photograph itself.[49]

In light of the conflicting verdicts of the US and German courts in relation to search engines' use of thumbnails, the visual search engine is left without the requisite legal certainty on which to build a stable business model.

A different issue, one which we shall address later, is whether there could be complicity on the part of the provider of the link in making the work posted on the linked-to site available.

CASES INVOLVING INDIRECT COPYRIGHT LIABILITY CAUSED BY THE CONTENT OF THE LINKED SITE

When considering the liability of intermediaries for linking to third party infringing sites the courts have not always succeeded in drawing a watertight distinction between primary and secondary liability. Also, in the context of the new Web 2.0 services that rely on the aggregation of content through the use of links and other information location tools, pure links are accompanied more and more by value-added content, such as extracts or thumbnail reproductions, appearing on the linking page, thus reinforcing the probability of a direct infringement of copyright in addition to the possible indirect liability for linking (to illicitly posted content). Besides, in the absence of being able to establish the requisite elements for secondary liability, the courts have tended to rely upon principles of direct copyright infringement in order to establish the liability of intermediaries.

---

[49] *Bidzerk LLC v Smith*, 2007 WL 3119445(D.S.C.) at 10.

Posting of URL Addresses

Mormon Church v Utah Lighthouse Ministry[50] This US case can be mentioned although it did not involve hyperlinking, but instead, the simple placement of URL addresses on a web page (the addresses were not activated as pointers). In this case, the Utah Lighthouse Ministry and Mr and Mrs Tanners (the founders of this association) operated a web site on which, initially, they had posted Mormon texts without the authorization of the right holder (the Intellectual Reserve Inc., as the owner of the rights in the texts of the Mormon Church). Following a formal notification from the latter, they had agreed to remove the texts at issue but kept the addresses of three other sites where visitors could find the texts that they had removed from their own site.

The Court began by confirming that the operators of the three web sites (who were not parties to the action) containing the texts at issue were infringing the Church's copyrights. To the question whether the defendants had incited, caused or physically contributed to the infringement by providing the three web site addresses, the Court replied in the negative; nevertheless, it went on to find the defendants liable on the grounds that they were contributing to the infringing transitory reproductions made by surfers who were encouraged to follow the addresses to browse the infringing material. In order to come to such a finding, the judge obviously had to accept that transitory reproductions of a work infringe copyright – a difficult topic, also beyond the scope here.[51] Rather than following this approach, the Court would probably have been more inspired to interpret the criteria for contributory infringement somewhat differently.

Links to Copyrighted File (MP3 Cases)

IFPI v T. Olsson In this Swedish case, IFPI, which represents the producers of phonograms, had filed a complaint prompting the Public Prosecutor to initiate criminal proceedings against Tommy Olsson for having provided hyperlinks to sites containing allegedly illegal MP3 files. After having noted that, when an MP3 file was downloaded by a user, no copy of the file was made by Olsson on a physical medium, including his own hard disk, the Göta Court of

---

[50] *Intellectual Reserve Inc. v Utah Lighthouse Ministry Inc.*, 75 F. Sapp. 2d 1290 (D. Utah 1999).

[51] In Europe, it is unlikely that such an approach would be taken as temporary reproductions will most likely be exempted under Article Art. 5.1 of the Directive on Copyright and Neighbouring Rights in the Information Society.

Appeal decided that he was not guilty of unlawful distribution of phonograms, and he had committed no infringement under Swedish copyright law.[52]

The Court that initially heard the case had not ruled out the possibility that Olsson might be held liable for contributory copyright infringement without taking a stand on the matter.[53,54] On the question of complicity, the Court of Appeal identified (as in the *Utah Lighthouse Ministry* case above) two possible charges. First, could Olsson be found guilty of contributory infringement with regard to the illegal acts of communication to the public committed by the operators of the linked-to sites? In this regard, the Court of Appeal held that Olsson could not be convicted of contributory infringement because it was not established that the MP3 files were infringing the copyright law applicable to sites hosted abroad. As in the case of P2P involving uploaders located all over the world, we believe it is very difficult to require a court to verify whether a primary copyright infringement occurred in all the foreign countries where the illicit files are located, and a 'de facto export' of national law is thus necessary in this regard. [55] Second, could Olsson be found guilty of contributory infringement as regards the copies of MP3 files made by Internet users who downloaded the files? Here the Court held that Olsson could not be convicted for complicity in the unlawful reproduction of phonograms because it had not been shown that the copies made by the Internet users could not benefit from the exception for private use.

The Supreme Court[56] handled the case differently. It first relied on primary liability and ruled that linking to music amounted to making music available to the public, an act prohibited under Swedish copyright law.[57] The Supreme Court then recalled that if, under Swedish law, an author has the right to prohibit any making available to the public of his or her work, producers of phonograms, such as the plaintiffs, only had a right to equitable compensation in the case of phonograms made available to the public. Therefore, plaintiffs could not prohibit the dissemination of their phonograms through T. Olsson's hyperlinks, regardless of whether such making available involved a legal or illegal copy. Without engaging in a discussion on Swedish law, we think that linking to content does not amount to a form of communication to the public

---

52 *IFPI v T. Olsson*, unreported, no. B 1009-99 (Göta, Court of Appeals 1999) (Swed.).

53 The public prosecutor had failed to state this claim.

54 *IFPI v T. Olsson*, unreported, no. B 824-99, (Tingsrätt Skövde 1999) (Swed.).

55 See on this particular issue, the contribution of G. Austin Chapter 5 in the present volume.

56 *IFPI v T. Olsson*, unreported, no. B 413-00, (Stockholm Supreme Court 2000).

57 See discussion of *Tono v Bruvik infra*.

and should thus be tackled under a secondary liability theory, as illustrated in the cases which follow.

KODA, NCB, Dansk Artist Forbund, Dansk Musiker Forbund & IFPI Denmark[58] The plaintiffs in this Danish case are organisations collectively representing artists and producers. The defendants are individuals who created homepages deemed to have infringed the rights of those represented by the plaintiffs. The two cases both consider whether the creation of deep links, which enable others to copy music tracks that are illegally made available on the Internet without permission from the rightful owners, infringes rights under the Danish Copyright Act. The deep links involved in these cases are characterised by automatic downloading of an MP3 file once the users activate the deep link, that is, clicking on the deep link creates a direct copying access to the MP3 file. The user is prompted with two options on activating a link: the user may choose to open the MP3 file at its present location, that is, the server in which it is placed; or may choose to save the file on hard disk. In the first instance, the file is copied to the 'cache' and may subsequently be used exactly as if the user had specifically selected where the file was to be saved.

The defendants' homepages consisted of alphabetical lists of collectively more than 446 Danish and foreign music tracks and direct links were created to the music tracks located on servers around the world. The Court upheld the claim that the defendants were not authorised to create direct links to music tracks or to copy and/or participate in other peoples' copying of music tracks, which are illegally made available on the Internet. The Danish High Court held that, by establishing direct links to the tracks, the defendants independently made the tracks available to the public in a manner that can be compared to public performance contrary to the Copyright Act. The Court then went on to discuss principles of secondary liability in order to establish the requisite intent to impose a fine on the defendants. As well as being held directly liable for making tracks available to the public, the Court found the defendants increased the possibility of those wanting to copy music of finding the music, facilitating faster and easier copying. On this basis, the Court found the defendants had aided the illegal copying. An instrumental factor in establishing the defendants *mens rea* was messages appearing on the defendants' homepages, such as the following: 'Some of the files must be renamed after downloading'; 'I have removed all banners because it takes longer to D/L pages with banners :) …'; and '…if you download some of these files, you

[58] *KODA, NCB, Dansk Artist Forbund, Dansk Musiker Forbund & IFPI Denmark,* Case Nos. V.L. B-1943-99 and V.L. B-2089-99 (High Ct. of Justice, Western Div., 20 April 2001).

must be aware that you violate Danish Law…'.[59] In establishing indirect liability, the Court's interpretation is more consistent with other cases (see the DeCSS cases discussed below), but to be established it requires additional elements such as the knowledge of the infringing element linked-to and the intention to promote its further dissemination.

IFPI v Beckers In this Belgian case, the finding of secondary liability was established in first instance and on appeal.[60] The president of the Antwerp Court of First Instance (in summary proceedings) held that the provider of links to sites containing MP3 files furnished Internet users with the means of infringing the neighbouring rights of record producers. The judge considered the following:

> A link is not a simple footnote. By activating a link, one has access to a site. To access a site, one must first be able to locate and activate it. The purpose of linking is precisely to provide this service to users. In this case, the defendant intended to establish links to sites from which music could be downloaded illegally, i.e., without paying any royalties to the copyright owner. Downloading pieces of music that are protected by copyright constitutes an offence. Even the defendant considers it illegal. The purpose of providing links – in this case a veritable discotheque of links – on a web site is helping users and to provide them with the key needed to download music illegally. The provider of such a key makes an offence directly possible and is liable as a result for doing so. The fact that it is possible to commit the same offence by other means and that a pirate does not necessarily have to follow the route proposed by the defendant – there are indeed many roads leading to MP3s – does not diminish or preclude the liability of the person who makes one particular path available to the public.[61]

Although the judge does not actually use the terms 'contributory infringement' or 'complicity', he applies the theory of the link provider's complicity to unlawful acts of reproduction committed by Internet users. As confirmed on appeal, the conduct of the link provider is (probably) not compatible with the obligation of 'due care' that can be deduced from the general principles of civil law. The Court of Appeal held that the balance of interest (in summary proceedings) weighs in favour of granting a provisional injunction against the link provider.

TONO v Bruvik[62] In 2005, the Norwegian Supreme Court established secondary liability for the act of creating links to copyrighted MP3 files. This

---

[59] The citations are taken from a translation of the original text.

[60] *Beckers v IFPI*, No. 2000/RK/27 (First Chamber, Court of Appeal, Antwerp, 26 June 2001) confirming Court of First Instance, Antwerp, 21 December 1999, RG 99/23830.

[61] Id. (authors' translation from original).

[62] *TONO v Bruvik*, Civil Case No. 2004/822 (S. Ct. Norway, 27 January 2005).

case concerned a student who created a web site, www.napster.no, which contained links to music files in MP3 format that were available at various Internet addresses. The site's opening page contained a link entitled 'add an MP3' where users were invited to enter the name of an artist, title and Web address of the relevant music file following which a new page would be created with a link to the music file.[63] Bruvik in this case did not upload the music files, but published links to the music files. It was considered to be a key issue in this case that the users of Bruvik's site obtained direct access to the music files by clicking the links he presented and that the downloads from the site where the music files were stored were automatically prompted. On clicking the link, the user was given the option of playing the music, downloading the music or aborting the download. Bruvik did not use the files himself, nor store or copy the files; he merely referenced sites where works were already made accessible.

In 2003, the District Court found the defendant guilty of directly infringing copyright holders' exclusive rights to make works available to the public pursuant to the Copyright Act by publishing links to the illegally uploaded music files. The Court of Appeal overturned this decision holding that the publication of links does not constitute making works available to the public nor render the defendant contributorily liable to the uploading of music files by others. By publishing links to music files, the defendant was held to contribute to the actions of downloaders in playing or copying such files. However, downloading for private use is not illegal in Norway, so no liability was established. The Supreme Court, upon further appeal, unanimously overturned the decision of the Appellate Court and affirmed the Court of First Instance's finding of liability but based on different reasons. The Supreme Court relied on principles of secondary liability to find Bruvik contributorily liable for infringement based on the presumption that his contributory action, that is, linking, alone does not need to be regarded as an act of making works publicly available. The Supreme Court established indirect liability finding that Bruvik's linking exacerbated the effects of the uploaders' actions by increasing the availability of the music. It also found his actions to have been intentional, wilful and committed with the knowledge that music was uploaded without the consent of the right's holders.[64]

Stichting BREIN v Techno Design[65] The Amsterdam Court of Appeal relied on the theory of indirect liability to establish liability in this case. Techno

---

63 The reference would be created under www.napster.no.

64 See also the contribution of A. Dixon Chapter 1 in the present volume.

65 *Stichting BREIN v Techno Design 'Internet Programming' BV,* (Ct. App. Amsterdam, 5th Civ. Div., 15 June 2006), overruling *Techno Design 'Internet Programming' BV v BREIN* (D. Ct. Haarlem, 12 May 2004).

Design was operating a web site called 'zoekMP3.nl' (in English 'searchMP3.nl') that facilitated the location of MP3 files on the Internet. A user could type in a request for a music file and the search tool would retrieve hyperlinks, in particular deep links, to the requested MP3 files. Clicking on the links would trigger the automatic downloading of the music files on the user's computer. The plaintiff who represents various copyright holders in the Netherlands sought to enjoin Techno Design's service. In first instance, the plaintiff's action relying on direct infringement was rightly dismissed: Techno Design had not committed any 'publication/communication to the public' in the sense of the Dutch Copyright Act.

On appeal, the Court of Amsterdam found Techno Design indirectly liable for facilitating the illicit acts of third parties. Three main elements are underlined in the Court's decision. First, Techno Design's service involves more than the mere provision of physical facilities for enabling or making a communication. It is not merely passive: the search service processes the collected data so as to facilitate the downloading of the MP3 files by the users. Secondly, the defendant had not convincingly proved it ignored that most of the files made available online were not authorized; by itself, the use of automatic tools such as web-spiders does not imply a lack of knowledge. A third element was also emphasized by the Court of Appeal: Techno Design was in fact benefiting from the illicit activities of third parties as (1) its search service relied on advertising revenues and (2) the increased traffic on its search pages would allow Techno Design to sell more ringtones (an ancillary service offered by the defendant). As stressed by the Court, the 'structural' use of the illicit MP3 files available on the web does not take into account the legitimate interest of the copyright holders and is not compatible with the 'duty of care' required from such an undertaking. Once those facts are present – the intermediary plays an active role, has sufficient knowledge of the illicit content and benefits from it – the fact that it is not possible for the search tool to distinguish between licit and illicit MP3 files is irrelevant for the outcome of such case.

Other jurisdictions have relied on alternative concepts of third-party liability. Examples from recent Australian and Chinese case law are discussed below.

Universal Music Pty. Ltd. v Cooper[66] This Australian case establishes secondary liability by relying on the alternative concept of 'authorising'

66 *Universal Music Pty. Ltd. v Cooper,* [2005] FCA 971 (Fed. Ct. Australia, 17 July 2005), http://www.austlii.edu.au/cgi-bin/disp.pl/au/cases/cth/federal%5fct/2005/972.html *Cooper v Universal Music Australia Pty. Ltd.,* [2006] FCAFC 187 (Fed. Ct. Full Court Appeal, 18 December 2006) http://www.austlii.edu.au/au/cases/cth/FCAFC/2006/187.html.

infringement.[67] A number of record companies, including Universal Music, Sony and EMI brought a claim for copyright infringement against Stephen Cooper, the registered owner of a web site. Claims were also brought against the Internet Service Providers, E-Talk Communications and Com-Cem,[68] as well as an employee of E-Talk and the Director of E-Talk and Com-Cem. Cooper's web site provided access to sound recordings via hyperlinks. A user clicking on a hyperlink would have the relevant music file transmitted directly to their computer from a remote server.

At first instance, Cooper was held liable for 'authorising' the infringement of copyright in the sound recordings, both by Internet users who downloaded the recordings and the operators of the remote web sites. E-Talk Communications and one of its employees were also found to be liable for their respective actions in hosting and assisting with the operation of Cooper's web site. Under s. 101 of the Australian Copyright Act 1968, a person infringes copyright where it authorises any act that infringes the copyright. In determining authorisation, the Court must take into account the following, non-exhaustive, factors:

> (a) the extent (if any) of the person's power to prevent the doing of the act concerned;
> (b) the nature of any relationship existing between the person and the person who did the act concerned;
> (c) whether the person took any other reasonable steps to prevent or avoid the doing of the act, including whether the person complied with any relevant industry codes of practice.[69]

On appeal, the Court considered the factors listed at subs. 101(1A) of the Australian Copyright Act 1968. In relation to the first factor, the power to prevent, the Court's decision was based on the fact that 'Mr Cooper deliberately designed the web site to facilitate infringing downloading of sound recordings'.[70] It was held that he could not rely on his indifference to the use of his web site to support his inability to prevent the infringement. Cooper's financial benefit from the advertising and sponsorship on his web site led the Court to assume a commercial relationship between Cooper and the users of his web site. Cooper included on his web site disclaimers, which misstated

---

67 See also the contributions of A. Dixon Chapter 1, J. Ginsburg Chapter 4 and M. Schlesinger Chapter 2 in the present volume.

68 A trading name of E-talk Communications.

69 Subsection 101(1A) of the Australian Copyright Act 1968, introduced by a 2000 Amendment.

70 *Universal Music Australia Pty. Ltd. v Cooper,* [2006] FCAFC 187 (Fed. Ct. Full Court Appeal, 18 Dec. 2006) at 149.

Australian copyright law. The Court did not find that Cooper took reasonable steps to prevent infringement. In fact, the intended purpose of the disclaimers was interpreted as purely cosmetic.

The Internet Service Provider E-Talk and its Director were also found liable for copyright infringement. E-Talk's actions were found to have gone beyond simply providing 'facilities for making, or facilitating the making of, a communication'[71] because it was aware of the copyright infringements, it hosted Cooper's web site (MP3s4free.net) for free in return for advertising on the site, and it had the power to prevent the infringing conduct by taking down the web site itself or declining to provide its host facilities. Conversely, the Appeal Court overturned the original decision in relation to the E-Talk employee. In his capacity of employee, he did not possess the power to, nor could he have taken reasonable steps to, prevent copyright infringement, and he had no relationship with the users of Cooper's web site.

Cooper sought to rely on the *Perfect 10* case (see below) and placed considerable weight on a suggested analogy between his web site and Google's general search facility. It should be noted that this analogy was rejected by the Court, and it clearly differentiated Cooper's site from a general search engine, stating 'Google is a general purpose search engine rather than a web site designed to facilitate the downloading of music files'.[72]

Baidu and Yahoo China cases The Chinese Courts have used the concept of 'assisting' infringement to establish the secondary liability of search engines providing links to copyrighted materials. The Beijing No 1 and the Beijing No 2 Intermediate People's Courts simultaneously reached opposing decisions regarding the liability of search engines for copyright infringement on providing links to infringing music files.[73]

China's most popular search engine, Baidu,[74] was accused by several record companies, including EMI, SonyBMG, Universal and Warner, of copyright infringement through its automated MP3 search engine.[75] The companies claimed that by providing links to music files, Baidu infringed their communication right under Chinese law. At issue in this case was whether Baidu had communicated MP3 songs to the public by allowing users to search and down-

---

71 Section 112E of the Australian Copyright Act 1968.

72 *Universal Music Australia Pty. Ltd v Cooper.* [2006] FCAFC 187 (Fed. Ct. Full Court Appeal, 18 December 2006) at 40.

73 See also the contribution of M. Schlesinger in the present volume.

74 Located at http://MP3.baidu.com.

75 *Gold Label Entertainment Ltd. v Beijing Baidu Network Information Scientech Co., Ltd.,* Civ. *v* No. (2005) 7965 Yi Zhong Min Chu Zi (Beijing No. 1 Intermediate People's Court, 17 November 2006).

load illegal MP3 files through the Baidu MP3 search engine service. Baidu did not directly upload MP3 files to their servers; they merely provided links to MP3 files stored on other servers.

Beijing No. 1 Intermediate People's Court held that, as the relevant MP3 files originated from other web servers and not the Baidu web site, the communication occurs between the users downloading the MP3 files and the web site that uploads the files.[76] The Court ruled that a web site providing links was not directly liable as it did not engage in the act of communication via the Internet under the Copyright Law of the People's Republic of China.[77] However, the Court confirmed that Baidu could be indirectly liable for participating in and assisting third-party sites in transmitting infringing music.[78]

The Baidu case was considered under an old law that is no longer in force, and therefore, this judgement can be considered as having been superseded by the *Yahoo! China* ruling.

The Beijing No. 2 Intermediate People's Court rejected Yahoo! China's[79] appeal against a decision holding it to be liable for 'assisting infringement' for linking to web sites offering illicit content.[80] The Court ruled that the provider of a searching or linking service is not liable for infringement where links to infringing material are disabled following receipt of notice from the rights owner. The Court clarified that a web site would not be liable where copyright owners had not sent adequate notices of infringements, however, it would be jointly liable for infringement if it is aware of or ought to know that the linked work, performance or phonogram product constitutes an infringement and fails to remove the link.[81]

Linking to File-sharing Programs

Phonefile v Startsiden[82] The facts in this Norwegian case differ from those

---

[76] See Wang Qian, 'A 'Direct' Decision vs an 'Indirect' Problem: A Commentary on Seven Record Labels vs Baidu.com' (2007) 1 *Journal of China Copyright*.

[77] This decision has been superseded by contemporaneous decision of the Beijing No. 2 Intermediary Court *infra*.

[78] Baidu was not held to be liable because the IFPI had brought the case against Baidu under outdated Chinese copyright law.

[79] Owned by Alibaba.

[80] *Go East Entertainment Co. Ltd. v Beijing Alibaba Information and Technology Co. Ltd.,* Civ. No. (2007) 02627 Er Zhong Min Chu Zi (Beijing No. 2 Intermediate People's Court, 24 April 2007).

[81] Article 'China Court Rejects Yahoo China's "Deep Linking" Appeal', December 20, 2007, By Steve McClure, Tokyo, http://www.billboard.biz/bbbiz/content_display/industry/e3i3ed206b8d3c0733b23120a461b4581f2.

[82] *Phonefile v Startsiden* (Oslo District court, Norway, 28 October 2003).

already discussed. The Court was asked to decide whether the Internet Portal ABC Startsiden[83] should be held liable for creating hyperlinks to file-sharing programs, such as Kazaa.[84] The defendant in this case provided links to file-sharing programs, which could be used to facilitate copyright infringement as well as other, lawful purposes, rather than directly to infringing materials. Extending the distance of the linker and the infringement, in terms of the chain of events, makes it more difficult to establish liability on the part of the linker. ABC Startsiden essentially acts like a directory by categorizing different types of services. The MP3 category presented links to file-sharing services. The Court considered ABC Startsiden's potential indirect liability for providing hyperlinks to web sites where programs allowing users to produce illegal copies of protected works can be downloaded. Relying on the principles of secondary liability, the discussion in the case focused on whether there was sufficient causation to make the defendant an accessory to the copyright infringements committed by end-users. Although the Court found the existence of a causal link between the links created by the defendant and the infringements committed by the end-users, this causal link was not sufficient to comply with the Norwegian legal theories on liability. As the user would be obliged to take steps subsequent to accessing the home page of the file-sharing service, the links were held to be of little importance in the chain of causation and no causal link was established. The Court noted that the file-sharing programs would still be available if ABC Startsiden were to remove its hyperlinks and that such programs can also be used for non infringing purposes.[85]

Hosting of Links to Illicit Content

Scientology v XS4all In the Dutch case *Scientology v XS4all*, the issue of hosting was addressed as well as linking. The Church of Scientology objected to its copyrighted writings (certain texts of Ron Hubbard, the founder of the Church of Scientology) being disseminated on the Internet and sued 22 hosting service providers (including XS4all and Dataweb), in addition to the operator of the site at issue, Mrs. Karin Spaink, who was primarily responsible for the online posting. As well as seeking an order enjoining the defendants from hosting its copyright material, the Church also asked the Court (as a preventive measure) to prohibit them from linking to other sites containing the copyrighted texts.

---

83 http://www.startsiden.no

84 http://www.Kazaa.com

85 See Article 'Decision on Linking to File Sharing Services', Jon Bing, Norwegian Research Centre for Computers & Law, Faculty of Law, University of Oslo, http://merlin.obs.coe.int/iris/2004/2/article33.en.html.

At first instance, the Court of The Hague ordered the defendants to desist from hosting or establishing links to the Church's texts, holding that the defendants were liable to the extent that they knew about the presence of the texts or of links on their servers, that the correct nature of the Church's notification could not reasonably be doubted, and that they did not act expeditiously to remove the texts or links in question.[86] The Court's reasoning concerning the liability of the defendants, including the provider of the link and the ISPs hosting the page with the link, was based on the general obligation of 'due care' ('zorvuldigheid') contained in the Dutch Civil Code.

On appeal, the Court of The Hague rightly considered that the freedom of expression protected by Art. 10 of the ECHR (see above) would be disproportionately restricted by such an injunction and thus reversed the first instance decision.[87] This is clearly a case where copyright is (mis)used in order to unduly limit the freedom to disseminate opinions that are particularly important to bring to the attention of the public. At length, the Court of Appeal's decision retraces the attempts of the Church of Scientology to restrict the public debate on the legitimacy of the Church and concludes that the claim against the publication of such protected documents, including through links, would not be a measure 'necessary in a democratic society' to protect 'the right of others', in this case the copyright held by the Church.[88]

IFPI v Skynet A further case involving IFPI had to do exclusively with the question of hosting hyperlinks.[89] The Belgian branch of IFPI issued a claim against a Belgian access provider, Skynet, for the presence of hyperlinks on some of its customers' sites leading to MP3 files that IFPI claimed were infringing. IFPI had not notified the operators of the sites containing the allegedly illegal MP3 files, nor their hosts, nor Skynet's customers who had established the links to the sites, but had directly addressed its requests to

86 Church of Spiritual Technology/Dataweb B.V., Rb. The Hague, 9 June 1999, available in Dutch at http://www.xs4all.nl/~kspaink/cos/verd2ned.html. See also Computerrecht, 1999/4, p. 200, note P.B., Hugenholtz; B.I.E., 1999, p. 458, note A. Quaedvlieg.

87 Court of Appeal, The Hague, 4 September 2003, *A&M*, 2004.1, pp. 44. On this decision, see G. Gathem and A. Strowel, *Droit d'auteur versus liberté d'expression et responsabilité des fournisseurs de service sur l'Internet*, *A&M*, 2004.1, pp. 50–52.

88 On the balance of copyright and freedom of expression, see A. Strowel and F. Tulkens, 'Freedom of Expression and Copyright under Civil Law: Of Balance, Adaptation and Access', *Copyright and Free Speech*, J. Griffiths and U. Suthersanen (ed), Oxford University Press, 2005, pp. 287–313; A. Strowel and Fr Tulkens, *Droit d'auteur et liberté d'expression. Regards francophones, d'Europe et d'ailleurs*, Larcier, 2006, p.161.

89 See also the discussion on *Universal Music Pty. Ltd. v Cooper infra.*

Skynet. Skynet, upon being asked to withdraw the links, had removed all of them from its servers, though not within time limits satisfactory to IFPI, who thus sought injunctive relief from the Court.

In his decision of 2 November 1999, the president of the Brussels Court of Commerce concluded that the hosting of links leading to copyrighted materials could trigger Skynet's liability if there were no reasonable grounds to doubt the correctness of IFPI's notification.[90] The president decided that there were no such grounds in this case, and thus enjoined Skynet from 'knowingly storing information on its server, giving rise to unlawful distribution of musical recordings'.[91]

The Brussels Court of Appeal adopted the opposite solution. In its ruling of 13 February 2001, the Court first addressed the issue of the liability of the link provider and stated quite clearly that links to MP3 files:

> [...] are a kind of key which, by clicking on it, allows reproductions of musical recordings made without the rightful parties' consent to be downloaded, copied and distributed. The creation of links to such unlawful files, when one knows or should know that they are illegal, constitutes an unlawful act.[92]

As regards the liability of the ISP, the Court of Appeal – duly informed about the relevant provisions of the US Digital Millennium Copyright Act and other existing foreign law and case law, and of the EC 2001/31 Electronic Commerce Directive – decided to first develop its own standards for a notice and take down procedure, and then to verify the application of such standards to the facts of the case, in order to decide whether Skynet had acted contrary to fair trade practices.

The notice and take-down procedure developed by the Court of Appeal implies that when IFPI informs Skynet of the existence of hyperlinks on sites that refer to illegal musical recordings posted on other sites, Skynet should remove these links or prevent access to them, provided the following conditions are met and the procedure indicated below is followed:

- IFPI must first, via an e-mail to the address indicated by Skynet, inform Skynet of these links, identify them by stating the page(s) on the site of Skynet's customer on which these links appear along with the musical recordings that form part of IFPI's repertoire and can be downloaded from the linked sites, and must expressly require that these links be removed or made inaccessible;

90 *IFPI v Belgacom Skynet*, Court of Commerce, Brussels, 2 November 1999.
91 Id. (authors' translation).
92 *IFPI v Belgacom Skynet*, Court of Appeals, Brussels, 13 February 2001.

- Such notification similarly should expressly include the facts that would, *prima facie,* lead a reasonable ISP to assume that the files to which the links refer are illegal;
- Skynet must remove these links or make them inaccessible within three working days following receipt of a notification meeting the above conditions, unless it can provide, within the same period, proof that the musical recordings to which the challenged links refer are legal;
- When submitting the request that links be removed or rendered inaccessible, IFPI must expressly agree to support the responsibility for the removal or rendering inaccessible of the links indicated by them and must guarantee Skynet against any claims from customers from whose web sites the indicated links have been removed or rendered inaccessible on IFPI's initiative, should it subsequently appear that this was done unlawfully.

The facts of the case proved that IFPI had not met these standards on several points. IFPI's notifications did not contain all the requested information and therefore, had not made it *prima facie* apparent to a reasonable ISP that the musical recordings to which the links referred were illegal.

Search Engine with Links to Illicit Content

Perfect 10. v Google[93] *and SAIF v Google* *Perfect 10. v Google* is a complex US case. It began in the District Court of the Central District of California in 2006 when Perfect 10 Inc., publisher of an adult magazine and subscription web site featuring photographs of nude models, sued Google for copyright infringement. Specifically, Perfect 10 sought a preliminary injunction against the search engine to stop generating and distributing thumbnails of Perfect 10 images in Google Image Search, and also to bar Google from indexing and linking third-party sites illegally displaying full-size images of Perfect 10 photos. The District Court deemed the thumbnails infringing but not the links. The Ninth Circuit Court of Appeals, on 16 May 2007, vacated the preliminary injunction on the thumbnail ruling and remanded the contributory infringement claim for links to the infringing third parties back to the district court. The Ninth Circuit found the thumbnail images themselves covered by the 'fair use' doctrine due to its transformative nature (as mentioned above in *Kelly v*

93 *Perfect 10 Inc. v Amazon.com Inc*, 508 F.3d 1146 (9th Cir. 2007). Because Google was a named defendant in this important case, and Google's service was more extensively discussed by the Court than Amazon.com's, we will refer to this case as *Perfect 10 v Google.*

Arriba). It then focused on secondary liability regarding Google's 'inline linking' to full size image.

To best understand how the courts addressed this issue, some background on the technology is necessary.

Google's thumbnail images serve as a link for the user to obtain more information about the image. Clicking on a thumbnail image opens a new page that uses the framing method to display two separate windows on the user's screen, one containing information from the Google web page, including the thumbnail image and text, and the other incorporating the full-size image from the third-party web site through the technique called 'inline'. Google does not store the (sometimes illicit) full-size images appearing in one window on the user's screen but only provides HTML instructions directing a user's browser to access a third-party web site. Because 'providing these HTML instructions is not equivalent to showing a copy', the Ninth Circuit held that Google cannot be directly liable for the appearance of the full-size images.

The Court considered both vicarious and contributory infringement based on the direct liability of the third-party web sites displaying the full-size images, not of the Google image search users.

In order to find Google vicariously liable, the test defined by the *Grokster* decision of the Supreme Court must be applied: one 'infringes vicariously by profiting from direct infringement while declining to exercise a right to stop or limit it'.[94] This means it would be necessary to establish that Google enjoyed a direct financial benefit from the infringing activities of third-party web sites that host and serve infringing copies of Perfect 10 photographs, and that Google declined to exercise the right and ability to supervise or control the infringing activity. According to the District Court and the Ninth Circuit, Google is not deemed to have sufficient control over or authority to stop or limit the infringing conduct of third parties to satisfy the second necessary prong of the test for vicarious liability. Thus, Perfect 10 was deemed unlikely to succeed in proving that Google can be held vicariously liable.

In order to establish contributory infringement, Google had to know the infringing activity and induce, cause or materially contribute to that activity. To ascertain Google's knowledge of the infringing activities, the District Court had considered the copyright notices placed on the original images, Google's monitoring activities and the notices of infringement that were sent from Perfect 10 to Google; however, it held that, alone, the inclusion of a copyright notice on the image is not sufficient for Google to ascertain whether the images were subject to copyright, and thus, Google's established monitoring

94 *MGM Studios Inc. v Grokster Ltd.* 545 US 913 (2005) at 930.

activities were not deemed to confer knowledge on it. The District Court did not reach a decision as to whether the notices of infringement sent from Perfect 10 to Google were sufficient to establish knowledge.

Assuming Google had knowledge of infringing materials available on its system, the District Court, when discussing material contribution, relied on the fact that Google does not offer the facility for its users to download the images in the same way that Napster enabled its users to download music files.[95] Focusing on the indirect liability in relation to the web sites offering the full-size images to which Google's system links (not in relation to the users of Google's system), the Court of Appeal dismissed the opinion of the District Court that had concluded that Google did not materially contribute to infringing conduct because it did not undertake any substantial promotional or advertising efforts to encourage visits to the infringing web sites. For the Court of Appeal, such analysis is not correct as Google substantially assists web sites in distributing their infringing copies to a worldwide market. While the Court of Appeal held that Google's activities do not meet the *Grokster* 'inducement test'[96] because it has not promoted the use of its search engine specifically to infringe copyrights, the Court did state that contributory liability could still be imposed under common law principles, which establish that intent can be imputed: 'an actor may be contributorily liable for intentionally encouraging direct infringement if the actor knowingly takes steps that are substantially certain to result in such direct infringement'.[97]

For Google to be held contributorily liable, it must be established that Google had knowledge that infringing Perfect 10 images were available using its search engine, that it could take simple measures to prevent further damage to Perfect 10's works and failed to do so. Because the District Court did not resolve the factual issues over the adequacy of the Perfect 10's notices and the availability of reasonable and feasible means for Google to refrain from providing access to the infringing images, the Court of Appeal remanded this claim back to it. Thus, there is no definite ruling in *Perfect 10 v Google* on whether Google is in fact contributorily liable for inline linking to full-size infringing images. The Court of Appeal rightly emphasizes that secondary liability in such a linking case requires 'fact-intensive enquiries'.

As for other issues considered in the present chapter, a case similar to Perfect 10 has found its way in continental Europe, allowing a comparison of views held in very different jurisdictions. A collective society (SAIF) representing well-known French photographers (Doisneau, Cartier-Bresson, etc.)

---

95 *Perfect 10 v Google Inc*, 416 F Supp 2d 828 (CD Cal, 2006) at 855.

96 See contribution of J. Ginsburg Chapter 4 in the current volume.

97 *Perfect 10, Inc. v Amazom.com, Inc.*, No. 06-55405 (9th Cir., 16 May 2007) at 54.

filed a case against Google France and Google Inc. for offering, through Google Image Search, links to illicit reproductions of those authors' pictures. On 20 May 2008, the Paris First Instance Court quite surprisingly ruled that US law should apply because Google's servers are located in California where the allegedly infringing acts also take place. The French court only focused on the alleged direct infringement for reproducing thumbnails on Google's pages. Applying the US fair use provision, the court considered that Google's use was non-commercial and did not negatively affect the exploitation of the photographs, and was thus deemed fair.[98] Strangely, the issue of indirect copyright liability for linking to illicit content was not addressed by the Paris court.

Links to Circumventing Devices

The 'DeCSS' cases As the Internet is a global and extremely rapid means of communication, it is very difficult to prevent the disclosure and subsequent dissemination of information on the network. The DVD Copy Control Association Inc. and the American film industry attempted to stop the online communication of information concerning the possibility of decrypting a program that is used to protect copyrighted films. Before marketing their films on DVDs, the major US film producers took steps to ensure that they could not be copied. The Content Scrambling System ('CSS') program was developed to prevent copying of films on DVDs. For obvious reasons of controlling the use of this technology, film producers gave a single company (the DVD Copy Control Association, Inc.) the right to license its corresponding decryption technology. No CSS license had been granted to enable DVDs to be played on Linux operating systems. However, a Norwegian Linux user, Jon Johansen, succeeded in reverse engineering the CSS code and created a program called 'DeCSS', enabling users to circumvent the CSS encryption system and thus copy DVDs. In record time, the DeCSS was disclosed on a profusion of web sites with an equally impressive number of web sites linking to them. In turn, the US film industry brought a number of lawsuits against operators of sites containing the DeCSS.

In one of these suits, *DVD Copy Control Ass'n v McLaughlin*, the film producers requested an injunction prohibiting the defendant not only from disclosing the DeCSS on his own site, but also from linking to sites containing the DeCSS. In its order granting a preliminary injunction, a California trial court ordered the defendant to remove the DeCSS from his site but did not

[98] *SAIF v Google France and Google Inc.*, TGI Paris, 20 May 2008, accessible on www.legalis.net.

deprive him of his freedom to establish links, claiming that such an injunction against linking would be 'overbroad and burdensome'.[99] The court added:

> Links to other web sites are the mainstay of the Internet and indispensable to its convenient access to the vast world of information. A web site owner simply cannot be held responsible for all the content of the sites to which it provides links. Further, an order prohibiting linking to web sites with prohibited information is not necessary since the Court has enjoined the posting of the information in first instance.[100]

In our view, the last consideration is mistaken: as long as the DeCSS continues to be available on the Internet, whether on the defendant's site or on other linked sites, it will be in the plaintiff's interest to apply for an injunction against linking. The real issue is rather the legal basis on which the plaintiff can seek an injunction against linking. Under US law, the Digital Millennium Copyright Act offers such a basis, as will be examined in the following case.

In the case on the merits, *Universal City Studios v Reimerdes*, the film industry sought a permanent injunction against the defendants' posting of the DeCSS on their web sites and against the linking to other web sites containing the DeCSS.[101] The discussion regarding posting of the DeCSS (which was declared to violate the DMCA) will not be further addressed here. More interestingly for this contribution, the court concluded that by linking to other web sites containing DeCSS, the defendants unlawfully 'offered, provided, or otherwise trafficked' in the described technology, and thus equally violated the DMCA.[102]

As regards the First Amendment defence, the court recognized the possible 'chilling effect' to the freedom of expression of a rule permitting liability for, or injunction against, hyperlinks (especially where the linked site would also offer content other than the DeCSS), and therefore, defined the standards to be applied in deciding whether the linking at stake should be declared illegal. The standards developed by the court are as follows:

> [T]here may be no injunction against, nor liability for, linking to a site containing circumvention technology, the offering of which is unlawful under the DMCA,

99 *DVD Copy Control Ass'n v McLaughlin*, No. CV 786804, 2000 WL 48512 (Cal. Super. Ct. 21 January 2000).

100 Id. at *4.

101 At first, the plaintiffs obtained, on 20 January 2000, a preliminary injunction, but only as regards the posting by defendants of DeCSS on their web sites (not for linking). *Universal Studios, Inc. v Reimerdes*, 82 F. Supp. 2d 211 (S.D.N.Y. 2000). Subsequent motions to expand the preliminary injunction to linking and to vacate it were consolidated with the trial on the merits.

102 *Universal City Studios, Inc. v Reimerdes*, 111 F Supp. 2d 294, 325 (S.D.N.Y. 2000).

> absent clear and convincing evidence that those responsible for the link (a) know at the relevant time that the offending material is on the linked-to site, (b) know that it is circumvention technology that may not lawfully be offered, and (c) create or maintain the link for the purpose of disseminating that technology.[103]

Knowledge of the infringing material on the linked-to site and the intentional placement of the link to disseminate the infringing material were therefore sufficient to conclude that the provider of the link was liable. In *Universal City Studios v Reimerdes*, the defendants had, upon issuance of the preliminary injunction enjoining them not to post the DeCSS on their web site, entered into a state of what they had themselves termed 'electronic civil disobedience' by attempting to defeat the preliminary injunction by linking users to other web sites still offering the DeCSS, and by encouraging other sites that had not been enjoined from posting the DeCSS to offer the DeCSS on their web sites. Based on such eloquent evidence of the defendants' intention, the court concluded that the abovementioned conditions for issuing a linking injunction were met.

The same outcome for linking to an anti-circumvention device has been reached in Germany (see below), although the legal grounds completely differ.

BMG Records v Heise Zeitschriften Verlag In this German case, which echoes the above DeCSS cases in the US, a respected online news service specialized in information technology had reported on a software ('AnyDVD') advertised for download from a third party's web site. The software was hosted on a server based in Antigua and was able to circumvent the encoding tools used to protect sound and video recording. Various German producers of recordings sued the online news service because its report contained a link to the web page from which the circumventing software could be downloaded. From reading the linked-to page, it was also clear that this software – whose ability to crack anti-copying devices used for DVDs was praised – was also prohibited in European countries. At the time this online report was made (in January 2005), Germany's 1965 Copyright Act had already implemented the European rules prohibiting the trafficking of circumventing devices, including promotion and advertisement to prevent such devices (Art. 6 of the EC 2001/29 Copyright in the Information Society Directive). At first instance and later on appeal, the Munich Courts held that the defendant was liable for assisting the infringement resulting from the traffic of circumventing technology.[104] The form of contributory infringement applied by the Appellate Court is known as 'disturbance liability' (*Störerhaftung*). It relies on a provision of

---

103 Id. at 341.

104 OLG München, 29 U 2887/05, 28 July 2005 (21 O 3220/05 Landgericht München I).

the German Civil Code (Article 830) dealing with torts, in particular acts of contributory tortfeasors. On this basis, liability exists where an act, even in the absence of intention or negligence, results in the violation of a legally conferred benefit. In such a case, only an injunction can be granted, not damages.[105] The plaintiffs obtained an injunction against the online service for assisting copyright infringement through the online publication and link.

As in other cases involving linking, the endorsement of the illicit content referred to is decisive in establishing liability. In various decisions, the German Supreme Federal Court (*Bundesgerichshof*) has emphasized that hyperlinking is not subject to specific rules for online liability (such as the German rules of the 'Telemedien' law implementing the provisions of the EC 2000/31 Electronic Commerce Directive on intermediaries), but to the general rules on liability. Applying these rules in two cases[106] involving linking to illicit material (such as pornographic content), the Supreme Federal Court ruled that the person who, through linking to the information provided by third parties, makes this information 'his own' is liable in the same way the provider of this information is. This 'appropriation' (endorsement or sponsoring) of third-party content exists when the link provider consciously and intentionally subscribes to the linked-to content.

SUMMARY

Secondary liability for copyright infringement has been widely debated in relation to P2P file sharing. It also plays an important role with regard to hyperlinking. In general, 'to link' does not raise any copyright liability. However, in certain circumstances, the links between web pages may prove 'dangerous'. Caution is necessary if 'good relations' are to be maintained. Hence the motto some commentators have proposed: 'Think before you link'.

The level of cautiousness needed and the liability risk firstly depend on the type of linking:

- *Use of protected pointers*. It is certainly necessary to think first before linking if, instead of an Internet address, the pointer takes the form of an image or other feature that may enjoy copyright protection in its own right. The use of headlines as pointers has in particular been condemned

105 See G. Westkamp (2006), 'Hyperlinks, circumvention technology and contributory infringement – a precarious tale from German jurisprudence', *JIPLP*, Vol. 1, p. 309.

106 BGH 1 April 2004 – I ZR 317/01 (Schöner Wetten) and BGH 18 October 2007 – 1 ZR 102/05.

in various cases. In those cases, direct copyright liability is involved as a copy is made by the linking site. Intermediaries such as search engines offering value-added services (for example, Google.News) have sometimes been held directly liable for using copyrighted elements as pointers or for adding and editing protected content on top of the simple links (for example, extracts or titles of press articles).

- *Deep links*. Caution is also called for if the link is made to a page that is not the homepage or front page of a site, as in the case of deep link, particularly, if the linked-to site is a commercial site supported by advertising revenues and if the advertising on the linked site is being replaced by that of the linking site. However, most deep links will not trigger any liability. The liability of the linking site will not be based on copyright infringement but would rely on other grounds of action such as unfair competition.
- *Embedded links*. Lastly, embedded links, which give the impression that the content of another site is being appropriated, should be avoided, especially in civil law countries where the tort of unfair competition and the protection of the author's moral interests will offer firm grounds for legal action.

Secondary liability for copyright infringement is mainly applied in the cases involving linking to illicit content (and to MP3 files in particular). The outcome of those cases largely depends on the specific facts and the behaviour of the link providers. Indirect liability for linking to illicit content relies on various legal grounds depending on the legal issues of the national law system: in common law countries, the notion of 'authorization' incorporated in the Copyright Acts has been used to oppose this form of linking; in the US, the case law doctrines of contributory infringement and liability for inducement are playing a role; in civil law countries, the general principle of due care, for example the rule of Article 1382 of the French and Belgian Civil Codes, will continue to be applied in various ways in the event of linking to illicit content.[107]

Secondary liability claims have not only been raised against the providers of links, but also against intermediaries who host links to illicit content or against other intermediaries who knowingly facilitate the identification of, and access to, illicit files. In the case of intermediaries who offer services directly connected to the presence of illicit content (for example, a (MP3) dedicated search tool), the active role in facilitating the infringements and the requirement of knowledge are easier to establish than in the case of hosting providers

---

107 See also the contribution of A. Dixon Chapter 1 in the present volume.

who offer a general purpose service and might legitimately ignore the presence of illicit content. However, even for hosting providers, who at first sight play a role remote from the directly infringing acts (the illicit uploading), some direct knowledge might result from adequate notifications, and this triggers an obligation to react expeditiously as in other cases involving the hosting of illicit content.

The review of the case law on those aspects has demonstrated the multiple issues raised by hyperlinking – but a certain convergence as well in the way courts have tackled those issues – although they are operating in very different legal contexts and with the help of various legal tools often deeply rooted in common law.

4. Copyright control v compensation: the prospects for exclusive rights after *Grokster* and *Kazaa*

Jane C. Ginsburg

INTRODUCTION

On the last day of the 2004 Term, the US Supreme Court announced its much-awaited decision in *MGM Studios, Inc. v Grokster Ltd.*[1] Songwriters, record producers and motion picture producers alleged that two popular file-'sharing' networks, Grokster and Streamcast (*dba* Morpheus) should be held liable for facilitating the commission of massive amounts of copyright infringement by the end-users who employed the defendants' peer-to-peer software to copy and redistribute films and sound recordings to each others' hard drives. The Court reversed the Ninth Circuit's grant of summary judgment for defendants, holding that the technology entrepreneurs could be held liable for 'actively inducing' the end-users' acts of infringement. As consumer-wielded digital media increasingly supplant the traditional intermediaries who made copyrighted works available to the public (and who traditionally were the targets of copyright enforcement), courts have struggled to balance meaningful protection for works of authorship against the progress of technological innovation. For some observers, the weakening of copyright control is the necessary price to pay for technological advancement.[2] For others, authors' ability to maintain exclusive rights remains a cornerstone of any copyright system as it adapts to accommodate new modes of exploitation.[3]

---

1 125 S. Ct. 2764 (2005).

2 See, e.g., id at 2793 (Breyer, J. concurring); Lawrence Lessig (2004), *Free Culture: How Big Media Uses technology and the Law to Lock Down Culture and Control Creativity*.

3 See, e.g., Stacey Dogan (2003), 'Code Versus the Common Law', 2 *Journal of Telecommunications & High Technology Law* 73; Jane C. Ginsburg (2001), 'Copyright and Control over New Technologies of Dissemination', 101 *Colum. L. Rev* 1613.

Grokster is the latest in a series of US decisions to address that balance by articulating the liability of an enterprise that does not itself commit copyright infringement, but instead makes it possible for others to infringe. To appreciate the Supreme Court's analysis, it helps to set the case in both domestic and international doctrinal context. Because unauthorized P2P distribution of copyrighted works extends well beyond the US, copyright owners have pursued legal actions in other countries, including the Netherlands[4] and Australia.[5] Thus, I will also consider another common law jurisdiction's analysis of the liability of those who provide goods or services to facilitate infringement. I will conclude with some (perhaps foolhardy) forecasts for the post-*Grokster* future of copyright enforcement.

SECONDARY LIABILITY IN THE US

Copyright infringement is a tort.[6] So is knowingly enabling or inciting another to infringe. Decisions dating back several decades recognize that one who supplies the means to infringe, and knows of the use to which the means will be put (or turns a blind eye), can be held liable for contributory infringement.[7] In the early cases, however, the relationship between the supplier and the user of the means was sufficiently close that there could be little doubt of either the knowledge or the nexus between the means and the infringement.[8] For example, in the 'make-a-tape' case, a record shop rented sound recordings to customers who would also purchase blank tape and then use a recording machine on the store premises to copy the rented recording onto the blank tape.[9] The storeowner's knowledge of the likely use of the blank tape was patent. When, however, the infringement-facilitating device leaves the direct

---

4 *Vereniging Buma, Stichting Stemra v Kazaa BV*, Supreme Court of the Netherlands (Hoge Raad), decision of 19 December 2003, AN7253 Case no.: C02/186HR.

5 *Universal Music Australia Pty Ltd v Sharman License Holdings Ltd.* [2005] FCA 1242.

6 See Latman and Tager (1963), 'Innocent Infringement of Copyright', 2 *Studies on Copyright* 139 (Fisher Mem. Ed.).

7 See generally *Goldstein on Copyright* § 8.1 (3d edn 2005) (citing cases).

8 See id. (advancing the general proposition that 'the closer the defendant's acts are to the infringing activity, the stronger will be the inference that the defendant knew of the activity').

9 *Elektra Records Co. v Gem Electronic Distributors, Inc.*, 360 F. Supp. 821 (E.D.N.Y. 1973). See also *RCA Records v A-Fast Systems, Inc.,* 594 F.Supp. 335 (SDNY 1984) (defendant's employees used 'Rezound' cassette recorder to make copies of sound recordings on customers' request).

control of the facilitator so that it no longer knows in fact what customers are up to, contributory infringement may be more difficult to establish. That, in essence, was the copyright owners' problem in the *'Betamax'* case.[10] Sony, the distributor of the video tape recorder, could well anticipate that consumers would use the record function to copy protected programs, but once the device was out of the manufacturer's hands, it could neither know precisely what the end-users were doing, nor limit their use to permissible copying.

In absolving Sony of liability, the US Supreme Court added a gloss to the prior standard: one who distributes an infringement-enabling device will not be liable for the ensuing infringements if the device is 'widely used for non-infringing purposes. Indeed it need merely be capable of substantial non-infringing use.'[11] This is so even though the distributor was aware that at least some of the use to which the device would be put would be infringing. The court then held that time shifting (recording for subsequent viewing and then erasure) of free broadcast television programs was a fair use.[12] On the record in the case, the 'primary use' of the VTR was for time shifting.[13] A use held to be non-infringing thus predominated, and certainly met the 'substantial' standard.

Cases subsequent to *Sony* endeavoured to apply the 'substantial non-infringing use' standard. But the standard did not again come into play with respect to mass-market means of copying until the *Napster* controversy.[14] There, an online peer-to-peer music 'sharing' service maintained a central database that allowed end-users to find other users currently online and to copy MP3 files from their hard drives. Napster evoked the *Sony* standard, asserting that not all the files were copied without authorization. Napster also asserted that P2P architecture could, in the future, spawn more non-infringing uses. The Ninth Circuit agreed that *Sony* required taking into account the service's capacity for future lawful use, but nonetheless held Napster a contributory infringer. In yet another gloss on the standard of liability, the *Napster* court held that courts should inquire into non-infringing uses when the distributor of the device lacks actual knowledge of and control over specific infringements. Where, however, it is possible to segregate and prevent

---

10 *Sony Corp. of America v Universal City Studios*, 464 US 417 (1984).

11 464 US at 442.

12 Id at 447–56.

13 Id at 493 (Blackmun J., dissenting).

14 *A&M Records, Inc. v Napster, Inc.*, 239 F.3d 1004 (9th Cir. 2001). But see *Vault v Quaid Software*, 874 F.2d 255 (5th Cir. 1988) (distributor of program designed to circumvent software copyright protection held not liable for contributory infringement because program could be used for non-infringing purpose of making back up copies authorized by 17 USC § 117).

infringing uses, it is not appropriate to exculpate the entire system by virtue of its capacity for non-infringing uses. In other words, the consequences to technology of enforcing copyright rules were different in *Sony* and in *Napster*. *Sony* presented the court with an all-or-nothing challenge: either the device would be enjoined, frustrating legitimate uses; or no liability would attach, despite the infringements the device enabled. In *Napster*, by contrast, the service could disable infringing uses by blocking access to listings of protected files, while allowing permissible uses to continue. *Napster* thus transformed *Sony* into an inquiry into knowledge of and ability to prevent specific infringements.[15]

Of course, *Napster* set out the instructions for its own demise: if Napster was liable because it could maintain control over its users' activities, then the next device or service would make sure to make it difficult if not impossible for the service to exercise control.[16] So were born Kazaa, and its US licensees, Grokster and Morpheus. Unlike Napster, these services had no centralized directory: they dispersed information about file location across computer 'nodes' around the world. Users could find each other, but the services disclaimed the ability to prevent infringements as they were occurring. Although it recognized that Grokster and Morpheus had intentionally built their systems to defeat copyright enforcement, the Ninth Circuit held that, without the ability to prevent specific infringements, the services could not be liable.[17] The court scarcely considered whether the services enabled substantial non-infringing use; it acknowledged that 90 per cent of the uses were infringing, but observed in footnote that 10 per cent could be substantial, particularly when the 10 per cent referenced many millions of uses. (That the other 90 per cent would be even more extensive seems not to have troubled the court.)[18]

A unanimous US Supreme Court reversed. It held that the Ninth Circuit had misapplied the *Sony* standard, or, more accurately, that the Ninth Circuit did not appreciate that the *Sony* standard does not even come into play when the defendant is 'actively inducing' copyright infringement. That is, a device might well be capable of substantial non-infringing uses. But if it can be shown that the distributor *intended* users to employ the device in order to infringe copyright, then the distributor will be liable as a matter of basic tort

---

15 For a criticism of the Ninth Circuit's approach, see *Goldstein, supra*, at § 8.1.2.

16 See, e.g., Fred Von Lohmann (2001), 'IAAL: Peer-to-Peer File Sharing and Copyright Law after Napster' available at http://www.gtamarketing.com/P2Panalyst/VonLohmann-article.html.

17 *MGM Studios, Inc. v Grokster Ltd.*, 380 F.3d 1154, 1165-66 (9th Cir. 2004), rev'd., 125 S. Ct. 2764 (2005).

18 380 F.3d at 1162 n. 10.

principles. In this light, *Sony* was a case articulating a standard for assessing liability when it cannot be shown that the device distributor sought to foster infringement. But if the defendant has actively induced infringement, there is no need to revisit the *Sony* standard in order to clarify what 'substantial non-infringing use' actually means.

The Court set out three elements probative of intent to induce infringement: (1) the defendant promoted the infringement-enabling virtues of its device; (2) the defendant failed to filter out infringing uses; (3) the defendant's business plan depended on a high volume of infringement. In Grokster's case, all three elements were easily demonstrated. Grokster had sent out emails extolling P2P copying, and it had 'aim[ed] to satisfy a known source of demand for copyright infringement, the market comprising former Napster users.'[19] Grokster not only declined to devise its own filters; it blocked third-party filters. And Grokster's business plan depended on advertising, whose rates would turn on the volume of users encountering the ads. The more Grokster could attract visitors, the better for its business, and the prospect of free music attracts more visitors than paid music. Taken together, these factors demonstrated a clear intention to foster infringement. As the Court declared: 'The unlawful objective is unmistakable.'[20]

Of course, inducement to infringe is actionable only if infringements in fact occur. Because the liability derives from primary infringing conduct, bad intent must join with unlawful end-user acts. Thus, for example, distributing a copying device together with an exhortation to use the device to engage in massive unauthorized copying does not give rise to liability if no one in fact so uses it. In *Grokster*, however, end-user infringement was never in doubt; plaintiffs' studies showed that 90 per cent of the works copied were copyrighted,[21] and even the Ninth Circuit acknowledged that the 'Copyright Owners assert, without serious contest by the Software Distributors, that the vast majority of the files are exchanged illegally in violation of copyright law.'[22] The Supreme Court thus could exclaim: 'The probable scope of copyright infringement is staggering.'[23]

Having ruled that bad intent, if proved, sufficed to find liability for infringements thus induced, the full Court declined to analyse what the standard for contributory infringement would be when intent to foster infringe-

---

19 125 S.Ct. at 2781. See also Sverker Högberg (2006), 'The Search for Intent-Based Doctrines of Secondary Liability in Copyright Law', 106 *Colum. L. Rev* 909 (discussing the post-*Grokster* dangers of targeting a 'risky demographic').

20 125 S.Ct. at 2782.

21 Id. at 2772, 2778.

22 380 F.3d at 1160.

23 125 S.Ct. at 2772.

ment cannot be shown. The full court opinion provided some indication of that standard, however, when it stressed that certain of the three indicia of intent could not, in isolation, establish inducement because basing liability solely on the defendant's business plan, or solely on the design of its product, would be inconsistent with *Sony*.[24] But the Court assiduously declined to offer further guidance on the meaning of '*substantial* non-infringing use.'

Two concurring opinions, each signed by three justices, ventured onto that terrain, advancing opposing analyses. For Justice Ginsburg, *Sony* requires that copyright protection be 'effective – not merely symbolic.'[25] Where the overwhelming use of the device is to infringe, to reject the distributor's liability would reduce copyright protection to the merely symbolic. The three justices also stressed factual differences between the facts of *Sony* and the activities of Grokster and Streamcast. In *Sony*, the 'time shifting' that the Court deemed fair use was in fact the primary use of the video tape recorder at the time. By contrast, the copies the Grokster and Streamcast users made were not ruled fair uses, and the defendants made no showing of significant actual non-infringing uses. The concurring opinion chided the Ninth Circuit for its failure to 'distinguish between uses of Grokster's and StreamCast's software products (which this case is about) and uses of peer-to-peer technology generally (which this case is not about).'[26] The evidence of non-infringing use presented by the defendants, and credited by the Ninth Circuit, addressed the general benefits of P2P, and not the particular application of P2P by Grokster and Streamcast.

Failure to distinguish between peer-to-peer in general and the exploitation made of that technology by Grokster and Streamcast characterizes the other concurring opinion by Justice Breyer, signed as well by Justices Stevens and O'Connor, who had authored or signed the majority opinion in *Sony*. This opinion urged a broad interpretation of *Sony*, in order to provide security to technology entrepreneurs against attacks by copyright owners allegedly harmed by the distribution of devices that enable end-users to make unauthorised uses of works of authorship. For these justices, the phrase 'capable of substantial non-infringing use' must be understood to excuse the distributor of a device whose lawful use is as low as 10 per cent, especially if non-infringing uses might develop in the future. Moreover, this concurrence stressed, the potential for non-infringing use should be assessed with respect to devices 'of this type,' and not specifically in relation to the defendant's device. Justice Breyer thus could assert that it did not matter that Grokster 'may not want to develop these other non-infringing uses. But *Sony*'s standard seeks to protect,

---

24 Id. at 2781–82 and n. 12.

25 Id. at 2783 (Ginsburg, J., concurring). Chief Justice Rehnquist and Justice Kennedy joined this concurrence.

26 Id. at 2786.

not the Groksters of this world (which in any event may well be liable under today's holding), but the development of technology more generally.'[27]

Justice Breyer emphasized the benefits of the *Sony* doctrine (as understood by the three concurring Justices): it is 'strongly technology protecting;' it is forward looking; and it does not require judges to evaluate the technology at issue.[28] The opinion does not hide its bias in favour of technological development. In weighing the disadvantages inflicted on technology against the advantages to authors and copyright owners that would flow from a stricter interpretation of *Sony* (such as that pressed by the Ginsburg concurrence), Justice Breyer's opinion does not allude to the interests of creativity, but to 'greater revenue security for copyright holders.'[29] In this perspective, the only creators who count appear to be the technology innovators, here confronted with the anonymous and oppressive financial interests of the 'copyright holders.' The opinion adds insult to injury by declaring that, in any event, 'the law disfavors equating the two different kinds of gain (copyright) and loss (technology); rather, it leans in favor of protecting technology.'[30] This striking affirmation is based neither on the text of 1976 Copyright Act nor in the Constitution. Its principal foundation is the *Sony* decision, which, as we have seen, can be understood in several different ways.[31]

But perhaps the disagreement over the *Sony* standard will not in fact matter very much because the *Grokster* inducement standard may displace inquiries into the substantiality of non-infringing uses. Speculation is hazardous, but one might predict that, where a device facilitates infringement on a massive scale, its distributor will likely be found to have intended that result. Where the infringement the device enables is relatively modest in scale, inducement will not be found; however, neither will the *Sony* threshold for liability be held to have been crossed, whatever its height. In other words, 'inducement' and

---

27 Id. at 2790 (Breyer, J., concurring).

28 Id. at 2791–92.

29 Id. at 2793.

30 Id.

31 Justice Breyer's declaration proposes a starker opposition than the Court's earlier dictum in *Twentieth Century Music Corp. v Aiken*, 422 US 151, 156 (1975) ('The limited scope of the copyright holder's statutory monopoly . . . reflects a balance of competing claims upon the public interest: Creative work is to be encouraged and rewarded, but private motivation must ultimately serve the cause of promoting broad public availability of literature, music, and the other arts. . . . When technological change has rendered its literal terms ambiguous, the Copyright Act must be construed in light of this basic purpose.'). The *Aiken* decision did not, however, concern new technologies; the question there was whether a small commercial establishment's playing of radio programming by means of a home style-receiving device was a 'performance' of the broadcast.

'substantial non-infringing use' will become legal conclusions, separating the Sony (good technology) sheep from the Grokster (evil entrepreneur) goats.

The following analysis supports the speculation. Suppose in each of the ensuing cases, the device made available to the public enables a very high volume of infringement.

> *Case 1.* The distributor, culture-wants-to-be-free.com, promotes the infringement-faciltating features of its device or service and does not filter out infringing uses. But it has no business plan because it does not seek revenues; rather it wishes to liberate content from copyright's clutches.

Although one of the three *Grokster* elements is missing, this still seems like a straightforward case of 'inducement,' and, assuming the device is used as intended, liability would be found.

> *Case 2.* The distributor, culture-for-me.com, neither promotes infringement, nor filters infringements out; its business plan requires a high volume of traffic to the site. Bloggers on the unaffiliated culture-wants-to-be-free.com site identify and promote the infringement-facilitating features of culture-for-me.com's device or service.

The most probative *Grokster* element, advertising, seems absent here. If culture-for-me.com merely benefits from, but is not in league with, culture-wants-to-be-free.com, then the question becomes whether failure to filter, plus an infringement-dependent business plan, suffice to establish inducement. *Grokster* tells us that each of these two in isolation will not, but neither did *Grokster* explicitly require all three elements to be present before inducement could be found. Moreover, as the Australian Federal Court in its Kazaa case recognized,[32] the distributor of a device or service is not likely to filter if to do so would reduce its economic benefit. In other words, the two go hand in hand. Other *Grokster* elements prove interdependent as well: a site that *does* filter is not likely to advertise an ability to facilitate infringement if it has in fact hampered that capacity. A site that does filter, moreover, will probably not be engendering massive infringement.

To determine whether advertising is the *sine qua non* of inducement, one might consider whether once it is shown that the distributor promoted infringing uses of the device, it necessarily follows that inducement will be found. The *Sony* case itself suggests not. There was considerable evidence that could have led to characterizing the Sony Corp. of America as an 'inducer.' Sony published advertisements encouraging consumers to build libraries of

---

[32] *Universal Music Australia Pty Ltd v Sharman License Holdings Ltd.* [2005] FCA 1242.

recorded television programming.[33] One advertisement depicted a television set next to a large bookcase fully stocked with hand-labelled boxes of Betamax tapes, and congratulated consumers on their creation of a home tape library of programs. But, despite this evidence of incitement to unauthorized copying – and retention – of protected works, the Court did not find Sony liable. As Prof. Litman's study also shows, a bare majority of the Court was unlikely to find Sony liable on any theory, convinced as Justice Stevens and his allies were that the primary consumer conduct should not be deemed wrongful. But recall that most of that conduct was in connection with an activity – time-shifting – that the majority held non-infringing. In other words, the Sony Corp. may have been proposing that consumers engage in an activity – librarying – whose characterization as a fair use was very doubtful, but most consumers in fact used the Betamax for a purpose the court deemed 'fair.' This suggests that incitement unaccompanied by substantial infringements does not give rise to liability.

If promotion standing alone does not necessarily amount to inducement, perhaps it is also true that non-filtering together with infringement-dependent business plans can so add up. With or without advertising, the economy of the operation depends on infringement. If that is so, it is difficult to see how the entrepreneur could not have intended to foster infringement. And *Grokster* tells us that where there is (realized) intent, there will be liability.

Does this prove too much? *Grokster* may instruct that technology entrepreneurs should not draw their start-up capital from other people's copyrights.[34] Pressing copyright owners into service as the principal (uncompensated) investors in a new technology seems rather problematic. But what if there are other investors? That is, let's assume that lawful uses account for some portion of the device or service's appeal, so that the service could start up thanks to the revenues derived from the lawful uses, although input from other people's copyrights may remain necessary to profitability. The *Grokster* goats are those technologists whose business plans would not exist but for the infringements

---

33 See Jessica Litman (2005), 'The Story of Sony Corp. of America v Universal City Studios: Mary Poppins Meets the Boston Strangler', in Jane Ginsburg and Rochelle Dreyfuss eds. *Intellectual Property Stories* 358, pp. 360–61 .

34 See Oral Argument Transcript at 36, *MGM Studios, Inc. v Grokster Ltd*, 125 S. Ct. 2764 (2005)(No. 04-480), available at http://www.supremecourtus.gov/oral_arguments/argument_transcripts/04-480.pdf.

> JUSTICE KENNEDY: – but what you have – what you want to do is to say that unlawfully expropriated property can be used by the owner of the instrumentality as part of the startup capital for his product.
>
> MR. TARANTO: I – well –
>
> JUSTICE KENNEDY: And I – just from an economic standpoint and a legal standpoint, which sounds wrong to me.

they enable. What barnyard characterization fits those whose business plans, albeit copyright-parasitic, contemplate mixing infringing and non-infringing sources of revenue? If we take *Grokster*'s treatment of the role of intent literally, then the partial foundation of the business plan (and the concomitant device design) on non-infringing uses should not matter; the entrepreneur still intends to foster some infringement. Liability, however, may turn on how much infringement. For we have posited that *Grokster* will supply the rule when the actual or potential volume of infringement is 'staggering'. Short of that (but how much short of that remains uncertain), the *Sony* standard reappears, with (as we have posited) the result that the challenged technology will be deemed lawful.[35]

If this prediction is incorrect, then we can expect further development of the *Sony* standard for exculpatory non-infringing use; in the absence of intent to induce infringement, will even trivial non-infringing use suffice to insulate the technology entrepreneur so long as the technology in the abstract is capable of future non-infringing use? Or will any device or service primarily used to infringe run afoul of the standard? Perhaps a glance at the analysis in a related jurisdiction might clarify the liability of infringement facilitators. The decision of the Federal Court of Australia in *Universal v Sharman* addressed the liability of the Kazaa network for 'authorizing' infringement, in violation of the Australian Copyright Act.

'AUTHORIZING' INFRINGEMENT IN AUSTRALIA

The Federal Court in Australia issued its decision on 5 September 2005, following more than a year of evidence gathering in defendant Sharman Networks' computers. Perhaps learning its lesson from the ruling by the Dutch Supreme Court rejecting liability on the ground that Buma-Stemra (the performing and mechanical rights society of the Netherlands) had failed to demonstrate that Kazaa (which had been located in the Netherlands before its move to Sydney and Vanuatu) was able to control the infringing activities of its customers,[36] the copyright owners obtained an

---

[35] If the sheep are to be divided from the goats based on volume of infringement, this poses challenges for the timing of any lawsuit. If suit is brought too soon, the record on actual use may not be sufficiently established. But if copyright owners wait to see how the device or service is used in fact, it may become difficult to dislodge; 'fair use' may reduce to a synonym for *fait accompli*.

[36] *Vereniging Buma, Stichting Stemra v Kazaa BV*, Supreme Court of the Netherlands (Hoge Raad), decision of 19 December 2003, AN7253 Case no.: C02/186HR.

'Anton Piller order'[37] authorizing pre-trial discovery of Sharman's computers. For over a year, the right holders monitored every transaction and every email transiting through the Sharman servers. This enabled them to establish an extensive record concerning both the measures that could be taken to control users, and Sharman's deliberate relinquishing of that control regarding its principal P2P service.

Unlike the US, where liability for facilitating infringement is grounded in the common law,[38] the Copyright Act of Australia (as well as of the UK[39] and NZ[40]) makes 'authorization' of infringement a direct violation of the statute. Subsection (1) of s 101 of the 1968 Australian Copyright Act provides that a copyright:

> is infringed by a person who, not being the owner of the copyright, and without the licence of the owner of the copyright, does in Australia, or authorizes the doing in Australia of, any act comprised in the copyright.

Subsection (1A), added in 2000, details the elements of 'authorization'. A court is to take into account:

> (a) the extent (if any) of the person's power to prevent the doing of the act concerned;
> (b) the nature of any relationship existing between the person and the person who did the act concerned;
> (c) whether the person took any other reasonable steps to prevent or avoid the doing of the act, including whether the person complied with any relevant industry codes of practice.

The Federal Court ruled that the statute did not require that the defendant in fact be able to prevent the infringement; the statutory language '(if any)' suggested the possibility that the extent of the power might be nil.[41] That would be the case where, for example, a defendant deliberately disabled itself from any ability to prevent the infringing uses it unleashed. Thus, the court

---

37 See *Anton Piller KG v Manufacturing Processes Ltd* [1976] Ch 55 (CA); [1976] 1 All ER 779; [1976] 2 WLR 162. An Anton Piller order, used primarily in copyright and patent infringement cases, is a court order, obtained *ex parte*, allowing a plaintiff to search a defendant's premises without prior warning. A plaintiff obtains an Anton Piller order to prevent an alleged infringer from destroying or hiding incriminating evidence.

38 Although in both *Grokster* and *Sony* the court analogized to § 271 of the Patent Act, which codifies contributory infringement.

39 Copyright, Designs and Patents Act 1988 s. 16(2).

40 Copyright Act 1994 s. 16(1)(i).

41 *Universal v Sharman, supra* at 360.

placed particular emphasis on the third element, focusing on the reasonable steps the defendant could have taken to avoid infringement.[42] On that score, the record of the defendant's calculated inactivity spoke starkly. As the court summarized its findings:

> (i) despite the fact that the Kazaa website contains warnings against the sharing of copyright files, and an end user licence agreement under which users are made to agree not to infringe copyright, it has long been obvious that those measures are ineffective to prevent, or even substantially to curtail, copyright infringements by users. The respondents have long known that the Kazaa system is widely used for the sharing of copyright files;
> (ii) there are technical measures . . . that would enable the respondents to curtail – although probably not totally to prevent – the sharing of copyright files. The respondents have not taken any action to implement those measures. It would be against their financial interest to do so. It is in the respondents' financial interest to maximise, not to minimise, music file sharing. Advertising provides the bulk of the revenue earned by the Kazaa system, which revenue is shared between Sharman Networks and Altnet;
> (iii) far from taking steps that are likely effectively to curtail copyright file-sharing, Sharman Networks and Altnet have included on the Kazaa website exhortations to users to increase their file-sharing and a webpage headed 'Join the Revolution' that criticizes record companies for opposing peer-to-peer file-sharing. They also sponsored a 'Kazaa Revolution' campaign attacking the record companies. The revolutionary material does not expressly advocate the sharing of copyright files. However, to a young audience, and it seems that Kazaa users are predominantly young people, the effect of this webpage would be to encourage visitors to think it 'cool' to defy the record companies by ignoring copyright constraints.[43]

The *Kazaa* decision's resemblance to *Grokster*'s three-point analysis is striking. Like the US Supreme Court, the Australian Federal Court addressed the defendant's promotion of the infringement-facilitating features of its service to a 'risky demographic'[44] of likely infringers; the defendant's deliberate failure to filter out infringing content; and its infringement-dependent business plan. The Australian court also noted the pretextual nature of such copyright-protective measures as Kazaa had taken (wink-and-nod website warnings not to commit infringement). Despite the similarity of the respective courts'

---

42 Id at 328, 330.

43 Court's summary; see also at 184 ('I do not doubt that some people use Kazaa only in a non-infringing way. However, it seems unlikely that non-infringing uses would sustain the enormous Kazaa traffic claimed by the respondents. The explanation of that volume of traffic must be a more populist use.'), 403–15 (legal conclusions concerning 'authorization').

44 I have borrowed this phrase from Sverker Högberg (2006), Note, 'Doctrinal Problems in the Judicial Expansion of Secondary Copyright Liability', 106 *Colum. L. Rev* 909.

approaches, however, the prospects of finding liability for enabling infringement may be greater in Australia than in the US, principally because there is no precedent in Australia equivalent to *Sony*; the UK and Australian cases addressing recording devices and media rejected 'authorisation' liability based on lack of control over the users' acts, not on the non infringing uses to which the recorders could be put.[45]

As a result, it is possible that, in the future, facilitators of online infringements may be more vulnerable in Australia than in the US. In the US, if bad intent is not shown (or not inferred from the scale of the enabled infringements), the prospect of non-infringing uses (albeit in still-undefined proportion) may relieve the technology entrepreneur of liability for contributory infringement. This may be true even where the entrepreneur relinquishes the ability to control end-user conduct, at least where that relinquishment is not probative of intent to induce. After *Kazaa*, by contrast, an entrepreneur who deliberately foregoes control that it could have exercised had it designed its service differently may well be found to have authorized the ensuing infringements. Whether the contrast is more theoretical than real may turn on whether there are bona fide reasons to decline to undertake measures to prevent or limit infringements. If there are not, the entrepreneur is likely to be held an inducer in the US and an authoriser in Australia. If there are, the *Sony* standard may protect the entrepreneur in the US; it is possible that an Australian court would require a more persuasive showing that the bona fide explanation in fact supplied the entrepreneur's reasons for declining to avoid infringements.

The possible difference in outcome poses some fascinating private international law consequences. Copyright law is generally territorial: liability in a given State arises out of wrongful acts occurring or impacting in that State. Unexcused copying in the US violates US copyright law, and unexcused copying in Australia violates Australian copyright law. Unexcused communication to the US public violates US law, and unexcused communication to the Australian public violates Australian law. But, unexcused communication from Australia to the public outside Australia also appears to violate Australian law.[46] This suggests that a technology entrepreneur who makes it possible for Australians to communicate works to the public outside Australia without the

---

[45] See, e.g., *CBS Songs Ltd v Amstrad Consumer Electronics plc* [1988] 1 AC 1013 (H.L.) (multiple-headed tape recorder); *WEA International Inc v Hanimex Corporation Ltd* (1987) 10 IPR 349 (blank tape); *Australian Tape Manufacturers Association Ltd v Commonwealth of Australia* (1993) 176 CLR 480 (High Court Aus.) (blank tape).

[46] See Copyright Act of 1968 (Aus), as amended, s. 10 ('to the public means to the public within or outside Australia').

right holders' permission may be violating Australian law, even if the entrepreneur would not be liable under the law of the recipients' countries.[47]

CONCLUSION

The *Grokster* and Australian *Kazaa* decisions illustrate the adaptation of general principles to problems spawned by new technologies. Even though *Kazaa* applies a statutory text, the reasoning draws on broader pre-statutory case law, and seems largely consistent with the US Supreme Court's federal common law analysis in *Grokster.* The two decisions may also have taken some of the wind out of the sails of proposals to substitute a P2P levy scheme for authors' exclusive rights.[48] At least to the extent those proposals were propelled by an *énergie du désespoir* at copyright's apparent inability to confront the latest technological challenge, an effective compensation right seemed more appealing than a hollow exclusive right. But if, as more recent decisions suggest, copyright can rein in the intermediaries who enable infringement for their own profit, then the climate may prove conducive to licensing P2P exploitations. The goal, after all, is not to extirpate new modes of exploitation, but to bring them within the zone of exclusive rights so that authors may avail themselves of technological advances for the benefit of both consumers and copyright owners.

---

[47] For extensive analysis of the international consequences of the *Kazaa* and *Grokster* analyses, see Graeme W. Austin (2006), 'Importing *Kazaa*–Exporting *Grokster*', *Santa Clara Computer & High Technology Journal*, Vol. 22, p. 577.

[48] For examples of these proposals, see Jessica Litman (2004), 'Sharing and Stealing', 26 *COMM/ENT* 1; Neil W. Netanel (2003), 'Impose a Noncommercial Use Levy to Allow Free Peer-to-Peer File Sharing', 17 *Harv J. L. & Tech.* 1.

Decisions subsequent to *Grokster* and *Kazaa* in other countries have also held against the facilitating intermediary. See A. Strowel and P.Y. Thoumsin (2005), 'Le P2P: un problème pressant en attente d'une réponse législative?', *Propriétés intellectuelles*, No. 17, pp. 428–434, citing developments in Taiwan, 'Kuro Conviction Threatens P2P', 10 September 2005.

5. Global networks and domestic laws: some private international law issues arising from Australian and US liability theories

Graeme W. Austin

INTRODUCTION

'[S]ervices that employ peer-to-peer technology create vast, global networks of copyright infringement',[1] observed the United States Register of Copyrights in a recent Congressional hearing on copyright law. While the networks are global, the law applicable to P2P networks remains tethered within domestic borders. Even so, the application of the law may have significant extraterritorial effects.

This chapter explores the international character of the emerging law on P2P networks in two common law jurisdictions: Australia and the United States. P2P networks are 'global' in many respects. Users of P2P products and services are present in many different jurisdictions. Technology entrepreneurs and their business partners are often geographically dispersed, and business structures can be 'split' to leverage advantages provided by different national legal systems. And the digital content, whose 'sharing' is facilitated by these products and services, regularly traverses back and forth across international borders. The global character of P2P networks makes it helpful to consider some of the private international law issues that may be raised by liability theories that are emerging in the P2P context.

The discussion in this chapter focuses on three recent cases: two from the Federal Court of Australia, the 2005 decision in *Universal Music Australia Pty Ltd v Sharman License Holdings Ltd*,[2] and the 2006 decision of the Full

1 'Protecting Innovation and Art While Preventing Piracy: Hearing on s 2560, The Intentional Inducement of Copyright Infringement Act of 2004, Before the Subcommittee on the Judiciary', 109th Cong (2004) (statement of Hon Marybeth Peters, Register of Copyrights).

2 *Universal Music Australia Pty Ltd v Sharman License Holdings Ltd* (2005) 220 ALR 1 [*Kazaa*].

Federal Court in *Cooper v Universal Music Australia Pty Ltd*,[3] and the famous decision of the United States Supreme Court in *Metro-Goldwyn-Mayer Studios Inc v Grokster*.[4] The second section of this chapter introduces the liability theories developed in the Australian cases and then discusses recently enacted Australian legislation that allows courts to apply Australian law to copyright material that reaches a 'public' outside its borders. It also explores other possibilities for extraterritorial application of relevant liability theories arising under Australian law.

The third section explores the opportunities for applying the 'inducement' theory of copyright infringement that was developed by the US Supreme Court in *Grokster* to conduct occurring in foreign jurisdictions. Copyright owners may have welcomed the new 'inducement' theory announced by the *Grokster* court.[5] Yet litigants may soon be embroiled in the task of determining how the theory might apply to conduct that occurs abroad. This section first identifies the potential, within the increasingly fluid doctrine on the territoriality of intellectual property rights,[6] for application of the *Grokster* inducement theory to activity occurring in foreign jurisdictions. It then considers the issue of *de facto* exporting of indirect liability theories, and examines Breyer J's concurring opinion in *Grokster* to explain this concept. The fourth section offers a brief exploration of the relevance of public international law to the development of a sound private international law regime for the P2P context.

P2P LIABILITY IN AUSTRALIAN LAW

Authorising Copyright Infringement: *Kazaa* and *Cooper*

The Australian Copyright Act of 1968 (Cth) provides that copyright infringement occurs when a defendant 'does … or *authorizes* the doing … of any act comprised in the copyright'.[7] The Copyright Act 1968 lists a

---

3 *Cooper v Universal Music Australia Pty Ltd v Sharman License Holdings Ltd* [2006] FCAC 187 (Full Federal Court of Australia) [*Cooper*].

4 *Metro-Goldwyn-Mayer Studios Inc v Grokster Ltd*, 125 S Ct 2764 (2005) [*Grokster*].

5 The *Grokster* court adapted this theory from US patent law. The Patent Act now codifies the inducement theory. See 35 USC § 271(b): 'Whoever actively induces infringement of a patent shall be liable as an infringer'.

6 *Quality King Distributors Inc v L'Anza Research International Inc*, 523 US 135 at 154 (1998) (Ginsburg J concurring) (describing copyright's territoriality principle as: 'Copyright protection is territorial. The rights granted by the United States Copyright Act extend no farther than the nation's borders' (quoting P. Goldstein (1998), *Copyright*, 2nd ed (Aspen Law and Business, New York).

7 Copyright Act 1968 (Cth) s. 101(1) (emphasis added).

number of non-exclusive factors that courts are required to take into account when considering liability for authorising copyright infringement:

> (a) the extent (if any) of the person's power to prevent the doing of the act concerned;
> (b) the nature of any relationship existing between the person and the person who did the act concerned;
> (c) whether the person took any other reasonable steps to prevent or avoid the doing of the act, including whether the person complied with any relevant industry codes of practice.[8]

These factors build on[9] judicial analyses in a long line of Australian and Commonwealth cases that have considered the scope of the concept of infringement by 'authorisation.'[10] The statutory factors are not exhaustive,[11] and they can be supplemented as the particular facts of cases demand. Significantly, the factors appear to provide for a finding of authorisation in situations in which the authorising defendant cannot control the end user, as is implied by the use of the words 'if any' in the first factor.[12]

In some Commonwealth jurisdictions, the interpretation of 'authorise' in the copyright infringement context had become fairly narrow. The House of Lords held in *CBS Songs Ltd v Amstrad Consumer Electronics plc*,[13] a case involving a dual audio cassette player, that 'to authorise' means 'a grant, or purported grant, which may be express or implied, of the right to do the act complained of'.[14] This standard was meant to be narrower than an earlier test that focused on whether the defendant 'sanctions, approves, or countenances' infringement by another.[15] Under this test, the purveyors of the tape deck were not liable for copyright infringement.

---

8 Copyright Act 1968 (Cth) s. 101(1)(A).

9 The explanatory memorandum accompanying the Bill that added these factors took the view that the inclusion of the factors 'essentially codifies' the common law development of the 'authorization' tort: Revised Explanatory Memorandum, Copyright Amendment (Digital Agenda) Bill 2000 (Cth).

10 See generally Y. Gendreau (2001), 'Authorization Revisited', 48 *Journal of the Copyright Society of the USA* 341 (surveying history of the 'authorisation' concept in Commonwealth jurisdictions).

11 See *Universal Music Australia Pty Ltd v Cooper* (2005) 150 FCR 1 at [81] (Tamberlin J.) (noting that the factors are 'not exhaustive and do not prevent the Court from taking into account other factors, such as the respondent's knowledge of the nature of the copyright infringement'.).

12 *Kazaa* (2005) 220 ALR 1 at 88–9.

13 [1988] AC 1013.

14 Ibid, at 1054.

15 The broader test had been articulated by Atkin L.J., as he then was, in *Falcon v Famous Players Film Co* [1926] 2 KB 474.

In Australia, the High Court maintained the broader test. It held in *University of New South Wales v Moorhouse*[16] that authorisation does not require the granting of express or active permission to infringe copyright. Under *Moorhouse*, the defendant will be liable for infringement if the defendant controls the means by which infringement takes place, makes that means available for the use of persons who might use it to infringe, and is indifferent as to whether or not they do in fact infringe.[17]

In *Kazaa*, the Court tailored the *Moorhouse* authorisation principle to the P2P context. It emphasised that providers of software that enabled the P2P system to operate were not liable for copyright infringement merely because they provided facilities used to infringe the applicants' copyrights.[18] 'Something more' was required. With respect to the Sharman defendants, the principal operators of the Kazaa system, the judge noted Sharman's promotion of the P2P file-sharing facility,[19] its exhortations to users to use the facility to share files, and its promotion of the 'Join the Revolution' movement on its website, a movement that, in the Court's words, 'is based on file-sharing, especially of music, and which scorns the attitude of record and movie companies in relation to their copyright works'.

The Court also paid close attention to the ability within the overall Kazaa system to monitor search requests by Kazaa users. Sharman had been involved in a joint enterprise with another firm, Altnet, with the intention of developing a business to distribute licensed content, which eventually would turn a profit.[20] From the user's perspective, this meant that both unlicensed and licensed copyright material, the latter accompanied by digital rights management information, were available on the Kazaa system. Licensed and unlicensed files were designated colours, 'gold' and 'blue' respectively. Altnet was able to disseminate licensed material to users of the Kazaa software in part by monitoring users' 'blue' file searches. Search for 'gold' files was facilitated by a TopSearch index, which was regularly 'pushed' to the computers acting as

---

16 (1975) 133 CLR 1.

17 Even in the United Kingdom, however, the narrower test has proven to be quite flexible, and has been more liberally applied in cases in which courts have identified a 'joint venture' between the supplier and the primary infringer that reveals a common purpose that a product be used in an infringing way. H. Laddie, P. Prescott and M. Vitoria (2000), *The Modern Law of Copyright and Designs*, vol 2, 3rd edn, (Butterworths, London), p. 1176.

18 *Kazaa* (2005) 220 ALR 1 at 98.

19 The Federal Court referred to a number of firms and one individual as the 'Sharman' defendants. *Kazaa* (2005) 220 ALR 1 at 11.

20 *Kazaa* (2005) 220 ALR 1 at 33 (Wilcox J.). Altnet was also licensed to use the 'Kazaa' trademarks.

Kazaa supernodes.[21] 'Gold' files were distributed by Altnet with metadata, regularly updated according to patterns of users' searches, which facilitated the sales of these files. If a Kazaa subscriber's 'blue search' search terms matched the terms included in the 'gold' file metadata, Kazaa users were offered 'gold' files along with the results of the 'blue' file search.

The Court enjoined most of the *Kazaa* defendants from authorising users to reproduce and publicly distribute copyright protected works, and from entering into a common design to 'carry out, procure, or direct the said authorisation'.[22] This technical information about the interrelationship between the Kazaa software and the Altnet search system also enabled the Federal Court to craft a ruling that would have allowed the Kazaa system to operate, albeit, on a different commercial basis, while implementing protections for the applicants' copyrights. The court's formal orders warrant reproducing in full:

> Continuation of the Kazaa Internet file-sharing system (including the provision of software programs to new users) shall not be regarded as a contravention of order 4 if that system is first modified pursuant to a protocol, to be agreed between the infringing respondents and the applicants or to be approved by the court, that ensures either of the following situations:
>
> (i) that:
>
> (a) the software program received by all new users of the Kazaa file-sharing system contains non-optional keyword filter technology that excludes from the displayed blue file search results all works identified (by titles, composers' or performers' names or otherwise) in such lists of their copyright works as may be provided, and periodically updated, by any of the applicants; and
>
> (b) all future versions of the Kazaa file-sharing system contain the said non-optional keyword filter technology; and
>
> (c) maximum pressure is placed on existing users, by the use of dialogue boxes on the Kazaa website, to upgrade their existing Kazaa software program to a new version of the program containing the said non-optional keyword filter technology; or
>
> (ii) that the TopSearch component of the Kazaa system will provide, in answer to a request for a work identified in any such list, search results that are limited to licensed works and warnings against copyright infringement and that will exclude provision of a copy of any such identified work.[23]

In 2006 in *Cooper v Universal Music Australia*,[24] the Full Federal Court (which decides appeals from cases in the Federal Court) confirmed these basic

---

[21] The system gave Altnet knowledge of the IP addresses of the Kazaa users. Ibid, at 36–7 (Wilcox J.).

[22] The court also made formal declarations that such infringement had occurred. Ibid, at 6–8 (Wilcox J.).

[23] *Kazaa* (2005) 220 ALR 1 at 7 (Wilcox J.).

[24] *Cooper* [2006] FCAFC 187.

rules on authorization. The principal defendant in *Cooper* operated a website ('MP3s4FREE') that listed user-generated hyperlinks to remote websites on which copies of copyright-protected musical works were loaded. Clicking on the hyperlink caused copies of the sound recordings to be downloaded to a browser's computer. Confirming that the operation of the website itself amounted to 'authorisation', one of the Justices drew the following analogy, which also underscores the 'viral' character of copyright infringement via digital networks:

> One person has a vial that contains active and highly infectious micro-organisms, which are ordinarily passed from human to human by the coughing of an infected person. He or she authorizes another person to break the vial in a crowded room knowing that this will result in some people in the room becoming infected with the micro-organisms. Most people would, I think, regard the first person as having authorised the infection not only of those in the room, but also of the wider group thereafter directly infected by them, notwithstanding that he or she had no power to prevent those who were in the room coughing.[25]

The Court concluded that the defendant had authorized copyright infringement by establishing and maintaining a website that 'was structured so that when a user clicked on a link to a specific music file a copy of that file was transmitted directly to the user's computer'.[26] It was 'immaterial' that the website 'operated automatically in the sense that, although [defendant] could edit links on the site, [defendant] did not control the usual way in which links were added to the site'.[27] The 'inexorable inference' from the evidence was that 'it was the deliberate choice of [defendant] to establish his website in a way that allowed automatic addition of hyperlinks'.[28]

In *Kazaa*, the Court did not distinguish between direct infringements or acts of authorisation that occurred in Australia and those that occurred outside Australia. The holding and remedy were only loosely tethered within territorial confines. For example, the modifications of the Kazaa system required by the court were directed at the software 'received by *all* new users of the Kazaa file-sharing system'. Similarly, *all* future versions of the Kazaa system were to include filter technology, and maximum pressure was to be placed on existing users without limitation to those in Australia to upgrade to a system that deploys these filters. There was no apparent restriction on the location of the users or to where new versions of the Kazaa system software were to be distributed. The record did disclose that there was a significant volume of

---

25 *Cooper* [2006] FCAFC 187 [32].
26 *Cooper* [2006] FCAFC 187 [42].
27 *Cooper* [2006] FCAFC 187 [43].
28 *Cooper* [2006] FCAFC 187 [43].

directly infringing activity occurring in Australia. Even so, there was no suggestion that the court was specifically concerned about the territorial limits of its holdings insofar as the acts of authorisation (as compared with the direct acts that were authorised) were concerned.

In *Cooper*, however, the Full Federal Court did address the territorial scope of the 'authorisation' tort. The Court noted that territorial restriction of copyright infringement in Australia concerns the direct infringement of reproduction and communication. This tracks the statutory definition of infringement, which imposes liability for copyright infringement on one who 'does *in Australia*, or authorizes the doing *in Australia* of, any act comprised in the copyright'.[29] Because the record in *Cooper* disclosed that vast numbers of primary acts of infringement occurred within Australia, the court was able to conclude that the elements of the 'authorisation' tort had been established.

Australian Copyright Law's Extraterritorial Reach

Australian copyright law offers some expressly 'extraterritorial' approaches to enforcing the rights of copyright owners. As part of a package of reforms enacted in 2000, the Australian Parliament added a new right to copyright owners' bundle of rights: the right to 'communicate' a work to the public, including outside Australia. Communicating a work also includes the making available of copyright protected works including, for instance, the uploading of a work to a generally accessible website. Among other things it achieved, the Copyright Amendment (Digital Agenda) Act (2000) enacted the legislation necessary for Australia to comply with the WCT.[30] Article 8 of the WCT provides:

> [A]uthors of literary and artistic works shall enjoy the exclusive right of authorizing any communication to the public of their works, by wire or wireless means, including the making available to the public of their works in such a way that members of the public may access these works from a place and at a time individually chosen by them.

Article 8 applies to the full bundle of rights of the copyright owner, and was intended to pave over gaps in the rights to disseminate copyright protected works provided in the Berne Convention.[31] The WCT is silent on the extra-

---

29 Copyright Act 1968 (Cth) s. 101 (emphasis added).

30 World Intellectual Property Organization Copyright Treaty, 20 December 1996, 36 ILM 65 (1997).

31 Berne Convention for the Protection of Literary and Artistic Works, 9 September 1886, as revised at Paris on 24 July 1971 and amended in 1979, S Treaty Doc No. 99-27, 99th Cong, 2d Sess 43 (1986) [*Berne Convention*]. Parties to the WCT

territorial reach of the communication right. As enacted into domestic Australian law, nonetheless, the communication right has an express extraterritorial reach. According to Australian law, '*to the public* means to the public within or *outside* Australia.'[32] The official commentary on the legislation made clear that the inclusion of this definition means that 'Australian copyright owners could control the communication from Australia of their material directed to overseas audiences'.[33] The Australian law on the communication right goes further than is required by the WCT in this aspect, and thus has the potential to be exported to – and, in effect, imported into – every nation in the world to which copyright protected material might be communicated without a license. Moreover, the communication right does not appear to require proof that the communication to users in foreign territories is *itself* infringing according to the laws of the countries where the communication is received.[34]

There are, however, some important limitations on the scope of the communication right under Australian law. Consistent with the 'Agreed statements concerning Article 8' of the WCT, which carve out a safe harbour for the 'mere provision of physical facilities for enabling or making a communication', the Copyright Act 1968 provides that a person, including an ISP,

> who provides facilities for making, or facilitating the making of, a communication is not taken to have authorised any infringement of copyright in a work merely because another person uses the facilities so provided to do something the right to do which is included in the copyright.[35]

---

were entitled to incorporate the treaty obligation into domestic law in their own way. The Australian Act applies the communication right broadly: '*communicate* means make available online or electronically transmit (whether over a path, or a combination of paths provided by a material substance or otherwise) a work or other subject matter, including a performance or live performance within the meaning of this Act'. Copyright Act 1968 (Cth) s. 10. The accompanying World Intellectual Property Organization Performances and Phonograms Treaty, 20 December 1996, 36 ILM 76 (1997) has a more layered approach to the media to which the 'communication' right is applied. See Agreed Statement Accompanying Article 15.

32 Copyright Act 1968 (Cth) s. 10 (emphasis added).

33 Digital Agenda Copyright Amendments: Exposure Draft and Commentary, Copyright Amendment (Digital Agenda) Bill at [28] (6 February 1999).

34 There are parallels in US case law on the 'predicate act' theory, which makes pecuniary relief available under US copyright law for foreign infringements facilitated by the making of an unlicensed copy within the United States. In an early case recognising this principle in the context of allegations of unlicensed exploitation of a copyright protected work in Canada, the Second Circuit imposed liability on the defendant in circumstances where the plaintiff had not established the content of the foreign law, observing '[t]he plaintiffs made no proof of foreign law, and we cannot say that the exhibition … abroad was a tort'. *Sheldon v Metro-Goldwyn Pictures Corp*, 106 F 2d 45 at 52 (2nd Cir, 1939), affirmed on other grounds: 309 US 390 (1940).

35 Copyright Act 1968 (Cth) s. 39B.

The Australian Act thus appears to limit direct liability for unlicensed communication by defining the person making the communication as 'the person responsible for determining the content of the communication'.[36] One cannot be held liable for communicating a work to the public merely by providing the facilities by which a communication is made; nor can one be held liable unless one is responsible for determining the content of the communication. Because users generally determine the content of communications facilitated by P2P networks, there may be significant obstacles to imposing liability on those responsible for providing P2P products or services that directly communicate a work to the public.

But if the territorially confined 'authorization' tort is layered onto the 'communication' concept, Australian law might offer copyright owners some quite powerful legal mechanisms capable of reaching many unlicensed foreign communications of copyright protected works. If the users of P2P services are considered responsible for the content of the communication by, for instance, making copyright protected works available for downloading by others (works they have at some stage selected themselves by downloading them from other users), they would appear to be primarily liable for all communications, domestic and foreign. If a party is liable for authorising those unlicensed communications, the indirect liability theory *also* has the potential to reach both communications within Australia *and* those made to P2P users in foreign territories. The leading English authority on authorisation, *Abkco Music & Records Inc v Music Collection International Ltd*,[37] is consistent with this point. The English Court of Appeal held that a foreign firm that authorised infringement of copyright by primary acts within the United Kingdom was liable for authorising infringement under the English copyright statute. If, under Australian law, the act of authorisation does not itself need to have occurred on Australian soil, a firm operating outside of Australia may, in some circumstances, be found to have authorised communications that begin from Australia, even if the communications themselves are directed or made available to users outside of Australia. Put another way, the Australian regime might imply that, so long as there's a 'communicator' located in Australia, Australian law can reach the conduct of, say, a British firm whose conduct can be characterised as 'authorizing' infringing communications to the United Kingdom and every other country to which they are transmitted.[38]

---

36 Copyright Act 1968 (Cth) s. 22(6).

37 [1995] RPC 657.

38 Because the communication principle also includes 'making available' a copyright work, it does not appear to be necessary for the work to reach anyone, so long as it is internationally accessible. However, at least in theory, remedies might be different where a work is actually downloaded by foreign users, as compared with mere 'exposure' for download.

Outside of Australia there may yet be further extraterritorial possibilities. In some jurisdictions, courts are willing to ascertain and apply foreign copyright laws. Some US appellate courts, for instance, have suggested that trial courts should determine and apply foreign intellectual property laws.[39] And the English Court of Appeal,[40] at least within the ambit of the (then) Brussels Convention, and probably further,[41] has suggested that foreign copyright laws are justiciable in domestic fora. Suppose such a court is seized of a dispute in which an Australian forum and application of Australian copyright law are appropriate and the allegations include unlicensed reproductions and distributions *in* Australia in addition to unlicensed communications *from* Australia. A foreign court that is willing to apply Australian copyright law at all will need to consider whether it is appropriate to apply those aspects of Australian law that have extraterritorial reach, as determined by the Australian parliament. This will involve the courts of one nation contending with the implications of another nation's express rebuttal of the premise that domestic legislation has no extraterritorial reach. The existing doctrine and statutory provisions appear to provide all the ingredients for this liability theory. It remains to be seen, however, if courts will be prepared to put the ingredients together.

GROKSTER ACROSS BORDERS

In *Grokster,* the Supreme Court of the United States famously held that those responsible for managing a P2P network may be liable for copyright infringement under the US Copyright Act on the basis that they 'induced' copyright infringement by others. The key factors that the Court considered relevant to a finding on 'inducement' were: (1) the defendants were aiming to satisfy a 'known source of demand for copyright infringement;' (2) no filtering or other tools were deployed to diminish the infringing activity of users of the defendant's software; and (3) the defendants' business plan, including its source of revenue from advertising, depended on high volume use of the system, 'which the record show[ed] is infringing.'[42]

---

39 See, e.g., *Boosey & Hawkes Music Publishers, Ltd v Walt Disney Co*, 145 F 3d 481 (2nd Cir, 1998).

40 *Pearce v Ove Arup Partnership Ltd* [2000] Ch 403.

41 The English Court of Appeal in *Pearce* considered the subject matter jurisdiction issue first under the Brussels Convention, and then according to general common law principles, suggesting that the ruling has significance outside of the European Union. See also *Lucasfilm Ltd v Ainsworth* [2008] EWHC 1878 (Ch) (31 July 2008).

42 549 U.S. at 939–40.

The *Grokster* Court was not required to consider any international issues. Were such issues to arise, the Court's statement of the holding would invite analysis of a number of questions. For example, are all uses 'promoted' by P2P services relevant to determining if the defendant induced copyright liability, including those that occur abroad? Would it matter if many of the former customers of an illegal service for which a defendant sought to substitute were also located abroad? Would it be relevant if the advertisements that supported defendants' business model were targeted only to US consumers?

On the facts of *Grokster*, these issues would likely have been regarded as moot. Even if analysis of the factual matrix supporting the *Grokster* holding were confined to purely domestic activity, there would almost certainly be enough domestic infringing acts, in terms of the sheer volume of primary infringers and targeted advertising, to make concern with the foreign conduct largely redundant. In the foreseeable future, however, purveyors of software tools facilitating the creation and maintenance of P2P networks may become more nimble, with services targeted more sharply at niche markets, both in terms of audience and content.[43] It is possible that numbers and geography may begin to have greater significance.

De jure Exporting of Intellectual Property Liability Theories

At first blush, extant US copyright doctrine appears to impede application of US copyright in cases where the primary infringers are located beyond the forum. In *Subafilms Ltd v MGM-Pathe Communications Co*,[44] for example, the US Court of Appeals for the Ninth Circuit has held *en banc* that the 'authorization' tort did not constrain authorisation in the United States of actions in foreign territories, regardless of whether the acts would have constituted infringements if done within the United States. The Court of Appeals grounded its analysis of the cross-border questions in the territoriality of domestic copyright law,[45] a concept that the Supreme Court had endorsed early in the 20th century.[46] The corollary of the Ninth Circuit's endorsement of the territoriality of copyright law is that the *lex protectionis* governs the

---

43 See, e.g., 'Irish Software Designer to Create P2P Network Secured from Official Monitoring', 1 August 2005, available at http://newsfromrussia.com/science/2005/08/01/60884.html (reporting on announcement by software designer, Ian Clark, to create a new P2P network that would include only invited, trusted users).

44 24 F 3d 1088 (9th Cir, 1994).

45 Ibid, at 1095–9.

46 See *United Dictionary Co v G & C Merriam Co,* 208 US 260 (1908); *Ferris v Frohman,* 223 US 424 (1912).

primary infringement aspect of the authorisation tort,[47] a principle that the Second Circuit has also endorsed in more recent case law.[48]

The Ninth Circuit did not rely solely on Supreme Court doctrine, however. It also acknowledged the connection between territoriality and the international copyright relations of the United States, reasoning that extraterritorial application of the US Copyright Act would cut across the territorial premise of international copyright treaties.[49] It considered that to accept that the US Copyright Act could apply to foreign activity would 'disrupt Congress's efforts to secure a more stable international intellectual property regime'.[50] The court observed, '[e]xtraterritorial application of American law would be contrary to the sprit of the *Berne Convention*, and might offend other member nations by effectively displacing their law in circumstances in which previously it was assumed to govern'.[51] As I have suggested elsewhere,[52] there may be an important normative component to the respect for the territorial integrity of different nations' intellectual property policies: extraterritorial application of intellectual property laws risks overriding domestic policy choices that may also be important to key aspects of domestic and social economic policy.[53]

If doctrine developed in the 'authorization' context is applicable to secondary liability generally, this may lead to the conclusion that *Grokster*'s inducement principle should not be applied where the primary infringements occurred outside the United States. Though the lines between various forms of domestic infringement may be blurry, a point recognised by the *Sony* court, geopolitical lines are not: the territoriality principle should preclude application of US liability theories where the primary acts of infringement occur abroad.[54]

---

47 For a meticulous exploration of the limits of the principle of *lex protectionis* in copyright law, see Mireille von Eechoud (2003), *Choice of Law in Copyright and Related Rights: Alternatives to the Lex Protectionis* (Kluwer Law International, London).

48 *Itar-Tass Russian News Agency v Russian Kurier Inc*, 153 F 3d 82 (2nd Cir, 1998).

49 *Subafilms Ltd v MGM-Pathe Communications Co*, 24 F 3d 1088 at 1097–8 (9th Cir, 1994).

50 Ibid, at 1097.

51 Ibid.

52 G.W. Austin (2002), 'Valuing "Domestic Self-Determination" in International Intellectual Property Jurisprudence', 77 *Chicago-Kent Law Review* 1155.

53 Ibid.

54 *Sony*, 464 US 417 at 435 n. 17 (1984): 'the lines between direct infringement, contributory infringement and vicarious liability are not clearly drawn…' quoting 480 F Supp 429 at 457–8.

The *Subafilms* approach is not universally endorsed, however.[55] Judge Wiseman of the US District Court for the Middle District of Tennessee made the following well-known retort to *Subafilms*, reasoning that authorisation does not require a domestic act of primary infringement:

> piracy has changed since the Barbary days. Today, the raider need not grab the bounty with his own hands; he need only transmit his go-ahead by wire or telefax to start the presses in a distant land. *Subafilms* ignores this economic reality, and the economic incentives underpinning the Copyright Clause designed to encourage creation of new works, and transforms infringement of the authorization right into a requirement of domestic presence by a primary infringer. Under this view, a phone call to Nebraska results in liability; the same phone call to France results in riches. In a global marketplace, it is literally a distinction without a difference.[56]

A district court in New Jersey has adopted a similar approach, reasoning that Wiseman J.'s analysis was more sensitive to the 'modern age of telefaxes, Internet communication, and electronic mail systems'.[57] The New Jersey court saw the authorisation tort as preventing infringement of copyright by an entity 'merely directing its foreign agent to do its "dirty work".'[58]

Subafilms is now over a decade old, and its analysis arose from a completely different context than P2P networks. It also predates the massive threats to copyright owners' interests posed by digitisation and the Internet, as did the Supreme Court cases on which the Ninth Circuit drew. One can sense in the district courts' analysis some frustration about domestic copyright owners' vulnerability to foreign piracy, which may be exacerbated by strict insistence on territoriality. Courts in the leading copyright circuits distinguish *Subafilms* where a predicate act of infringement occurring within the United States facilitates infringement abroad.[59] Rightly or wrongly, the predicate act theory has the potential to be quite protective of domestic copyright owners' interests in foreign territories, even in cases in which liability under the copyright laws of the relevant foreign state(s) has not been established.[60]

---

55 P. Koneru (1996), 'The Right "to Authorize" in US Copyright Law: Questions of Contributory Infringement and Extraterritoriality', 37 *IDEA – The Journal of Law and Technology* 87 (criticising the Ninth Circuit in *Subafilms* for inappropriately adopting the requirement in contributory infringement that there be an infringing primary act).

56 *Curb v MCA Records Inc*, 898 F Supp 586 at 595 (MD Tenn, 1995).

57 *Expediters International of Washington Inc v Direct Line Cargo Management Services Inc*, 995 F Supp 468 at 477 (DNJ, 1998).

58 Ibid.

59 See, e.g., *Los Angeles News Service v Reuters Television International, Ltd*, 149 F 3d 987 (9th Cir, 2005).

60 *Sheldon v Metro-Goldwyn Pictures Corp*, 106 F 2d 45 (2nd Cir, 1939).

Moreover, because temporary digital storage is considered a legally cognisable copy according to US copyright law, the predicate act theory has the potential to catch a significant amount of foreign copying.[61] Because P2P networks are usually not geographically segregated, temporary copies of files to 'pass through' local 'nodes' quite often. If a liability theory can catch an unauthorised copy that occurs in the United States, then it would seem to be consistent with the predicate act theory for it too provides pecuniary relief for *all* the further foreign infringements that the 'local' copy facilitates.

Without definitive guidance from the Supreme Court, lower courts' willingness to apply *Grokster* in cases that involve foreign conduct, and in which litigants have questioned the geographical scope of the liability theory at issue, will likely depend on how rigidly future courts view the territoriality principle. Arguably, application of the predicate act theory will very often be an affront to a strict understanding of the territorial premise of the international copyright treaty regime, as much as extraterritorial application of the 'authorization' tort.[62] Further extension of the theory may be even more so.[63] With this in mind, however, one should also question whether it is always contrary to the spirit of the Berne Convention to adapt liability theories to stem the tide of massive copyright infringement over international communications networks.

Before considering that question in detail, it may be helpful first to consider briefly the rapidly evolving doctrine on the territorial reach of US patent and trademark laws. This doctrine may shed some helpful light on US courts' attitude towards the territoriality issue in intellectual property generally. In the patent context, recent decisions from both the Federal Circuit and the Supreme Court evince some hostility to plaintiffs who seek to use US fora to or invoke US patent law police infringing activities in foreign territories. In a much-awaited 2007 decision, *Voda v Cordis Corporation*,[64] the Court of Appeals for the Federal Circuit declined to exercise jurisdiction over a plaintiff's allegations of infringement of foreign patents. Though the decision was limited to a particular species of US federal jurisdiction,[65] the Federal Circuit held, over a

---

61 J.C. Ginsburg (1998), 'The Private International Law of Copyright in an Era of Technological Change', 273 *Recueil Des Cours* 239 at 341.

62 G.W. Austin (1999), 'Domestic Laws and Foreign Rights: Choice of Law in Transnational Copyright Infringement Litigation', 23 *Columbia-VLA Journal of Law and the Arts* 1.

63 Ginsburg, above n. 61, at 347.

64 476 F.3d 887 (Fed.Cir. 2007).

65 Technically, the holding in *Voda* was limited to 'supplemental' subject matter jurisdiction arising under 28 USC §1367. In *Baker-Bauman v Walker*, 2007 WL 1026436, a district judge in the Southern District of Ohio distinguished *Voda* in a case involving diversity jurisdiction under 28 USC § 1332(a), but noting that such a case could still be dismissed on *forum non conveniens* grounds.

strenuous dissent, that considerations of comity, judicial economy, convenience, fairness and other exceptional circumstances provided 'compelling reasons' to decline jurisdiction over the allegations of foreign patent infringement. If this approach becomes generally applicable, it will be necessary for parties to litigate allegations of patent infringement occurring in a number of different territories *seriatim* – that is, in each of the different jurisdictions in which each national patent is alleged to have been infringed.

The US Supreme Court has recently been engaged with a related set of questions concerning the territorial scope of US patent law. In *Microsoft v AT&T Corp.*,[66] an April 2007 decision, the Court held that the US Patent Act did not apply to a situation in which a defendant sent computer software from the United States (either on a disk or by electronic transmission) to a foreign manufacturer for installation on computers made and sold abroad. Generally, there is no infringement under the US Patent Act where a product is made and sold in another country. However, an exception enacted in 1984 applies where a party 'supplies…from the United States,' for 'combination' abroad a patented invention's 'components'.[67] In *AT&T*, the Court reasoned, in essence, that 'copies' of software supplied from the United States could qualify as components, but that liability did not attach merely to supply of the program 'in the abstract'. Accordingly, supply of a single copy from the United States did not qualify under the section. The copies that were loaded onto the machines manufactured abroad were not therefore supplied 'from' the United States; rather they were supplied from 'places outside the United States'. The Court's reasoning suggests that the 1984 amendment envisaged the supply of 'things;' the ease of copying software did not make the supply of a single copy the supply of 'components' from the United States for the purposes of assembly abroad. In other words, because the copies 'did not exist until they were generated by third parties outside the United States', the statute did not apply.

In *AT&T*, the Court accompanied its statutory interpretation analysis with a statement about the propriety of extending the reach of US law to conduct in foreign territories. Any doubt about the statutory interpretation point, the Court reasoned:

> would be resolved by the presumption against extraterritoriality, on which we have already touched. The presumption that United States law governs domestically but does not rule the world applies with particular force in patent law. The traditional understanding that our patent law 'operate[s] only domestically and d[oes] not extend to foreign activities', is embedded in the Patent Act itself, which provides that a patent confers exclusive rights in an invention within the United States.

66 127 S Ct 1746 (2007).
67 35 USC § 271(f)(1).

> [...]
> As a principle of general application, moreover, we have stated that courts should 'assume that legislators take account of the legitimate sovereign interests of other nations when they write American laws.' Thus, the United States accurately conveyed in this case: 'Foreign conduct is [generally] the domain of foreign law', and in the area here involved, in particular, foreign law 'may embody different policy judgments about the relative rights of inventors, competitors, and the public in patented inventions.' Applied to this case, the presumption tugs strongly against construction of [the statute] to encompass as a 'component' not only a physical copy of software, but also software's intangible code, and to render 'supplie [d] ... from the United States' not only exported copies of software, but also duplicates made abroad.[68]

A possible implication of the Court's statement is that there may need to be fairly clear statutory guidance before US intellectual property laws would be interpreted as reaching conduct occurring in foreign territory.

In the trademark context, however, the Supreme Court has been far more receptive to application of US trademark law to foreign conduct. The 1952 decision in *Steele v Bulova,*[69] involved a US resident's marketing of 'Bulova' branded watches in Mexico. The defendant had been the first to register the mark in Mexico, but by the date of the Supreme Court's decision, that registration had been annulled in separate Mexican judicial proceedings. Arguably, this meant that the extraterritorial application of the Lanham Act presented less of an affront to the foreign trademark laws and the decisions of the foreign trademark officials who had registered the defendant's trademark. The Fifth Circuit, however, would have allowed the case to proceed, even where imposition of liability under US trademark law could have conflicted with rights granted by a foreign sovereign.[70] While other circuits have adopted slightly different responses to the application of the Lanham Act in cases of alleged infringement of trademark rights in foreign territories,[71] the general trend has been toward increased flexibility and enhancing opportunities for US trademark law to be applied to conduct occurring in foreign territories.

Bulova is now over fifty years old, and the Supreme Court has not had the opportunity to reconsider the territorial scope of the Lanham Act in the light of the concerns articulated in 2007 in *AT&T* about the territorial confines of US statutory law. As a general matter, the law on the extraterritorial application of

---

68 127 S Ct at 1758 (citations omitted).

69 *Steele v Bulova Watch Co*, 344 US 280 (1952).

70 *Bulova Watch Co v Steele*, 194 F 2d 567 (5th Cir, 1952).

71 The leading case is *Vanity Fair Mills, Inc v T Eaton Co*, 234 F 2d 633 at 642 (2nd Cir, 1956). See also *McBee v Delica*, 417 F 3d 107 (2005); *Wells Fargo v Wells Fargo Express Co*, 556 F 2d 406 at 428–9 (9th Cir, 1977); *Star-Kist Foods, Inc v PJ Rhodes & Co,* 769 F 2d 1393 (9th Cir, 1985).

US law, and on the related topic of the receptiveness of US courts to allegations of infringement that implicate foreign laws, appears to be pulling in a number of different directions. In P2P cases, and indeed in any intellectual property case involving foreign conduct, parties on each side should consider whether it may be advantageous to raise the issue of the location of any activities that are relevant to the applicable liability theory.

De facto Export of Liability Theories

The doctrinal developments discussed immediately above all involve issues of *de jure* applications of US intellectual property law, applications that directly confront the territoriality of domestic laws. In the networked environment, however, domestic laws do not necessarily have to be deliberately applied to foreign conduct to have effects in other jurisdictions. Justice Breyer's concurring opinion in *Grokster* illustrates that there is also potential for *de facto* application of US copyright law.

Justice Breyer joined the Court's unanimous opinion holding that inducement of copyright infringement was a viable liability theory for the P2P context. If the inducement theory were not available on the facts, however, Justice Breyer, and two Justices who joined his opinion, O'Connor and Stevens JJ, would have upheld the granting of summary judgment based on the test articulated in the famous decision in *Sony Corp of America v Universal Studios Inc*[72] in favour of the *Grokster* defendants. *Sony* provides a 'safe harbour' for those who, without more, market products that are capable of uses that infringe copyrights as well as substantial non-infringing uses. Justices Breyer disagreed with Justice Ginsburg, who authored another concurring opinion, as to the evidence required to establish whether a product complied with the *Sony* standard for purposes of summary judgment. These Justices also disagreed about how to characterise the *volume* of non-infringing uses that the *Sony* safe harbour requires, a question that the *Sony* court did not directly address. Justice Breyer suggested that a product would fall outside of the *Sony* standard if it 'will be used almost exclusively to infringe copyrights'.[73] Justice Ginsburg and the two justices who joined her opinion, Rehnquist CJ and Kennedy J, cited cases indicating that lower courts have required 'substantial' and 'predominant' non-infringing uses to enable a defendant to qualify.[74] On this view, the relative amounts of infringing and non-infringing conduct may be more important for the application of the *Sony* standard.

72 464 US 417 (1984).
73 Ibid, at 442.
74 *Grokster*, 125 S Ct 2764 at 2791 (2005).

Justice Breyer's opinion emphasised the 'balancing' implicit in the *Sony* test, between facilitating the development of new technology and providing meaningful protection for the rights of copyright owners. He argued that the *Sony* standard 'seeks to protect not only the Groksters of this world … but the development of technology more generally'.[75] He concluded that, if there is a choice between protecting copyrights and facilitating technological development, the law 'leans in favour of protecting technology'.[76] In support of this conclusion, Breyer J pointed to the ability to bring copyright infringement actions against individual infringers, and technological tools – such as digital watermarking and encryption – that copyright owners can use to prevent further illicit copying.

Others will debate whether the balance struck in Breyer J's analysis between technology and copyright is sensible, and whether it finds much genuine support in US copyright law and the federal Constitution.[77] But if we consider this reasoning in light of international relationships between different nations' copyright laws, this reasoning betrays both an *insular* conception of the problems of cross-border infringement of digital material, and a *unilateralist* imposition on other jurisdictions of a localised vision of the appropriate balance between technological development and copyright protection. Most significantly, Breyer J's analysis leaves little room for the possibility that other nations might see the balance differently. Given the ease with which digital files cross international borders and can interfere with foreign markets for copyright protected materials, perhaps one unforeseen corollary of 'technology-friendly' policies developed in the US may be their 'export' into foreign copyright systems, accompanied by the risk of upsetting whatever balance other nations' copyright regimes have established. Different nations and regions are in the process of developing legal and economic policies to respond to the problem of P2P networks, policies that will be formulated against the key question Breyer J articulated: whether 'gains on the copyright swings would exceed the losses on the technology roundabouts'.[78] It is not clear that all, or even most, would resolve the uncertainties by adopting a policy that 'leans in favour of protecting technology'. Some might favour protecting copyright more.

---

75 Ibid, at 2784.

76 Ibid, at 2790.

77 See J.C. Ginsburg (2005), 'Nouvelles des Etats Unis: Responsabilité pour complicité de contrefaçon – La décision de la Cour Suprême du 27 juin 2005 dans l'affaire MGM v Grokster', 11 *Auteurs & Médias* 290 (suggesting that Breyer J's assertion that copyright law favours technology is warranted by neither the Copyright Act 1976 nor the Copyright Clause in the Federal Constitution).

78 *Grokster*, 125 S Ct 2764 at 2793.

Justice Breyer's analysis also betrays a conventional understanding of the role of the author in copyright law. Most obviously, his analysis does not focus on authors at all; his balancing analysis pitches the developers of technology against the revenue interests of copyright *owners*. And, as between copyright owners and those who develop new technologies 'in the garage, the dorm room, the corporate lab, or the boardroom',[79] copyright owners are to take second place. Imposing the costs of technological self-help on copyright owners risks entrenching traditional relationships between individual authors and publishers. Those who seek to protect copyrights will likely be forced to use ever stronger technological protections against P2P products and services developed in the nations' board- and dorm-rooms, and authors may be driven back into relationships with firms that can provide those kinds of services. Because few individual authors are likely to have the required technological expertise, some relationships between authors and those purveying technological protection services are likely to endure. But the doctrine developed by Breyer J would increase the need for authors to seek out firms providing such services and enter into licensing arrangements with them, which may make it even more difficult for authors to market their works independently.

Justice Breyer's opinion underscores the problem that a liability standard that favours technological development over the rights of copyright owners risks *de facto* export of these domestic policies.[80] That is, if the *Sony* 'safe harbour' is capacious, we should expect more copyright protected works to be 'shared' without compensating copyright owners. Furthermore, we could also expect those copies to circulate in foreign jurisdictions, including those that adopt more copyright-protective policies, or which, for example, are more concerned with ensuring an author's ability to forge more direct relationships with the public, without the need to search for firms that market the highest-end technological protections. Justice Breyer provided no indication in his opinion that the *Sony* balance was an appropriate policy choice for any nation other than the United States; nor did he identify what the international effects of such a policy balance might be.

---

79 *Grokster*, 125 S Ct 2764 at 2793.

80 See generally, P. Samuelson (2004), 'Intellectual Property Arbitrage: How Foreign Rules Can Affect Domestic Protections', 71 *University of Chicago Law Review* 223 (discussing how low protection rules in one jurisdiction can undermine the force of higher protections in other jurisdictions).

TOWARD A PRINCIPLED DEPARTURE FROM TERRITORIALITY IN THE P2P CONTEXT

Of course *de jure* application of domestic copyright law to conduct in foreign territories can also seem unilateral in its approach to international copyright relations. For example, the Australian approach to unlicensed communication of copyright protection works 'from Australia' that was discussed above cuts right across the territoriality premise. Moreover, if the *Grokster* liability theory were applied in a way that was indifferent to the place of the primary infringement, it too might create significant tension with the basic territorial premise. A strict territorialist might insist that analysis of the *Grokster* liability standard, and the conditions for its application, should take into account the location of the various actions constituting infringement, both direct and indirect infringement.

For a strict territorialist, it *should* matter where the primary acts of infringement take place, where the advertising touting the infringing uses is directed, and most importantly, whether the direct acts of infringement are unlawful in the place where the users of the P2P products and services are located. These issues may also be relevant for the *Sony* safe harbour, depending on which version applies: if numbers of infringing uses as compared with non-infringing uses are critical to a finding of substantial non-infringing uses, where the users of the P2P products and services are located might also be dispositive.

Contesting Territoriality in the P2P Context

Liability for direct infringement of copyright is based on a relationship between the indirect and the direct defendants, a relationship that is now decidedly international in character. Indirect liability, whether based on authorisation or inducement, is determined by inferring the defendants' mental state with respect to both their *own* actions in the development of business plans, advertising strategies, and the like, *and* the actions of primary infringers located everywhere the Internet can reach. Where the liability theory itself depends on defendants' communication of signals, express or implied, to P2P users everywhere, strict adherence to the territoriality principle seems artificial. If domestic courts really need to concern themselves with exactly where the primary acts of infringement occurred, or are likely to occur, the legal analysis is likely to become unmanageable. Unyielding insistence on the territoriality principle could impose significant impediments to a viable domestic copyright scheme that can respond to massive amounts of copyright infringement facilitated by technologies that link primary infringers in every nation where there is Internet access. In this aspect, *Grokster* and *Kazaa* present the antithesis of the kind of fact pattern that engaged the US Supreme Court recently in *F Hoffmann–LaRoche Ltd v Empagran SA*,[81] a case where plaintiffs urged the court to mandate application of US antitrust law to foreign conduct. *Empagran* was premised on an assumption that the commercial activity in the relevant markets was independent of the effects on United States commerce.[82] In contrast, it is hard to imagine a case in which domestic and foreign effects are more intertwined than one involving P2P products and services in which no geographical or other filtering devices have been applied by the designers.

P2P products and services distil a paradox: practical steps to enforce the rights of copyright owners under domestic law will almost inevitably lead to application in foreign territories of the applicable law, something that is most pertinently demonstrated by the *silence* of both the *Grokster* and the *Kazaa* courts on the international reach of their holdings. On the other hand, as the discussion above of Breyer J's *Grokster* concurrence attempts to demonstrate, lower levels of enforcement of copyright is also very likely to have significant effects on other nations' copyright regimes. Faced with this paradox, perhaps the best that we can do is to work toward identifying 'common values' that may assist in guiding tribunals and legislatures that must contend with the interrelationship between different legal systems in the international copyright context.[83]

Public and Private International Law

In a technological and legal context where legal standards developed in one nation can easily affect policies developed in others, it may be appropriate to look to public international norms for guiding principles. The idea that public international law principles should influence the development of domestic law, particularly where one nation's acts affect others, has a long legal pedigree, and in the copyright context, reflects a broad consensus among many[84] nations about appropriate legal ordering for copyright matters.[85]

---

[81] 542 US 155 (2004).

[82] The DC Circuit confirmed this assumption on remand: *F Hoffman-LaRoche Ltd v Empagran* SA 417 F 3d 1267 (DC Cir, 2005) (holding that, for the purpose of 15 USC § 6(a), the foreign conduct was not sufficiently connected with the effects on the US market caused by the defendants' conduct).

[83] R. Higgins (1994), *Problems and Process: International Law and How We Use It* (Oxford University Press), New York, pp. 74–7.

[84] Perhaps not all, see, e.g., A. Story (2003), 'Burn Berne: Why the Leading International Copyright Convention Must Be Repealed', 40 *Houston Law Review* 763 at 764.

[85] See R.G. Steinhardt (1990), 'The Role of International Law as a Canon of Domestic Statutory Construction', 43 *Vanderbilt Law Review* 1103.

For copyright questions, an obvious source for principles is the *Berne Convention*. In most cases, adherence to the territoriality principle is consistent with dominant international norms reflected in the Convention. The Ninth Circuit's emphasis in *Subafilms* on the role of international obligations in the shaping of domestic doctrine is consistent with the underlying national treatment premise of the international copyright regime: each nation's laws should govern issues of infringement for the places where the infringing activity interferes with the market that is created by each nation's copyright laws.[86] The territoriality principle is also consistent with normative principles that require accountability to the citizenship that is required to bear the costs of intellectual property enforcement. The *Subafilms* approach is more than 'invocation of sovereignty for its own sake', to borrow Rosalyn Higgins' phrase.[87] Moreover, the Ninth Circuit's approach reflects the principle that public international law obligations have a role in shaping domestic doctrine. The Supreme Court recently emphasised the importance of 'prescriptive comity' in the antitrust context,[88] and recent copyright jurisprudence emphasises the role of international obligations of the United States in the interpretation of the Copyright Clause.[89]

In the present context, however, it is also important to recognise that the Berne Convention emphasises *both* territoriality as a structural matter and effective protection of the rights of authors as a governing substantive concern. As the Ninth Circuit in *Subafilms* pointed out, national treatment and territoriality are important premises upon which the international copyright regime is built. But they are not the only ones. The Berne Convention sprang from a desire to *protect* authors' rights. This is suggested, for example, by the 1883 statement from the Swiss government, inviting other nations to participate in the process of drafting an international copyright treaty:

> The protection of the rights of authors in their literary and artistic works (literary and artistic property) is becoming more and more the object of International Conventions. It is, in fact, in the nature of things that the work of man's genius, once

---

86 See also H. Ullrich (1995), 'TRIPs: Adequate Protection, Inadequate Trade, Adequate Competition Policy', 4 *Pacific Rim Law and Policy Journal* 153 at 160 (arguing that extraterritorial application of domestic intellectual property law distorts competition).

87 Higgins at 77.

88 *F. Hoffman-La Roche Ltd v Empagran SA*, 542 US 155 at 169 (2004): '…if America's antitrust policies could not win their own way in the international marketplace for such ideas, Congress, we must assume, would not have tried to impose them, in an act of legal imperialism, through legislative fiat'.

89 See *Luck's Music Library, Inc v Gonzales* 407 F 3d 1262 (DC Cir, 2005) (international bargaining leverage secured by membership of the Berne Convention achieved by copyright legislation relevant to the constitutionality of that legislation).

> it has seen the light, can no longer be restricted to one country and to one nationality. If it possesses any value, it is not long in spreading itself in all countries, under forms which may vary more or less, but which, however, leave in its essence and its principal manifestations the creative idea. This is why, after all civilized States have recognised and guaranteed by their domestic legislation the right of writer and of artist over his work, the imperative necessity has been shown of protecting this right in international relations, which multiply and grow daily.[90]

That general purpose, internationalist in its aspirations, is affirmed by the preamble of the Berne Convention, which now states that the nations of the Berne Union are 'equally animated by the desire to protect, in as effective and uniform a manner as possible, the rights of authors in their literary and artistic works literary and artistic works.'[91] While the national treatment principle was adopted quite early in the treaty drafting process,[92] and as a structural and normative matter, remains critical to international intellectual property relations, we should be wary of the possibility that formalistic adherence to territoriality might undermine meaningful protection of authors' rights, which is precisely the idea that explicitly animates the Convention.

If public international law norms are to influence the development of domestic conflict of laws principles, courts should not always be impeded in imposing liability for indirect infringement in contexts in which the decision might have extraterritorial effects. Greater cognisance of the international legal context might also prompt reticence about developing policy positions such as those adopted by Breyer J in *Grokster*. In cases where the development of liability standards will have obvious extraterritorial effects, it might be appropriate to give more consideration to the extraterritorial implications of doctrinal commitments and their likely impacts on the international copyright regime in which the United States now plays such a significant part.

CONCLUSION

Promoters of P2P products and services, along with other groups including activists, litigants, and a number of academics, have made sustained efforts in recent years to challenge the idea that copyright protection, and intellectual

---

[90] December 1883, circular note from the Swiss government to the governments of 'all civilized nations'. Reprinted in *Actes de la Conférence internationale pour la protection des droits d'auteur réunie à Berne du 8 au 19 Septembre 1884* (1884) pp. 8–9, cited in S. Ricketson (1987), *The Berne Convention for the Protection of Literary and Artistic Works: 1886–1986* (Kluwer, London), p. 54.

[91] Berne Convention, above n. 31, Preamble.

[92] See Ricketson at 74.

property protection generally, is founded on unassailable societal norms. This is part of the politics of contemporary intellectual property law, and may make the argument that failure to provide robust copyright protection in global markets being an offence against the 'international order' seem somewhat more difficult to sustain.[93]

Equally, however, a sustainable '*Kazaa* Revolution' is unlikely to be one that defies the international copyright system. Whatever its rhetorical appeal, the rallying cry of 'it's cool to infringe' is not the stuff from which coherent governing norms are likely to develop in an increasingly interconnected world – not, at least, of the type that will appeal to most legal actors. One of the major criticisms levelled at the *Kazaa* and *Grokster* decisions is that they are not 'technology-friendly'.[94] But technological friendliness has not yet caught on as a principle around which an international judicial or legislative consensus has coalesced that would justify undermining the more established consensus focused on protecting authors' rights in international commerce.

---

93 Higgins at 58.

94 This criticism of the Australian decision was quickly made by Prof. Kim Weatherall in her regular blog on IP issues: http://weatherall.blogspot.com/2005_09_01_weatherall_archive.html#112592939140783823.

6. A bipolar copyright system for the digital network environment

Alexander Peukert*

INTRODUCTION

Digital technology and global networks have led to the so-called 'digital dilemma'.[1] On the one hand, digital technology and the Internet facilitate the global dissemination of information at a very low cost. This feature favours static efficiency in the use of existing works because works as public goods are distributed as widely as is economically feasible. On the other hand, digital technology and global networks diminish the control of copyright owners over their copyrighted works. If a single digital copy made available on the Internet, especially in a peer-to-peer network, theoretically suffices as a master for an indefinite number of identical, unauthorized clones, right holders fear that they will not be able to recoup their investment in producing the work in the first place. Without this promise, it is argued, fewer works will be created. Beneficial dynamic effects of intellectual property protection will be lost. It is thus not surprising that copyright owners try to condition access to information on the basis of digital rights management (DRM) systems. These measures rely on digitization and therefore on the very same technology that makes widespread dissemination of information possible. From its very beginning, copyright has had to cope with and has addressed[2] the tension between the public interest in increasing the storehouse of knowledge and authors'

* A more comprehensive version of Alexander Peukert's article was published in (2005) 28 *Hastings Comm. & Ent. L. J.* 1.

1 See Committee on Intellectual Property Rights and the Emerging Information Infrastructure (2000), *The Digital Dilemma*; Congress of the United States, Congressional Budget Office (CBO) (August 2004), *Copyright Issues in Digital Media*; William W. Fisher III (2004), *Promises to Keep: Technology, Law, and the Future of Entertainment*, pp.11–37; Raymond Shih Ray Ku (2002), 'The Creative Destruction of Copyright: Napster and the New Economics of Digital Technology', 69 *U. Chi. L. Rev.* 263, 270–276.

2 The search for a balance in copyright is already inherently articulated in US Const. art. I, § 8, cl. 8: 'To promote the Progress of Science . . . by securing for limited Times to Authors . . . the exclusive Right to their respective Writings . . . '.

interests in obtaining compensation to secure their investment. Digitization and the Internet carry this tension to extremes because they optimize both static and dynamic efficiency.

The current paradigm of this dilemma is P2P file sharing.[3] Indeed, the conflict that arose out of P2P network development has already been called a 'war'.[4] It is taking place between copyright owners, and users and their proponents, who want to retain the benefits of this technology for themselves and for society at large. This dispute is far from being resolved. Besides court proceedings over the liability of users and mere facilitators of file sharing for copyright infringement, different proposals for future amendments of the respective laws have been made. In particular, several commentators and institutions have suggested a solution where non-commercial file sharing in P2P networks would be lawful and the copyright owner would be compensated indirectly through a collective licensing scheme, a tax or a levy.[5]

In this chapter, I ask whether these proposals are in accordance with obligations under the Berne Convention (BC),[6] the TRIPS Agreement[7] and the WCT.[8] This question is not only of theoretical relevance. The US has ratified all three treaties. Overall, 157 countries are party to the Berne Convention,[9] 148 to the WTO and thus the TRIPS Agreement,[10] and 50 to the WCT.[11] Given that countries must adhere to their obligations under this 'supranational copyright law',[12] every proposal that wants a chance at being enacted has to be

---

3 See Lawrence Lessig (2004), *Free Culture: The Nature and Future of Creativity* p. 296; Peer to Peer Networks in OECD Countries, *OECD Information Technology Outlook 2004*, available at http://www.oecd.org/dataoecd/55/57/32927686.pdf, 2.

4 See, for example, (2004) 'Streaming Media', 12 *Wired* 6, 148–9; Lessig, *supra* n. 3, at 10; Fisher, *supra* n. 1, at 82; Daniel J. Gervais (2004), 'The Price of Social Norms: Towards a Liability Regime for File-Sharing', 12 *J. Intell. Prop. L.* 39, 40.

5 See *infra* 'non-voluntary licenses regarding P2P file sharing' at p. 154.

6 Berne Convention for the Protection of Literary and Artistic Works, Paris Act of 24 July 1971, as amended on September 28, 1979.

7 Agreement on Trade-Related Aspects of Intellectual Property Rights of 15 April 1994.

8 WIPO Copyright Treaty and Agreed Statements Concerning the WIPO Copyright Treaty, adopted in Geneva on 20 December 1996.

9 See Berne Convention for the Protection of Literary and Artistic Works, http://www.wipo.int/treaties/en/ip/berne/index.html.

10 See the WTO, http://www.wto.org/english/thewto_e/thewto_e.htm.

11 See WIPO Copyright Treaty, http://www.wipo.int/treaties/en/documents/pdf/s-wct.pdf.

12 See Daniel J. Gervais (2005), 'Towards a New Core International Copyright Norm: The Reverse Three-Step Test', 9 *Marquette Intell. Prop. L. J.* 1, available at http://ssrn.com/abstract=499924, at 33; Jane C. Ginsburg (2001), 'Toward Supranational Copyright Law? The WTO Panel Decision and the "Three-step Test" for

tested for conformance with these requirements under international law. For example, the German Ministry of Justice already declined to adopt a new limitation to copyright with regard to non-commercial file sharing, explicitly referring to the three-step test under Berne.[13]

Further, the dispute settlement system of the GATT/WTO, makes it possible to enforce rules of an international treaty on intellectual property for the first time.[14] When one country adopts a trade policy measure or takes some action that one or more fellow WTO members consider to be breaking the WTO agreements, including TRIPS,[15] a dispute settlement procedure can be instituted. According to the Uruguay Round Understanding on Rules and Procedures Governing the Settlement of Disputes (DSU), the Dispute Settlement Body may authorize the imposition of trade sanctions if the target of the complaint does not follow the recommendations of the panel report or the appeals report.[16] As of October 2005, the WTO homepage lists 24 dispute settlement procedures relating to TRIPS,[17] including a procedure concerning US copyright law. The WTO Panel held that 17 USC § 110(5) was a violation of US obligations under the TRIPS Agreement.[18] As a result the US, as a temporary arrangement between the US and the EC, agreed to make a lump-sum payment in the amount of $3.3 million to a fund to be set up by performing rights societies in the European Communities for the provision of general assistance to their members and the promotion of authors' rights for a three-

Copyright Exceptions', 187 *Revue Internationale du Droit d'Auteur* (RIDA) 3; but see Pierre Sirinelli, 'Exceptions and Limits to Copyright and Neighbouring Rights', Workshop on Implementation Issues of the WIPO Copyright Treaty (WCT) and the WIPO Performances and Phonograms Treaty (WCCT), WIPO Document WCT-WPPT/IMP/1 of 3 December 1999, available at http://www.wipo.int, 42 (stating that the three-step test 'is far from providing harmonization').

[13] See Bill for a 'Second Act on Copyright in the Information Society' of 27 September 2004.

[14] In a WTO Dispute Settlement Proceeding, the one invoking the restriction to minimum rights under TRIPS bears the burden of proof. See Panel Report, *United States-Section 110(5) of US Copyright Act*, WT/DS160 (15 June 2000), para. 6.9-16; Panel Report, *Canada-Patent Protection of Pharmaceutical Products*, WT/DS114/13 (17 March 2000), para 7.16.

[15] See Art. 64 TRIPS.

[16] See 'Understanding on Rules and Procedures Governing the Settlement of Disputes', 15 April 1994, Marrakesh Agreement Establishing the World Trade Organization, Annex 2, Legal Instruments-Results of the Uruguay Round, 33 I.L.M. 1226 (1994).

[17] See Index of Dispute Issues, http://www.wto.org/english/tratop_e/dispu_e/dispu_subjects_index_e.htm#bkmk137.

[18] See Panel Report, *United States-Section 110(5) of US Copyright Act*, *supra* n. 14.

year period commencing on 21 December 2001.[19] Thus, an amendment of national copyright law that is in violation of TRIPS may have to be abandoned to avoid trade sanctions by other WTO members.

Therefore, international copyright law must be considered in the discussion about the future of copyright in the digital network environment. If a proposal does not comport with treaty obligations, it is then necessary to either amend respective international rules or to terminate membership, which, in the case of the TRIPS Agreement, would mean leaving the WTO. Obviously, neither of these alternatives are likely to become reality. The amendment of an international treaty requires international consensus of all contracting parties.[20] To quit membership in the WTO will not be taken as a serious option in a global economy by any country.

Nevertheless, discussion of the digital dilemma, especially in the US, focuses on the admittedly central search for an effective, preferably balanced, solution. Models are developed for the future. Current law is not the yardstick. Obligations under international copyright law are merely considered as details.[21] Admittedly, proposals that start from scratch are essential to both fuel the discussion and to finally come to an acceptable solution for all players involved. The aim of this article, in contrast, is to contribute to this discussion by adopting a strictly positivistic view. This will help to outline a model for future copyright in the digital online environment that has not yet been clearly articulated which I call the *bipolar copyright system.* This system follows from the proposals already on the table. However, it also claims to be in line with international copyright law, and thus is actually available to national legislatures.

COPYRIGHT AND PEER-TO-PEER NETWORKS

The advent of P2P network technology and the ability of users all over the world to exchange digital files intensified the conflict between right holders and users about the future of copyright in cyberspace. Much is at stake for both sides. Copyright owners fear not being able to establish a market for digital

---

19 See Notification of a Mutually Satisfaction Temporary Agreement, *United States-Section 110(5) of the US Copyright Act*, WT/DS160/23 (26 June 2003).

20 On the difficulties amending the TRIPS Agreement see Gervais, *supra* n. 12, at p. 28 ('far from simple politically'); Gervais, *supra* n. 4, at 71 ('any proposal to license P2P should take account of applicable international treaties'); Peter Eckersley (2004), 'Virtual Markets for Virtual Goods: The Mirror Image of Digital Copyright?', 18 *Harv. J.L. & Tech.* 85, 157.

21 See *infra* 'international copyright law' at p. 159.

products. Users want to benefit from cheap, worldwide, and unrestricted access to information contained in published works. It is no wonder that when even the facts are controversial[22] the possible solutions will be even more so.

In light of these developments, one commentator rightly describes the current situation as a 'kind of logjam'.[23] On the one hand, P2P networks are still intensely used and technologically improved for the sharing of digitized content, some of which is copyrighted. On the other hand, right holders are trying everything to bring an end to this allegedly harmful institution. This, however, is not to say that nobody has an idea of how to resolve this conflict. On the contrary, postulations cover the whole spectrum, from 'abolish copyright' to 'abolish P2P networks'.

Two of these approaches would not require legislative actions. First, a 'wait-and-see approach' argues that the market will provide an efficient result, especially in the form of differential pricing, even if the legislature refrains from stepping in.[24] Second, several commentators and the Electronic Frontier Foundation plead instead for *voluntary* collective licensing of exclusive rights. Under the EFF's proposal, the music industry would form a collecting society and then offer file-sharing users the opportunity to 'get legit' by making a reasonable regular payment (the EFF specifies $5 per month). So long as they pay, users would be free to download whatever they like, using whatever software works best for them.[25]

---

[22] It is not undisputed, on an empirical level, whether at all, and if so, to what extent, file sharing causes declines in sales of music and other copyrighted products. See *MGM Studios, Inc. v Grokster Ltd.*, 125 S.Ct. 2764, 2794 (2005) (Breyer, J., concurring); Felix Oberholzer & Koleman Strumpf (March 2004), 'The Effect of File Sharing on Record Sales. An Empirical Analysis', at 24–25, available at http://www.unc.edu/~cigar/papers/FileSharing_March2004.pdf; Martin Peitz & Patrick Waelbroeck (January 2004), 'The Effect of Internet Piracy on CD Sales: Cross-Section Evidence', *CESifo Working Paper Series No. 1122*; Stan J. Liebowitz (2005), 'Pitfalls in Measuring the Impact of File-Sharing', 51 *CESifo Economic Studies* 435, 471–472.

[23] Neil Weinstock Netanel (2003), 'Impose a Noncommercial Use Levy to Allow Free Peer-to-peer File Sharing', 17 *Harv. J.L. & Tech.* 1, 19–22.

[24] See CBO, *supra* n. 1, at 28–33.

[25] See Electronic Frontier Foundation (2004), 'A Better Way Forward: Voluntary Collective Licensing of Music', available at http://www.eff.org/share/collective_lic_wp.pdf; Daniel J. Gervais (2004), 'Copyright, Money & the Internet', paper presented at the 'Copyright Office Comes to California' Conference San Francisco, March 3, 2004, available at http://www.commonlaw.uottawa.ca/faculty/prof/dgervais/CopyrightMoneyAndTheInternet.pdf, at 22–23 (proposing a voluntary licensing system for file sharing, especially in light of international copyright treaties); Gervais, *supra* n. 4, at 71; Fisher, *supra* n. 1, at 252–258 (describing a voluntary licensing regime to be implemented if the government was not willing to step in to impose the tax-based system that Fisher prefers).

The problem with both approaches is that they have not yet become reality. Copyright owners establish more and more commercial online ventures where users can stream and download legally and pay for these uses individually. But neither these lawful alternatives to file sharing, nor civil and criminal actions have lead to a decrease of traffic in P2P networks.[26] Thus, uncontrolled use of copyrighted works takes place as ever without generating revenues for artists and right holders. The market has not solved the problem. Whether it ever will is uncertain. Interestingly enough, the failure to stop unauthorized file sharing has not put enough pressure on copyright owners to agree on a voluntary collecting and licensing scheme as proposed by the EFF and others. Right holders are still betting on exclusivity in cyberspace.[27]

Not surprisingly, therefore, both parties have turned their attention to the legislature.[28] Several proposals have been put forward, differing substantially with respect to the aim and the practical solution suggested. At the extremes, 'anti-copyright' models plead for a complete or nearly complete abandonment of copyright as an exclusive right in the digital network environment, arguing that exclusive rights in cyberspace would do more harm than good.[29] The 'beyond copyright model' instead proposes a 'digital lock up' to stop infringing uses on the net.[30] Looking for a middle ground that acknowledges the need of right holders to enforce their exclusive rights effectively against illegal uses in P2P networks without banning these technologies altogether, Mark A. Lemley and R. Anthony Reese have outlined a streamlined and largely online administrative proceeding overseen by the Copyright Office that gives copyright owners a quick, low-cost alternative to enforcing their rights against individual large-scale uploaders on P2P networks.[31]

---

26 See 'Streaming Media', *supra* n. 4.

27 This reluctance of copyright owners is telling with regard to the acceptance of proposals to establish a non-voluntary licensing regime.

28 See also *MGM Studios, Inc. v Grokster Ltd.*, 380 F.3d at 1166–67 (holding that to fix the flow of Internet innovation is a question to be resolved by Congress and not by the courts); *AT&T Corp. v City of Portland*, 216 F.3d 871, 876 (9th Cir. 1999) (pointing to Congress as the right addressee for a re-examination of copyright principles in cyberspace).

29 See, e.g., Shih Ray Ku, *supra* n. 1; Mark S. Nadel (2004), 'How Current Copyright Law Discourages Creative Output: The Overlooked Impact of Marketing', *19 Berkeley Tech. L.J.* 785.

30 For an overview on different approaches, see Lionel S. Sobel (2003), 'DRM as an Enabler of Business Models: ISPs as Digital Retailers', 18 *Berkeley Tech. L.J.* 667, 670 et seq.; Netanel, *supra* n. 23, at 7–22, pp. 74–83; Aric Jacover (2002), 'I Want My MP3!', 90 *Geo. L.J.* 2207, 2209–11; Eckersley, *supra* n. 20, at 86 ('information anarchism and information feudalism'). On filters that stop infringing uses in P2P networks, see Mark A. Lemley and R. Anthony Reese (2004), 'Reducing Digital Copyright Infringement Without Restricting Innovation', 56 *Stan. L. Rev.* 1345, 1385.

31 Lemley and Reese, *supra* n. 30, at 1354 et seq. For a dispute resolution mech-

Also somewhere in the middle of this spectrum of control are proposals for future copyright models regarding P2P networks that would replace exclusive rights in copyrightable subject matter with mandatory remuneration rights. The fundamental notion of these concepts is that efficient control of the use of P2P network technology is not possible without banning the technology altogether or without severe drawbacks with regard to monitoring and privacy. To avoid these disadvantages, non-commercial file sharing would be legalized under a limitation of or exception from copyright. Right holders would be compensated by a levy or tax on products and services used for file sharing. The congeniality of this solution rests upon the fact that it preserves the benefits of P2P network technologies while at the same time guaranteeing authors compensation. In Lawrence Lessig's words, it is 'compensation without control'.[32]

NON-VOLUNTARY LICENSES REGARDING P2P FILE SHARING

Whereas non-voluntary licenses have for a long time been an important instrument in balancing the private interest of the right holder with the public interest in the dissemination of knowledge, a non-voluntary license covering P2P file sharing does not yet exist in any national copyright law.[33] However, several commentators advocate models that permit non-commercial file sharing in exchange for a levy or tax that is meant to compensate the losses incurred by the right holder.

Without going into detail, German and Swiss commentators state that copyright in the digital network environment will at least partially have to be replaced or supplemented by levies because exclusive rights would either not be enforceable or their exercise would constrain the free flow of information on the Internet.[34] In his French dissertation, Christophe Geiger discusses

anism through a form of non-binding arbitration which could rapidly resolve copyright infringement cases on the Internet at low litigation expense, see also Alan R. Kabat (1998), 'Proposal for a Worldwide Internet Collecting Society: Mark Twain and Samuel Johnson Licenses', 45 *J. Copyright Society of the USA* 329, 341.

32 Lawrence Lessig (2001), *The Future of Ideas: The Fate of the Commons in a Connected World*; Shih Ray Ku, *supra* n. 1, at 263.

33 Netanel, *supra* n. 23, at 32.

34 See Philipp Wittgenstein (2000), *Die digitale Agenda der WIPO-Verträge*, p. 162 (stating that copyright on the Internet should be transformed from an exclusive right to a mere remuneration right); Artur-Axel Wandtke (2002), 'Copyright und virtueller Markt in der Informationsgesellschaft', *Gewerblicher Rechtsschutz und Urheberreht* (GRUR) 1, 7 (arguing that the future protection of authors will probably amount to mere remuneration rights).

several solutions addressing the fact that copyright, as it exists today, does not meet the needs of a functioning information society. Among these solutions, the author lists compulsory licenses, especially for *sui generis* rights in databases,[35] and mandatory collective administration of exclusive rights, where collecting societies woould be required to license certain uses on a non-discriminating, fair basis,[36] a model that ultimately is very similar to a statutory, non-voluntary license.[37]

Interestingly, a richer set of proposals for non-voluntary licenses applied to P2P file sharing can be found in recent US literature.[38] Glynn S. Lunney argues that a levy or limited tax on copying technology and storage media for private copying is 'inescapable', taking into account the dangers of an 'encryption-based approach'.[39] Raymond Shih Ray Ku is very much in line with this reasoning with his proposal of a 'Digital Recording Act' as a second-best solution if the abolishment of copyright would hamper the incentive to be creative. This Act would allow file sharing, but would introduce statutory levies on subscriptions for Internet services and on the sales of computer, audio, and video equipment. In order to measure the extent of downloads and other uses

---

35 Christophe Geiger (2004), *Droit d'auteur et droit du public à l'information. Approche de droit, compare* para. 370–380 (R.D.T.I.); see also Christophe Geiger (2005), 'Right to Copy v Three-Step Test', *Computer L. Rev. Int'l* (CRi) 7, 10 (stating that it would be preferable to admit private copying as an enforceable right against technical devices and to solve the problem by a working system of equitable remuneration).

36 Geiger, *supra* n. 35, at para. 381–84; Lucie M.C.R. Guibault (2002), *Copyright Limitations and Contracts. An Analysis of the Contractual Overridability of Limitations on Copyright*, pp. 26–27.

37 See Guibault, *supra* n. 36, at 26–27. On mandatory collective administration of exclusive rights without the obligation of the collecting society to license certain uses, see Silke von Lewinski (2004), 'Mandatory Collective Administration of Exclusive Rights – A Case Study on Its Compatibility with International and EC Copyright Law', *UNESCO e.Copyright Bulletin*, No. 1.

38 See also the proposals by Jim Griffin (April 2001), 'At Impasse: Technology, Popular Demand, and Today's Copyright Regime', available at http://www.62chevy.com/at_impasse.htm; Bennett Lincoff (22 November 2002), 'A Full, Fair and Feasible Solution to the Dilemma of Online Music Licensing', available at http://www.quicktopic.com/boing/D/uhAMNwVb8yfkc.html; Philip S. Corwin & Lawrence M. Hadley (2004), 'P2P: The Path to Prosperity', 24 *Loy. L. A. Ent. L. Rev*. 649, 669; Eckersley, *supra* n. 20, at 92 ('virtual market reward/remuneration system'). Lionel Sobel's 'Digital Retailers' model (Sobel, *supra* n. 30, at 667, 673 et seq.) should not be listed among the proponents of a non-voluntary license for non-commercial file sharing; see Lemley & Reese, *supra* n. 30, at 1410 (stating that Sobel's model is not a levy at all, because it depends on identifying and collecting from infringers).

39 Glynn S. Lunney (2001), 'The Death of Copyright: Digital Technology, Private Copying, and the Digital Millennium Copyright Act', 87 *Va. L. Rev*. 813, 910–918.

of digital works on the Internet, these activities would be technologically tracked and monitored.[40] Speaking in favour of exclusive rights in works as a means to ensure adequate compensation for artists and right holders, Aric Jacover pleads for a similar levy or tax system as a second-best solution if the strategy of 'aggressively employing traditional copyright policies in the Internet distribution market' should not ensure compensation for the use of works.[41] Even these few examples show that a levy/tax solution forms a compromise between ever-expanding exclusivity and the abandonment of copyright. Advocates of both extremes refer to levies as the second-best solution.

Others plead for a levy/tax system as regards P2P file sharing, not only as the second-best, but as the primary solution. Among these ranks Neil Netanel with his proposal for a 'Noncommercial Use Levy'.[42] His model permits – as a right protected by law that cannot be waived contractually – non-commercial copying, online distribution in P2P networks (downloading), streaming, and adaptation of published copyrighted works (except software), provided that the derivative creator clearly identifies the underlying work and indicates that it has been modified, in return for a levy which is – provided that negotiations have failed – set by a Copyright Office Tribunal at a 'fair return/fair income' rate (some 4 per cent of the retail price of the goods/services). The levy has to be paid by providers of products and services whose value is enhanced by file swapping (Internet access, P2P software and services, computer hardware, consumer electronic devices such as CD writers, MP3 players, digital video recorders and storage media such as blank CDs). The allocation of the collected money is made in accordance with the actual use of the content as measured by technology that tracks and monitors the use. Apparently Netanel does not concede to copyright holders the right to withdraw their works from the levy system and to opt for exclusive exploitation on the basis of digital rights management instead.

In a proposal that bears much resemblance to Netanel's 'Noncommercial Use Levy,' William Fisher outlines an administrative compensation system,[43] even providing detailed figures on the amount of taxes that would be needed

---

[40] Shih Ray Ku, *supra* n. 1, at 311–15; Raymond Shih Ray Ku (2003), 'Consumers and Creative Destruction: Fair Use Beyond Market Failure', 18 *Berkeley Tech. L.J.* 539, 566 n.160.

[41] Jacover, *supra* n. 30, at 2250–54, with reference to Kabat, *supra* n. 31, at 336–37, who proposed a Worldwide Internet Collecting Society (WICS) which, contrary to the proposals discussed in this chapter, was meant to administer the exclusive rights of authors in cyberspace.

[42] Netanel, *supra* n. 23, at 4, 35–59.

[43] Fisher, *supra* n. 1, at 199–251.

to compensate the losses to be expected from the reduction of exclusive rights.[44] Fisher sketches his model as follows:

> The owner of the copyright in an audio or video recording who wished to be compensated when it was used by others would register it with the Copyright Office and would receive, in return, a unique file name, which then would be used to track its distribution, consumption, and modification. The government would raise the money necessary to compensate copyright owners through a tax – most likely, a tax on devices and services that consumers use to gain access to digital entertainment. Using techniques pioneered by television rating services and performing rights organizations, a government agency would estimate the frequency with which each song and film was listened to or watched. The tax revenues would then be distributed to copyright owners in proportion to the rates with which their registered works were being consumed. Once this alternative regime were in place, copyright law would be reformed to eliminate most of the current prohibitions on unauthorized reproduction and use of published recorded music and films.[45]

Fisher allows right holders a hybrid marketing strategy, that is, to sell copy-protected CDs while simultaneously distributing unencrypted versions of the song, receiving shares of the tax for these uses.[46] In addition, copyright owners would be free to implement DRM without registering their work for the tax system.[47] The statutory default, however, would be a limitation for non-commercial file sharing. It would also apply to works not registered.[48]

In *The Future of Ideas*, Lawrence Lessig argued that file sharing should be empowered by recognizing a system of compulsory licenses similar to those used in cable retransmission, the fee being set by a policy maker striking the right balance.[49] In his 2004 book *Free Culture*, he still agrees with Fisher's proposal, but he also stresses that the current P2P network technology might become irrelevant when faster and easier Internet access will empower users to switch from downloading to streaming content from a commercial service to which they subscribe. Due to this possible technological development, Fisher's

---

44 Fisher, *supra* n. 1, at 214 ($2.389 billion would have to be raised for copyright owners in movies, musical works and sound recordings).

45 *Id.* at 9.

46 *Id.* at 248.

47 *Id.* On the potential of this solution to comply with international copyright law treaties, see *infra* 'Conflicts with a normal exploitation' at p. 164 and 'Features and benefits' on p. 181.

48 See *id.* at 204 (stating that if a work was not registered, the use would be lawful but uncompensated), at 247 ('. . .if a copyright owner opted out of the system entirely, releasing only an encrypted version of his or her recording. . .').

49 Lessig, *supra* n. 32, at 254–55.

system would only serve in the interim period, to the extent that actual harm is demonstrated.[50]

Jessica Litman differentiates between 'sharing' and 'hoarding' as the two possible ways to exploit works on the Internet.[51] By that, she means that right holders can choose between letting their works be shared in P2P networks in exchange for a blanket fee or levy/tax disbursed primarily to the musicians and composers, or hoarding their works in exclusively exploited online ventures, protected by DRM. Sharing would be the legal default rule.[52] However, right holders would be able to opt out of the levy system. To this end, they would have to make their work available in a *.drm format capable of conveying copyright management information, as defined in 17 USC § 1202, that incorporates and facilitates digital rights management.[53] If they had already released their works in other formats, they still could – after a 24-month grace period before any withdrawal would take effect – withdraw it from the levy/tax system. In order to do so, however, the right holders would have to recall copies of the work released in other formats and offer any consumers who own authorized, commercial copies in a non-*.drm format the opportunity to exchange those copies for *.drm copies at no charge.[54]

Summing up, these concepts take the same starting point: 'compensation without control' is considered to be the best way to reap the fruits of the digital network technologies for authors and the general public alike. Nevertheless, important differences can be observed. For example, not all models afford the copyright owner the right to withhold his or her work from the levy/tax system and to go for exclusivity in cyberspace instead. Even those that do so, such as the models of Jessica Litman and William Fisher, advocate 'sharing' as the legal default. As will be shown in the following sections, these differences are important when it comes to the question of compliance with international copyright law. Finally, it should be noted that the mentioned proposals are already influencing current political debates about copyright and file sharing. Whereas content holders propose the application of software filters that check files on the fly and order the user's computer to terminate a download if a file's 'fingerprint' matches that of a restricted song contained in

---

[50] Lessig, *supra* n. 3, at 298, 301; see also Paul Goldstein (2003), *Copyright's Highway. From Gutenberg to the Celestial Jukebox*, pp. 202–03 (2nd edn.).

[51] Jessica D. Litman (2004), 'Sharing and Stealing', 27 *Hastings Comm. & Ent. LJ* 1, 39–50.

[52] Litman, *supra* n. 51, at 41. On the consequences of this solution for the compliance of the proposal with international copyright law see *infra* 'Compliance with international copyright law' at p. 182.

[53] Litman, *supra* n. 51, at 46–48.

[54] *Id.* at 48.

an online database, providers of P2P network software and services advocate a collective licensing regime similar to that currently applied to broadcast radio and web casting under US copyright law.[55]

INTERNATIONAL COPYRIGHT LAW

The following section will adopt a positivistic view in analysing the above-mentioned proposals. In particular, it will discuss whether the three-step test conflicts with the implementation of the suggested regimes in national copyright law. The three-step test limits the extent to which national legislatures may impose limitations on and exceptions to exclusive rights. In other words, it marks the border between exclusivity and non-voluntary licenses.[56] Additionally, this section will consider the obligation of contracting parties to the WIPO Copyright Treaties to provide adequate legal protection and effective legal remedies against the circumvention of effective technological measures.[57]

The proposals for levy/tax systems to cover non-commercial file sharing deal with these questions of compliance with international treaty obligations marginally at best. Some papers do not attend to this question at all.[58] Lawrence Lessig acknowledges that 'some of the changes' he proposes would require amendments to 'or the abrogation of some treaties', listing the BC, the WIPO Treaties and TRIPS.[59] William Fisher briefly explicates that his proposed limitation to exclusive rights[60] would necessitate amendment of the

---

55 See 9 BNA Electronic Commerce & Law Report 204-05 (2004); Netanel, *supra* n. 23, at 35–36.

56 On the functions of the three-step test, see Martin Senftleben (2004), *Copyright, Limitations and the Three-Step Test. An Analysis of the Three-Step Test in International and EC Copyright Law*, pp. 118–124.

57 See Art. 11 WCT, Art. 18 WPPT.

58 See Lunney, *supra* n. 39, at 910–18; Sobel, *supra* n. 30, at 673; Shih Ray Ku, *supra* n. 1, at 311–15; Shih Ray Ku, *supra* n. 40, at 566 n. 160; Lemley and Reese, *supra* no. 30, at 1414–31 (hinting only at the widespread adoption of TRIPS and the Berne Convention).

Eckersley, *supra* n. 20, at 152–58, is the only proponent of a tax/levy system for file sharing who offers a more detailed discussion of Art. 13 TRIPS.

59 Lessig, *supra* n. 32, at 251 n. 14.

60 Fisher, *supra* n. 1, at 247 proposes a new section 107A of the US Copyright Act that would permit:

- Reproduction of a musical composition, sound recording, or motion picture for noncommercial purposes (i.e. consumption, not resale);
- Preparation of a derivative work of a sound recording or motion picture registered pursuant to the new scheme, provided that the derivative work is also so registered before it is made available to the public;

BC and the TRIPS Agreement. Only Art. 13 BC allows some flexibility with regard to music.[61] According to Jessica Litman, a model in which the right holders can withdraw their work from the levy system would 'at least arguably' be 'compliant' with treaty obligations under the BC and WIPO treaties.[62] She apparently doubts, however, whether her proposal for a levy/tax system as the statutory default rule with an opt-out-procedure for right holders to be eligible for exclusive exploitation comports with the prohibition of formalities for copyright protection under the BC.[63] Finally, Neil Netanel states that the levy he proposes would comport with Art. 13 TRIPS because it would be limited to non-commercial uses and would provide a solution to the practical implausibility of enforcing proprietary copyrights in the global P2P arena.[64] The following section will analyse which of these clearly differing assessments is at least arguably correct.

Overview

All of the aforementioned proposals draw upon a limitation of or exception to exclusive rights. With some differences in detail, the concepts permit non-commercial reproduction, distribution and public performance (streaming) of a musical composition, sound recording, or motion picture via the Internet.[65] Thus, they restrict both the reproduction right and the right of communication to the public, which includes the right to make protected content available to the public. Both rights are regulated as mandatory minimum rights in international copyright law.[66]

- Distribution of a sound recording (including a musical composition embodied therein) or motion picture via the Internet;
- Public performance of a sound recording (including a musical composition embodied therein) via a digital audio transmission; and
- Public performance of a motion picture via a digital video transmission.

61 Fisher, *supra* n. 1, at 248–49.

62 Litman, *supra* n. 51, at 45–46.

63 Litman, *supra* n. 51, at 46 n. 166.

64 Netanel, *supra* n. 23, at 60 n. 199.

65 Fisher, *supra* n. 1, at 247; Netanel, *supra* n. 23, at 37–38 (non-commercial copying, distribution, and streaming over digital networks); Sobel, *supra* n. 30, at 683 (copying and redistribution online). Fisher's and Netanel's concepts additionally permit derivative creations, see Fisher, *supra* n. 1, at 234–36, 247 and Netanel, *supra* n. 23, at 38–40. Since this form of use is not necessarily involved in file sharing, this chapter does not dwell on this proposal.

66 See Art. 9 BC; Art. 9(1) TRIPS; Agreed Statement concerning Art. 1(4) WCT (reproduction right); Arts. 11, 11bis(1), 11ter(1), 14(1), 14bis(1) BC; Art. 8 WCT; Arts. 10, 14 WPPT (right of communication to the public).

These exclusive rights are subject to the three-step test, which was adopted in 1967 in Art. 9(2) BC[67] and later in Art. 13 TRIPS,[68] Art. 10 WCT[69] and Art. 16(2) WIPO Performances and Phonograms Treaty (WPPT).[70] It proclaims that contracting parties may, in their national legislation, provide for limitations of or exceptions to the rights granted to authors

1. in certain special cases
2. that do not conflict with a normal exploitation of the work and
3. that do not unreasonably prejudice the legitimate interests of the author.

The named provisions are regulated in different international conventions and treaties, which have partially differing goals. This is especially true regarding the TRIPS Agreement, which was intended to reduce distortions of and impediments to international trade.[71] Nevertheless, this chapter will not analyse the provisions individually because each wording is practically identical and all

---

67 Report on the Work of Main Committee I of the Conference in Stockholm 1967, reprinted in: WIPO, *The Berne Convention for the Protection of Literary and Artistic Works from 1886 to 1986* (Centenary) 196–97 (1986) [hereinafter Report in Stockholm 1967]. Art. 9(2) BC applies only to the reproduction right as regulated in paragraph one of that article.

68 Art. 13 TRIPS is not confined to the rights newly introduced by the TRIPS Agreement, but also applies to the rights provided for under the BC. See Panel Report, *United States-Section 110(5) of US Copyright Act, supra* n. 14, at para. 6.80; Mihály Ficsor (2002), 'How Much of What? The Three-Step Test and Its Application in Two Recent WTO Dispute Settlement Cases', 192 *Revue Internationale du Droit d'Auteur* 111, 153, 163; Sam Ricketson, 'WIPO Study on Limitations and Exceptions of Copyright and Related Rights in the Digital Environment', *Standing Committee on Copyright and Related Rights, Ninth Session*, Geneva, 23 to 27 June 2003, WIPO Document SCCR/9/7 of 5 April 2003.

69 Art. 10(1) WCT covers the rights added by the WCT. Jörg Reinbothe and Silke von Lewinski, *The WIPO-Treaties 1996* Art. 10 WCT no. 26 . Art. 10(2) WCT 2 relates to the rights provided for in the BC. See WCT, Agreed Statement to Art. 10(2) ('It is also understood that Article 10(2) neither reduces nor extends the scope of applicability of the limitations and exceptions permitted by the Berne Convention.'); Reinbothe and von Lewinski, at no. 6.

70 For the purpose of this chapter, I assume that the country that considers implementing one of the proposals is a member of or contracting party to the BC, the TRIPS Agreement and the WIPO Copyright Treaties.

71 According to the preamble of the TRIPS Agreement, it is also 'taking into account the need to promote effective and adequate protection of intellectual property rights.' In this respect, TRIPS parallels the WCT ('to develop and maintain the protection of the rights of authors in their literary and artistic works in a manner as effective and uniform as possible') and the BC ('to protect, in as effective and uniform a manner as possible, the rights of authors in their literary and artistic works').

provisions derive from Art. 9(2) BC.[72] Moreover, this article does not attempt a comprehensive interpretation of the three-step test according to the Vienna Convention on the Law of Treaties.[73] Rather, it summarizes how national courts, the WTO Panel and legal literature construe the elements of the test. It then applies these definitions to the concepts underpinning a levy/tax system for P2P file sharing.

Interpretation of the Three-step Test

As regards the interpretation of the three-step test, it is undisputed that the three steps have to be applied cumulatively[74] and successively.[75] In addition, it is generally acknowledged that in construing the provisions of the three-step test, one has to keep in mind the overall aim of the conventions: to provide for adequate, balanced copyright protection.[76]

Certain special cases

The first condition established by the three-step test is that limitations of or exceptions to exclusive rights may be introduced only in *certain special cases*. As with all other elements of the test, divergent opinions exist as to what this requirement means in detail. Some argue that a restriction in national law must be clearly defined and should be narrow in its scope.[77] The scope of the excep-

---

[72] With regard to Art. 13 TRIPS, see Art. 2(2), 9(1) TRIPS and Daniel Gervais (2nd ed. 2003), *The TRIPS Agreement: Drafting History and Analysis* 2.124; Panel Report, *United States-Section 110(5) of the US Copyright Act*, *supra* n. 14, at para. 6.66; Ginsburg, *supra* n. 12, at 35; Senftleben, *supra* n. 56, at 99 et seq. But see Gervais, *The TRIPs Agreement*, at 2.11.

[73] See Panel Report, *United States-Section 110(5) of the US Copyright Act*, *supra* n. 14, at para. 6.43–46; Sam Ricketson (1987), *The Berne Convention for the Protection of Literary and Artistic Works: 1886–1986*, pp. 134–44; Ricketson, *supra* n. 68, at 5–9; Senftleben, *supra* n. 56, at 99–114.

[74] Failure to comply with any one of the three conditions results in the limitation/exception being disallowed. See Panel Report, *United States-Section 110(5) of the US Copyright Act*, *supra* n. 14, at para. 6.74, 6.97; Reinbothe and von Lewinski, *supra* n. 69, Art. 10 WCT no. 14.

[75] See the records of the WCT negotiations, reproduced in Mihály Ficsor (2002), *The Law of Copyright and the Internet: the 1996 WIPO Treaties, Their Interpretation and Implementation* 5.134; Ficsor, *supra* n. 68, at 120–21; Ginsburg, *supra* n. 12, at 40–41.

[76] With regard to the BC see Ricketson, *supra* n. 73, at 47–48 (a pure 'maximalist' view is mistaken); Ficsor, *supra* n. 75, 5.06–8. Regarding Art. 7 and 8 TRIPS see Panel Report, *Canada-Patent Protection of Pharmaceutical Products*, *supra* n. 14, at para. 7.26. Regarding the WCT see Reinbothe & von Lewinski, *supra* n. 69, Art. 10 WCT no. 7.

[77] Panel Report, *United States-Section 110(5) of the US Copyright Act*, *supra* n. 14, at para. 6.112; Ricketson, *supra* n. 731, at 482; Ficsor, *supra* n. 68, at 129, 227;

tion has to be known and particularized so that it becomes foreseeable whether a given use will be subject to the limitation/exception.[78] Though it seems clear that this condition does not rule out concepts like fair dealing or fair use, 'an incalculable, shapeless provision exempting a wide variety of different uses' is deemed to be impermissible.[79] Moreover, the WTO Panel has held that the business exemption of 17 USC § 110(5)(B) is not a 'certain special case' because a 'substantial majority of eating and drinking establishments and close to half of retail establishments' are covered by the exemption.[80] Thus, the panel adopted a quantitative view regarding the first step.[81]

Regarding the 'specialness' of the limitation or exception, some commentators ask whether some clear reason of public policy or a rational basis for justification need exist for the restriction;[82] whether there is an understandable need for the reconciliation of the user's interests with the author's interests.[83] However, the WTO Panel views the legitimacy of public policy as only of subsidiary relevance in applying the first element of the test.[84]

In my view, a non-voluntary license in national copyright law privileging non-commercial file sharing on the Internet could in fact constitute a special case under the three-step test. First, a limitation or exception that is geared towards non-commercial reproduction and communication to the public with

---

Reinbothe and von Lewinski, *supra* n. 69, Art. 10 WCT no. 15. With regard to Art. 30 TRIPS ('limited exceptions') see Panel Report, *Canada-Patent Protection of Pharmaceutical Products*, *supra* n. 14, at para. 7.30; Gervais, *supra* n. 72, at 2.125; Ficsor, *supra* n. 75, at 151 (extensive use of compulsory licensing not in line with Art. 13 TRIPS).

[78] Panel Report, *United States-Section 110(5) of the US Copyright Act*, *supra* n. 14, para. 6.108; Senftleben, *supra* n. 56 at 137.

[79] Senftleben, *supra* n. 56 at 133–137. Due to the fact that few countries would act in a purely arbitrary way and any exception short of a complete repeal of the Copyright Act would arguably be a certain special case. Gervais, *supra* n. 12, at 17, argues that only the second and third step really embody a restriction to future limitations and exceptions.

[80] Panel Report, *United States-Section 110(5) of the US Copyright Act*, *supra* n. 14, para. 6.133. *Contra* Senftleben, *supra* n. 56, at 140–44 (disapproving of the quantitative approach of the WTO Panel because the outcome of the second criterion is predetermined).

[81] But see Panel Report, *Canada-Patent Protection of Pharmaceutical Products*, *supra* n. 14, para. 7.49 (holding that the first step does not directly address the issue of economic impact); Ficsor, *supra* n. 83, at 229 (critical of this pure statistical approach).

[82] Ricketson, *supra* n. 73, at 482 ; Ficsor, *supra* n. 75, at 129–32, 227; Reinbothe and von Lewinski, *supra* n. 69, Art. 10 WCT no. 15; but see Ricketson, *supra* n. 68, at 22.

[83] Senftleben, *supra* n. 56 at 144–52.

[84] Panel Report, *United States-Section 110(5) of the US Copyright Act*, *supra* n. 14, para. 6.102-13; Ginsburg, *supra* n. 12, at 39-43 (no normative inquiry at this point); Ricketson, *supra* n. 68, at 22.

regard to P2P networks is clearly defined and can easily be distinguished from impermissible uses. For example, posting a work on a website or running a 'P2P dark net' where users have access only on a subscription basis would not be privileged, because these uses have nothing to do with P2P technology (posting a work on a web site) or are made for commercial purposes (running a 'dark net'). Second, advocates of non-voluntary license regimes raise several justifications: namely, their concepts would preserve the promising advantages of global digital networks for instant and global dissemination of knowledge, especially for those works that are not adequately exploited and offered by the right holder.[85] Third, the 'quantitative' approach taken by the WTO Panel misconceives the scope of the limitation/exception and its consequences, on the basis that the proprietary exploitation of the work in general must be analysed under the second step, not the first.[86]

Conflict with a normal exploitation

Proceeding to step two, the proposals must not conflict with a *normal exploitation* of the work. This is probably the element of the three-step test that raises the most doubts regarding the scope of application and its effect on national copyright legislation.

First, it is of utmost importance to note that, according to a nearly uniformly accepted understanding based on the wording and structure of the test, a non-voluntary license may only be introduced in national law if it clears this hurdle. In particular, the implementation of a levy cannot cure a conflict of the underlying limitation/exception with the second step, even if it compensates for the losses of the copyright owner. This aspect of compensation is relevant only with regard to step three.[87]

---

85 On the assets of the proposals see Lessig, *supra* n. 3, at 296–97. But see Ricketson, *supra* n. 68, at 75 (unqualified assertion of 'public interest' is not enough); similarly Senftleben, *supra* n. 56, at 162 (with regard to digital private copying).

86 Senftleben, *supra* n. 56, at 140–144.

87 Report in Stockholm 1967, *supra* n. 67, at 197 (the sequence would afford a more logical order for the interpretation of the rule); Panel Report, *United States-Section 110(5) of the US Copyright Act*, *supra* n. 14, para. 6.73–4; Ginsburg, *supra* n. 12, at 45–53; Claude Masouyé (1978), *Guide to the Berne Convention for the Protection of Literary and Artistic Works* (Paris Act, 1971), pp. 55–56; Ricketson, *supra* n. 73, at 483–485; Ricketson, *supra* n. 68, at 27; Henri Desbois et al. (1976), *Les Conventions Internationales du Droit d'Auteur et des Droit Voisins,* para. 173; Ficsor, *supra* n. 75, at 5.58; Senftleben, *supra* n. 56, at 130–1; *Contra* Geiger, *supra* n. 35, at para. 418–420; Christophe Geiger (2005), 'Comment', 36 *International Review of Intellectual Property and Competition Law* (IIC) 151, 157 (proposing to read the three-step test backwards and to start with the third step in order to accomplish a flexible, balanced system).

In defining 'normal' exploitation, it is accepted that something less than full use of an exclusive right has to be meant in order not to render every restriction impermissible and thus the provision itself superfluous.[88] Moreover, 'normal' implies both an empirical and a normative element.[89]

Regarding the empirical element (the degree of market displacement following from the restriction), different standards have been articulated. It has been variously maintained that a limitation/exception conflicts with normal exploitation:

> if it causes a serious loss of profit;[90]
> if it covers uses for which the author would ordinarily expect to receive a fee;[91]
> or if it applies to those forms of exploitation that currently generate significant or tangible revenue or which, with a certain degree of likelihood and plausibility, could acquire considerable economic or practical importance as opposed to uses that do not compete with non-exempted uses (actual and potential effects).[92]

According to the prevailing opinion, the existence of a conflict with normal exploitation for each exclusive right is judged separately.[93] In contrast, Senftleben refers to a deprivation of an actual or potential market, which typically constitutes a major source of income, which carries weight within the *overall commercialization* of works of the relevant category and, consequently, belongs to the core of copyright.[94]

Whether additional aspects can be derived from the often referred-to normative element of 'normal exploitation' is still largely unclear.[95] In light of the fact that DRM systems enable the right holder to exploit a work even on a

---

88 Panel Report, *United States-Section 110(5) of the US Copyright Act, supra* n. 14, para. 6.167.

89 Panel Report, *United States-Section 110(5) of the US Copyright Act, supra* n. 14, para. 6.166–78; Panel Report, *Canada-Patent Protection of Pharmaceutical Products, supra* n. 14, para. 7.54; Ficsor, *supra* n. 68, at 139.

90 Masouyé, *supra* n. 87, at 56.

91 Ricketson, *supra* n. 73, at 482–3; Ricketson, *supra* n. 68, at 23; critical of this 'subjective' approach: Kamiel J. Koelman (2003), 'De nationale driestappentoets', 17 *Tijdschrift voor Auteurs-, Media- & Informatierecht* (AMI) 6, 7 (noting that this argument tends to be circular).

92 Panel Report, *United States-Section 110(5) of the US Copyright Act, supra* n. 14, para. 6.181–87; Ricketson, *supra* n. 68, at 24; Gervais, *supra* n. 12, at 18; Ficsor, *supra* n. 68, at 137.

93 Panel Report, *United States-Section 110(5) of the US Copyright Act, supra* n. 14, para. 6.173; Reinbothe and von Lewinski, *supra* n. 69, Art. 10 WCT no. 18.

94 Senftleben, *supra* n. 56 at 177–94.

95 See Panel Report, *United States-Section 110(5) of the US Copyright Act, supra* n. 14, para. 6.178 (holding that the normative approach to defining normal exploitation includes '*inter alia* a dynamical element capable of taking into account technological and market developments').

pay-per-use basis, it is argued that market failure considerations and decreasing transaction costs cannot be the sole line of argument. Otherwise, generally accepted restrictions for, say, criticism, parody, or scholarship could be argued to contravene step two.[96]

Applying these definitions to the proposals raises severe doubts regarding their compatibility with this step of the three-step test. This is because the uses covered by the proposed non-voluntary license, that is, copying and distributing content online by way of up- and downloads or streaming, are a source of income today and will probably become even more important in the future. Right holders are increasingly establishing commercial platforms to offer their content for download or streaming.[97] Assuming that a complete shift to commercial online distribution by way of streaming is plausible, at least for music and perhaps motion pictures, even Senftleben's restrictive interpretation, according to which a significant effect on the overall commercialization of the work is necessary, to run afoul of this step would arguably assume a conflict. It thus appears non-voluntary licenses covering non-commercial file sharing can hardly be considered to be in line with the second criterion of the three-step test.[98]

This conclusion, however, does not exhaust the problem as the aforementioned application of the three-step test relies upon a new 'type' of protection and factual exclusivity that Stefan Bechtold has called 'copyright cast in silicon'[99] – DRM systems. This technology enables right holders to launch commercial services in the digital network environment. With the advent of technological protection measures, the copyright owner not only enjoys exclusivity based on the rights granted to him or her in national and international copyright law, but DRM systems also make it possible to establish an additional, factual exclusivity supplemented with legal protection against the circumvention of those technological measures.[100]

As already indicated, contracting parties of the WIPO Copyright Treaties are obligated to provide legal protection of technological measures and rights management information systems. Are the tax levy proposals in accordance

---

96 Ginsburg, *supra* n. 12, at 50–51; Ricketson, *supra* n. 68, at 25.

97 *MGM*, 125 S.Ct. at 2795–96 (Breyer, J., concurring).

98 This is also true in respect of Sobel's Digital Retailer Model (*supra* n. 30), which aims at preserving for the right holder the ability to set the rates for a download, because setting the price is only one feature of exclusivity apart from when, to what extent, and how (e.g. via streaming or via download) an asset may be used by others.

99 Stefan Bechtold (2002), *Vom Urheber- Zum Informationsrecht*, p. 279.

100 See Art. 11, 12 WCT, Art. 18, 19 WPPT; 17 USC Chapter 12; Art. 6, 7 Directive 2001/29/EC of the European Parliament and of the Council of 22 May 2001 on the Harmonisation of Certain Aspects of Copyright and Related Rights in the Information Society, OJ L 167/10 of 22 June 2001 (hereinafter Copyright Directive).

with these international requirements? And how does this legal protection relate to the specifications of the three-step test?

Regarding rights management information, most of the proposals actually draw upon 'fingerprinting' and 'watermarking' technologies. They do so in order to monitor the ongoing uses in P2P networks for determining the shares of each right holder. The establishment of a levy/tax system thus benefits from, and relies upon, the mandatory protection of rights management information systems according to Art. 12 WCT. A violation of this treaty obligation is not apparent.

Much more problematic in this context is the mandatory protection of technological measures required by Art. 11 WCT. A complete prohibition of technological measures in national law would obviously be in conflict with this requirement. However, none of the proposals discussed in this article suggests that.

Neil Netanel's 'Noncommercial Use Levy', however, rests upon the idea that all works are covered by the limitation/exception to copyright and are thus lawfully available in P2P networks. This premise can only be fulfilled if right holders do not have the opportunity to withhold their works from this system. Consequently, Netanel's proposal suggests that right holders would not be entitled to employ technological DRM controls to block the privileged uses or, at the very least, it would be legal for users to circumvent DRM controls and for suppliers to distribute circumvention tools needed to engage in privileged uses.[101] Would such a limitation of the legal protection of technological protection measures be in accordance with the WIPO copyright treaties? This raises the very fundamental question of how this additional protection layer for copyright,[102] as regulated in Art. 11 WCT, relates to the three-step test (Art. 10 WCT), which historically corresponded solely to exclusive *rights* granted by law.

As both provisions are regulated in the same treaty, they must not be construed separately. Adopting this view, it is certainly in accordance with this treaty to provide for narrow limitations/exceptions in line with Art. 10 WCT and to restrict the legal protection of technological measures to the remaining

---

[101] Netanel, *supra* n. 23, at 40. Sobel does not address this question expressly, but it seems that his model is meant to comprise all copyrighted works and that it implies that works can be downloaded, which would also require a prohibition of certain restrictive technologies, e.g. those that facilitate pay-per-use models. See Sobel, *supra* n. 30, at 683–93.

[102] See *Chamberlain Group, Inc. v Skylink Techs., Inc.*, 381 F.3d 1178, 1192, 1202 (Fed. Cir. 2004) (holding that 17 USC § 1201 *et seq.* do not establish a new, highly protective alternative regime for copyrighted works and a new property right, but instead prohibit forms of access that bear a reasonable relationship to the protections that the Copyright Act otherwise affords as an additional protection layer).

(broad) scope of exclusive rights.[103] For example, it would not be a violation of the WCT to limit copyright as regards quotations and to legislate that a person may circumvent a technological measure for the sole purpose of copying a part of the work in order to make a quotation. Consider the example of incorporating sequences of movie A, available only on copy-protected DVDs, into movie B for the purpose of commenting on movie A's statements.[104]

But what about also applying a limitation/exception for non-commercial file sharing to the anti-circumvention provisions, as Netanel suggests? Article 11 WCT proclaims that contracting parties shall provide adequate legal protection of effective technological measures that restrict acts in respect of works not authorized by the authors concerned *or permitted by law*. At first glance, it seems that this wording would not require contracting parties to provide legal protection for technological measures that restrict uses covered by such a limitation/exception, as the obligation under Article 11 WCT does not extend to acts *permitted by law*. Thus, if a national legislature implemented a broad limitation/exception, for example, for file sharing, that country would consequently be free to confine the anti-circumvention provisions accordingly. Obviously, this reasoning would open the door for contracting parties to chip away at both legal *and* factual exclusivity in the digital online environment, particularly regarding file sharing.

This solution, however, would amount to a violation of obligations under the WCT. As outlined above, a limitation/exception for non-commercial file sharing would run afoul of the three-step test as the privileged P2P networks would compete with commercial online ventures licensed by the right holders.[105] This latter kind of 'hoarding' in cyberspace rests upon DRM. There is no indication that this mode of exploitation may not be regarded as 'normal' under the three-step test. On the contrary, the WCT acknowledges that the adoption of DRM is crucial for exclusive exploitation in cyberspace. This can be shown by the fact that it prohibits circumvention of technological measures. Considering the possibility of DRM-based pay-per-use business models, one could even argue that any restriction to copyright contravenes the three-step test because *any* use of the work forms part of this 'normal' exploitation.[106] Even if one does not want to go that far, a *combination* of a broad limitation/exception with limited legal protection of DRM systems (that is, circum-

---

103 Ficsor, *supra* n. 75, at C11.10. This is the approach of the DMCA that gives users a right to hack, but only under very restricted circumstances. See 17 USC § 1201(d)-(j).

104 For example, critics of Michael Moore considered making a point-by-point rebuttal of his movie 'Fahrenheit 9/11'.

105 *Supra* 'Conflict with a normal exploitation' at p. 164.

106 See Koelman, *supra* n. 91, at 7.

vention is legal if done to engage in privileged uses, for example, non-commercial file sharing) or even a prohibition of technological measures that restrict these permitted uses is not in line with the three-step test and the mandatory protection of technological measures.

This result, however, does not render all ideas for a levy/tax system covering non-commercial file sharing unlawful. Accounting for DRM systems when applying the three-step test might result in an even greater freedom of contracting parties to structure their national copyright law: the idea behind this consideration is that right holders feature a new kind of exclusivity if they implement DRM systems that eventually prevent the work from being used without permission, for example, 'shared' online. There are now two protection layers for a copyrightable work. The first one is exclusive rights under copyright. The second one is the application of technological measures and the legal rules against circumventing this factual exclusivity. The legislature can limit both layers in parallel. For example, national copyright law can limit exclusive rights and the legal protection of technological measures with regard to quotations.

Both protection layers can, however, also be treated differently. By 'differently', I mean that national copyright law would, on the one hand, grant nearly limitless anti-circumvention protection to DRM systems in order to enable proprietary business models in cyberspace (exclusivity/'hoarding'). On the other hand, a limitation/exception would allow non-commercial file sharing under a levy/tax system, *provided that the right owner does not implement DRM*. The copyright owner would thus be free to choose which kind of protection to adopt. With that freedom to choose, exclusivity as the fundamental feature of current international copyright law is not restricted by a statutory limitation/exception imposed by national law, but voluntarily by the right holder. This is the basic notion of the *bipolar copyright system* and the reason why this approach – if implemented in national copyright law – would not be a violation of the three-step test or the obligation to protect technological measures.

One nevertheless has to consider some possible counter-arguments in view of international copyright law. Article 31(3)(b) of the Vienna Convention on the Law of Treaties proclaims that 'there shall be taken into account, together with the context . . . any subsequent practice in the application of the treaty which establishes the agreement of the parties regarding its interpretation.' An agreement of the contracting parties regarding the permissibility of a 'bipolar system' cannot yet be observed. Broad non-voluntary licenses have, until now, only been accepted to the extent that the exercise of exclusive rights is practically impossible (as in the case of private copying in the analog world). They have not been adopted in situations where the copyright owner simply refuses to implement readily available enforcement mechanisms. In addition, legal protection of technological measures is dealt with only in the WIPO Copyright Treaties and not in the TRIPS Agreement. This may be one reason why the WTO Panel has generally refused to consider the failure of right holders to exercise their rights (due to a lack of effective or affordable means of enforcement) when deciding what constitutes normal exploitation.[107]

However, these arguments are not persuasive. Many copyright owners, for example, small start-up record labels and single creators, do not currently and most likely will not in the future adopt DRM to exploit a work in cyberspace simply because it is too difficult or expensive for them. At the same time, modern technologies and P2P networks enable these right holders to cheaply produce and publish their works for a worldwide audience.[108] Copyright law as the conventional protection layer, however, cannot be effectively enforced to generate sufficient income. Therefore, commercialization of works in cyberspace can be said to be impossible or extremely impractical for these right holders. In acknowledging this problem, some authors state that the three-step test actually obliges contracting parties to impose a levy in order to compensate for the losses incurred by the right holder if exercising the right is impossible.[109]

Moreover, if the right owner, for whatever reason, does not implement restrictive DRM systems but instead prefers to benefit from a levy or tax for statutorily privileged uses in cyberspace, there cannot be a conflict with the 'normal,' that is, DRM-based, exploitation. P2P networks simply will not compete with proprietary business models because, if applied, technology prevents the respective work from being available at all in unrestricted P2P networks. Admittedly, this assumption will work only if technological measures prevail over existing restrictions to exclusive rights. In other words, any circumvention of technological measures must be prohibited, even if the intended use is permitted by law. If the right holder chooses exclusivity, this exclusivity has to be far-reaching, as it is under current US and European copyright law. Only in this case can the copyright owner effectively build a pay-per-use business model on DRM systems.[110] Additionally, only this

---

[107] Panel Report, *United States-Section 110(5) of the US Copyright Act, supra* n. 14, para. 6.188.

[108] This notion can be traced back to the digital dilemma stemming from digitization and the Internet. See *supra* 'Introduction' at p. 148.

[109] See Ficsor, *supra* n. 75, at C10.34; Sirinelli, *supra* n. 12, at 28; Ricketson, *supra* n. 68, at 75; Netanel, *supra* n. 23, at 60 n. 199.

[110] With regard to European copyright law see Alexander Peukert, 'Der Schutzbereich des Urheberrechts und das Werk als öffentliches Gut. Insbesondere: Die urheberrechtliche Relevanz des privaten Werkgenusses', in Reto M. Hilty and Alexander Peukert (ed.)(2004), *Interessenausgleich im Urheberrecht* p. 11, 25 *et seq.* (explaining how the copyright directive expanded exclusivity to listening, reading, and watching a work even if the consumer does not acquire a copy of the work).

approach lets one expect that a work is technologically shielded from file sharing. This approach is also fruitful with regard to the interpretation of the WCT. A contracting party providing for protection beyond the obligations established by Art. 11 WCT regarding technological measures (because circumvention is also prohibited if the intended uses fall under a limitation/exception to copyright) may draw upon a more flexible interpretation of Art. 10 WCT regarding the three-step test, as opposed to a contracting party that seeks narrow limitations to/exceptions from both the legal and the technological protection layer.

Finally, the three-step test is not geared towards single copyright owners but instead addresses national legislatures. Right holders have always been free to decide to what extent they want to benefit from the exclusivity granted by law. This freedom is exactly where the bipolar copyright system begins. Right holders may opt for exclusivity and individual licensing ('hoarding'), but under the bipolar copyright system, they have an additional option: they would also be able to earn a levy/tax share by accepting certain privileges of users, in particular, the non-commercial use of their work in P2P file sharing systems.[111] Seen from this perspective, the bipolar copyright system is nothing more than an additional compensation mechanism beyond what is available today. At present, right holders may try to recoup their investment by individually licensing the use of their work. File sharing is copyright infringement. It is not compensated for if the right holder does not enforce exclusive rights in difficult and expensive litigation in every single case. Under the bipolar copyright system, these uncompensated uses would potentially fall under the levy/tax system and would therefore generate income. It would be up to the right holder to decide which compensation mechanism promises more revenues. Therefore, the levy/tax system essentially is not a non-voluntary license, but instead a voluntary option.[112]

It has to be stressed, however, that this discussion relates to the second step of the three-step test: the bipolar copyright system does not conflict with normal exploitation of the work. The limitation/exception to exclusive rights under the levy/tax system still has to meet the requirements of the first and third steps. This way, the legal protection layer 'copyright' may not be removed completely. A bipolar copyright system would have to be limited to certain special cases (first step) and would have to be modelled in a way not to prejudice the legitimate interests of the author (third step).

---

[111] On the lawfulness of the opt-in and opt-out alternatives, see *infra* 'Compliance with international law' at p. 182 and 'Features and benefits' at p. 181.

[112] On the differences to voluntary collective licensing as proposed by the EFF (*supra* n. 25), Daniel Gervais (*supra* n. 25) and others, see *infra* 'The opt-in model compared to collective licensing' at p. 191.

In summary, the bipolar system rests upon the two pillars, which represent the layers of today's copyright protection. One pillar is the law that prohibits the circumvention of technological protection measures in order to establish exclusivity in the digital realm. The other pillar is a limitation/exception that permits digital uses (for example, non-commercial file sharing) in the case of the right holder opting out of the 'silicon copyright'. The bipolar model (in accordance with the three-step test) is thus a levy/tax for non-commercial file sharing as an *alternative* to exclusivity based on law and technology. This follows the approach of William Fisher and Jessica Litman. According to their concepts, the copyright owner is free to choose 'hoarding' instead of 'sharing'.[113]

Fischer and Litman suggest the levy/tax system as the statutory default rule, thereby requiring right holders to *opt out* of the levy/tax system if they prefer proprietary exploitation. The pros and cons of this alternative and its compliance with international copyright law treaties will be discussed later on in this chapter.

Unreasonable prejudice to the legitimate interests of the right holder

Before these details of the bipolar copyright system can be addressed, one must still consider the third element of the three-step test. This element sets out that the limitation/exception must *not unreasonably prejudice the legitimate interests of the right holder.*

Only if a non-voluntary license overcomes the first two hurdles must this last condition be assessed. It establishes a flexible standard of reasonableness, balancing the interests of right holders versus that of the beneficiaries of the restriction to exclusive rights.[114] It calls for protection of interests that are 'justifiable' in the sense that they are supported by relevant public policies or other social norms.[115] The crucial questions are whether the interests at stake are legitimate, and at what point the degree or level of prejudice to the interests of the right holder may be considered 'unreasonable'.[116] The payment of remuneration under a non-voluntary license may prevent the prejudice from reaching an 'unreasonable' level.[117]

---

113 Litman, *supra* n. 51, at 39–50 ('sharing' *or* 'hoarding'); Fisher, *supra* n. 1, at 248. For a more detailed discussion of the bipolar system, *see infra* 'How a bipolar copyright system would function' at p. 175.

114 Ficsor, *supra* n. 68, at 145; Ricketson, *supra* n. 68, at 27; Ginsburg, *supra* n. 12, at 57; Senftleben, *supra* n. 56, at 210–44; Gervais, *supra* n. 12, at 19–20.

115 Panel Report, *Canada-Patent Protection of Pharmaceutical Products*, *supra* n. 14, at para. 7.69; Gervais, *supra* n. 12, at 19–20.

116 Senftleben, *supra* n. 56, at 226–41.

117 German Federal Supreme Court, Gewerblicher Rechtsschutz und Urheberrecht (GRUR) 963, 967 (2002); Reinbothe and von Lewinski, *supra* n. 69, Art. 10 WCT no. 23; Ginsburg, *supra* n. 12, at 53; Senftleben, *supra* n. 56, at 237–41.

Deciding whether a levy/tax system covering P2P networks on a non-commercial scale presents an unreasonable prejudice to the right holders' interest depends, to a large extent, upon the architecture of the system. It would obviously present a prejudice to right holders if they were not allowed to technologically prevent file sharing, or if circumvention for the purpose of file sharing were not prohibited.[118]

Relying on technological measures to exploit works online is a legitimate interest of right holders,[119] as that is just what Arts. 8, 10 and 11 WCT are meant to facilitate. Whether such an encroachment upon authors' rights is seen as unreasonable depends on whether national legislatures find that the public interests benefited by this regime are equal to the interests of authors,[120] and whether the tax/levy actually compensates for the losses. In that regard, it must be observed that the third requirement remains open-ended, leaving it for the national legislature to strike the balance in particular cases that have passed the first and second step.[121] Considering the positive effects of a levy/tax system for the dissemination of knowledge as well as for the compensation of the accruing uses, it could certainly be argued that it would be a justified, and not unreasonable prejudice to the interests of the right holders. However, the problem with a proposal that restricts both protection layers (copyright and DRM plus anti-circumvention provisions) with regard to file sharing is that it does not fulfil the requirements of the second step. Neil Netanel's concept, therefore, would not survive for consideration of the third step.

As explained above, a tax or levy system as an optional alternative to exclusive exploitation in cyberspace, the bipolar system, does not run afoul of the first two steps of the three-step test. Regarding the third step, the beneficial effects of not outlawing P2P technology, improving the dissemination of knowledge and guaranteeing compensation for authors, justifies the adoption of this system. The bipolar system does not limit exclusivity as such; it simply

---

118 This reflects Neil Netanel's proposal. See *supra* 'Non-voluntary licenses regarding P2P file sharing' at p. 154.

119 In this regard, it is important to determine whether only the interests of the author count or also the interests of intermediaries as derivative right holders; see Reinbothe and von Lewinski, *supra* n. 69, Art. 10 WCT no. 8 (safeguarding of investments of intermediaries is an aspect to be considered in applying Art. 10 WCT); Senftleben, *supra* n. 56, at 216–21.

120 The dominant opinion prioritizes author's *rights* v user's *interests*; see e.g. Guibault, *supra* n. 36, at 90–110; Reinbothe and von Lewinski, *supra* n. 69, Art. 10 WCT no. 8 (referring to the preamble of the WCT that speaks of 'rights of authors' but only of the public 'interest'); *contra* Geiger, *supra* n. 35, paras. 225–26 (regarding limitations justified by fundamental rights); *CCH Canadian Ltd. v Law Society of Upper Canada*, 2004 SCC 13 (Supreme Court of Canada 2004), paras. 12, 48 (finding that fair dealing is a right of users).

121 Ricketson, *supra* n. 68, at 26.

offers right holders an additional business model to generate income from uses of their work in cyberspace. The mere necessity of making a choice between the two alternatives cannot be said to be a 'prejudice' to the legitimate interests of right holders because it is nothing other than an everyday business decision. This illuminates the fact that limiting only one protection layer (copyright) to a mere remuneration right and leaving the other layer (DRM plus anti-circumvention rules) untouched is consistent with international copyright law. In any event, the levy/tax revenue must be sufficiently high to at least arguably substitute for a potential exclusive exploitation on the basis of DRM in cyberspace.[122]

Agreed Statement to Article 10 WCT

The previous analysis has revealed that it is more than doubtful whether, for example, Neil Netanel's 'noncommercial use levy' for P2P file sharing fulfils the obligations laid down in international copyright law because this levy also denies the right holder the option of individual licensing using DRM. A different view could be derived from the Agreed Statements regarding Art. 10 WCT,[123] which reads:

> It is understood that the provisions of Article 10 permit Contracting Parties to carry forward and appropriately extend into the digital environment limitations and exceptions in their national laws, which have been considered acceptable under the Berne Convention. Similarly, these provisions should be understood to permit Contracting Parties to devise new exceptions and limitations that are appropriate in the digital network environment.[124]

The delegations that proposed this statement wanted to express concerns that the three-step test might become a straightjacket for adopting limitations and exceptions in the digital environment.[125] It is worth noticing the differences between the two sentences: whereas the first sentence corresponds to already existing restrictions and the digital environment in general, the second sentence, dealing with *new* exceptions/limitations, relates to the digital *network* environment and thus to the Internet context addressed by this article.

---

[122] For a discussion of the amount of tax/levy due, see Fisher, *supra* n. 1, at 205–15; Netanel, *supra* n. 23, at 44–52.

[123] Since it applies to both paragraphs of Art. 10 WCT, it not only relates to the rights provided for in the WCT (especially the right of communication to the public, Art. 8 WCT), but also to the rights granted under the BC (the reproduction right).

[124] For a discussion on the relevance of the Agreed Statements with regard to the application of the three-step test in general, see Ricketson, *supra* n. 68, at 62.

[125] For the remarks of the delegations of the USA, Denmark, India, and the United Kingdom, see Ficsor, *supra* n. 75, at 5.137.

Does this statement thus constitute a charter for contracting parties to devise new exceptions and limitations in the digital network environment without taking account of the three-step test?

For a number of reasons, the answer has to be in the negative. One of the main goals of the WCT was to establish a new, exclusive 'Internet right' as a minimum right in international law. It would be inconsistent with this purpose to read the agreed statement as giving contracting parties discretion to restrict exclusivity in the digital network environment as they see fit. Had the contracting parties wanted to exclude online uses from the three-step test, they would have done so in the treaty. Finally, since the reproduction right is also subject to Art. 13 TRIPS, which does not contain a similar statement, this interpretation would produce a severe discrepancy in international copyright law in general. Thus, the statement has to be understood, not as a broad enabling clause, but as a clarification that exceptions and limitations may indeed be adopted in the digital network environment[126] and that they still are subject to the three-step test.[127]

HOW A BIPOLAR COPYRIGHT SYSTEM WOULD FUNCTION

Complexity of the System

A fundamental reservation against a bipolar copyright system for the digital network environment is its complexity.[128] Even without going into the details of how the freedom of the right holder to choose between those two alternatives might be accomplished in practice, it is certain that it would involve considerable effort to establish and organize the system. It is certainly true that there are less complex answers to the digital dilemma.[129] For example, a shorter term than life plus 50 or even life plus 70 years would flush many

126 Ficsor, *supra* n. 75, at C10.10 (correlating the statement to limitations and exceptions justified specifically in view of the digital network environment, e.g. temporary reproductions).

127 Reinbothe and von Lewinski, *supra* n. 69, Art. 10 WCT no. 33; Ficsor, *supra* n. 75, at C10.09; Sirinelli, *supra* n. 12, at 42; Ricketson, *supra* n. 68, at 63 ('If a distinct regime for new limitations and exceptions is envisaged under the WCT, this would need to be the subject of an express provision of that treaty.').

128 For a discussion on a necessary 'new simplicity' in dealing with copyright, see Stefan Bechtold, *Das Urheberrecht und die Informationsgesellschaft*, in Reto M. Hilty and Alexander Peukert (2004) (ed.), *Interessenausgleich im Urheberrecht*, p. 67, pp. 84–86.

129 For the definition of the term 'digital dilemma,' see *supra* 'Introduction' at p. 148.

works into the public domain without significantly diminishing the incentive of authors to create new works. A similar result could perhaps be achieved by requiring registration for the renewal of the copyright term.[130]

The problem with these proposals is – and that brings us back to the aim of this paper – that they require the amendment or abrogation of international copyright treaties.[131] It has been pointed out that these steps are extremely difficult to achieve or simply unrealistic on a political level.[132] It is therefore reasonable to seek a solution that is superior to the logjam we have right now without conflicting with Berne, TRIPS or the WIPO Treaties. One proposal that fulfils this fundamental requirement and looks for middle ground in the battle over copyright in the digital network environment is a streamlined enforcement mechanism as outlined by Lemley and Reese.[133] Another option would be a voluntary collective management system as suggested by the EFF and others.[134] However, as long as these solutions are not adopted and have therefore not yet proven that they actually solve the problems they are supposed to address, it is worth asking what a bipolar copyright system would look like – in spite of its complexity.

Switching Between Individual Licensing and the Levy System

Does the choice make sense?

The most important feature of the bipolar system is that the right holder may freely choose between exclusive, proprietary exploitation on the basis of DRM ('hoarding') or participating in the levy/tax system ('sharing') as regards non-commercial file sharing. One of the advantages of this system is that the decision must be made for *every single subject matter* by the copyright owner

---

[130] See Lessig, *supra* n. 32, at 251–52; William M. Landes and Richard A. Posner (2003), 'Indefinitely Renewable Copyright', 70 *U. Chi. L. Rev.* 471, 476; Epstein, *supra* n. 1, at 33–37; Public Domain Enhancement Act, H.R. 2601 108th Cong. (2003), available at http://thomas.loc.gov/cgi-bin/query/z?c108:H.R.2601:.

[131] For the duration of copyright, see Art. 7 BC, Art. 12 TRIPS. For the formalities of copyright, see Art. 5(2) BC.

[132] See *supra* 'Introduction' at p. 149. In the end, national lawmakers have to make a choice between negotiations on a political level to amend international copyright law, and systems like the bipolar copyright system that do not require changes of international law. Complexity is involved in either strategy. It only relates to different aspects, that is, politics on the one hand and the legal and technological architecture of the approach in line with current international copyright law on the other (be it a bipolar copyright system or a streamlined enforcement mechanism).

[133] *Supra* n. 30. The authors also think it possible that their proposed system could be part of a levy system, be it on an opt-in or opt-out basis; *id.* at 1424.

[134] See *supra* 'Non-voluntary licenses regarding P2P file sharing' at p. 154.

according to the particular circumstances of each case. No governmental agency is involved. It is thus a market-based, decentralized concept. To leave the choice to the right holder recognizes self-determination as a core value of copyright in general.

The following examples are meant to show that it makes sense to provide for both alternatives in the digital online environment. In doing so, one has to distinguish between two scenarios. Either the choice will be made at the time of first publication of the work, or the copyright owner withdraws the work from one system and releases it into the other after the time of first publication.

Decision at the time of first publication A recognized artist who has already had some commercial success may decide in favour of the proprietary system just as it is today – unauthorized use of his or her works in P2P networks infringes the copyright in the works. To increase the probability that possible infringers actually face consequences, a streamlined enforcement procedure as proposed by Lemley and Reese[135] might be advisable.

The situation is completely different if a newly created work does not promise commercial success.[136] This might be the case if the author is not yet known to the public,[137] or the work is geared at a very small market for which there is not yet an intermediary offering commercial distribution. In these scenarios, the author does not and cannot expect significant revenue from the proprietary system. Authors often do not find an intermediary who will agree to handle commercial exploitation. In this situation, the levy/tax system will be much more appealing. The work, once produced and ready for distribution as a digital file in P2P networks, can be registered as eligible for distribution of the tax/levy. It is then up to the author or a commercial supplier of this service to promote the work among potential consumers. To this end, the Internet and modern technologies, especially preference-matching engines,[138]

---

[135] *Supra* n. 30.

[136] The distinction between popular works and less popular works also plays a role in the discussion on the optimal level of DRM protection. See Jeevan Jaisingh (2004), 'Piracy on File Sharing Networks: Strategies for Recording Companies', available at http://ssrn.com/abstract=567681, 19 (stating that 'protecting the latest album by Michael Jackson or the latest Lord of the Rings (movies and artists which already do, or are more likely to create a "buzz") makes more sense than protecting an album, which is less likely to be popular.').

[137] See *MGM*, 380 F.3d 1154, 1161 (9th Cir. 2004) ('Indeed, the record indicates that that thousands of other musical groups have authorized free distribution of their music through the Internet.'); *MGM*, 125 S.Ct. 2772 ('Some musical performers . . . have gained new audiences by distributing their copyrighted works for free across peer-to-peer networks. . .').

[138] See Lessig, *supra* n. 32, at 132–34.

provide promising tools for cost-effective promotion, lowering the barriers to entering the market. The interested user may download and redistribute the work without being obliged to pay for every use directly.[139] Instead, the creator receives a share of the levy/tax according to the use of the work as monitored by technology. Thus, failing to get a contract in the entertainment industry does not automatically mean that authors must offer their work 'for free'. Instead, simply by opting for the other business model, authors still have the possibility to earn money from their creations. It should be added that the levy/tax system can be attractive not only for newcomers or artists who create works for markets too small to be served by intermediaries of today. For example, a newly released album may be promoted with a pre-released single that is registered for the levy/tax system and then lawfully and unrestrictedly 'shared' in P2P networks. If the song proves successful, it can afterwards be exploited in the proprietary system together with the rest of the album and additional material such as video sequences.

Switch-over from one system to the other The last example gives rise to the second scenario, which is much more difficult to handle. Until now, this chapter has only dealt with works that are deliberately channelled into either the proprietary or the levy/tax system at the time of first publication. Are there cases imaginable where the copyright owner would decide to switch from one system to the other?

The first variant under this switch-over scenario is where the author initially chose proprietary exploitation on the basis of DRM. If it becomes clear that there will not be significant additional revenue from exclusive exploitation – be it because consumers did not like the work or because the commercial life cycle of the work has already passed – the copyright owner can at least try to gain additional revenue by registering the work and making it freely available in P2P networks.[140] The author is thereby able to reach consumers who are not willing to pay for the song or other work on an individual basis. The levy/tax system can thus form part of a strategy that relies on price discrimination.[141] To offer the work for non-commercial file sharing, not

---

[139] This is the approach of the so-called Potato System, which was developed by the German Company '4FO AG' together with the Fraunhofer-Institute for Digital Media Technology IDMT in Ilmenau, Germany; see http://www.potatosystem.com/info/eng/index.html.

[140] The copyright owner may still try to sell copies of the work. While commercial online ventures will face significant competitive pressure from the freely available versions in P2P networks, CDs and other offline mediums may still be successfully offered.

[141] There is no considerable risk that consumers will willfully abstain from

to require direct payment for such uses, and to still receive revenue is an alternative business model not available today.

Moreover, the fact that this switch to the levy/tax system will often take place after a certain period of proprietary exploitation reflects current criticisms of the copyright term. In many jurisdictions, copyright currently lasts 70 years *post mortem auctoris*.[142] It is rightly argued that such a long copyright term, compared to a copyright term of 50 years p.m.a. or even shorter terms, does not generate economic incentives meaningful for initial creativity.[143] As Justice Breyer put it in his dissenting opinion in *Eldred v Ashcroft*, 'no potential author can reasonably believe that he has more than a tiny chance of writing a classic that will survive commercially long enough for the copyright extension to matter. After all, if, after 55 to 75 years, only 2 per cent of all copyrights retain commercial value, the percentage surviving after 75 years or more (a typical pre-extension copyright term) must be far smaller.'[144] The bipolar copyright system can be understood as a flexible answer to that problem. Releasing works into P2P networks after an initial exploitation in proprietary systems gives users nearly as much freedom as with works in the public domain. In addition, to provide for a significantly shorter copyright term would again require the amendment of international copyright law. Finally, no statutory modification of the copyright term would ever make it possible to consider the commercial life cycle of each work individually. This, however, is just what the bipolar copyright system does.

At first glance, it seems that the second variant of the switch-over scenario, to switch from the levy/tax system to the proprietary system, is not likely to be of practical relevance. After all, digital files of the unportected work are available in P2P networks. Given the current state of the art, it would hardly be possible to prevent further use of these files technologically. The *Grokster* decision of the Ninth Circuit Court, however, offers a telling example that

purchasing or licensing copies of newly released songs or movies because they hope that these works will soon be available in P2P networks, as cultural works exert considerable attraction on consumers if they are – admittedly, for a limited period of time – a 'must-have.' Think, for example, of number one hits or movies that consumers simply have to know in order to be able to take part in everyday conversation. This notion relates particularly to younger consumers.

142 See, for example, 17 USC § 302(a); Art. 1(1) Council Directive 93/98, 1993 OJ (L290) 9-13 (EC).

143 See *Eldred v Ashcroft*, 123 S.Ct. 769, 792–93 (Stevens, J., dissenting), 808 (Breyer, J., dissenting) (2003).

144 *Id.*; Lessig, *supra* n. 32, at 292–94; for a European perspective on *Eldred* see Reto M. Hilty (2003), 'Eldred v Ashcroft: Die Schutzfrist im Urheberrecht – eine Diskussion, die auch Europäer interessieren sollte', *Gewerblicher Rechtsschutz und Urheberrecht International* (GRUR Int.), 201–204.

teaches the opposite. Explaining why the P2P software at issue was 'capable of substantial' or 'commercially significant noninfringing uses,' the court states:[145]

> One striking example provided by the Software Distributors is the popular band Wilco, whose record company had declined to release one of its albums on the basis that it had no commercial potential. Wilco repurchased the work from the record company and made the album available for free downloading, both from its own website and through the software user networks. The result sparked widespread interest and, as a result, Wilco received another recording contract.

Thus, experience shows that proprietary exploitation is not at all eliminated if the respective work has already been available in P2P networks in an unprotected digital format. The strategy to exclusively commercialize such works could become even more attractive under the bipolar copyright system. First, the proprietary system could be strengthened by an improved enforcement system on the Internet in order to deter users from further 'sharing'.[146] Second, the monitoring technology that counts lawful uses in P2P networks could also be employed to curtail file sharing. For example, one could imagine an automatic indicator that the work is no longer available for 'free' if a user wants to stream or download a work after withdrawal. It should be added in this context that one important consequence of the differentiated approach of the bipolar copyright system may well be that consumers would be more likely to respect copyright enforcement if it applies only to commercially valuable works, and not to potentially any content available.[147] In any event, it would be up to the copyright owner to take the risk. Again, new business models and improved offers (for example additional versions of a song, etc.) may help to make this strategy valuable.[148]

---

[145] *MGM*, 380 F.3d 1154, 1161 (9th Cir. 2004). The Supreme Court did not refer to this example expressly but stated that 'some musical performers . . . have gained new audiences by distributing their copyrighted works for free across peer-to-peer networks . . .'; *MGM*, 125 S.Ct. 2764, 2772 (2005). Justice Ginsburg declared that 'there has been no finding of any fair use and little beyond anecdotal evidence of noninfringing uses'; *id.* at 2785.

[146] See Lemley and Reese, *supra* n. 30.

[147] Litman, *supra* n. 51, at 49.

[148] One could even consider allocating, for a certain period of time, a fraction of the money due under the levy/tax system to the copyright owner after the work has been withdrawn to account for the ongoing uses. This option, however, has severe legal pitfalls. In the end, the uses are unlawful. After the work has been withdrawn, uploads and downloads infringe the copyright in the work. They can be prevented by exercising exclusive rights. If the copyright owner fails to do so, it does not seem justified to nevertheless assign his or her shares of the levy/tax revenue.

These examples show that both systems will be used for different classes of works. While some works will be exploited (often for a limited time only) in commercial online ventures, others will from the time of first publication be available for non-commercial file sharing in P2P networks. The question remains, however, as to which system should or must form the legal default. Two alternatives are imaginable. In the first, the levy/tax system is the legal default and the copyright owner must opt out of it. This is the variant proposed by Jessica Litman and William Fisher. Alternatively, exclusivity is the rule and the right holder may deliberately opt into the levy/tax system. The following section addresses both alternatives, again emphasizing the question of whether both approaches are in line with international copyright law.

Opting Out of the Levy/tax System

Features and benefits

The first alternative to be considered here is the opt-out model. According to the suggestions of Jessica Litman and William Fisher, the levy/tax system should be the legal default.[149] Any work still under copyright and every newly published work would fall under the new limitation from or exception to exclusive rights, and would at the same time be eligible for shares of the levy/tax, unless the right holder opted for exclusivity on the basis of DRM. With regard to new works, Litman proposes a notice-based opt out mechanism. In order to inform consumers that a particular work does not fall under the levy/tax system, the copyright owners would have to release the work in a '*.drm' format.[150] The right holders would lose any claims under the levy system. Additionally, they would have to take affirmative steps to exclude their work from the network and 'enable consumers to quickly and painlessly ascertain that those works may not lawfully be shared.'[151] For works that have already been released in another, free, format, Litman would make it even more burdensome to withdraw a work from 'sharing'.[152] Without explaining

149 See Litman, *supra* n. 51, at 45 et seq.

150 Litman, *supra* n. 51, at 46–47.

151 *Id.* at 45.

152 See Litman, *supra* n. 51, at 48:

'All owners of the copyright in the work, as well as the work's creators, would be required to join in the decision to withdraw. First, the copyright owners would need to recall copies of the work released in formats other than *.drm, and offer any consumers who own authorized, commercial copies in a non-*.drm format the opportunity to swap those copies for *.drm copies at no charge. Second, the law should incorporate a 24-month grace period before any withdrawal of a work could take effect. (In the meantime, withdrawn works could collect payments from the common fund.) Finally, in order to recover in an infringement suit for consumer-to-how the implementation of technological measures and privileged uses under the alternative compensation system relate to each other, Fisher would allow that a copyright owner 'opted out of the tax system entirely, releasing only an encrypted version of his or her recording.'[153]

Obviously, this concept aims at encouraging 'sharing' instead of 'hoarding'.[154] It thus relies on the positive effects of levy/tax systems. Moreover, it accepts that virtually every work published today can be accessed in P2P networks, and that many works are not commercialized and are instead released for free on the Internet.[155] If 'sharing' is the default today, Litman reasons, it should be the default of tomorrow. It would simply be transformed from illegal use to lawful and compensated use. One final aspect of Litman's proposal that should not be underestimated: a tax or levy system would be imposed upfront on services and devices in use for file sharing. It would not be collected on an individual basis, as under a collective license where the user or the facilitator has to pay according to the number of works actually being used or at least available for use in the network.[156] The imposition of a levy/tax high enough to generate funding that encourages authors to choose the levy/tax system can hardly be justified if there are only very few works registered for lawful use in P2P networks. The opt-out model would make sure that all copyrighted works are presumptively legally available for up- and download. It would thus provide the prospect of something of value for the society at large. Without this prospect, there will be strong resistance against the adoption of a levy/tax system as a mere alternative to exclusive exploitation.

Compliance with international copyright law

However, there are severe doubts whether this concept is in accordance with international copyright law, for two main reasons.

First, one must ask whether exclusivity as only the secondary option is still in line with the three-step test. As already outlined, the bipolar copyright system *as such* arguably complies with this treaty obligation because it simply

---

consumer dissemination of a withdrawn work, the copyright owner would need to show knowledge that the work had been withdrawn.'

153 Fisher, *supra* n. 1, at 247–48.

154 Litman, *supra* n. 51, at 41; Fisher, *supra* n. 1, at 237.

155 See *MGM*, 380 F.3d 1154, 1161 (9th Cir. 2004) ('Indeed, the record indicates that that thousands of other musical groups have authorized free distribution of their music through the Internet.'); *MGM Studios, Inc. v Grokster Ltd.*, 125 S.Ct. 2764, 2772 (2005) ('Some musical performers . . . have gained new audiences by distributing their copyrighted works for free across peer-to-peer networks . . .'); see also *id.* at 6 (Breyer J., concurring) (explaining the significant future market for non-infringing uses of Grokster-type peer-to-peer software).

156 Fisher, *supra* n. 1, at 252.

offers the right holder an additional business model. Exclusivity in cyberspace is limited only insofar as copyright is one of the two layers of exclusivity available to the right holder. The other option, that is, exclusive exploitation based on DRM systems, remains unaffected. What has not yet been answered, however, is whether exclusivity has to be the legal default under the three-step test.

Second, if the right holder has to opt out of the levy/tax system in order to enjoy full exclusivity, it could be argued that this model establishes a formality requirement.[157] Article 5(2) BC reads that '[t]he enjoyment and exercise of these rights shall not be subject to any formality. . . .' The formulation 'these rights' refers to paragraph 1 of Article 5 BC, which provides that 'authors shall enjoy, in respect of works for which they are protected under this Convention, in countries of the Union other than the country of origin, the rights which their respective laws do now or may hereafter grant to their nationals, as well as the rights specially granted by this Convention'.[158]

As both the TRIPS Agreement and the WCT stipulate that contracting parties have to comply with Articles 1 through 21 of the Berne Convention, the prohibition of formalities has to be observed by parties to these treaties as well.[159] An alleged violation of this obligation is consequently subject to WTO dispute settlement proceedings. Moreover, these references entail that not only the right of reproduction according to Art. 9 BC must not be subject to formality requirements, but also that the right of communication to the public, including the right of making works available to the public under Art. 8 WCT, must not be subject to formality requirements. These rights are minimum rights granted by the Berne Convention and the WCT. They are thus 'rights specially granted' under these treaties, so their enjoyment or exercise must not be subject to formalities.[160] In order to establish a levy/tax system where 'sharing' is the legal default rule, however, the right of reproduction and the

---

[157] See Litman, *supra* n. 51, at 46 n. 166.

[158] Historically, the acts of the Berne Convention moved away from formality requirements for copyright protection. Article 2(2) of the 1886 act provided that 'the enjoyment of these rights shall be subject to the accomplishment of the conditions and formalities prescribed by law in the country of origin of the work. . . .' It was only at the 1908 Berlin Conference that this requirement was abolished. Article 4(2) BC 1908 already had the same wording as Art. 5(2) of the current version. The 1967 Stockholm Conference simply rearranged the legal material in Arts. 4 to 6. It did not alter Art. 4(2) but simply gave it a new number, Art. 5. See Ricketson, *supra* n. 73, at 5.82; Fritz Schönherr (1981), 'On the Interpretation of Article 5(2) of the Berne Convention, Taking as an Example the Greek Antipiracy Law of July 15, 1980', *Copyright* 295–97; Alfred Baum (1932), 'Berner Konvention, Landesgesetze und internationals Privatrecht', *Gewerblicher Rechtsschutz und Urheberrecht* (GRUR) pp. 923–27.

[159] See Art. 9 (1) TRIPS (excluding Art. 6bis BC), Art. 1(4) WCT.

[160] Wilhelm Nordemann, Kai Vinck and Paul W. Hertin (1990), *International Copyright and Neighboring Rights Law*, Art. 5 BC no. 6.

right of communication to the public would be limited with regard to non-commercial file sharing unless the right holder fulfills certain requirements.

The three-step test and the prohibition of formalities are closely related to each other. If exclusivity has to be the default under the three-step test, the opt-out mechanism can well be said to act as a formality requirement. If not, the right holder would in principle[161] enjoy automatic protection under the levy/tax system without further conditions or formalities. In this latter case, Art. 5(2) BC would not be violated by this solution. To explain this distinction, one must look to the general goals of the convention and the relevant provisions, because there is no precedent for an opt-out mechanism under a bipolar copyright system. The idea of two layers of exclusivity that are treated differently was not known in 1971, the year of the last amendment of the Berne Convention.

To begin with, it can certainly be argued that the necessary acts for opting out of the levy/tax system are *formalities* under Art. 5(2) BC. Jessica Litman suggests that the work would have to be published in a certain *.drm format and that the right holder would have to take care that consumers are informed about this choice. One could alternatively imagine a notice with the competent authority that the work shall not be lawfully available for file sharing.[162] Both requirements are state-required, formal preconditions, similar to the notice and registration system under former US copyright law, which was one of the major obstacles to the US joining the Berne Convention.[163] This is obvious in the case that a declaration or registration is necessary.[164] It also holds true for the requirement to use a digital format (*.drm). While one might question whether this requirement is a 'formality,' it certainly can be said to impose a 'condition' in a more general sense that has to be complied with in order to ensure that the work does not fall under the limitation/exception for non-commercial file sharing.

Originally, Art. 2(2) of the 1886 Berne Act referred to formalities *and* conditions. 'Conditions' meant material requirements such as providing a

---

161 It has to be noted that naturally only those right holders can receive a share of the incurred levy/tax who register their work with the competent authority that distributes the money.

162 See Fisher, *supra* n. 1, at 242 (discussing an opt-out mechanism as regards the preparation of derivative works).

163 See 17 USC § 401(a); Nordemann et al., *supra* n. 160, Art. 5 BC no. 7.

164 Other formalities are the obligation to affix a copyright symbol and to make a legal deposit of money or a copy of the work under penalty of losing rights. See Daniel Gervais (2003), 'Application of an Extended Collective Licensing Regime in Canada: Principles and Issues Related to Implementation', Study Prepared for the Department of Canadian Heritage, available at http://www.canadianheritage.gc.ca/progs/ac-ca/progs/pda-cpb/pubs/regime/regime_e.pdf, 19; Ricketson, *supra* n. 73, at 5.83; Nordemann et al., *supra* n. 160, Art. 5 BC no. 7.

translation of the work in the language of the country where protection was sought.[165] When the need to comply with conditions and formalities was abolished at the 1908 Berlin Conference, the term 'conditions' in the new provision 4(2) was deleted as well. The documents of the conference, however, show that the delegations understood the new wording 'formalities' as covering both the 'conditions and formalities' referred to in the 1886 Act.[166] Thus, the requirement to use a certain format for publication in order to enjoy exclusivity in cyberspace is also a 'formality' under Art. 5(2) BC.[167]

With this insight, however, the interpretation of Art. 5(2) BC is not complete. The second element of this provision is *that the enjoyment or exercise* of the right of reproduction and the right of communication to the public as minimum rights under the named conventions be subject to the formality. The necessity of addressing this element separately becomes obvious in light of a statement at the Diplomatic Conference of 1884 that explains the meaning and reach of the provision. During the discussion, one of the German delegates put forward an interpretation that was approved by the Conference and was reproduced verbatim in the Conference records. According to the statement of Dr. Meyer, 'the words "formalities and conditions" comprise everything which must be complied with in order to ensure that the rights of the author with regard to his work may come into existence [in German: "*Voraussetzungen*"], while the effects and consequences of protection [in German: "*Wirkungen*"], in particular the extent of that protection, should remain subordinated to the principle of treatment equal with nationals.'[168] As was already shown, the current version of Art. 5(2) BC can be traced back to Art. 2(2) of the 1886 Act.[169] Hence, the distinction between prohibited formalities relating to the *genesis* of the right, and formalities that concern only the *scope* of copyright is still valid for the interpretation of the provision.[170]

Adopting this reading of Art. 5(2) BC, it could be argued that the opt-out mechanism establishes only a formality requirement as regards the *scope* of copyright, in Dr. Meyer's words the *consequences of protection*, but not its genesis. As a result, these formalities would not fall under Art. 5(2) BC and would therefore not conflict with this international obligation. For example, it

---

165 Ernst Röthlisberger (1906), *Die Berner Übereinkunft zum Schutze von Werken der Literatur und Kunst und die Zusatzabkommen*, p. 101.

166 Ricketson, *supra* n. 73, at 5.83.

167 The same holds true for other requirements Litman proposes. See Litman, *supra* n. 51, at 48.

168 Ricketson, *supra* n. 73, at 5.82.

169 See *supra* 'Compliance with international copyright law' at p. 182.

170 See Ricketson, *supra* n. 73, at 5.83; Masouyé, *supra* n. 87, at 35; Nordemann et al., *supra* n. 160, Art. 5 BC no. 7; see also Baum, *supra* n. 158, at 927 for further references.

is held that Art. 5(2) BC does not apply[171] to provisions in national copyright law that grant a longer copyright term for pseudonymous works if the author registers his or her true name in a register for authors[172] or if the law provides for a presumption in favour of the person who is designated as author on a copy of the work.[173] Similarly, the opt-out mechanism does not deprive the author of copyright protection completely. Copyright still comes into existence without any formalities. Only with regard to non-commercial file sharing is the legal default not exclusivity, but a levy/tax system, which still generates income for the author. True, copyright owners still have to register their work with the competent authority in order to actually have the prospect of receiving a share of the accrued money. But this could be said to be a mere factual necessity.[174] It is not required by law. Basically, the protection under the levy/tax system is afforded without any formalities.

Moreover, it has to be kept in mind that the bipolar copyright system is generally admissible under the three-step test. A national copyright law establishing this model could thus be said to grant authors the minimum rights under Berne. If this is true, both pillars of the bipolar system are valid default rules. Art. 5(2) BC would only prohibit *both* layers of protection being subjected to formalities. Therefore, if right holders opt for exclusivity, they are, according to this view, only extending the scope of copyright protection, just like authors of pseudonymous works who register their true names to enjoy the full copyright term.

---

171 See Ricketson, *supra* n. 75, at 5.82; Röthlisberger, *supra* n. 165, at 108; Baum, *supra* n. 158, at 928; Willy Hoffmann (1935), *Die Berner Uebereinkunft zum Schutze von Werken der Literatur und Kunst* 92; Schönherr, *supra* n. 158, at 297.

172 See, e.g., Sec. 66(2) German CA.

173 See, e.g., Sec. 10(1) German CA: In the absence of proof to the contrary, the person designated in the customary manner as the author on copies of a work which has been published or on the original of a work of fine art shall be deemed the author of the work; the same shall apply to a designation which is known as the author's pseudonym or the artist's mark.

174 For a discussion on the contrary view and the duty of the competent authority to search for authors who did not register, although their works are being shared, see *infra* n. 183. It is furthermore interesting in this context that the 'extended collective management' of exclusive rights by collecting societies is said to be in line with Art. 5(2) BC. Extended collective management of rights means that national copyright law entails a presumption in favour of collecting societies. According to this presumption, all authors whose works are actually used under the collective licensing scheme grant rights, even if this is true only for a substantial number but not all authors. Without this presumption, smaller collecting societies would not be able to offer a comprehensive repertoire for users. Authors are therefore obliged to expressly object to this administration of their rights in order to regain control over the exercise of their exclusive rights. See Gervais, *supra* n. 164, at 19; Gervais, *supra* n. 4, at 72.

Finally, the formalities proposed for opting out of the levy/tax system do not relate to the *exercise* of the exclusive rights. With exercise, Art. 5(2) BC refers to the enforcement of copyrights, that is, to the remedies available in the case of an infringement. For example, the bringing of proceedings or the award of damages must not be dependent on formalities or conditions.[175] The formalities at stake here do not centre on infringement and remedies, but primarily on the enjoyment of rights. Additionally, the whole idea of a bipolar copyright system strongly implies a choice to be made by the right holder. This choice has to be expressed and registered in some form to give the public, or at least the competent authority, notice about the status of the work. If 'exercise' of rights were to cover this notification, even a system that starts from exclusivity and provides for a voluntary opt-in mechanism as regards the levy/tax system would not comply with Art. 5(2) BC. Even the requirement to file written documents in order to institute an infringement proceeding would run afoul of the Berne Convention. Obviously, this cannot be true. A formality requirement as to the exercise of rights has to impose additional obstacles not necessarily inherent in the copyright system.

For the following reasons, however, these arguments in favour of an opt-out mechanism as the default are unconvincing. First and most importantly, it has to be restated that the bipolar copyright system is also subject to the three-step test. The arguments above only help to avoid a conflict with the second step, that is, the normal exploitation of the work in the digital network environment. The first and third step still have to be observed. From this it follows that a bipolar copyright system has to be confined to certain special cases (non-commercial file sharing), and that the levy or tax has to compensate the privileged uses in order not to cause an unreasonable prejudice to the legitimate interests of the right holder. If it is true that the three-step test applies, its primary purpose has to be observed. This fundamental goal is to guarantee certain minimum *exclusive* rights in works, and to confine the scope of limitations to or exceptions from exclusive rights in national copyright law. The bipolar copyright system already downgrades exclusivity to an alternative, on par with a mere right to remuneration under a levy/tax system. This right to remuneration relies on limitations/exceptions to copyright, which would conflict with the normal exploitation of the work if the copyright owner did not have the option to choose exclusivity. A paradigm shift like this only conforms with the purpose of the three-step test if exclusivity at least forms the statutory default rule.

Second, this consideration can be rested upon the evaluation of other cases where the copyright owner is obliged to fulfil formalities in order to enjoy exclusivity. One example can be found in the BC itself. Art. 10bis(1)(1) reads:

---

175 Ricketson, *supra* n. 73, at 5.84.

> It shall be a matter for legislation in the countries of the Union to permit the reproduction by the press, the broadcasting or the communication to the public by wire of articles published in newspapers or periodicals on current economic, political or religious topics, and of broadcast works of the same character, *in cases in which the reproduction, broadcasting or such communication thereof is not expressly reserved* [emphasis added].

The emphasized qualification enables right holders to avoid the limitation. In order to enjoy exclusivity, they have to expressly reserve their rights. Under German copyright law, the statement 'all rights reserved' has to be expressed in connection with every single published article.[176] Obviously, this solution bears great resemblance to the bipolar copyright system, and particularly to the opt-out model as proposed by Jessica Litman. Ricketson and other commentators, however, reason that Art. 10bis (1) BC contains a formality requirement in that the genesis of the exclusive right at stake depends upon making an express reservation.[177] They argue that it is justified only because it is acknowledged in the convention itself as a *lex specialis* to Art. 5(2) BC.[178]

Another situation similar to the opt-out model is mandatory or extended collective licensing, where the authors must withdraw their rights from the collecting society in order to handle their rights individually. Again, the authors have to either make a declaration or fulfil other conditions to enjoy exclusivity. However, mandatory collective licensing is found to be in conflict with the three-step test if it pertains to exclusive rights[179] or, at any rate, if the collecting society is required by law to grant exploitation rights or authorizations to any person so requesting.[180] In the latter case, the exclusive rights are in fact reduced to a mere right to remuneration administered by a collecting society.[181] This, however, is exactly the case under the opt-out model where

---

[176] See Ferdinand Melichar in Gerhard Schricker (ed.), *Urheberrecht*, Sec. 49 German CA no. 10.

[177] Hoffmann, *supra* n. 171, at 91.

[178] Ricketson, *supra* n. 73, at 5.85.

[179] See Schönherr, *supra* n. 158, at 295 with further references; Nordemann et al., *supra* n. 160, Art. BC no. 77.

[180] This is the case according to the German 'Law on the Administration of Copyright and Neighboring Rights (Copyright Administration Law)'. According to Sec. 11 of the Copyright Administration Law, '[C]ollecting societies shall be required to grant exploitation rights or authorizations to any person so requesting on equitable terms in respect of the rights they administer.'

[181] See von Lewinski, *supra* n. 37, at 5 ('The mandatory collective administration however does not affect the exclusive right itself; the covered uses are not authorized by law. Rather, the author is only restricted in the options of exercising the right: he is left with the only possibility to exercise the exclusive right through the collecting society, whereas the right itself is not limited as such, in particular not in favor of any such interest of the public at large.'); *contra* Gervais, *supra* n. 4, at 72.

participation in the levy/tax system is the statutory default. Taken together, these examples demonstrate that the Berne Convention has been interpreted as obliging national copyright laws to vest the author with exclusive rights as the statutory default rule. A diverging subsequent practice in the application of the treaty cannot be ascertained.[182]

It should finally be added that right holders have to register their works with the competent authority in order to actually participate in the levy/tax system. Thus, even the statutory default under the opt-out model requires compliance with formalities.[183]

Summary

In summary, the opt-out model as suggested by Jessica Litman and William Fisher is a state-required formality for the enjoyment of minimum exclusive rights. It is thus not in line with Art. 5(2) BC, as international copyright law persists in the notion of exclusive rights, even in the digital network environment. These exclusive rights must come into existence without further formalities as the statutory default. To provide for exclusivity only under the condition that the right holder opts out of a levy/tax system does not meet this requirement.

The only way to go forward would be to confine the opt-out approach to works for which the respective country (for example, the US) is the country of origin as defined in Art. 5(4) BC,[184] because the obligation to provide for certain minimum rights and the formality requirement of Art. 5(2) BC do not apply in this situation.[185] Such a limited adoption of the opt-out model, however, does not seem to be practical. First publication determines the country of origin of a work. Right holders could easily evade the system if they published the work in a country other than, for example, the US for the first time. Users of P2P networks could not be sure whether the work they were using was lawfully available in the network even if it was not in a *.drm format, because it could still be a foreign work, which does not fall under the

---

182 See Vienna Convention on the Law of Treaties, Art. 31(3)(b) May 23, 1969 n. 55 U.N.T.S.331.

183 In order to address this problem, the authority distributing the money would have to check whether all works that are being used are registered and would have to contact the respective right holders if this were not the case. This solution obviously entails significant administrative costs that diminish the prospects of the whole system.

184 Litman, *supra* n. 51, at 46 n. 166.

185 See Art. 5(1) BC ('[I]n countries of the Union other than the country of origin'); Ricketson, *supra* n. 73, at 5.81; Masouyé, *supra* n. 87, at 5.6; von Lewinski, *supra* n. 37, at 5 n. 13. This is the reason why 17 USC § 411(a) limits registration as a condition to instituting an infringement action to 'United States works.' See Paul Goldstein (2002), *Copyright* at § 3.15 (2nd ed.).

system anyway. The opt-out model as such would lose its most important advantage, that the levy/tax system presumptively covers all works available in the network. Finally, it would be even more difficult to persuade the legislature to implement a general levy/tax up front if the amendment discriminates against national authors as compared to foreigners.[186]

If the opt-out model is not in line with international copyright law and admissible modifications of this concept do not seem reasonable as to their consequences, it shows promise to turn one's attention to the legal and practical aspects of an opt-in model.

Opting in to the Levy/tax System

Features and benefits

Under the opt-in model, to get paid a share of the levy/tax based on the monitored use of the work in P2P file-sharing systems, the right holder has to register the work with the competent authority. So as long as the work has not been registered and technologically tagged, use is unauthorized and thus infringes on the author's rights.[187] This means that exclusivity is the legal default – just as it is today. The levy/tax system would provide an additional business model, available for those right holders who think that this mode of exploitation is more attractive than individual licensing on the basis of DRM.

Obviously, this solution does not raise doubts as to whether it is in accordance with treaty obligations under Berne, TRIPS or the WCT. It does not limit the enjoyment or exercise of exclusive rights by law. Moreover, these rights come into existence without formalities or other conditions. Accordingly, neither the guarantee of normal exploitation under the three-step test[188] nor the prohibition of formalities is affected. This concept only gives the copyright owner an incentive to accept lawful non-commercial file sharing by providing a distribution channel where 'compensation without control' can become a reality.

Contrary to the opt-out model, the questions relating to this approach are not of a positivistic and legal, but of a practical nature: is it persuasive to

---

186 See Ricketson, *supra* n. 73, at 5.81 (explaining that the convention invariably has a decisive effect on the content of the domestic laws of its members).

187 Fisher, *supra* n. 1, at 204, proposes a different solution. If the work is not registered, it would be deemed to be dedicated to the public domain ('*Would each creator be obliged to register his or her creations?* No. Unlike cars, songs and films could be unlicensed. Creators who wished for whatever reason to dedicate their products to the public domain could do so.').

188 Still, however, the first and third requirements of the three-step test have to be observed.

implement a levy or tax on devices and services up front if it is still up to the right holder to reserve 'all' rights or only 'some'? And how is this different from a voluntary collective licensing scheme as proposed *inter alia* by the EFF if the right holder is free to choose exclusivity?[189]

The opt-in model compared to collective licensing

The difference and, at the same time, the advantage that makes the opt-in model more attractive than voluntary collective licensing relates to the funding of the system and how lawful uses are compensated: collective licensing relies on a voluntary agreement of right holders to form a collecting society, which then offers consumers the opportunity to use works online in exchange for a regular payment. This system functions successfully only under the condition that most, if not all, works are covered. Otherwise, consumers have no incentive to pay a subscription fee if they are not offered a variety of content. If it is not certain that enough users will subscribe, right holders have no incentive to agree on collective licensing instead of exploiting their works individually in different commercial online ventures while trying to stop unauthorized file sharing in P2P networks. This may be the reason voluntary collective licensing has not been adopted in the digital network environment.[190]

A levy/tax system provides funds to be distributed among right holders without requiring them to establish a collective society and without relying on the readiness of consumers to pay a subscription fee. Instead, the levy/tax is imposed upfront on services and products whose value is increased by file sharing.[191] Thereby, a significant amount of money will be collected. All right holders who register their works are entitled to a share of this revenue. The primary difference between a levy/tax system and collective licensing is that a levy/tax system generates funding as an incentive for choosing 'sharing' instead of 'hoarding.' With registration, the work becomes available for lawful non-commercial file sharing. This, in turn, increases the readiness of consumers to pay more for Internet access or devices used for file sharing. In other words, the government would step in to offer an incentive for copyright owners to accept 'compensation without control.' This is necessary because

189 For the EFF proposal, see *supra* 'Non-voluntary licenses regarding P2P file sharing' at p. 154.

190 See Fisher, *supra* n. 1, at 257–58.

191 See Netanel, *supra* n. 23, at 35–59. The levy/tax would have to be imposed on all services and products offered in the respective country. Therefore, it would not severely affect competition in the relevant markets because all manufacturers or suppliers of services would have to pay the levy/tax. It has to be admitted, however, that newly developed substitutes would have to be covered quickly by the levy/tax.

'contracting into liability rules'[192] obviously does not take place automatically. The government, however, cannot force right holders into liability rules, since that would be incompatible with international copyright law. Instead, it establishes a system for indirect compensation of non-commercial file sharing. Whereas in the short run, not all works will be available for lawful file sharing, the fact that at least some will be will probably change consumers' attitude towards the way works on the Internet can be legally accessed. This 'soft' pressure and change of consumer behaviour is likely to make the levy/tax system ever more appealing for copyright owners.

That the levy/tax system may grow due to network effects, however, also reveals important drawbacks of the opt-in model. The levy or tax has to be imposed without the guarantee that all works will be lawfully available in P2P networks. Works that promise particular commercial success will not likely be registered, at least in the beginning. Thus, the ones who have to pay the levy/tax, consumers and manufacturers of devices and suppliers of services used for file sharing, will claim that they are being burdened while the public benefit is uncertain. In fact, this value judgment will be at the core of the political discussion surrounding an opt-in model: is it justified to raise prices for devices and services at the heart of the information and knowledge society in order to establish an additional business model for the distribution of copyrighted content online?

As right holders retain their freedom to decide about the use of their work, it will not be them, but manufacturers of devices and suppliers of services who will primarily argue against the implementation of this proposal.[193] The opt-in model shifts the pressure away from copyright owners towards a party that neither creates nor consumes content. This view, however, neglects the fact that manufacturers and suppliers of services profit from unauthorized use of copyrighted works in P2P networks because they commercialize the very services and devices necessary for file sharing. Thus, they cannot claim to be uninvolved.

To sum up, there are many good reasons for a bipolar opt-in model, even if it is uncertain how many works will be lawfully available for non-commercial file sharing in the end. Most importantly, it is the only model that brings a levy/tax system in the digital network environment into line with international copyright law.

---

[192] See Robert P. Merges (1996), 'Contracting Into Liability Rules', 84 *Cal. L. Rev.* 1293 (explaining why right holders will automatically establish systems like collective licensing if individual licensing does not work).

[193] Fisher, *supra* n. 1, at 242. This repudiation can also be observed in the course of the discussion about the future of the limitation and the levy for private copying in Germany; see e.g., Bernd Rohleder (2004), *Für eine zukunftsfähige Urhebervergütung*, Zeitschrift für Urheber- und Medienrecht (ZUM), p. 1061 (proposing to abolish the levy for digital private copies).

CONCLUSION

As long as P2P file-sharing technology is not declared illegal[194] and is not substituted by other technologies, it is here to stay. If copyright owners fail to integrate this technology into business models to generate revenue from the consumer's use of copyrighted works (as in the case of the VCR[195]), the discussion about alternatives to exclusive exploitation in cyberspace will become ever more important. Proposals for tax or levy systems covering non-commercial file sharing are among the most promising approaches to take advantage of this technology for authors and society at large because this model secures compensation for authors without hindering P2P networks and the innovation that this technology brings about: *compensation without control*.[196]

This chapter has shown, however, that none of the currently discussed models is in accordance with obligations contained in international copyright law. The BC, TRIPS and WCT rest upon the notion of legal and technological exclusivity enjoyed by the copyright owner. These international instruments are opposed to the implementation of statutory, non-voluntary licenses covering non-commercial file sharing. Only if the right holder is free to decide whether he or she wants a work to be subject to a levy/tax system is exclusivity as the fundamental requirement of international copyright law satisfied. As a result, exclusive rights and individual licensing have to be the legal default. Therefore, only an opt-in model, in which the right holder has to register the work for the levy/tax system, can be implemented in national law without the need to either amend international copyright treaties or terminate membership.

Although this approach has some significant drawbacks, particularly with regard to the number of works available for lawful sharing, it nevertheless provides a business model not available today, to accept file sharing in exchange for indirect compensation. It is also superior to voluntary collective licensing in that it generates funding up front and thereby gives copyright owners an incentive to opt for 'sharing.' In sum, the bipolar opt-in copyright system caters to a permanent coexistence of – speaking in economic terms – property and liability rules in cyberspace. Whereas the architecture of proprietary exploitation is constructed by the copyright owner, the levy/tax system has to be established by the government. Neither form of exploitation is outlawed.[197] Instead, the choice

---

194 For the limited holding of *MGM*, 125 S.Ct. 2764 (2005), see *supra* 'Copyright and peer-to-peer networks' at p. 151.

195 See Lessig, *supra* n. 32, at 195; Shih Ray Ku, *supra* n. 40, at 553–57.

196 Lessig, *supra* n. 32, at 201.

197 See also Einhorn and Rosenblatt (2005), 52 *J. Copyright Society of the USA*.

between the two is up to the copyright owner. As a result, this approach enhances freedom and triggers competition between the two alternatives for the exploitation of works in the digital network environment. All in all, it supports creative pursuits through exclusive rights *and* innovation in and development of new communication technologies.[198]

What this chapter finally shows is that in thinking about new approaches, existing copyright law must be considered as it is rooted in international law to a large extent, which in turn is binding upon national and even supranational legislatures such as the EC. The crucial question to be answered is what this chapter tells us about the harmonization of copyright law in general. In my opinion, it is necessary to carefully examine the drawbacks of international harmonization as regards the flexibility of copyright legislation.[199] This is true not only for developing countries,[200] but also for highly industrialized nations. Copyright in general is directly linked to and has always reacted to technological changes. Accepting this insight, modern national copyright laws provide for expiration dates of certain provisions,[201] for specific measures to quickly amend the law,[202] or at least for obligatory, regular reports on the effects of the law.[203] Even if one does not call into question the international

---

239, 271('In other words, P2P and DRM technologies should be left to evolve together . . .').

[198] These were the two seemingly opposing policy considerations at the heart of the *Grokster* decision; see *MGM*, 125 S.Ct. 2764, 2775 (2005) ('The more artistic protection is favored, the more technological innovation may be discouraged. . .'); *id.* at 11, n. 8 ('The mutual exclusivity of these values should not be overstated, however.'); see also *id.* at 2 (Breyer, J., concurring) (referring to the need for the law to 'strike a balance between a copyright holder's legitimate demand for effective – not merely symbolic – protection of the statutory monopoly, and the rights of others freely to engage in substantially unrelated areas of commerce.').

[199] See generally Annette Kur (2004), 'A New Framework for Intellectual Property Rights – Horizontal Issues', 35 *IIC* 1, 20; *contra* Sirinelli, *supra* n. 12, at 26–27 (pleading for additional harmonization); Reinbothe & von Lewinski, *supra* n. 69, Art. 10 WCT no. 11 (recognizing the need to flexibly interpret the three-step test in light of changing market conditions, focusing, however, solely on strengthening the position of authors); Goldstein, *supra* n. 50, at 209–11.

[200] See the preamble of TRIPS: 'Recognizing also the special needs of the least-developed country Members in respect of maximum flexibility in the domestic implementation of laws and regulations in order to enable them to create a sound and viable technological base.'

[201] See 17 USC § 119(a)(1), (e); Sec. 52a, 137k German CA (proclaiming that one limitation to copyright – Sec. 52a German CA – expired on 1 January 2007).

[202] See 17 USC § 1201(a)(B)-(D) (rulemaking of the US Copyright Office regarding certain classes of works that are exempted from the legal protection of technological measures).

[203] See 17 USC § 1201(g)(5); Art. 12 Copyright Directive, *supra* n. 100 (both concerning the legal protection of technological measures).

harmonization of copyright law in general,[204] it is necessary to discuss whether and how we can achieve a balance between the need for adequate minimum protection on a global scale, and the flexibility to react to perhaps fundamental changes in the way works are exploited and used.[205] This call for flexibility in international copyright law not only relates to technology-specific rules, like those on technological protection measures, but also to the three-step test as an open, technology-neutral and central aspect of international intellectual property law.[206] A narrow construction of the three-step test may prevent the implementation of a concept that addresses new problems (file sharing) in a way that favours most if not all parties involved. If reality proves even the initial point of a given concept wrong, it must be possible to modify this concept as a whole.[207]

---

[204] See Kur, *supra* n. 199, at 20 (naming soft law and recommendations as an alternative).

[205] This applies even to the proposals discussed herein. These may become obsolete, just like today's file sharing, because of easier Internet access which enables information from commercial databases to be streamed; see Lessig, *supra* n. 3, at 300–04.

[206] Ficsor, *supra* n. 75, at 5.50; Senftleben, *supra* n. 56, at 304–11.

[207] But see Senftleben, *supra* n. 56, at 304 (arguing that the three-step test lends sufficient weight to the interests of authors and users alike and that it was wise to embrace the three-step test to circumscribe the ambit of operation of permissible limitations in the digital environment).

7. Sharing out online liability: sharing files, sharing risks and targeting ISPs

Robert Clark

THE FILE-SHARING PHENOMENON

The use of the Internet to distribute sound recordings now forms a significant proportion of music sales.[1] The use of the Internet to facilitate music file transfers has spawned new ways of commercialising music, which benefits most sectors of the music copyright industries. The use of file-sharing technology to enable musicians to distribute music for promotional purposes shows that original musical compositions and sound recordings can be exchanged over a network using MP3 technology without infringing any rights. A startling demonstration of this is the success of the Arctic Monkeys. Early sound recordings and original compositions of the band were available for free download, creating a strong fan base and a reputation for 'integrity'.[2] The Gnarls Barkley single *Crazy* has been available as an illegal download since Autumn 2005 but proved so popular that, when it became available for legal download in March 2006, the track went to no. 1 in the charts on the basis of downloads alone.[3] Even the back catalogues of major record companies have benefited from the availability of single tracks for legal download, though there is a negative impact in the sense that the buying public is less likely to

1 The International Federation for the Phonographic Industry (IFPI) estimates that in 2005 some 420 million single tracks were downloaded, more than 20 times the figure for 2003. Estimates for 2006 total 795 million single track downloads. The market for music downloads to mobile phones (ring tones, full track downloads, etc.) is estimated to be not far behind music downloads in value. These digital sales brought in \$1.1 billion globally, tripling in value from 2004 during 2006 total sales had nearly doubled to \$2 billion: see *IFPI: 06 Digital Music Report p 3* and *IFPI: 07 Digital Music Report p.4.*

2 'Arctic Monkeys race to top of the tree', *The Times* 30 January 2006; 'Stage Graft'. *The Independent* 3 February 2006. Songs from *Whatever People Say I Am, That's What I'm Not*, their no. 1 album, are not available as ring tones, nor are their compositions offered for advertising.

3 'Record buyers Go Crazy for new Number 1', *The Times* 1 April 2006.

buy an entire 'classic' album rather than purchase individual tracks.[4] Other developments in the British music industry indicate a shift away from traditional models of music distribution. Radiohead initially released the album *In Rainbows* via digital download only, with fans being able to decide how much to pay for the album. While surveys indicate that fans may, on average, have paid as little as £4 (with one third of fans paying nothing at all),[5] it is generally thought that by stripping away the margins normally afforded to the record companies and retailers, Radiohead still netted increased profits as well as considerable kudos amongst Internet music users. Nor is this kind of marketing model being used exclusively by major and established acts who have, like Radiohead, been able to break free from record labels. Indie band The Crimea gave away its second album, *Secrets of the Witching Hour* in 2007, the band being only one of many acts which have realized that the revenue opportunities being afforded to touring, live performances and merchandising outstrip record sales by some distance.[6] Any perusal of social networking sites such as Facebook will show up the importance of this kind of marketing and distribution mechanism, often encapsulated in the fact that fans are able to access music legally and for free. Indeed, bands likes Koopa have broken into the singles charts without a record deal of any kind, relying heavily on social networking sites to publicise and distribute their works, often by actively encouraging fans to share music files with friends as part of their social experience that Facebook, etc. seek to foster. Of course, where a sound recording copyright is involved, MySpace and Facebook etc. will no doubt seek and obtain licenses, but this may not always be necessary

File sharing is not *per se* illegal; it also benefits creators and right holders by meeting consumer demand. Some right holders and other entities in the entertainment products distribution chain may not like the way in which digital distribution and greater consumer choice have challenged traditional markets – for example, the impact of direct download and on-demand services on the retail industry – but the process is irreversible.

This chapter seeks to explore the file-sharing phenomenon in the context of international copyright norms and the response that the activities of file sharers have provoked from the music industry and national courts. Its focus, given that the legal response is rooted in individual jurisdictions, is the law of the UK and Ireland, although case law from other jurisdictions is examined.

---

4 'Downloads make hit singles again'. Available at www.washingtonpost.com/wp-dgn/article/2006/02/07

5 'How much is Radiohead's online album worth? Nothing at all, say a third of fans'. *The Times* 11 October 2007.

6 'Album giveaway could ignite music revolution', *The Guardian* 30 April 2007.

What emerges is a much more complex picture of the liability issues that litigation has generated, with a greater number of potential actors being caught up in potential liability scenarios than was previously thought. While many commentators have rightly questioned whether right holders have sufficiently appreciated the opportunities afforded by new methods of music transfer – often blaming market failure for encouraging illegal copying by users – there are signs that the courts are coming to grips with file sharing. However, signs of structural change are appearing in the way in which issues of online liability and immunity are addressed, with consequences for the future operation of ISPs. Indeed, some decisions explore the possibility of allocating both the risk and liability in a much more horizontal way than the early stages of the debate on file sharing could possibly have anticipated, drawing attention in numerous jurisdictions to the possibility that acts of infringement of copyright can be impeded, if not negated entirely, by technical measures at a variety of levels.

A KEY COPYRIGHT CONCEPT

Apart from protection under traditional copyright laws, in national legislation, Art. 8 of the 1996 WIPO Copyright Treaty provided additional protection to the authors of works, this being the following:

> the exclusive right of authorising any communication to the public of their works by wire or wireless means including the making available to the public of their works in such a way that members of the public may access these works from a place and at a time individually chosen by them.

This provision, replicated in the WIPO Performances and Phonograms Treaty, Arts. 10 and 14 for performers[7] and phonogram producers[8] respectively, is reinforced by the European Union Information Society Directive.[9] And von Lewinski, commenting on the 1996 Treaties shortly after they were agreed, opined that, as to their application to new technologies, 'the WIPO treaties are probably even more advanced and adapted to the current technologies than any national law'.[10]

---

7 See Art. 2(a) for the definition of performers.

8 See Arts. 2(b) and 2(d) for definitions of 'phonogram' and 'phonogram producer' respectively.

9 Directive 2001/29, Art. 3. Earlier EU legislation in the form of the Rental and Lending Right Directive, Directive 92/100, contained in Art. 9 a distribution right limited to the physical distribution of a work or copies of the work.

10 (1997) 28 IIC 203, 207–208.

These Articles provide a clear basis for protecting authors' works and sound recordings from piracy and unauthorised online transfer. Before the adoption of the WIPO Treaty, online dissemination (to use a legally neutral word) of copyright works created several conceptual difficulties for judges as definitions and terms of art that were apt earlier in the previous century do not make sense in a digital environment. The reproduction of a work, the publication of a work, the distribution of a work, and the broadcasting of a work are the four cornerstones of liability, but their late 20th century relevance was problematical. When a work exists solely in an electronic format, some jurisdictions have found it difficult to hold that the replication of the work in that form is an infringing act.[11] While these cases reflect in part the failure of national legislatures to keep statutes in step with international treaties, delays in the implementation of treaty obligations can and do occur. Moreover, on the difficult political issue of defining reproduction, the international community failed to produce a definition (the 1996 Geneva treaties contain something less than a satisfactory outcome on this point).[12] On the issue of ISP liability through the communication of a work to the public, however, Art. 8 of the WIPO Copyright Treaty is fleshed out by an Agreed Statement which provides that the provision of physical facilities does not amount to a communication within the treaty or the Berne Conventions. The Hague Court of Appeal referred to this in *Church of Spiritual Technology v Dataweb BV* in dismissing copyright infringement actions against website hosts, the court holding that 'service providers only provide the technical facilities for others to expose information. Therefore it does not seem right to consider them as being equivalent to publishers'.[13] A French court reached a similar conclusion,[14] but it is the Supreme Court of Canada that has most authoritatively analysed the legal characteristics of online distribution of copyright works. This decision is important, given that Canada at the relevant time had not ratified the 1996 Treaties.

[11] See e.g. Ireland in cases like *News Datacom Ltd v Lyons* [1994] 1 ILRM 450 (smartcards) and *Gormley v EMI* [1999] 1 ICRM 154 (tape recorded speech not a work).

[12] The failure of the 1996 WIPO Diplomatic Conference to flesh out the reproduction right was in part ameliorated by the Agreed Statement concerning Art. 1(4).

[13] [2004] ECDR 258 [269].

[14] *Perathoner v S. Joseph Société Free* [2003] ECDR 76. See generally Gervais (2001) 34 *Vand J Transnat'l L* 1363.

SOCAN: THE COPYRIGHT BOARD AND APPEAL COURT DECISIONS

Canadian Association of Internet Providers v Society of Composers, Authors and Music Publishers of Canada (SOCAN)[15] resulted from SOCAN's application to the Canadian Copyright Board for approval of a tariff scheme that permitted access to the SOCAN repertoire via an ISD telecommunications service at a time and place selected by the subscriber/user. Initially, SOCAN argued that virtually everyone involved in the transmission chain would be required to pay royalties to SOCAN. SOCAN later resiled from this position vis-à-vis infrastructure service providers (for example, Bell), the 'backbone service providers', but the claim was prosecuted against ISPs. SOCAN also claimed entitlement to collect the tariff against all ISPs located in Canada, irrespective of where the transmission originated.

The legislative background to the SOCAN proceedings can be found in the Canadian Federal statute, The Copyright Act,[16] a traditional copyright statute based on the UK's Copyright Acts 1911 (the Imperial Statute) and 1956. However, although Canada had not then adopted the 1996 WIPO Treaties on the 'making available' right,[17] SOCAN argued that the ISPs were communicating works to the public – individual end-users – or authorising content providers to infringe copyright by 'hosting' unauthorised files on servers. In addition, SOCAN argued that certain acts by the ISPs infringed the reproduction right: when an ISP gives an end-user access to a website end-user via a telecommunications network, the end-user's request creates a stored copy, which is made as a matter of technical necessity. While these copies are normally deleted within hours, the effect of another user requesting access to the same work may be that the browser of the ISP directs that second user to the cached copy rather than the original website on the remote server, this being cheaper and faster. The effect of caching on liability was, thus, an important element in the SOCAN proceedings.

The Canadian Parliament provided in s. 2.4(1)(b) of the Copyright Act that, in relation to the act of communication of a work to the public by telecommunication,

> a person whose only act in respect of the communication of a work or other subject-matter to the public consists of providing the means of telecommunication neces-

---

15 Copyright Board of Canada (1999) 1 CPR (4th) 417: Federal Court of Appeal, (2002) 215 DLR (4th) 118.

16 RSC 1985, c C-42, amended by 1988, c 65.

17 The treaties had been signed but not ratified.

> sary for another person to so communicate the work or other subject matter does not communicate that work or other subject-matter to the public.[18]

The Copyright Board considered that an Internet communication occurs when the work is transmitted from the host server to the end-user's computer and that the end-user's access to the file is irrelevant. As to whether the ISP participates in the transmission, the Board held that s. 2.4(1)(b) directs that an ISP does not communicate the work if its only act is to provide the means of communication necessary for another person to communicate. The Board however extended the immunity to ISP activities vis-à-vis the cached files where the cache is created solely for improving system performance. The Board also held that proof that the ISP knew that its facilities might be used by others to infringe copyright did not constitute 'authorising' infringement. SOCAN sought judicial review of this decision. The Federal Court of Appeal, by a 2:1 majority, ruled that s. 2.4(1)(b) did not provide immunity for the ISP in respect of caches of music files; such caches are not a practical necessity. S. 2.4(1)(b) directs that the communication must be necessary, while merely effecting improvements in terms of speed and cost of access are not within the section.

SOCAN in the Supreme Court of Canada

The Supreme Court of Canada,[19] by an 8:1 majority (Le Bel J dissenting in part), dismissed the appeal on the jurisdictional issue of when an Internet communication takes place in Canada, but upheld the ISPs' arguments on the scope of s. 2.4(1)(b). The Court's analysis clarifies many issues addressed later in the file sharing cases. The judgment of the majority, delivered by Binnie J, reflects an awareness of the approach adopted in jurisdictions that have specifically legislated for ISP immunity and liability, the provisions of s. 2.4(1)(b) being interpreted in accord with the more 'tailored' foreign legislative texts.

Binnie J did not view s. 2.4(1)(b) as providing an ISP with immunity. Rather, the section says that:

> such intermediaries are deemed, for purposes of the Copyright Act, not to communicate the work to the public at all. Whether or not intermediaries are parties to the communication for legal purposes other than copyright is an issue that will have to be decided when it arises.[20]

---

18 RSC 1985, c C-42.

19 (2004) 240 DLR (4th) 193.

20 18 ibid 224.

Binnie J viewed s. 2.4(1)(b) as requiring a 'balanced reading', suggesting that this provision's roots lay in the innocent dissemination defences in defamation.[21] After focusing on the word 'necessary' in the section and the legislative history, he concluded that an act is necessary 'if the means are reasonably useful and proper to achieve the benefits of enhanced economy and efficiency'. Agreeing with the Board that 'means' are not to be confined to routers and other hardware but could extend to software connection equipment, hosting and other facilities and services, Binnie J observed:

> So long as an Internet intermediary does not itself engage in acts that relate to the content of the communication, i.e. whose participation is content neutral, but confines itself to providing a 'conduit' for information communicated by ethers, then it will fall within section 2.4(1)(b).[22]

He cited, with apparent approval, the Board's conclusions that, with respect to most transmissions, 'only the person who posts a musical work communicates it' and that 'the content provider effects the communication'.

Binnie J then suggested that 'mere conduit' status will be scrutinized by the courts in appropriate cases, citing both Art. 8 of the WIPO Copyright Treaty and Recital 42 of the EC Electronic Commerce Directive.[23] Noting that lack of knowledge is not a defence to copyright liability, the opposite could well be a basis for denying protection under s. 2.4(1)(b): the presence of such knowledge [that illegal files are held] would be a factor in the evaluation of the conduit status of an Internet Service Provider. [24]

Thus, the Supreme Court of Canada both provided an analysis of who is an infringer in an online transmission and proposed that any immunity, whether based on a specific statute or as a matter of general law, may need a 'balanced' analysis rather than a blanket application in favour of either right owner or ISP.

SOCAN bridges earlier case law, in which conduit status generally afforded an immunity,[25] and the more pragmatic position reached in the file-sharing cases. Binnie J clearly considered that the balance of interests of users and right holders could best be served by following the knowledge of infringing materials and notice and take down procedure found in the Electronic Commerce Directive.[26] Viewed in this light, the file-sharing cases are more

---

21 (2004) 240 DLR (4th) 193 [224].

22 (2004) 240 DLR (4th) 193 [226].

23 Directive 2000/31.

24 (2004) 240 DLR (4th) 193 [232].

25 See in particular the *Supreme Court of Canada, Electric Despatch Co. of Toronto v Bell Telephone* (1891) 20 SCR 83 at 91, cited at (2004) 240 DLR (4th) 193 [227].

26 (2004) 240 DLR (4th) 193 [232].

straightforward because those who provide website links to software, or to music files, often do so knowing that there is a high probability that the content is illegal; motivation may often be attributed to personal gain via advertising revenues that require users to access illegal files in order to maximize revenue.

RELEVANT INFRINGEMENT PROVISIONS IN UK AND IRISH LAW

Both UK and Irish copyright law follow the same pattern in making provision for acts of primary and secondary infringement. The copying of a work, the making available to the public of a work, and the adaptation of a work are primary infringing acts.[27] Acts of secondary infringement involve dealings with infringing copies through acts of importation, sale, or other distribution.[28] In the context of electronic transmission, common law courts have been asked to consider whether the use of information, or a work, falls within a particular word or phrase. For example, in *Reform Party of Canada*,[29] it was held that the posting of a work on a website could be 'publishing' or 'broadcasting', although a later decision of the Ontario Court of Appeal cast some doubt on this vis-à-vis the issue of broadcasting: *Bahleida v Santa*.[30] In *CCH Canadian Ltd v Law Society of Upper Canada*[31] the Supreme Court of Canada ruled that the facsimile transmission of the single copy of a work is not a communication to the public of that work, while the Supreme Court of New South Wales held that the sending by an employee of copies of confidential documents from his workstation to his home computer was not an act of communication to the public – but the transfer of the file may be an act of 'reproduction' until such time as the file is opened or deleted: *Woolworths Ltd v Olson*.[32]

While the 'making available' right in Art. 8 of the 1996 WCT goes some way towards clarifying that authors enjoy such rights, this provision does not resolve questions of when, how, and by whom the making available right is engaged. Several European decisions demonstrate that the courts struggle to

27 Copyright Designs and Patents Act 1988, ss. 22–27, as amended; (UK) Copyright and Related Rights Act 2000, ss. 37–43 (IRL).

28 Copyright, Designs, and Patents Act 1988, ss. 22–27 (UK); Copyright and Related Rights Act 2000, ss. 44–48 (IRL).

29 *Reform Party of Canada v Western Union Insurance Co.* (1998) 3 CPR(4th) 289.

30 (2003) 233 (4th) 382.

31 (2004) 236 DLR (4th) 395; see Gervais (2004) 18 IPJ 131.

32 (2004) 63 IPR 258 (New South Wales).

fit file sharing into pre-Internet terminology such as acts of 'performance' and 'distribution'[33] of a work. Even where the 'making available' right is transposed into national law, the trend in most common law jurisdictions is to use the concept of authorization of infringement, a concept that exists independently[34] of primary infringement in the legislation of jurisdictions such as Ireland, Australia, Canada, and the UK.[35] The attraction of using the 'authorisation' concept is that the defendant may not actually participate in the infringing act but, where that person facilitates infringement by others, or sanctions or approves of such conduct, liability may result. In a recent case, a party who instructed the employees of another to 'data mine' the plaintiff 's database had committed an act of authorisation for which he could be personally liable.[36] The utility of the 'authorisation' concept is evidenced by the fact that, in the US file-sharing cases, the courts have had to resort to basic common law concepts such as vicarious infringement and contributory infringement, as well as devising a notion of inducement, in order to visit liability on the defendants.[37] In many European jurisdictions, the courts also had to rely on general principles of civil liability, such as whether the facilitation of file sharing can provide the basis for liability as an accessory.[38] The general result appears to be that liability will be imposed if the primary infringer, in this case, the downloader, does not have a defence such as private use (the conclusion reached in Bruvik, which also discussed the possibility of contributory infringement). Thus, the gap between civil law solutions to this new problem and the line of authority in the US may not be significant, at least in terms of finding common approaches to the issues.

CIVIL LIABILITY FOR ONLINE TRANSMISSIONS GENERALLY

The general issue of civil liability for online transmissions containing illegal

---

33 See e.g. *Bruvik v EMI Norsk SA* [2005] ECDR 331; see also Krog (2006) 22 CLSR 73.

34 Gummow J in *WEA International Inc. v Hanimex Corporation* (1987) 17 FCR 274.

35 Authorization of infringement first appeared in the Copyright Act 1911, s. 1(2).

36 *Nominet UK v Diverse Internet* (2004) 63 IPR 543 (Western Australia).

37 US Senate Bill s. 2560 posited a new basis for liability. For a discussion of this Bill in the context of Grokster see Band (2005) *Computer and Internet Lawyer* 22: 1

38 *KODA v Lauritzen and Egeberg* [2002] ECDR 25 (Denmark); *Bruvik v EMI Norsk* [2005] ECDR 332 (Norway).

material, before the Electronic Commerce Directive,[39] generally arose from defamation actions. Early US case law on website postings employed an analogy with established principles. Was the ISP a publisher or merely the equivalent of the news vendor or delivery boy? The conclusion was that an ISP that transmitted content of which it had no knowledge, or which it did not create or control (for example, by editing content), could not lead to liability. Clearly, the content provider would be liable but ISP immunity was initially afforded via case law in the USA[40] and later put onto a firmer statutory footing.[41]

In the UK, defamation was addressed by legislation in the Defamation Act 1996, s. 1(1) of which provided a network provider or a service provider with a defence in defamation proceedings if it could show that it was not the author, editor, or publisher of the statement, had taken reasonable care in relation to the publication and did not know, and had no reason to believe that it had caused or contributed to a defamatory statement. Morland J considered that provision in *Godfrey v Demon Internet*,[42] where an ISP sought to rely on it in proceedings concerning defamatory material in an email posted on a server maintained by the defendant. The defendant did not respond to the claimant's requests to take down the statement, which was deleted automatically 10 days after being posted. Morland J held that, under English common law, the ISP was liable as a publisher and that, while s. 1 of the 1996 Act afforded a defence, the defendant did not come within it because it could not show that it had taken reasonable care in relation to the publication and could not show that it did not know, and had no reason to believe, that what it did caused or contributed to the defamatory publication.[43] More recently, the English High Court, in *Bunt v Tilley*[44] distinguished Godfrey on the basis that the three ISP defendants merely afforded access to the Internet with the defamatory content complained of being hosted by entities such as Google via a Usenet service. Eady J took the view that common law liability would require a plaintiff to establish 'knowing involvement in the process of the publication of the relevant words' and whether the defendants had been notified of the words complained of in such a way as to render them subsequently responsible for the publication. On the facts, none of the three ISP defendants triggered these tests, unlike the defendant in Godfrey. It is particularly noteworthy that, in

---

39 Directive 2000/31.

40 The classic cases are *Stratton Oakmont v Prodigy Services Co.* (1995) 23 *Media L.Rep.* 1794 and *Cubby v Compuserve* 776 F Supp 135 (1991).

41 Communications Decency Act 1996 (47 USC s 230 et seq.). See generally Voelzke (2003), *Computer and Internet Lawyer* 22: 4.

42 [2001] QB 201.

43 As required by s. 1(5).

44 [2006] EWHC 407 QB.

Godfrey, Morland J considered that both US case law and the US statutory immunity were much broader than that afforded to an ISP under English law but the Defamation Act 1996 solution, as well as US legislative initiatives, clearly influenced the shaping of the European 'solution' to online civil liability in the form of the Directive.

THE ELECTRONIC COMMERCE DIRECTIVE

The European Commission, influenced by other jurisdictions (especially the US) towards affording either limited or general immunities to network providers and ISPs, promoted what eventually became the Electronic Commerce Directive.[45] The relevant UK regulations[46] apply, inter alia, to the Copyright, Designs, and Patents Act 1988. In essence, these regulations, and their Irish counterpart,[47] provide the following:

- there is no liability where an ISP does not initiate the transmission, select the recipient or select or modify the information ('mere conduit' defence);
- there is no liability for the automatic, intermediate and temporary storage of information for the sole purpose of more efficient onward transmission (caching defence);
- there is no liability for storing information at the request of another if an ISP does not have actual knowledge of the activity and, where damages are sought, is not aware of facts or circumstances from which the unlawful activity is apparent, or when informed or aware of the illegal content acts expeditiously to remove or disable access to the information (the hosting defence).

While there are some textual differences between the Irish and UK regulations in terms of the mode of expression, the Directive clearly was intended to provide some form of protection against claims that an ISP may be liable for infringement of copyright by, inter alia, storing, transmitting, or caching illegal music files or audio-visual works. Insofar as there is no case law on ISP liability per se, the Directive has been successful, but the obiter statements of Eady J in *Bunt v Tilley* are extremely important in the light of subsequent

---

[45] 2000/31.

[46] The Electronic Commerce (EC Directive) Regulations 2002 (2013/2002) (as amended by 1178/3005) Articles 17–19.

[47] European Communities (Directive 2000/31/EC) Regulations 2003 (SI 2003/68).

developments such as *SCRL Société Belge des Auteurs Compositeurs et Editeurs v SA Scarlet*[48] (hereafter *Scarlet*). In dealing with the complainant's observations that the Directive denied him justice by extending too broad a form of immunity, Eady J responded:

> the regulations would not preclude the grant of an injunction in a proper case. It is concerned to restrict financial and penal sanctions. ... looking at the matter more broadly, it is clear to me that the injunctive relief sought by the claimant is wholly disproportionate to any conceivable legitimate advantage. He seems to be applying for an order preventing any supply of services to the relevant defendant. That would be draconian and pointless, since the individual defendants would be able to obtain such services with great ease elsewhere.

PRE-DIRECTIVE EUROPEAN CASE LAW

Before the Directive's Article 14 hosting 'shelter', ISPs faced significant exposure in Europe. In *Hi Bit Software GmbH v AOL Bertelsmann Online GmbH,*[49] the Landgericht Munich 1 observed that, while knowledge of illegal content being downloaded was within the capacity of the ISP (by use of text editors to open files), no such capacity or knowledge could per se be imputed to the uploading of files. On appeal,[50] the Oberlandesgericht Munich rejected this distinction, holding that AOL, 'opening a forum to facilitate its subscribers in exchanging musical works and sound recordings',

> was issuing nothing short of an invitation to infringement of copyright and ancillary rights on a grand scale ... the defendant's conduct thus amounted in general and with regard to the titles which are the subject matter of the dispute to gross negligence, if not even eventual intent.[51]

However, liability will not result if the ISP merely hosts content without, as in *Hi Bit*, having any knowledge of illegal copyright material, and the ISP acts expeditiously to disable access when furnished with adequate details of unlawful material. French case law[52] suggests a distinction between defendants who host content as distinct from providing a link to content hosted elsewhere. The common law jurisdictions reflect this distinction between positive inducement of others to file share (as in *HiBit*) and a general awareness that the defendant's

---

48 [2007] ECDR 320.

49 [2001] ECDR 375; see also *Koubareli v Volotas and Forthnet* SA [2003] ECDR 19.

50 [2001] ECDR 375.

51 [2001] ECDR 375, 393–394, 14 December 2000.

52 *Perathoner v S. Joseph Société Free* [2003] ECDR 76 (Paris).

facilities may be used by others to share files. While there has been no reported case law on file sharing in the UK, other common law jurisdictions have been hotbeds of file-sharing litigation. The US decisions in *Grokster*[53] and *Napster*[54] have the most high profile in the file-sharing arena, but recent Australian case law may be of greater clarity and relevance than *Grokster,* for example, at least to common law jurisdictions

THE AUSTRALIAN CASES AND EUROPEAN COUNTERPARTS

The Federal Court of Australia, in Universal Music *Australia Pty Ltd v Cooper*[55] was first to consider issues of liability, where an ISP could not be shown to have directly loaded infringing files on to his server, but it could be shown that users had access to facilities, provided at the behest of the defendant, enabling users to exchange files containing infringing works. Cooper operated a website under the domain name mp3s4free.net. Cooper made a commercial arrangement with an ISP that gave him free hosting facilities in exchange for revenue-sharing in respect of 'hits' made to mp3s4free.net and advertising royalties paid to Cooper. The evidence indicated that users accessed music files by logging on to the website, accessing and downloading music by clicking hyperlinks that transferred the user to 'free' songs on the basis of criteria such as 'Billboard 50', 'Popular Artist', or the alphabetical arrangement of an artist's name or song title. The files in question were not held on Cooper's website. In the view of Tamberlin J, Cooper could not be held to have communicated the work to mp3s4free.net's users. Tamberlin J was *not* satisfied that:

> the Cooper website has 'made available' the music sound recordings within the meaning of that expression. It is the remote websites which make available the sound recordings and from which the digital music files are downloaded as a result of a request transmitted to the remote website.[56]

Similar reasoning has also been applied in Europe. In *KODA v Lauritzen and*

---

[53] 125 S Ct 2764. The subsequent reaction to *Grokster* was immense; e.g. Blakeney [2006] CTCR 55; Ganley [2006] EIPR 15; Hogberg (2006) 106 *Col LR* 909; Radcliffe 22 CLSR 137. 50.

[54] *A&M Records, Inc. v Napster* 239 F 3d 1004 and 284 F 3d 1091 (2002).

[55] (2005) 65 IPR 409, exhaustively reviewed by Hyland at (2005) 10(5) *Comms. Law* 157.

[56] (2005) 65 IPR 409 [424].

Egeberg,[57] the Vestre Landset, Denmark, found that when two children who maintained their own websites created links directly to infringing music files, they were liable as principals and accessories to infringement. The reasoning on principal liability is difficult to reconcile with the Swedish Supreme Court decision in *Public Prosecutor v Olssen*[58] where it was held that making a link is not an act of distribution. The controversial Dutch decision in *Vereniging Buma, Stichting Stemra v Kazaa*[59] may have broader precedent value, the Court of Appeals holding that Kazaa was not liable for the actions of others because the facilitation of infringement by third parties was not of itself an act of publication, nor was such conduct an act of reproduction in its own right.

The best-known 'first generation' file-sharing decision is that of the Ninth Circuit Court of Appeals in *A&M Records, Inc. v Napster*,[60] the leading decision arising out of 'the notorious file-sharing service Napster'.[61] Napster permitted members of the Napster Community of users, following sign-up and the downloading of free software from site, to search and download music from the hard drives and servers of other Napster users. Napster provided both user support and indexing facilities via its central registry. While it was not in dispute that Napster was a primary infringer, Napster sought to counteract allegations of contributory and vicarious infringements by arguing that, since its users did not infringe copyright, no case for its secondary liability could be made out. Fair use defences in respect of the sampling of music files were rejected, as was a defence of time shifting.

The Court of Appeals for the Ninth Circuit has handed down a fairly pro-user decision on linking, *Kelly v Arriba Soft Corporation*.[62] Although fair use did not feature in the Ninth Circuit's later decision in *Grokster*,[63] *Napster* is rooted in the factual link between the activities of Napster in directly stimulating infringement by its users and the common law concepts of contributory and vicarious infringement as the basis of civil liability. So, while the US approach to issues of secondary liability is constrained to use common law concepts to visit liability on file-share facilitators, other jurisdictions have specific statutory provisions than can be used in such context. The Copyright Act 1911 being the basis of Irish, Canadian, Australian, and New Zealand statutory traditions, the concept of infringement by authorising others to commit acts of primary infringement is an extremely important means of redress.

---

57 [2002] ECDR 25.
58 [2001] EDCR 303.
59 [2004] EDCR 183.
60 239 F 3d 1004 (2001); 284 F 3d 1091 (2002).
61 Per Souter J in *MGM v Grokster* 125 S Ct 2764 (2005).
62 336 F 3d 811 (2003).
63 380 F 3d 1154 (2004).

In the classical sense, authorisation of infringement is made out by showing that the primary infringer has the benefit of another person's 'sanction, approval or countenance'. Case law makes it clear that mere knowledge that another person may infringe copyright is not enough to constitute acts of authorisation and that the person having authorised infringement may only do so where he or she has the necessary power to control the infringing act. Thus, hiring out sound recordings in the knowledge that hirers may make copies in the privacy of the home will not make the hirer an authoriser,[64] nor does the sale of a tape recorder, even on the foot of advertising copy that refers to copying, make the seller of that equipment an authoriser (although this decision is borderline[65]). Nevertheless, *Universal Music Australian Pty Ltd v Cooper*[66] supports the view that the provision of file-sharing facilities may be acts of authorisation if the putative authoriser is shown to have sufficient control over both the user accessing the website and any remote operator placing hyperlinks on it. Cooper did not monitor users to see if the files being downloaded were legal, nor did he scrutinise those linking to his site for illegal content. As such, Cooper was held to have infringed copyright by authorising both downloading by users and of the making available of illegal files by operators of remote websites.

At the heart of *Cooper* is a notion of authorisation that is rooted in the failure to exercise control over others. The Australian cases in particular stress the possibility that authorisation may occur by omission: where a defendant has 'abstained from action which under the circumstances then existing it would have been reasonable to take, or . . . exhibited a degree of indifference . . . ',[67] permission may be inferred. Canadian case law has specifically rejected this reasoning[68] and it has yet to find favour in England because it is incompatible with *Amstrad*. However, as a recent New Zealand Court of Appeal decision points out, *Amstrad* was a case on its particular facts, where the defendant had no control over the domestic use of a technology that could be put to substantial non-infringing uses as well as infringing ones.[69] In the file-sharing cases,

---

64 *CBS Inc. v Ames Records and Tapes* [1982] Ch 91.

65 *CBS Songs v Amstrad Consumer Electronics* [1988] AC 1013. Sale of smart cards that may be used to illegally decrypt a broadcast signal may also infringe according to Canadian case law (which is generally more pro-user that Australian case law): see *Columbia Pictures Industries Inc. v Frankl* (2004) 36 CPR (4th) 342, *Columbia Pictures Industries Inc. v Gaudreault* [2006] FCA 29.

66 (2005) 65 IPR 409. For a recent Dutch counterpart, see *BREIN v Techno Design 'Internet Programming' BV* [2006] ECDR 21 (Court of Appeal, Amsterdam).

67 Knox CJ in *Adelaide Corporation v APRA* (1920) 40 CLR 481 at 488, approved in Moorhouse (1975) 133 CLR 1 and *Cooper* (2005) IPR 409.

68 *Moorhouse v University of New South Wales* (1975) 133 CLR 1.

69 *Heinz Wattie's Ltd v Spantech Property* (2005) 67 IPR 666.

the courts have held that the defendant had the capacity both to monitor use and restrict (albeit imperfectly) access to illegal files. *Amstrad* does not represent a barrier to the use of the authorisation of infringement concept by an English court and the obiter statements of Binnie J in *SOCAN*[70] do not suggest an aversion to finding that an ISP has authorised infringement in specific circumstances.

GROKSTER AND AUSTRALIAN LAW

In *Grokster*, the Supreme Court borrowed heavily from patent law to formulate an inducement test that could form the basis of secondary liability (while retaining the earlier *Sony* decision on dual use[71]). The critical issues that led to expanding liability far beyond *Napster* were the defendants' desire to benefit from the termination of Napster's unlawful service, the failure to use filtering technologies to frustrate infringing use by Grokster users, and a revenue model that incentivised high volume use, much of which was directed at replicating copyright material without permission. Although the Australian Federal Court in *Universal Music Australia Pty Ltd v Sharman License Holdings Ltd*[72] found *Grokster* 'to be of little assistance',[73] given legal and factual differences between the US and Australian litigation, the result and conclusions reached are virtually identical. In both, the court concluded that provision of facilities per se will not trigger liability, but knowledge of third-party use of a service that in terms of cumulative use may threaten a copyright industry, may require the service provider to adopt measures to restrict infringing use. This will certainly be so where the service provider advertises or publicises the service as having this illegal capacity, and the success of its business model adopted is predicated on levels of infringing use.

For a service provider seeking to avoid liability for copyright infringement, the critical feature of Kazaa technology was the apparent absence of a central register of infringing copies, and that no infringing copies were held by Kazaa. The technological problem of facilitating a Kazaa 'node' to access a music file, without a central register, was solved by building into Kazaa the capacity to use the networking capacity of high capacity computers to which the individual 'node' was already linked (such as those of large corporations and universities). Such a facility, known as a 'supernode', provided the physical and geographical context within which groups of Kazaa users could both

70 (2004) 240 DLR (4th) 195, especially at 232–235.
71 *Sony Corp. v Universal City Studios Inc* 464 US 417 (1984).
72 (2005) 65 IPR 289, reviewed by Hyland at [2006] CTLR 98.
73 (2005) 65 IPR 289 at 301.

develop and interchange files. Kazaa technology also permitted a degree of information transfer between 'supernodes' in order to collate information on the number of Kazaa users and downloads.[74]

Wilcox J did not find that Sharman operated a central register (though he thought that this was a possibility); nor could the infringing acts of users be visited upon the defendants simply because the latter supplied the technology. There was however ample material on which liability as an authoriser could be made out. Wilcox J identified positive acts of approval[75] in the form of website promotions exhortations to users to use the facility and share shares, as well as promotional material that criticised right holders and their use of copyrights. When these statements were made, Sharman knew that most files accessed via Kazaa were illegal. As to whether Sharman infringed by tacit acts of authorisation, Wilcox J followed *Cooper*, holding that Sharman's financial interests were best served by not regulating user access as advertising revenues depended on high volume, use, and access restrictions would earn lower revenues. Like *Cooper*, some technical restrictions and other measures such as keyword filtering and allowing access to gold files predominantly would have reduced illegal file sharing, but Sharman took no such steps. While Sharman was given two months to put a number of technical and non-technical measures in place, the deadline came and went. Kazaa.com sought to restrict Australian users from downloading the software, the website carrying the banner notice: 'If you are in Australia, you must not download or use the Kazaa Media Desktop'. The Full Court of the Federal Court of Australia dismissed Sharman's appeal and proceedings for contempt of court have since commenced. Sharman Holdings may also face judicial proceedings in other jurisdictions.[76] Grokster itself has agreed to pay the entertainment industry US$50 million and close down its operations.[77] But while the record industry

74 Supernodes identified by the plaintiffs included a number of universities; for secondary infringement by universities see Harris (2004) 31 *Rutgers Computer and Tech. L.J.* 187.

75 This conclusion is not dissimilar to that reached in the German case of *Hi Bit Software GmbH v AOL Bertelsmann Online GmbH* [2001] ECDR 375.

76 *2005/2006 Copyright World No. 156, End of three-year battle.* The website www.grokster.com currently carries a message stating 'There are legal services for downloading music and movies. This is not one of them. Your IP address is [number] AND HAS BEEN LOGGED. Don't think you can't get caught. You are not anonymous'.

77 In California in 2003, proceedings against Sharman Networks brought by RIAA and MPAA persuaded the District Court to exercise jurisdiction. But, applying *Sony*, the court said that StreamCast was no different from a VCR or a photocopier; judgment of 25 April 2003 by California District Judge Stephen Wilson. In July 2006, Sharman Networks announced a $100 million settlement of worldwide litigation brought by the music and motion picture industries, opening the door to legitimate use of Kazaa technology to distribute works on a P2P basis.

continues to pursue software providers, persons providing links, and so on, following the somewhat belated success of the US *Grokster* case, and the *Sharman* decision in late 2005, the music industry has been fighting downloading on other fronts – in the offices, bedrooms, and studies of Internet users throughout the world.

FILE SHARERS AND PERSONAL LIABILITY

Those engaged in unauthorised file sharing are personally liable as copyright infringers in the absence of any defence such as private copying. The user who makes a copy of a music file available to others even if that file is legal[78] is likely to have authorised others to make an illegal copy or be responsible as a secondary infringer. A file sharer using Kazaa, for example, may also infringe the reproduction right by way of the copy made and held in 'my shared folder' file, as well as the making available right. But this author is unaware of any reported decisions in which these points have been finally determined.

The international music industry, particularly its representative organizations, has actively pursued file sharers in many jurisdictions. The International Federation of Phonogram and Videogram Producers (IFPI), an international record industry organization representing nearly 1500 record producers in 75 countries, has actively promoted litigation against file sharers. In April 2005, the CEO of IFPI, John Kennedy announced 950 new actions in 11 countries against file sharers. In April 2006, nearly 2000 new actions in 10 countries around the world were announced and by the end of 2006 legal actions were brought by IFPI affiliates against more than 10,000 individuals in 18 countries, including Brazil, Mexico, Poland and Portugal for the first time. The IFPI reproduce survey evidence that in Germany, for example, the proportion of Internet users frequently file sharing copyright music fell back from 13 per cent in 2004 to 'just' 8 per cent in 2006. While in the UK, the percentage in both 2004 and 2006 is some 11 per cent of Internet users.[79] The use of the courts to both educate and deter, a key consideration in IFPI strategy is highly visible but these claims to effectiveness are hard to measure.

It may be doubted whether these actions have this effect, at least in terms of the statistics. The Internet measurement company Big Champagne estimated that those engaged in P2P activity more than doubled from an estimated

---

[78] The US music industry apparently conceded that, if a music CD is lawfully purchased, it will be lawful for the purchaser to load it onto a PC or MP3 player, but copyright legislation in the USA and elsewhere does not reflect this. See comment by DB Verrilli, Counsel for MGM in *Grokster*, cited by Ganley [2006] EIPR 15 [19].

[79] *IFPI: 07 Digital Music Report* p. 18.

4,319,182 in September 2003 to 9,284,558 in September 2005.[80] Even at the level of national enforcement, civil actions may only have a temporary impact. For example, in Ireland, high profile proceedings brought against 17 alleged copyright infringers led to a judgment ordering ISPs to give the names and addresses of those individuals to the recording industry. The plaintiffs themselves conceded[81] that, while the campaign culminating in that judgment had some deterrent effect in early 2005, by July–September 2005 file sharing had actually increased, leading to a second round of actions against new downloaders. Even judges have opined that actions against users may not produce a deterrent effect. Wilcox J in *Sharman* considered that few Kazaa users knew or even cared about copyright law and that pursuit of individuals was ultimately a futile exercise.[82]

This tactic was undoubtedly used by industry in response to the negative decisions handed down in several high profile actions against Kazaa in the Netherlands, as well as to the position taken in the US courts before *Grokster* in June 2005. While *Grokster* and *Sharman* suggest that actions against software distributors now have an increased chance of success, the record industry appears to continue pursuing file sharers. However, the pursuit of 'serial infringers' is expensive, time-consuming, and potentially legally complex.

ANONYMITY AND THE INTERNET

The file sharer's identity is initially unknown to the right holder who has reason to believe that a user is engaged in illegal file sharing. The right holder must formulate a legal basis upon how to obtain the name and address of the subscriber from the ISP with whom the subscriber has contracted. In the common law world, applications to require an ISP to reveal the name and address of the subscriber rely on civil procedural rules of discovery, as in Canada,[83] or because the ISP is in possession of information which it is required to disclose. In the UK, an application procedure has evolved from the seminal decision in *Norwich Pharmacal v Customs and Excise Commissioners*[84] in which the House of Lords ruled that a person who, even

[80] See www.pcpro.co.uk/news/.
[81] Statement to High Court, Dublin, 23 January 2006.
[82] (2005) 65 IPR 289 at 372 per Wilcox J.
[83] See the equitable Civil Bill procedure in *BMG Canada Inc. v John Doe* (2005) 252 DLR (4th) 726.
[84] [1974] AC 13.

innocently,[85] gets mixed up in wrongdoing is obliged to assist the injured party by providing information about the identity of other persons, or other vital information.[86] The remedy is flexible: the courts set off the interest in ensuring that justice is done against the need[87] not to involve third parties in avoidable litigation.

The Irish Norwich Pharmacal File-sharing Decision

The balancing exercise required for *Norwich Pharmacal* applications takes on a specific character where the application is brought against ISPs.

In the context of file sharing, case law establishes that an ISP is not liable for copyright infringement by others[88] (the transposition of the Electronic Commerce Directive[89] affords ISPs in Ireland and elsewhere in the EU with a statutory immunity from liability for copyright infringement). But immunity does not excuse an ISP from compliance with the notice and take down procedure to remove infringing files from servers, given that such procedures have little or no impact upon the availability of identical files posted on other servers.

ISPs are engaged in the telecommunications industry. Irish law, for example, recognizes that, in respect of the provision of telecommunications services to citizens, the expectation of privacy enjoys constitutional status[90] and is afforded through statute.[91] While Irish case law suggests the privacy right arises in the context of voice telephony, there is no reason to confine that right. The Data Protection Acts 1988–2003 recognise that the right to privacy of personal data must be respected through the data protection principles, in particular that personal data must not be disclosed for purposes other than

---

85 The relief is available against wrongdoers also: *CHC Software Care v Hopkins and Wood* [1993] FSR 241; *Arsenal Football Club plc v Elite Sports* [2003] FSR 26.

86 *Carlton Film Distributors Ltd v MGN Ltd* [2002] FSR 47.

87 *Ashworth Hospital Authority v MGN Ltd* [2002] 1 WLR 2003; *Mitsui & Co. Ltd v Nexen Petroleum UK Ltd* [2005] EWHC 625 (Ch).

88 See e.g. *Perathoner v S. Joseph Société Free* [2003] ECDR 76; *Church of Spiritual Technology v Dataweb BV* [2004] ECDR 258.

89 Directive 2000/31, as transposed by SI 68 of 2003 in Ireland and by SI2002/2013 in the UK.

90 See *Kennedy v Ireland* [1987] IR 587; *Haughey v Moriarty* [1999]3 IR 1; *Cogley v RTE* [2005] 2 ICRH 529.

91 Section 98 of the Postal and Telecommunications Services Act 1983 makes it an offence, without lawful authority, to intercept a telecommunications message. On 7 July 2006, the Irish Government published a Privacy Bill (no 44 of 2006) that introduces a statutory tort of violation of privacy. A relevant defence is that the action was undertaken by way of court (or other lawful) process – clause 5(1)(b).

those for which the personal data was legitimately obtained. Other data protection principles such as the security principle are also relevant.

The fact that ISPs may compile user records that reveal a considerable amount of information about an individual user was recognized in 2001 when the Irish government added ISPs to the list of data controllers who must register with the Data Protection Commissioner.[92] *In BMG Canada Inc v John Doe*,[93] the Canadian Federal Court of Appeal indicated that the balance between the protection of privacy and the rights of intellectual property owners would generally turn upon the force of the perceived threat to the integrity of intellectual property rights. BMG Canada Inc. sought Norwich Pharmacal-type orders against numerous ISPs (the applicants). Having identified 29 file sharers who had each downloaded over 1000 songs, BMG sought the names and addresses of those persons, providing the ISPs with the users' pseudonyms.[94] Noting that the traditional *Norwich Pharmacal* approach requires a balance between maintaining the integrity of confidential information and the protection of clearly established intellectual property rights which have been infringed, the Court lowered the threshold by requiring the plaintiff to establish a bona fide claim to be pursued and not a prima facie case of infringement of an intellectual property right. Sexton JA reasoned:

> Intellectual Property laws originated in order to protect the promulgation of ideas. Copyright law provides incentives for innovators – artists, musicians, inventors, writers, performers and marketers to create. It is designed to ensure that ideas are expressed and developed instead of remaining dormant. Individuals need to be encouraged to develop their own talents and personal expression of artistic ideas, including music. If they are robbed of the fruits of their efforts, their incentive to express their ideas in tangible form is diminished.
>
> Modern technology such as the Internet has provided extraordinary benefits for society, which includes faster and more efficient means of communication to wider audiences. This technology must not be allowed to obliterate those personal property rights which society has deemed important. Although privacy concerns must also be considered, it seems to me that they must yield to public concerns for the protection of intellectual property rights in situations where infringement threatens to erode those rights.[95]

Sexton JA emphasized that, if privacy rights are to be invaded, they must be invaded in the most minimal way. The order is unlikely to be granted if the applicant's proofs reveal a time lag between the investigation and the application because of the risk of 'stale' evidence of identity.

---

92 SI 2001/2.

93 (2005) 39 CPR (4th) 97 and (2005) 252 DLR (4th) 726, reversing the Motions Court decision at (2004) 239 DLR (4th) 726.

94 See e.g. *Geekboy@Kazaa.*

95 (2005) 39 CPR (4th) 97 at 115.

In making the order, the Court may be expected to impose strict conditions upon the applicant. In *BMG Canada,* the Federal Court stressed that the information disclosed should not be unrelated to copyright infringement and that specific directions should be given as to the type of information disclosed and its manner of use. Privacy should be respected by an order that the user be identified by initials or protected by a confidentiality order. Kelly J endorsed this approach in the Irish High Court in *EMI Records (Ireland) Ltd and Others v Eircom Ltd and BT Communications Ireland Ltd*[96] where four major record companies sought *Norwich Pharmacal* orders in respect of 17 habitual downloaders. Granting the orders, Kelly J found that the plaintiffs had established *prima facie* infringement and that no other recourse was available to obtain the names and addresses of the users. Noting the importance of duties of confidentiality owed by the defendants to their subscribers and the subscribers' rights of privacy, Kelly J held that these duties and rights:

> cannot be relied on by a wrongdoer or a person against whom there is evidence of wrongdoing to protect his or her identity. The right to privacy or confidentiality of identity must give way where there is prima facie evidence of wrong doing.[97]

Kelly J then built 'safeguards' into the order. The plaintiffs were required to undertake to use the information disclosed in compliance with the order only to obtain redress in respect of copyright infringement in the sound recordings covered by the plaintiff 's Irish license; thus, indicating that the information could not be transferred to a UK or US counterpart. The plaintiffs also undertook not to disclose the identities of the subscribers until the plaintiffs began to enforce their copyrights against those persons. Kelly J explained:

> This is being done in protection of the rights and entitlements of the subscribers because it may turn out that they were not in fact guilty of any wrongdoing or that the named person was not the operator at the time when the wrongdoing was in fact carried out.[98]

The defendants were held entitled to costs of the action (including the costs of actually making the disclosure) from the applicant.[99]

---

96 [2006] ECDR 40. For a robust Hong Kong counterpart, see *Cineplay Records Co Ltd v Hong Kong Broadband Network Ltd* [2006] 1 HKLRD 255.

97 Ibid 43.

98 Ibid 44. A second phase of actions commenced in late 2005, culminating in similar orders being made on 26 January 2006 (unreported).

99 Following the Court of Appeal (England and Wales) in *Totalise plc v Motley Fool Ltd* and *Interactive Investor* [2001] EWCA Civ 1897. A second set of proceedings brought in the Irish High Court in 2007 led to disclosure orders against seven ISPs: see IRMA to get web users' details' *Irish Times* 8 June 2007.

Some European Decisions on Discovery of Identity Orders

While these applications are part of the general law in the common law world, similar mechanisms are found in other jurisdictions. The Dutch courts have considered whether they have power to compel ISPs to disclose the identity of subscribers. The first such case was *BREIN and others v UPC Nederland BV, trading as Chello and Others.*[100] BREIN, an authors' collecting society, acting in conjunction with 50 record companies, sought orders against five ISPs for the names and addresses of file sharers with whom the ISPs had contracts and to whom IP addresses has been allocated. The Utrecht Court ruled that both the Electronic Commerce Directive[101] and the Enforcement Directive,[102] as well as Art. 6:196c of the Dutch Civil Code, required disclosure; even without a statutory basis for the application, 'under special circumstances it may be unlawful vis-à-vis Brein to refuse to make known these details because it constitutes a violation of a social obligation to exhibit due care that a service provider must bear in mind'. A later Dutch Supreme Court decision, *Lycos v Pessers,*[103] upheld the decision of the Court of Appeal as to whether a general duty exists. The Supreme Court endorsed this four criteria test:

1. it must be sufficiently plausible that the information is wrongful and harmful;
2. the third party must have a real interest in the information;
3. it must be plausible that the injured party does not have a less drastic method to retrieve the information; and
4. the interests at stake of the third party, the provider and the website owner must be weighed and the third party's interest must prevail.

These Dutch decisions are important because they demonstrate that the right to operate as an ISP can involve the observance of a duty of care and that the Electronic Commerce Directive far from creating an immunity in respect of these operations, will incline in the opposite direction. Recent Italian case law had inclined in favour of ISP disclosure orders although a definitive appellate decision is expected shortly.[104]

---

[100] Decision of the District Court of Utrecht of 12 July 2005, judgment translated into English by SOLV Advocaten: www.solv.nl.

[101] 2000/31.

[102] 2004/48.

[103] Decision of 25 November 2005. See the February 2006 newsletter of Kennedy Van der Laan available at www.kvdl.nl.

[104] See Prosperetti [2007] *Ent. L.R.* 280.

The Privacy Interest

It is widely reported that the French Data Protection Authority has ruled[105] that the automated monitoring of users of P2P file-sharing systems may not be permitted as it results in the accumulation of 'a massive collection of personal data' on the basis of exhaustive and continuous surveillance' of P2P sites that goes 'beyond that which is necessary for the fight against piracy'. [While the impact of the new French Copyright law remains to be assessed, the IFPI is optimistic[106] that data protection law does not bar discovery of identity orders in French courts.]

In contrast, when the issue of a right holder's ability to compel disclosure of the details of the person standing behind an IP address arises, personal privacy arguments have not succeeded in either the Irish or Canadian courts. In particular, the view of the English and Irish courts is that, because data protection legislation in each jurisdiction permits personal data to be obtained following court orders,[107] as long as the right holder uses a *Norwich Pharmacal* or similar civil procedure,[108] the ISP will be able to disclose personal data about suspected file sharers. In *EMI v Eircom*[109] Kelly J said, of the rights of privacy:

> the statutory entitlements, whether they arise under the Data Protection legislation of the Postal and telecommunications legislation are subject to a provision which permits the confidentiality to be legitimately breached by an order of the Court.[110]

While he conceded that the law did not prescribe the conditions under which an order may be made, the 'necessity' test vis-à-vis *Norwich Pharmacal* is flexible enough to afford a basis for such an order.

What may remain unexplored is the difficulty right holders may have in some jurisdictions in collecting evidence. Case law suggests that the standard methodology is to engage the US agency MediaSentry to monitor volume uses of MP3 files, taking a 10 minute snapshot of real-time users in order to identify

---

105 CNIL decision, 24 October 2005. See generally Richardson (2002) 13 JLIS 90 on misuse of discovery procedures.

106 See www.ifpi.org. A more pertinent issue is the survival of the private copying defence under French law, the current debate being reviewed by Hugo and Hugot [2006] *Ent L. R.* 139.

107 Data Protection Act 1998, s. 35 (UK); Data Protection Act 1988, s. 8(e) (Ireland).

108 See e.g. the relevant rules of civil procedure, discovery, etc. In England and Wales, see the Civil Procedure Rules.

109 [2006] ECDR 40.

110 Ibid 43.

potentially infringing file sharers on a high volume basis. In *BREIN*, the collection of personal data by MediaSentry on behalf of BREIN was held unlawful as MediaSentry had not signed up to the EU/US Safe Harbour Agreement. The Utrecht Court's ruling was upheld on appeal on the basis of MediaSentry's infringement of privacy and because the agency's software was not sophisticated enough to identify users or acts of infringement correctly.[111] This manner in which information is collected was also considered in *Sharman*, when Wilcox J put it to the MediaSentry witness: 'so what you are doing is, you are in effect spying on a person who is in the act of downloading'.[112]

In the context of Irish law, intrusive methods of collecting data may be challengeable under the privacy provisions in the EU Telecommunications Data Protection Directive,[113] as well as under the constitutional guarantee of privacy in respect of the communication of messages.[114] It is also uncertain whether right holders are illegally using telecommunications technology to intercept communications as MediaSentry, at the time of the interception, clearly had no authority to do this. Thus, one may need to distinguish between activities that employ privacy intrusive techniques to collect evidence[115] (no legal process having yet taken place) and a subsequent court application to complete the chain of evidence, to secure the names and addresses of persons behind the IP address. In the former case, serious statutory and constitutional law issues may need to be addressed.[116] Until more light is cast on the methods of data collection used initially to identify suspects by organizations such as MediaSentry, this uncertainty will remain.

At the level of national law, some European jurisdictions are alive to the possibility that right holders may seek to use rules of criminal procedure to compel the disclosure of personal data relating to suspected file sharers. For

---

111 Available at www.theregister.com/2006/07/14fileswappers_protected.

112 (2005) 65 IPR 289 at 348. The evidence admitted in *Sharman* revealed for example that users may be able to shelter behind firewalls. Some software applications to ensure anonymity are being researched. See e.g. www.freenet.sourceforge.net and www.relakks.com; Comber and Staple [2007] ECL & P 9(7), 9–11.

113 2002/58, as amended by Directive 2006/24, transposed in Ireland by SI 2003/535; for UK transposition see SI 2003/2426.

114 *Kennedy v Ireland* [1987] IR 587; *Atherton v DPP* [2006] 2 ILRM 153.

115 In the UK, see the Regulation of Investigatory Powers Act 2000, ss. 1–2.

116 For example, if the evidence is illegally or unconstitutionally obtained, English law contains an exclusionary discretion, case law indicating that any privacy intrusion is a relevant consideration for the court: see *Jones v University of Warwick* [2003] 3 All ER 760. In Irish law, there is a discretion in relation to illegally obtained evidence but a complete bar in unconstitutionally obtained evidence: see McGrath, *Evidence* (2005) Chapter 7. The leading case is *Universal City Studios v Mulligan* [1999] 3 IR 392.

example, even taking applications at face value, some German prosecutors have balanced the nature of the criminal offences relating to unlawful file sharing – often characterised as minor offences – with the need to protect personal privacy, finding that the balance rests in favour of refusing to order disclosure. Just as important is a willingness to look behind the criminal application in order to test the real motives of the right holder. The chief public prosecutor for Berlin, in an opinion dated 18 October 2006 accused the right holders of trying 'under cover of pretending to want to initiate criminal proceedings to obtain for free and by exploiting the limited resources of the prosecuting authorities and at the expense of the budget of the federal state of Berlin the personal data required for the successful pursuit of civil claims'.[117]

This balance has been recently explored by Advocate General Kokott, in *Productores de Musica de Espana Promusicae v Telefonica de Espana Sau.*[118] The net point that the Advocate General's Opinion makes is that Community law does not require that the privacy protections afforded by Directives 95/46/EC and 2002/58/EC are to be superseded by Enforcement Directive 2004/48/EC unless one of the overriding considerations in Art. 15(1) of Directive 2002/58/EC are satisfied such as public security or the investigation of criminal offences, although the Opinion is not very compelling on this point as Spanish law did not render file sharing a criminal offence, per se. What remains to be seen is whether the European Court of Justice will read into the process of reconciling the Enforcement Directive with the Data Protection Directives a requirement of proportionality: will the ECJ follow the Irish/Dutch view that file sharing is such a serious threat to property rights so as to require data protection to be brushed aside, or will a more cautious approach prevail, such as that favoured in Germany where infringement offences are not seen as heinous and the right holder is encouraged to pursue civil reliefs rather than seeking to transfer enforcement costs to the public purse in the form of 'bogus' criminal proceedings. It is of course in the very nature of right holders to lobby and press for greater clarity in the law and it might be that right holders may be aware that some collection techniques are legally suspect. In November 2005, the Creative and Media Business Alliance attempted to persuade the members of the European Parliament to extend the draft Data Protection Directive[119] to cover offences that arise from copyright infringement. This attempt failed,[120] the lobbying being attacked as both an

---

117 http//www.heise.de/English/newsticker/news/93759.

118 Case C – 275/06: Summarised at [2007] ECDR 390.

119 In 2005, the European Institutions put forward two texts, a Framework decision and a draft Directive. The Framework decision was rejected by the European Parliament.

120 The obligations to retain data and provide such data is reserved for 'the

infringement of civil liberties and an attempt to transfer the cost of protecting copyright from well funded industries to European taxpayers and telecoms subscribers.[121]

The advantage of data retention laws is that no court application is necessary – the entire process operates in a secretive environment. Lumping even serial file sharers into the same category as members of al-Qaeda shows just how irrational the file-sharers debate has become. Nevertheless, in the UK, the pursuit of individual file sharers continues.[122] The British Phonographic Industry launched a campaign to require disclosure of the names and addresses of 31 subscribers whose IP addresses had been used to engage in high volume file sharing in May 2005; while some subscribers settled subsequent claims for damages – estimated at around £2500 – others did not.[123] The High Court later ordered two men to pay a combined amount of £6500 in damages after both were held to have infringed the claimants' sound recording copyrights. A second phase of infringement proceedings commenced in December 2005 against another list of suspected file sharers.[124]

FILE SHARING: ISPS IN THE DOCK

Until recently, the position of ISPs in Europe has been relatively comfortable, enjoying a degree of immunity from liability due to the Electronic Commerce Directive and a widespread belief that ISPs have little or no knowledge or control over materials hosted or accessed by users of their services. *BREIN* in the Netherlands, and a highly publicized decision of the Danish Supreme Court, have raised the conflict to another level. In the Danish decision, the Danish Supreme Court ordered the telecommunications company TDC to

---

competent national authorities': Directive 2006/24 on the retention of data generated or processed in connection with the provision of publicly available electronic communications services or of public communications networks, 15 March 2006.

[121] See Music Industry seeks access to private data to fight piracy, *The Guardian*, 26 November 2005; Entertainment Industry trying to hijack data retention directive, available at www.news.zdnet.co.uk.

[122] This has attracted considerable publicity and comment, for example, in *The Guardian*, 25 June 2005, and in particular 'Is your child an Internet pirate? That'll be £4000' *The Times*, 7 June 2005.

[123] Subsequent claims for £4000 in damages were brought.

[124] Apart from music file-sharing actions brought by the music industry, the Federation Against Software Theft (FAST) obtained court orders against 10 ISPs, including Tiscali, BT, and Telewest requiring disclosure of the identities of persons who had loaded illegal software onto the networks of these ISPs: see theregister.co.uk, 1 February 2006 and 'On the FAST Track to Success', *Copyright World* No. 158, March 2006, p. 9.

discontinue the provision of services to subscribers who, rightholders believed, engaged in file sharing, with an injunction being granted to the rightholders if the ISP should fail to react expeditiously.[125] More recently, the British Phonographic Industry (BPI) provided Tiscali with 17 subscribers' IP addresses and Cable and Wireless with 42 IP addresses, which BPI believed were used for P2P file sharing. BPI did not seek *Norwich Pharmacal* relief, but proceeded directly to the 'cease and desist' provisions in the Electronic Commerce Directive:

> Both Tiscali and Cable & Wireless state in their terms of use for subscribers that Internet accounts should not be used for copyright infringement,' said BPI general counsel Roz Groome. 'We now invite them to enforce their own terms of use.[126]

Tiscali responded that the information provided is not evidence of infringement and that, without a court order, Tiscali will respect the privacy and data protection rights of its subscribers.[127]

Again, ISPs are in a difficult position. While an ISP must act expeditiously, must it take the right holder at its word? Under the standard cease and desist case law in the UK,[128] the person served with the notice must have the opportunity both to consult the alleged infringer and to take legal advice; it is hoped that this is part of the notice and take down procedure under the Electronic Commerce Directive. Further, it would be appropriate for the right holder to agree to indemnify the ISP in the event of the complaint against the subscriber being ill-founded. However, without, any judicial process, it is difficult to see how this mechanism can evolve. It is perhaps best if the courts continue to require right holders to employ discovery or *Norwich Pharamacal* principles, possibly allowing the court to hold that there is sufficient prima facie evidence of infringement to warrant withdrawal of service to the user. The integration of discovery or *Norwich Pharmacal* procedures into notice and take down powers may be expensive and cumbersome but any alternative puts ISPs in a predicament.

---

125 Court ruling confirms Internet Service Providers must act to stop piracy, available at www.ifpi.org/site-content/PRESS20060215.html.

126 Available at www.pcpro.co.uk/news/90078/bpi-pressures-isps-to-suspend-filesharing-accounts.html?searchString=news+90078 (last accessed 1 November 2008).

127 Available at www.pcpro.co.uk/news/bpi-pressures-isps-to suspend-filesharing-accounts.html?searchString=news+90078 (last accessed 1 November 2008). Tiscali instead provided evidence of infringement in the form of screenshots and user connections.

128 *Infabrics Ltd v Jaytex Shirt Co* [1978] FSR 451; *Vermaat v Boncrest* (No 2) [2002] FSR 21.

Is this all worth the effort? Serial file sharers can be expected to take out new subscriptions with other ISPs, change IP addresses, and resort to firewalls and other technical ways of avoiding detection. Research projects in the pipeline will allow users to go online with some assurance of privacy[129] while the encryption of files raises the computer forensics exercise to a new level. But the music and entertainment industries must be seen to be doing something to tackle the P2P problem[130] and the emphasis that the recording industry appears to be placing on ISPs seeks to both erode the safe harbour immunities and make ISPs civilly and even criminally liable for third-party wrongdoings.[131] Some organisations in the UK are pressing for the expansion of copyright in the form of a 'value recognition right' that would make 'unlicensed' ISPs liable in damages for third-party file sharing amongst its customers, and while this initiative is unlikely to progress, the record industry may be getting its way via a more indirect route.

The Weakening of ISP Immunity in UK Law

In *Bunt v Tilley*,[132] Eady J noted concern over distinguishing between the shelter from damages and penal sanctions that the Electronic Commerce Directive affords, while leaving open the exposure to injunctive reliefs that the Directive does not close down; the ISP defendants were not party to meaningful injunctive proceedings in that case, and on the facts, Eady J held that injunctive relief would not have been forthcoming as the ISPs had cancelled contracts and taken other remedial measures anyway. But within the UK, the signs are that the ISP 'immunity' is unlikely to survive for much longer. This is not simply because of judicial proceedings such as the *Bunt v Tilley* dicta or the 2006 *Tiscali* proceedings, outlined above. A number of straws in the wind are pointing towards a convergence of technical 'solutions' and a changing regulatory climate. In 2005, the (then) UK Department of Trade and Industry (DTI) initiated a consultation exercise[133] on the possibility of expanding 'mere conduit' type immunities to hyperlinkers and the providers of location tool services and

---

[129] See footnote 112 above.

[130] The use of software such as BitTorrent to transfer files containing television programmes and films, as well as music, is the most highly visible example of P2P file sharing, but actions are being brought against BitTorrent entrepreneurs. BREIN closed down the Dutch BitTorrent site Torrentit.com in April 2006, only one of many successful BREIN actions.

[131] See Henry [2007] *Ent L.R.* N-7.

[132] [2006] EWHC 407 QB.

[133] DTI Consultation document on the Electronic Commerce Directive: www.berr.gov.uk/files/file13986.pdf.

data content aggregators, but the DTI concluded[134] that there was insufficient evidence to justify the expansion of any 'safe harbour' immunity. Indeed, industry had expanded, even absent such immunity, and it may be that this conclusion has contributed to an 'awareness' that the Electronic Commerce Directive of 2000 does more than is actually necessary to stimulate the growth of the Information Society.

A parallel development from the area of child pornography and Internet content regulation has also fuelled the view that ISP 'immunity' is in need of revision. The UK, in 1996, established the Internet Watch Foundation (IWF) charged with developing a safer Internet environment, specifically in relation to counteracting on-line child pornography. In 2004, the largest ISP, British Telecom, launched BT Cleanfeed, a blocking service that relies upon the IWF providing a list of URLs, on a daily basis, and Cleanfeed blocking access to suspect sites on the list. This 'blocking' technology is regarded by critics as being crude and mechanical, but it has caught the attention of both the public and law enforcement as having a measure of effectiveness. In fact, the Gowers Review on Intellectual Property, published in 2006,[135] clearly had one eye on this kind of 'technology' when recommending the development of a negotiated code of practice between UK rightholders and ISPs, setting a deadline of one year for such a code to emerge. More recently still, the House of Lords Science and Technology Committee, in its report, *Personal Internet Security*, published on 10 August 2007,[136] suggested that it is now appropriate 'to take a nibble out of the blanket immunity'[137] afforded by the 'mere conduit' defence. This recommendation was framed in the context of requiring ISPs to monitor customer traffic that may, perhaps unwittingly, contain a virus or spam. The Science and Technology Committee took the view that it is unrealistic to place the onus for ensuring Internet service safety onto the shoulders of the end-user. The Committee recommended, at paragraph 3.69 that:

> the 'mere' conduit immunity should be removed once ISPs have detected or been notified of the fact that machines on their network are sending out spam or infected code. This would give third parties harmed by infected machines the opportunity to recover damages from the ISP responsible. However, in order not to discourage ISPs from monitoring outgoing traffic proactively, they should enjoy a time-limited immunity when they have themselves detected the problem.

---

134 Summary of responses, December 2006 www.dti.gov.uk/files/file35905.pdf.

135 *Gowers Review of Intellectual Property 2006*, available at www.hm-treasury.gov.uk: see photographs 5.99 and 5.100 and recommendation 39.

136 HL Paper 165-I.

137 The phrase is attributed to Zittrain in paragraph 3.62, see Zittrain (2006) 119 *Harvard Law Review* 2029.

What we are witnessing here is a not-so-subtle shift away from the principle that merely providing a facility that might be used by others to infringe the criminal or civil law will not, of itself, produce liability for the service provider. This principle is apparently being replaced with a statistical analysis of levels of illegal Internet traffic, informed by technical evidence that some forms of blocking or filtering will diminish the flow of illegal music or audio-visual files. When this analysis is combined with evidence that an ISP is indifferent to file-sharing activities and that the ISP could adopt countervailing measures (in terms of practical steps and actions that would be contractually possible), the fact that an actual complaint may have been made is likely to derail any 'mere conduit' defence.

The SABAM v Scarlet Decisions

Insofar as injunctive relief is sought to this extent, the controversial decision *SCRL Société Belge des Auteurs Compositeurs et Editeurs v SA Scarlet*[138] may be a harbinger of the Europe-wide emasculation of the Electronic Commerce Directive safe harbours. Here, the plaintiff, SABAM, obtained judgment against Tiscali, later renamed as Scarlet, in November 2004 as a result of cease and desist proceedings brought against Tiscali as an ISP whose network was being used by third parties for P2P file sharing of illegal music files. The Brussels Court of First Instance appointed an expert to advise on technical measures that Tiscali could adopt to stop copyright infringement by users. Although the expert noted that the most appropriate form of filtering technology, Copysense Network Appliances' Audible Magic, was educational software not designed to deal with ISP traffic or encrypted files, the Court noted that MySpace and Microsoft had either used or announced an intention to use Audible Magic. The Court also brushed aside evidence that the software in question could throw up false positives (that is, block legitimate transmissions) and found that the cost of installation (some 0.50 per subscriber per month over a three-year period) meant that a technical solution was possible, giving Tiscali six months to install the relevant technical solution. The Court indicated that this decision did not set aside the Electronic Commerce Directive's provision that an ISP has no duty to monitor content, noting that the Directive does not touch upon the jurisdiction of a 'cease and desist' judge and that Recital 40 of the Directive specifically approves of 'technical surveillance instruments'. This decision is under appeal. While distinguishing immunity from damages and

---

138 [2006] EWHC 407 QB.

criminal sanctions from injunctive relief was legitimate – Eady J in *Bunt v Tilley*[139] did much the same – the Brussels Court, by imposing a penalty of 25,000 per day if the technical surveillance solution was not in place, somewhat erodes the distinction. Other European jurisdictions such as Italy have also produced similar results in case law, the cases also being under appeal.[140]

In the United Kingdom in recent months, there have been industry led initiatives and a number of Government reports seeking to clear the way for a file sharing solution. On 29 January 2009, the Government published *Digital Britain: Interim Report*, promoting the idea of a 'Rights Agency' to facilitate stakeholder led solutions. The report also suggests ISPs become proactive in informing right holders about suspected illegal file sharing. In Ireland, recent litigation between EMI and Eircom, Ireland's largest ISP, has gone even further. EMI started this litigation looking for blocking software to be put on Eircom's network the *Scarlet* litigation being cited. The case was settled with Eircom agreeing a 'three strikes' solution, subscribers being afforded a number of opportunities to challenge allegations of misuse, with disconnection being the ultimate sanction in appropriate and practicable cases. Other Irish ISPs are under pressure to give similar undertakings to those found in the 28 January 2009 Eircopme settlement, specific reference being made to disabling access to Pirate Bay in correspondence originating from Irish record industry lawyers.

CONCLUSIONS: WHERE ARE WE NOW?

A review of the impact of the Electronic Commerce Directive is to be published by the European Commission. The review must address the relationship between that Directive and the community *acquis* on data protection as well as the Enforcement Directive. The Opinion of the Advocate General in *Telefonica*[141] is helpful in this regard, but it suggests that national laws are capable of being used to allow a civil procedure to require ISPs to disclose subscriber details and, as we have seen from the Irish and Dutch cases, both data protection and anti-wiretapping legislation at the national level tend to be subordinated to the interests of the music industry. There is an even more fundamental objection to the direction that the law is going in. The distinction between P2P software distributors and ISPs is being overlooked. Software distributors like Kazaa rely upon a business model that requires

139 [2007] ECDR 320.
140 Prosperetti [2007] *Ent L.R.* 280.
141 [2007] ECDR 390.

file sharing to take place; such entities encourage and incite file sharing – in the language of Irish and UK copyright law, they 'authorise' others to infringe. Unlike ISPs, such entities are not permitted to resort to the 'safe harbour' of the Electronic Commerce Directive. On the other hand, the ISP should not monitor content. But as a result of the *SABAM* decision, the ISP now only has to be served a notice that illegal content is being transmitted via its service and, if evidence of some kind of technical solution is presented, the ISP will not only have to install it, the ISP will have to charge its subcribers also. The convergence of the reasoning in the Australian *Sharman*[142] case and the Belgian *SABAM* decision overlooks the critical differences in relation to culpability, and in jurisprudential terms, undervalues and threatens civil liberties. All the right holder needs to invoke are injunctive proceedings in order to sidestep the Electronic Commerce Directive and impose upon an ISP proactive duties to place filtering technology onto the ISPs services – and pay for it too. Add to this mixture the confusion at the level of national law and criminal and civil litigation, and it is hard not to escape the conclusion that single market harmonization of Intermediary Service Providers through the Electronic Commerce Directive has been a complete failure.

142 (2005) 65 IPR 289.

8. A reverse notice and takedown regime to enable public interest uses of technically protected copyrighted works

Jerome H. Reichman, Graeme B. Dinwoodie and Pamela Samuelson*

The WIPO Copyright Treaty (WCT), concluded in 1996, recognizes 'the need to maintain a balance between the rights of authors and the larger public interest, particularly education, research and access to information' in updating international copyright norms to respond to challenges arising from advances in information and communications technologies, including global digital networks.[1] The WCT implements this balance by affirming that existing exclusive rights, as well as exceptions to and limitations on those rights, can and should be applied to copyrighted works in digital forms.[2] Indeed, nations

* A prior version of this chapter appeared in (2007) *Berkeley Technology Law Journal*, 22 (Summer), pp. 981–1060. This chapter is based in part on a paper entitled 'Digital Copyright: Third Party Liability and The Outer Limits of Protection,' which Professor Reichman initially wrote and presented at a SOFTIC conference in Tokyo, Japan, in November 2005. The authors wish to thank Thomas Kearney and Assad Rajani for their valuable research assistance. Professor Reichman also gratefully acknowledges the support of the National Human Genome Research Institute and the Department of Energy (CEER Grant P50 HG003391, Duke University Center of Excellence for ELSI Research).

1 WIPO Copyright Treaty, Preamble, 20 December 1996, WIPO Doc. CRNR/DC/94, available at http://www.wipo.int/documents/en/diplconf/distrib/pdf/94dc.pdf [hereinafter WCT].

2 Id., Arts. 6–8; Agreed Statements Concerning the WIPO Copyright Treaty, statement concerning Art. 1(4), Dec. 20, 1996, WIPO Doc. CRNR/DC/96 (published 23 December 1996), available at http://www.wipo.int/documents/en/diplconf/distrib/pdf/96dc.pdf [hereinafter Agreed Statements]. The WCT also reflects an international consensus that nations are entitled 'to carry forward and appropriately extend into the digital environment limitations and exceptions in their national laws which have been considered acceptable under the Berne Convention.' Id., statement concerning Art. 10.

are free 'to devise new exceptions and limitations that are appropriate in the digital network environment.'[3]

The treaty also calls for nations to 'provide adequate legal protection and effective legal remedies against the circumvention of effective technological measures that are used by authors in connection with the exercise of their rights,'[4] although such rules should not impede acts that are 'permitted by law' or otherwise beyond the authority of copyright owners.[5] The treaty gives no guidance, however, about how nations might implement this anti-circumvention norm so as to enable privileged and other public interest uses of copyrighted works.

While the WCT embodies a negotiated balance between copyright owners and users of digital works, the translation of this balance into the domestic laws of the United States and the member states of the European Union has not been fully successful.[6] When enacting the Digital Millennium Copyright Act (DMCA) of 1998 as the US implementation of the WCT,[7] Congress achieved a reasonable balance of competing interests in its creation of safe harbours from copyright liability for Internet service providers and other intermediaries for the infringing acts of others.[8] However, contrary to its apparent intention, Congress failed to achieve a similar balance of interests when establishing new rules forbidding circumvention of technical protection measures (TPMs) used by copyright owners to control access to their works and in regulating the manufacture and distribution of technologies primarily designed or produced to enable circumvention of copyright-protective TPMs.[9]

---

3 Agreed Statements, *supra* n. 2, statement concerning Art. 10.

4 WCT, Art. 11. See, e.g., Pamela Samuelson, *The US Digital Agenda at WIPO*, 37 *Va. J. Int'l L.* 369, 409–15 (1997) (discussing the evolution of the WCT anti-circumvention provision).

5 WCT, Art. 11.

6 Maintaining a balance between the interests of copyright owners in having adequate protection for their works and the public in having access to and the freedom to use these works in non-infringing ways has long been a 'bedrock principle' of US copyright law and policy. See, e.g., H.R. Rep. No. 105–551, at 18 (1998); *Chamberlain Group, Inc. v Skylink Techs., Inc.,* 381 F.3d 1178, 1196 (Fed. Cir. 2004) (quoting legislative history of the DMCA).

7 Digital Millennium Copyright Act, Pub. L. No. 105–304, 112 Stat. 2860 (1998) (anti-circumvention rules codified at 17 USC. § 1201).

8 17 USC. § 512 (2000).

9 17 USC. § 1201 (2000). 'Checks and balances in the ISP safe harbours and anti-circumvention rules' (at p. 234) will discuss various limitations on and exceptions to the DMCA anti-circumvention rules, including authorization of the Library of Congress to develop new exceptions and limitations; it will also show that these limitations and exceptions do not accomplish the needed balance.

Although the EU followed the US lead in adopting DMCA-like rules that forbid circumvention and trafficking in circumvention tools,[10] it diverged from the US approach by explicitly requiring member states to fulfil a normative commitment to ensuring that certain public interest uses can be made of technically protected works. Article 6(4) of the EU Copyright Directive provides that member states must take 'appropriate measures' to ensure that right holders enable lawful users of copyrighted works to exercise certain exceptions or limitations provided for by national law, even when the works in question are technically protected.[11] Unfortunately, the Directive contains some limits that seemingly undermine this commitment,[12] and like the WCT, it provides little guidance about how member states might achieve this goal. National implementations of this Directive thus far have not, in our judgment, adequately facilitated public interest uses of technically protected content nor fulfilled the normative commitment to parity in the ability to exercise exceptions and limitations.[13]

The resulting imbalance in US and EU member state anti-circumvention rules harms legitimate interests of the public in making fair uses, privileged uses, and other non-infringing uses of copyrighted works (which collectively we deem to be 'public interest uses' of copyrighted works).[14] We believe that

---

[10] Directive 2001/29/EC on the Harmonisation of Certain Aspects of Copyright and Related Rights in the Information Society, Art. 6, 2001 O.J. (L 167) 10 [hereinafter Copyright Directive]. This Directive is more restrictive than the DMCA in at least two ways. First, it bans all acts of circumvention, not just circumventions of access controls. Compare id. with 17 USC. § 1201(a)(1)(A). Second, it lacks a set of built-in exceptions and limitations such as those in the DMCA. Compare Copyright Directive, *supra*, Art. 6, with 17 USC. § 1201(c)–(j).

[11] Copyright Directive, Art. 6(4). We recognize that other commentators have been more skeptical than we are about the will to carry through with this normative commitment. See e.g., Severine Dusollier (2003), 'Exceptions and Technological Measures in the European Copyright Directive of 2001—An Empty Promise', 34 IIC 62; Inst. for Info. Law, Univ. of Amsterdam, 'Study on the Implementation and Effect in Member States' Laws of Directive 2001/29/EC on the Harmonisation of Certain Aspects of Copyright and Related Rights in the Information Society', Final Report 73 (2007) [hereinafter Copyright Directive Implementation Study].

[12] See *infra* nn. 295–298 and accompanying text.

[13] See id.; see also *infra* nn. 334–340 and accompanying text.

[14] Numerous commentators have noted the imbalance of the DMCA anti-circumvention rules and their deleterious effects on fair, privileged, and other non-infringing uses of copyrighted works. See, e.g., Timothy K. Armstrong (2006), 'Digital Rights Management and the Process of Fair Use', 20 *Harv. J. L. & Tech.* 49; Yochai Benkler (1999), 'Free as the Air to Common Use: First Amendment Constraints on Enclosure of the Public Domain', 74 *N.Y.U. L. Rev.* 354; Dan L. Burk and Julie E. Cohen (2001), 'Fair Use Infrastructure for Rights Management Systems', 15 *Harv. J. L. & Tech.* 41; Julie E. Cohen (1997), 'Lochner in Cyberspace: The New Economic

practical judicial and administrative measures can and should be devised to implement the spirit of the WCT in both the US and EU without reopening the contentious debates that engulfed the process leading up to enactment of the DMCA and the EU Copyright Directive. To this end, we propose adoption of a 'reverse notice and takedown' procedure to help achieve some of the balance in anti-circumvention rules that the WCT endorsed, but which implementing legislation has thus far failed to deliver.[15] Under this regime, users would be able to give copyright owners notice of their desire to make public interest uses of technically protected copyrighted works, and right holders would have the responsibility to take down the TPMs or otherwise enable these lawful uses.

We call this a 'reverse notice and takedown' process because, in an inversion of the notice and takedown procedure first developed through common law adjudication about ISP liability for wrongful acts of users,[16] it is the user who will be giving notice and the content owner who will have a responsibility to take something down. A reverse notice and takedown regime would

---

Orthodoxy of Rights Management', 97 *Mich. L. Rev.* 462; Jacqueline D. Lipton (2005), 'Solving the Digital Piracy Puzzle: Disaggregating Fair Use from the DMCA's Anti-Device Provisions', 19 *Harv. J. L. & Tech.* 111; Tricia J. Sadd (2001), 'Fair Use as a Defense Under the Digital Millennium Copyright Act's Anti-Circumvention Provisions', 10 *Geo. Mason L. Rev.* 321; Pamela Samuelson (1999), 'Intellectual Property and the Digital Economy: Why the Anti-Circumvention Rules Need to Be Revised', 14 *Berkeley Tech. L.J.* 519; Jane C. Ginsburg, 'The Pros and Cons of Strengthening Intellectual Property Protection: Technological Protection Measures and Section 1201 of the US Copyright Act', (*Columbia Law Sch. Pub. Law & Legal Theory Working Paper Group*, Paper No. 07-137, Feb. 1, 2007), available at http://ssrn.com/abstract=960724.

[15] See *infra* 'Implications for public interest uses of technically protected content' at p. 264 and 'The lock-out technology cases: Chamberlain, Lexmark, and StorageTek,', at p. 270.

[16] *Religious Tech. Ctr. (RTC) v Netcom On-Line Commc'n Servs., Inc.*, 907 F. Supp. 1361 (N.D. Cal. 1995). *Netcom* opined that Internet access and service providers were not liable for user infringements unless and until they had received notice about the existence of infringing materials on their sites and failed to investigate and take infringing materials down. Id. at 1373–76. (The *Netcom* decision is discussed *infra* nn. 36–42 and accompanying text.) This notice and takedown approach was later legislatively adopted in the US and EU. Three of the four DMCA safe harbors for ISPs, for example, employ the judicially devised notice and takedown framework set forth in *Netcom.* See 17 USC. § 512(b)–(d). (The fourth, s. 512(a), creates a safe harbor for copies made in the course of transitory digital network transmissions for which notice and takedown is infeasible.) See also Directive 2000/31/EC on Certain Legal Aspects of Information Society Services, in Particular Electronic Commerce in the Internal Market, Arts. 12–14, 2000 O.J. (L 178) 1, available at http://eurlex.-europa.eu/LexUriServ/site/en/oj/2000/l_178/l_17820000717en00010016.pdf [hereinafter E-Commerce Directive].

achieve for the anti-circumvention rules a comparable symmetry to the balance embedded in the ISP safe harbour rules. It would also effectuate the nascent, but not fully realized, legislative intent to permit public interest uses of technically protected digital content, while at the same time protecting copyright owners against circumvention of TPMs that would facilitate or lead to massive infringements.[17]

The chapter will demonstrate that a reverse notice and takedown mechanism is best understood as a principle capable of numerous implementations. In the US, the most likely way to achieve this goal is through judicial interpretation of the anti-circumvention rules through case-by-case adjudication. It was, after all, the judicial branch that introduced the fair use doctrine into US law and also pioneered the notice and takedown rules to govern ISP liability. In the heated political climate in which the DMCA was enacted, the measured analysis developed in *Netcom* was invaluable in shaping ISP liability rules. Unfortunately, no similarly careful judicial assessment was available in the late 1990s to guide Congress about how to achieve an appropriate balance in the anti-circumvention rules. We believe that courts in the US can and should be enlisted in bringing about a balanced approach for dual-use circumvention technologies akin to that developed for the dual-use technologies and services of ISPs. Recent decisions, moreover, provide a theoretical base upon which this case law evolution could occur.

In the EU, by contrast, member states could implement a reverse notice and takedown regime in the course of fulfilling their obligations under the Copyright Directive, including Art. 6(4), which requires them to ensure that users of technically protected works can exercise certain public interest exceptions. Although it is not possible in either the US or the EU to write anti-circumvention rules on a completely blank slate, there is flexibility in the legal cultures of both entities to implement a reverse notice and takedown procedure to achieve needed balance in anti-circumvention regulations. Nations that have yet to implement the WCT may find our proposed reverse notice and takedown regime provides a far more balanced way to comply with the treaty than the approach being promoted by US trade negotiators.[18]

Part II discusses the legislative history of the DMCA and the checks and balances embodied in its ISP safe harbour and anti-circumvention rules. It shows that the notice and takedown regime under section 512 has achieved a reasonable balance in the regulation of ISPs for wrongful acts of users, but that

---

17 This proposal is developed in 'The reverse notice and takedown framework' at p. 277.

18 See, e.g., Anupam Chander (2006), 'Exporting DMCA Lock-outs', 54 *Clev. St. L. Rev.* 205 (discussing imbalanced anti-circumvention rules that the US has insisted on in trade agreements with several nations).

s. 1201 lacks a similar balance. Certain case law interpretations of s. 1201 have, moreover, made the DMCA anti-circumvention rules seem even more imbalanced than its express provisions require.[19]

'Setting the stage for a reverse notice and takedown regime' at p. 255 argues that a reverse notice and takedown regime would provide a needed balance in the US anti-circumvention rules and shows that there is sufficient flexibility in the existing US legal framework for courts to fashion such a regime. 'Reverse notice and takedown as a mode of implementing Article 6(4) of the EU Copyright Directive' at p. 284 argues that member states of the EU should likewise consider adopting a reverse notice and takedown regime as a sound way to effectuate the duty that the Copyright Directive imposes on them to ensure that users are able to enjoy copyright exceptions and limitations that have been granted under national laws, notwithstanding the use of TPMs to control access to and uses of copyrighted works.[20]

Because the EU imposed this duty, yet deferred to national judgments about how to fulfil it, EU member states would seem to have more flexibility to experiment with different ways to implement a reverse notice and takedown regime than the US presently does. Some of the available options are discussed later on in this chapter.

CHECKS AND BALANCES IN THE ISP SAFE HARBOURS AND ANTI-CIRCUMVENTION RULES

The WCT was the end product of an international conversation about updating copyright laws for the digital age that began when the Clinton Administration published its 'White Paper' on Intellectual Property and the National Information Infrastructure in September 1995.[21] No checks and balances were built into that document. Among other things, the White Paper opined that Internet service and access providers were and should be strictly liable for copyright infringement of their users on account of the temporary copies made in the random access memory of their computers.[22]

---

[19] See, e.g., *Universal City Studios, Inc. v Reimerdes*, 111 F. Supp. 2d 294, 324 (S.D.N.Y. 2000), aff'd sub nom. *Universal City Studios, Inc. v Corley*, 273 F.3d 429 (2d Cir. 2001).

[20] Copyright Directive, Art. 6(4).

[21] See Working Group on Intellectual Prop. Rights, Info. Infrastructure Task Force, Intellectual Property and the National Information Infrastructure (1995), [hereinafter White Paper]. Imbalance in the White Paper's interpretation of digital copyright issues was widely noted at the time. See, e.g., Pamela Samuelson, 'The Copyright Grab', 4.01 *Wired* 96 (1996).

[22] White Paper, at 114–24. The White Paper analyzed ISP liability based on

ISPs were, in the White Paper's view, in a far better position to monitor and control user infringements than copyright owners.[23] The prospect of liability would give them strong incentives to ensure that their sites were not used for infringing purposes and to develop technologies to deter infringements.[24]

The White Paper also recommended legislation to outlaw technologies the primary purpose or effect of which was to bypass TPMs that copyright owners used to protect their works.[25] Without such protection, the drafters warned, copyright owners would not be willing to make their works available in digital form. The White Paper contemplated no public policy exceptions to or limitations on the proposed anti-circumvention rules, a strategy that generated considerable opposition and criticism.[26] This section will discuss the different ways that Congress responded to criticisms of the White Paper's proposed ISP and anti-circumvention liability rules.

ISP Safe Harbour Provisions

Congress had already begun to consider whether ISPs should be liable for wrongful acts of their users, such as libellous postings on bulletin board services, at the time the White Paper was published.[27] In 1996, as part of a telecommunications regulation reform measure, the telecom industry obtained

---

temporary copies made in the random access memory of computers as direct infringements of copyright. The White Paper discussed contributory and vicarious liability in a different section. Id. at 109–14.

23 Id. at 117.

24 Id. at 117–18.

25 Id. at 230–34.

26 See, e.g., Jessica Litman (2001), 'Digital Copyright: Protecting Intellectual Property on the Internet' 122–65 (discussing the controversy). See also *supra* n. 21.

27 The ISP immunity provision was first introduced in Congress on 4 August 1995. See 141 Cong. Rec. H8468-69 (daily ed. 4 August 1995). Prior to this, the case law on ISP liability for tortious acts of users was mixed. Compare *Cubby, Inc. v CompuServe Inc.*, 776 F. Supp. 135 (S.D.N.Y. 1991) (rejecting a defamation claim against CompuServe because it did not monitor user postings) with *Stratton Oakmont, Inc. v Prodigy Servs. Co.*, 1995 WL 323710 (N.Y. Sup. Ct. 1995) (refusing to dismiss a lawsuit similar to *Cubby* because, by monitoring some user postings for harmful speech, Prodigy had shown it could monitor for defamation as well). The telecommunications industry became concerned that it would routinely be held liable for wrongful acts of users insofar as it policed its sites for any reason. The telecom industry lobbied hard for Congressional preemption of decisions such as *Stratton Oakmont*. The House Conference report makes clear that '[o]ne of the specific purposes of [the immunity provision] is to overrule . . . decisions which have treated such providers and users as publishers or speakers of content that is not their own.' H.R. Rep. No. 104-458, at 94 (1996) (Conf. Rep.).

a broad grant of immunity from liability for user wrongs.[28] The industry successfully argued that imposing liability on ISPs for wrongful acts of which they were unaware was unfair and unwise. Requiring them to monitor their sites for wrongful activity would not only interfere with user privacy and freedom of expression interests, but it would also increase dramatically the cost of Internet access.

Self-regulation was deemed a more effective way to create incentives for ISPs to ensure that their sites were being used for lawful purposes.[29] At the copyright industry's insistence, Congress carved out an exception to the Communications Decency Act's (CDA) immunity provision for intellectual property violations.[30]

Having won a broad grant of immunity in the first round of the fight over ISP liability for wrongful acts of users, the telecom industry believed that, by advancing the same arguments used to gain immunity under the CDA, it could persuade Congress to reject the White Paper's contention that that industry should be held strictly liable for copyright infringements.[31] ISP technology platforms were, moreover, 'dual-use' technologies, in the sense that they could be as easily used for lawful as for unlawful purposes. Under the Supreme Court's decision in *Sony Corp. of America v Universal City Studios, Inc.*, ISP platform technologies seemed to qualify for the safe harbour that *Sony* carved out for technologies having substantial non-infringing uses.[32]

The telecom industry's chances for averting the strict liability rule proposed in the White Paper were substantially enhanced by two pre-DMCA developments. One was the *Netcom* decision, which rejected the White Paper's strict liability theory against ISPs.[33] A second was an international repudiation of a similar proposed strict liability rule for Internet intermediaries that the US had initially supported at the diplomatic conference that

---

[28] Telecommunications Act of 1996, Pub. L. No. 104–104, 110 Stat. 56. Title V of this Act was the Communications Decency Act. The immunity provision is now codified at 47 USC. § 230(c)(1) ('No provider or user of an interactive computer service shall be treated as the publisher or speaker of any information provided by another information provider.').

[29] The rationale for this grant of immunity is discussed in *Zeran v America Online*, 129 F.3d 327 (4th Cir. 1997).

[30] 47 USC. § 230(e)(2). The Ninth Circuit has recently ruled that this limitation on CDA immunity applies only to federal intellectual property laws. See Perfect 10, Inc. v. CCBill LLC, 481 F.3d 751, 768 (9th Cir. 2007) (applying CDA immunity provision to state right of publicity claims).

[31] See *supra* text accompanying n. 29 for the rationale for the CDA immunity.

[32] *Sony Corp. of Am. v Universal City Studios*, 464 US 417, 442 (1984).

[33] *Religious Tech. Ctr. (RTC) v Netcom On-Line Commc'n Servs., Inc.*, 907 F. Supp. 1361, 1370 (N.D. Cal. 1995).

produced the WCT.[34] An Agreed Statement on the treaty further clarified that 'mere provision of physical facilities for enabling or making a communication does not in itself amount to communication' under the treaty.[35] ISPs could accordingly point to the international consensus against a strict liability rule when arguing for a more balanced approach before Congress.

The *Netcom* decision was a pivotal development in the legislative drama that spawned the DMCA safe harbours.[36] In response to the copyright owner's direct infringement claim against Netcom, the alleged infringer's Internet access provider, Judge Whyte identified the question in the case as 'whether possessors of computers are liable for incidental copies automatically made on their computers using their software as part of a process initiated by a third party.'[37] Judge Whyte decided that RTC's direct infringement theory was an unreasonable interpretation of copyright law because it would logically lead to imposing liability on owners of 'every single Usenet server in the worldwide link of computers transmitting Erlich's message to every other computer.'[38] Before an Internet access provider could become directly liable, there needed to be proof of 'some element of volition or causation', proof 'which is lacking where a defendant's system is merely used to create a copy for a third party'.[39]

---

[34] The Clinton Administration had supported a draft treaty provision under which ISPs would have been strictly liable for temporary copies of infringing materials passing through their computers. See Samuelson, *supra* n. 4, at 383–92 (discussing debate over ISP liability at the WIPO diplomatic conference).

[35] Agreed Statements, statement concerning Art. 8.

[36] *RTC*, 907 F. Supp. at 1364–66. Litigation ensued after Dennis Erlich, a former minister of the Scientology religion turned vocal critic, posted portions of the writings of L. Ron Hubbard in the alt.religion.scientology Usenet newsgroup. RTC, owner of the relevant copyrights, sued Erlich, Thomas Klemesrud (the operator of a bulletin board service (BBS) on which Erlich had made the postings), and Netcom (the Internet access provider for Klemesrud's BBS), for copyright infringement. Id. at 1366.

[37] Id. at 1368. In support of its direct infringement claim, RTC relied upon the White Paper; the Ninth Circuit's decision in *MAI Systems Corp. v Peak Computer, Inc.*, 991 F.2d 511 (9th Cir. 1993), which held that temporary copies of copyrighted works made in the random access memory of computers were infringing reproductions of the works unless authorized by the copyright owner or the law, id. at 518; and *Playboy v Frena*, 839 F. Supp. 1552 (M.D. Fla. 1993), which held the operator of a BBS directly liable for infringing copies of Playboy bunny pictures that users had uploaded to and downloaded from the BBS. The White Paper had also relied upon *MAI* in support of its view that making temporary as well as permanent copies of works in digital form were copyright-significant acts and upon *Frena* in support of its view that ISPs were directly liable for user infringements. See White Paper, at 64–69, 120.

[38] *RTC*, 907 F. Supp. at 1369.

[39] Id. at 1370. Judge Whyte also granted Netcom's motion for summary judgment on RTC's vicarious liability claim. Although the judge was skeptical of Netcom's claim that it lacked the ability to supervise and control users' postings, the vicarious

Although Judge Whyte also agreed with Netcom that it should not be held contributorily liable for Erlich's infringement before receiving notice about this risk, he took issue with Netcom's assertion that RTC's notice of Erlich's infringement was 'too equivocal given the difficulty in assessing whether registrations are valid and whether a use is fair.'[40] While 'a mere unsupported allegation of infringement by a copyright owner may not automatically put a defendant on notice of infringing activity,' Judge Whyte declared, 'Netcom's position that liability must be unequivocal is unsupportable.'[41] Upon receipt of a proper notice, Judge Whyte thought that Netcom should have a duty to investigate the claim of infringement and to take the material down if the claim was valid. Failure to do so amounted to a substantial contribution to user infringement that, if proven, would justify contributory infringement liability.[42]

Two of the DMCA safe harbours are codifications of the *Netcom* ruling: s. 512(a) exempts service providers from liability for incidental copies made in the course of network transmission of digital content on behalf of users;[43] and s. 512(c) exempts copies made in storing information for users except when providers have received proper notice of infringement from the copyright owner and failed to investigate the charges and remove infringing materials.[44] Congress also created safe harbours for caching of digital content to enable faster service to users and for information locating tools (for example, search engines) that might connect users to infringing materials.[45] The information storage, caching, and information location tool safe harbours have notice and takedown requirements akin to those articulated in *Netcom*.[46]

---

claim was unsustainable because Netcom had not received any direct financial benefit from user infringements. Id. at 1375–77.

[40] Id. at 1373. 'To require proof of valid registration would be impractical and would perhaps take too long to verify, making it impossible for a copyright holder to protect his or her works in some cases. . . .' Id.

[41] Id. at 1374.

[42] Id. at 1374–75. There being a triable issue of fact on the adequacy of RTC's notice to Netcom and the reasonableness of Netcom's response, the latter's motion for summary judgment on the contributory infringement claim failed. Id. The White Paper had not considered a notice and takedown regime as a way to balance competing interests in ISP liability cases.

[43] 17 USC. § 512(a).

[44] Id. at § 512(c).

[45] Id. at § 512(b) (caching safe harbour), § 512(d) (information location tool safe harbour). As mentioned above, the EU found notice and takedown to be a balanced approach to ISP liability in its E-Commerce Directive, which, like the DMCA, provides a safe harbour for transmission, caching, and information storage. It has no counterpart, however, to s. 512(d). E-Commerce Directive, *supra* n. 16, Arts. 12–14.

[46] 17 USC. §§ 512(b)(2)(E)(i), (c)(1)(A), (d)(1)(A).

The DMCA safe harbours represented a major victory for telecom and Internet industry groups, given that powerful copyright industry groups had wanted service providers held strictly liable for infringing acts of users. Other legislative concessions to ISPs included: a specification of what constitutes adequate notice from copyright owners before the duty to investigate arises;[47] a counter-notice regime so that users can ask to restore information initially taken down in response to a complaint of infringement;[48] an immunity for taking information down based on a good faith belief that such action was proper;[49] limitations on injunctive relief;[50] and a clarification that service providers were not obliged to monitor their sites for infringing materials.[51]

Copyright industry groups obtained some concessions as well. ISPs could rely on the safe harbours only if they had adopted and reasonably implemented policies to terminate repeat infringers, and if they accommodated standard technical measures that might be developed in the future for the protection of digital copyrighted works.[52] ISPs were obliged to publicly designate an agent to whom notices of infringement could be sent.[53] The DMCA also authorized copyright owners to seek subpoenas to require service providers to disclose names and other identifying information about ISP subscribers whom copyright owners alleged were infringers.[54]

---

47 Id. at § 512(c)(3). The Ninth Circuit gave this requirement some teeth in a recent secondary liability case:

> In order to substantially comply with sec. 512(c)(3)'s requirements, a notification must do more than identify infringing files. The DMCA requires a complainant to declare, under penalty of perjury . . . that he has a good faith belief that the use is infringing.. . . Permitting a copyright holder to cobble together adequate notice from separately defective notices . . . unduly burdens service providers.

Perfect 10, Inc. v CCBill LLC, 481 F.3d 751, 761–62 (9th Cir. 2007).

48 17 USC. § 512 (g)(2)–(3).

49 Id. at § 512(g)(1).

50 Id. at § 512(j)(1)–(2).

51 Id. at § 512(m).

52 Id. at § 512(i). See *Perfect 10, Inc.*, 481 F.3d at 758–64 (discussing the reasonable implementation requirement).

53 17 USC. § 512(c)(2).

54 Id. at § 512(h). But see *Recording Indus. Ass'n of Am. v Verizon Internet Servs., Inc.*, 351 F.3d 1229 (D.C. Cir. 2003) (holding RIAA not authorized to obtain subpoena identifying information as to file sharers whose communications Verizon transmitted; s. 512(h) allows subpoenas as to s. 512(c) storage of information, not as to s. 512(a) transmissions of information).

The DMCA safe harbours have generally been efficacious in run-of-the-mill copyright infringement cases involving users and their ISPs.[55] Copyright owners have incentives to monitor Internet sites for infringing materials and to provide appropriately detailed information to ISPs so that the infringing material can be taken down. Copyright owners are deterred from sending false or overreaching notices of infringement not only by provisions of the DMCA that penalize wrongful notices,[56] but also by the prospect of 'bad' publicity and judicial sanctions if they send improper or overreaching notices.[57] ISPs have incentives to cooperate with copyright owners in the notice and takedown process and to terminate repeat infringers lest they forfeit the safe harbours provided by the DMCA.

While there is some empirical evidence that ISPs are perhaps quicker than they should be to take materials down upon receipt of notice and that the counter-notice procedures are too rarely invoked,[58] ISPs and copyright owners have generally adapted to conducting businesses within the framework of the notice and takedown regime of the DMCA safe harbours.[59] Viacom's pending copyright infringement lawsuit against YouTube will test how secure the DMCA safe harbours really are,[60] but it will not be surprising if the court tells Viacom that it should take its complaint to Congress, as Viacom is essentially trying to achieve through litigation what the copyright industry was unable to obtain from Congress in 1998.[61] Leaving aside the Viacom lawsuit, the past

---

55 See, e.g., Christian C.M. Beams (1999), 'Note: The Copyright Dilemma Involving Online Service Providers: Problem Solved . . . For Now', 51 *Fed. Comm. L.J.* 823, 846; Heidi Pearlman Salow (2001), 'Liability Immunity for Internet Service Providers – How Is It Working?', 6 *J. Tech. L. & Pol'y* 31, 49–50.

56 17 USC. § 512(f). This provision has some teeth, as is illustrated by *Online Policy Group v Diebold, Inc.*, 337 F. Supp. 2d 1195 (N.D. Cal. 2004) (sanctioning an electronic voting technology firm for knowing misrepresentations when giving notice to an ISP to take down allegedly infringing materials).

57 See e.g., Free Speech Battle Over Online Parody of 'Colbert Report,' http://www.eff.org/news/archives/2007_03.php#005176 (Mar. 22, 2007) (challenging Viacom notice and takedown demand as to parody available on YouTube).

58 See e.g., Jennifer Urban and Laura Quilter (2006), 'Efficient Process or 'Chilling Effects'? Takedown Notices Under Section 512 of the Digital Millennium Copyright Act', 22 *Santa Clara Computer & High Tech. L.J.* 621. For examples of notice and takedown letters that have had chilling effects on users, see http://chillingeffects.org/copyright/.

59 See, e.g., Kevin M. Lemley (2003), 'Comment: Protecting Consumers From Themselves: Alleviating the Market Inequalities Created by Online Copyright Infringement in the Entertainment Industry', 13 *Alb. L.J. Sci. & Tech.* 613, 620.

60 See Complaint, *Viacom Int'l, Inc. v YouTube, Inc.*, No. 07 Civ. 2103 (S.D.N.Y. 12 March 2007).

61 See, e.g., *CoStar Group, Inc. v LoopNet, Inc.*, 373 F.3d 544 (4th. Cir. 2004)

decade of experience with the DMCA notice and takedown regime suggests that a relatively balanced and workable solution to this particular dual-use technology problem has been found.[62]

Anti-circumvention Provisions

In addition to endorsing a strict liability rule against ISPs, the White Paper anticipated that many copyright owners would find it desirable to use technical protection measures for digital media products or services intended for distribution via global digital networks; yet, it also recognized that clever technologists could build tools to bypass these TPMs, which would thereby render digital works vulnerable to infringements.[63] To offer greater security to technically protected content, the White Paper recommended enactment of a ban on technologies, 'the primary purpose or effect of which is to avoid, bypass, remove, deactivate, or otherwise circumvent' technical measures used by copyright owners to protect their works.[64]

The White Paper offered very little policy analysis in support of this ban.[65]

(rejecting copyright owner arguments for intermediary liability as having been resolved by DMCA safe harbors).

62 See, e.g., Beams, *supra* n. 55, at 841; Tim Wu, 'Does YouTube Really Have Legal Problems?', Slate.com, 26 October 2006, http://www.slate.com/id/2152264/ (arguing that 'the content industry actually likes section 512 more than anyone will admit'). See also Michael L. Rustad & Thomas H. Koenig (2005), 'Rebooting Cybertort Law', 80 *Wash. L. Rev*. 335, 397 (praising the balance of the notice and takedown rules).

63 White Paper, at 230.

64 The White Paper's proposal was:

> No person shall import, manufacture or distribute any device, product, or component incorporated into a device or product, or to offer or perform a service, the primary purpose or effect of which is to avoid, bypass, remove, deactivate, or otherwise circumvent, without authority of the copyright owner or the law, any process, treatment, mechanism, or system which prevents or inhibits the exercise of any of the exclusive rights under section 106.

Id., Appendix 1 at 6.

65 The White Paper did state:

> The Working Group finds that prohibition of devices, products, components, and services that defeat technological methods of preventing unauthorized use is in the public interest and furthers the Constitutional purpose of copyright laws. Consumers of copyrighted works pay for the acts of infringers; copyright owners have suggested that the price of legitimate copies of copyrighted works may be higher due to infringement losses suffered by copyright owners. The public will also

It dismissed as misguided expressions of concern about the effects of anti-circumvention rules on the public domain and on fair and other privileged uses of copyrighted works.[66] Clinton Administration officials also proposed that a virtually identical provision should be included in the WCT.[67]

The Sony Safe Harbour was the pre-DMCA default rule for dual-use technologies

The radical nature of the White Paper's proposed anti-circumvention rule can best be appreciated by contrasting it with the safe harbour for technologies with substantial non-infringing uses set forth in *Sony Corp. of America v Universal City Studios, Inc.*[68] *Sony* was the first case to consider whether copyright owners could hold technology developers indirectly liable for user infringements on the ground that the primary purpose or effect of the challenged technologies was to facilitate unauthorized copying of copyrighted works.[69]

Universal sued Sony for contributory infringement in 1976, shortly after Sony introduced the Betamax video tape recorder (VTR) to the market, claiming that Sony knew that the primary use of its Betamax machines would be to make unauthorized, and hence infringing, copies of copyrighted works, such as movies shown on broadcast television.[70] Indeed, Sony's advertisements encouraged the public to purchase its VTRs in order to copy favourite programs.[71] In 1981, the Ninth Circuit Court of Appeals ruled in Universal's favour, on the grounds that making copies of copyrighted television programmes, even for time-shifting purposes, was direct infringement, and that Sony had knowingly contributed to that infringement because the primary

---

have access to more copyrighted works if they are not vulnerable to the defeat of copy protection systems.

Id. at 230.

[66] Id. at 231–32.

[67] See Samuelson, *supra* n. 4, at 409–15 (discussing proposed WIPO treaty anti-circumvention provision).

[68] *Sony Corp. of Am. v Universal City Studios, Inc.*, 464 US 417 (1984). The White Paper did not mention that its anti-circumvention rule would partially overturn the *Sony* safe harbor for technologies with substantial non-infringing uses. The White Paper mischaracterized *Sony* as a case in which the absence of a market for home-taping had led the Court to conclude that time-shift copying of television programs was fair use. White Paper, at 79.

[69] For a well told history of the lawsuit, see generally James Lardner, 'Fast Forward: A Machine and the Commotion It Caused' (rev. ed. 2002).

[70] *Sony*, 464 US at 459.

[71] Id.

use of Betamax machines was to make such copies.[72] In 1984, the Supreme Court reversed, holding that time-shift copying of TV programmes was fair use and that Sony was not liable for contributory infringement on account of the substantial non-infringing uses to which the Betamax machines could be put.[73]

Justice Stevens, writing for the Court in *Sony*, observed that the only theory on which Sony could be held liable was 'that [it has sold] equipment with constructive knowledge that its customers may use that equipment to make unauthorized copies of copyrighted material.'[74] There was, however, 'no precedent for imposition of [secondary] liability on such a theory,'[75] nor any basis in the copyright statute.[76] Holding Sony liable on this theory was unwarranted, moreover, because of the significant effects it would have on other parties, including copyright owners who approved of time-shift copying of their programmes by Betamax users, members of the public who wanted access to such technologies to make authorized and fair uses of them, and of course, Sony and other technology developers who wanted to make and sell these technologies.[77] 'When a charge of contributory infringement is predicated entirely on the sale of an article in commerce that is used by the purchaser to infringe [an intellectual property right], the public interest in access to that article is necessarily implicated.'[78]

Sony recognized that Congress had resolved a similar tension in patent law by imposing contributory liability on technology developers only when they made and sold devices that had been 'especially made or especially adapted

---

72 *Universal City Studios, Inc. v Sony Corp. of Am.*, 659 F.2d 963, 971-72 (9th Cir. 1981).

73 *Sony*, 464 US at 447–56.

74 Id. at 439.

75 Id.

76 Justice Stevens pointed out that US copyright law 'does not expressly render anyone liable for infringement committed by another.' Id. at 434. Universal argued that '*Kalem* [*Co. v Harper Bros.*, 222 US 55 (1911)] stands for the proposition that supplying the "means" to accomplish an infringing activity and encouraging that activity through advertisement are sufficient to establish liability for copyright infringement.' *Sony*, 464 US at 436. This was, Justice Stevens opined, a 'gross generalization that cannot withstand scrutiny.' Id.

77 Id. at 434–42.

78 Id. at 440. This statement was particularly significant because by the time the Court heard oral argument in *Sony* for the second time, 9.5 million American households had Betamax machines; under Universal's theory, virtually every Betamax user was a copyright infringer, and Sony's potential liability was vast. Counsel for Sony led off his oral argument with this fact. See Jessica Litman (2005), 'The Sony Paradox', 55 *Case W. Res. L. Rev.* 917, 940. The potential for statutory damages for which Sony and/or owners of Betamax machines might be liable if Universal's theory was accepted was staggeringly large.

for use in an infringement of . . . a patent.'[79] Congress had created a statutory safe harbour from contributory liability for dual-use technologies, that is, for 'staple articles of commerce,' which applies to technologies 'suitable for substantial non-infringing use.'[80] This safe harbour recognized a legitimate public interest in having the ability to access and enjoy staple articles for their non-infringing purposes.

Invoking an 'historic kinship' between the copyright and patent laws,[81] the Court decided such a safe harbour was appropriate for copyright law as well as for patent law. 'The sale of copying equipment, like the sale of other articles of commerce, does not constitute contributory infringement,' *Sony* opined, 'if the product is widely used for legitimate unobjectionable purposes.'[82] Indeed, 'it need merely be capable of substantial non-infringing uses.'[83] Because the Betamax had substantial non-infringing uses for time-shift copying of television programmes, the Court ruled that Sony could not be held secondarily liable for any infringing acts of users of these machines.[84]

In the twenty-some years since the *Sony* decision, information technology developers and the copyright industries have flourished.[85] The *Sony* safe harbour has been an important contributor to the success of both industries. Consumer electronics industry representatives speak of the *Sony* safe harbour as the 'Magna Carta' for their industry.[86] Universal and other motion picture

---

[79] 35 USC. § 271(c).

[80] Id. For a highly informative discussion of the case law on the staple article of commerce rule, see Donald S. Chisum, *Chisum on Patents* § 17.03 (2004).

[81] *Sony*, 464 US at 439. For an argument that the Court was justified in borrowing this rule from patent law, see, for example, Brief of Amici Curiae of Sixty Intellectual Property and Technology Law Professors and US-ACM Public Policy Committee, to the US Supreme Court in *MGM v Grokster*, 20 *Berkeley Tech. L.J.* 535 (2005) [hereinafter IP Professor Amicus Brief]. But see Peter S. Menell and David Nimmer (2007), 'Unwinding Sony', 95 *Cal. L. Rev.* 941, 985 (questioning the historic kinship justification).

[82] *Sony*, 464 US at 442.

[83] Id.

[84] Id. at 456.

[85] See e.g., Pamela Samuelson (2006), 'The Generativity of Sony v. Universal: The Intellectual Property Legacy of Justice Stevens', 74 *Fordham L. Rev.* 1831, 1850–51 (discussing the legacy of *Sony*).

[86] Litman, *supra* n. 78, at 951. There is considerable support for the *Sony* safe harbour among academics as well as among technology developers. See e.g., IP Professor Amicus Brief, *supra* n. 81; Brief of Intel Corp. as Amicus Curiae Supporting Affirmance, *Metro-Goldwyn-Mayer Studios, Inc. v Grokster, Ltd.*, 545 US 913 (2005) (No. 04-480), available at http://www.eff.org/IP/P2P/MGM_v_Grokster/20050301_intel.pdf [hereinafter Intel Amicus Brief]. However, there are also some critics. See e.g., Menell and Nimmer, *supra* n. 81; Douglas Lichtman and William Landes (2003), 'Indirect Liability for Copyright Infringement: An Economic Perspective', 16 *Harv. J. L. & Tech.* 395.

producers greatly benefited from the installed base of Betamax and other VTRs, which created opportunities for a wholly new lucrative market for copyrighted motion pictures, such as the sale of video cassettes of movies that could be played in VTR machines.[87] Many other new technologies, including notably the iPod, have similarly allowed both information technology and copyright industries to achieve mutual success.[88]

Although Congress has been persuaded on two occasions to deviate from the *Sony* safe harbour in very narrowly drawn circumstances,[89] it has rejected other legislative proposals aimed at giving copyright owners greater control over dual-use technologies.[90] Courts have also denied relief to some who sought to expand technology developer liability.[91] Yet, when presented with technologies lacking in substantial non-infringing uses, courts followed *Sony* and imposed liability for infringements thereby enabled.[92]

The White Paper had sought to establish a new rule for technology developer liability with respect to so-called circumvention technologies based on the 'primary use' of the technology.[93] This approach resembled the technology developer liability rule that the Supreme Court rejected in *Sony* as too unbalanced. Soon after enactment of the DMCA, the entertainment industry commenced litigation against peer-to-peer ('P2P') file-sharing software developer Napster with the aim of overturning the *Sony* safe harbour for technologies with substantial non-infringing uses.[94] In cases against P2P file-sharing

87 Lardner, *supra* n. 69, at 297–313.

88 See e.g., Intel Amicus Brief, *supra* n. 86.

89 See 17 USC. § 1002 (prohibiting manufacture and sale of digital audio recording technologies unless they incorporate serial copy management technologies); 47 USC. § 605(e)(4) (outlawing development and distribution of satellite cable decoder boxes). These narrow exceptions to the *Sony* safe harbour are discussed in Samuelson, *supra* n. 85, at 1858–62.

90 See e.g., Nicholas E. Sciorra (1993), 'Note, Self-Help and Contributory Infringement: The Law and Legal Thought Behind a Little Black Box', 11 *Cardozo Arts & Ent. L.J.* 905.

91 In *Vault Corp. v Quaid Software, Ltd.*, 847 F.2d 255 (5th Cir. 1988), for instance, the maker of the Prolok copy-protection software sued Quaid, the maker of Ramkey software that bypassed Prolok, claiming Quaid was a secondary copyright infringer because the primary use of its software was likely to be making infringing copies of Prolok-protected software. The court invoked the *Sony* safe harbour as a basis for denying Vault's claim because Ramkey was a dual-use technology that enabled purchasers of software products to make lawful backup copies. Id. at 262.

92 See e.g., *A&M Records, Inc. v Abdallah*, 948 F. Supp. 1449 (C.D. Cal. 1996) (imposing secondary liability because alleged non-infringing uses were insubstantial).

93 See *supra* n. 25 and accompanying text.

94 See *A&M Records, Inc. v Napster, Inc.*, 114 F. Supp. 2d 896 (N.D. Cal. 2000), aff'd in part, rev'd in part, 239 F.3d 1004 (9th Cir. 2001), discussed *infra* 'The dissemination technology cases: *Napster*, *Aimster* and *Grokster*' at p. 255.

technology developers, the entertainment industry once again urged the courts to adopt a 'primary use' theory of technology developer liability for user infringements.[95] Part III will discuss why the latter effort was unsuccessful, but for now, it suffices to say that the White Paper proposal for regulating technologies based on their primary purpose or use was a radical departure from the *Sony* safe harbour default rule in place since 1984.[96]

TECHNOLOGY DEVELOPER RESPONSES TO THE WHITE PAPER'S ANTI-CIRCUMVENTION RULE

Information technology developers raised numerous concerns about the White Paper's proposed anti-circumvention rule in addition to objecting to its incompatibility with the *Sony* safe harbour for technologies with substantial non-infringing uses.[97] For one thing, the proposed provision was vague about what kinds of 'processes' and 'treatments' it was designed to protect. For another, its willingness to penalize technology developers based on 'primary effect' meant that developers risked liability for what users did with the technology, rather than for what the technology had been designed to do. The proposed rule also lacked exceptions for legitimate acts, such as building tools to bypass TPMs for law enforcement, national security, or computer security research purposes. It could, moreover, be interpreted as outlawing the development of reverse engineering technologies to enable interoperability among computer programs.

---

[95] See e.g., Petition for a Writ of Certiorari at 15-20, *Metro-Goldwyn-Mayer Studios Inc. v Grokster, Ltd.*, 545 US 913 (2005) (No. 04-480) (interpreting *Sony* as a 'primary use' case), available at http://www.eff.org/IP/P2P/MGM_v_Grokster/20041008_Grokster_final_petition.pdf.

[96] Although the White Paper did not acknowledge that its proposal would have any impact on the *Sony* safe harbor, Marybeth Peters, the Register of Copyrights, did so in the course of the legislative debate that led up to the DMCA. See *WIPO Copyright Treaties Implementation Act and On-Line Copyright Liability Limitation Act: Hearing on H.R. 2281 and H.R. 2180, Before the Subcomm. on Courts and Intellectual Property of the House Comm. on the Judiciary*, 105th Cong. (1997) (statement of Marybeth Peters, the Register of Copyrights), available at http://www.copyright.gov/docs/2180_stat.html.

[97] The technology industry objections to the White Paper proposed anti-circumvention rule are discussed at length in Samuelson, *supra* n. 14, at 531–534, 546–557. Some in the technology industry, including the Business Software Alliance and its members, ultimately supported the DMCA anti-circuvmention rules because they were more narrowly tailored than the White Paper proposal and because these developers sometimes use TPMs to control access to their works and did not want others to build tools to circumvent them.

The greatest concern of technology developers, however, was that the provision might be construed as imposing a duty on them to detect and enforce any TPM that copyright owners might use to protect their works in digital form. The most vigorous technology industry lobbying about anti-circumvention rules concentrated on getting statutory clarification that they had no obligation to design technologies to respond to copyright-protective TPMs.

The technology industry's opposition to the proposed anti-circumvention rule contributed to a stall in the initial legislative efforts in 1995 and 1996 to enact the White Paper's recommendation.[98] Another setback for copyright industry groups occurred in December 1996 when opposition to a White Paper-like ban on circumvention technologies caused it to be dropped from the final version of the WCT.[99] Many delegations at the WIPO diplomatic conference were concerned that the proposed anti-circumvention rule would chill development of dual use technologies and impede fair and other non-infringing uses of copyrighted works and public domain materials.[100] To avert these undesirable effects, the treaty required only that contracting parties provide 'adequate protection' and 'effective remedies' against circumvention of TPMs,[101] which seemingly left the mode and extent of implementation of this norm to national discretion.

Congressmen Tom Campbell and Rick Boucher proposed to implement this treaty obligation in the U.S. with a minimalist anti-circumvention rule aimed at outlawing circumvention of a TPM for purposes of facilitating or engaging in infringing activities.[102] This bill was unacceptable to copyright industry groups, who favored adoption of a broad ban on circumvention technologies, akin to the proposal that had been rejected at WIPO, to serve as a standard for international implementation of the WIPO treaty's anti-circumvention norm.[103]

The Clinton Administration's post-treaty anti-circumvention proposal responded to technology industry concerns in several ways: by becoming more precise about the technical measures the rule was designed to protect;[104] by defining circumvention;[105] and by outlawing only technologies that were

98 Id. at 523.

99 See Samuelson, *supra* n. 4, at 409–416 (discussing opposition to the proposed WIPO treaty anti-circumvention provision).

100 Id.

101 WCT, *supra* n. 1, art. 11.

102 See H.R. 3048, 105th Cong., § 8 (1997).

103 See, e.g., Chander, *supra* n. 18, at 206–07 (discussing stronger than DMCA anti-circumvention rules being negotiated by the U.S. in free trade agreements with other nations).

104 17 U.S.C. § 1201(a)(3).

105 Id.

'primarily designed or produced' to circumvent TPMs, that had only limited uses other than for circumvention, or that had been marketed as circumvention tools.[106] It also contained an exception for national security and law enforcement activities.[107] Further lobbying led to the creation of exceptions for encryption research, computer security testing,[108] and reverse engineering to achieve interoperability.[109] The technology industry also obtained the 'no mandate' clause that had been its top priority. Section 1201(c)(3) provides that the law does not 'require that the design of, or design and selection of parts and components for, a consumer electronics, telecommunications, or computing product provide for a response to any particular technological protection measure.'[110]

Given how hard the copyright industries fought against inclusion of any exceptions to § 1201 – beyond that for law enforcement and national security activities – especially the 'no mandate' rule, it is notable that technology industry objections led to substantial changes in the circumvention technology rules.

Still, it was a major victory for the entertainment industry that the DMCA anti-circumvention rules premised technology developer liability on a 'primarily designed or produced' standard.[111] Copyright industry representatives were pleased with the DMCA also because, on its face, § 1201 does not appear to require any proof that the availability of a circumvention tool enabled copyright infringement or even created a grave risk of infringement.[112] The exceptions are, moreover, complex and ambiguous enough to be susceptible to dismissive interpretations.[113]

---

106 Id. at §§ 1201(a)(2), 1201(b)(1).

107 Id. at § 1201(e).

108 Id. at §§ 1201(g), 1201(j).

109 Id. at § 1201(f).

110 Id. at § 1201(c)(3).

111 Id. at §§ 1201(a)(2)(A), 1201(b)(1)(A).

112 For a discussion of numerous examples of the ill effects arising from the overbreadth of the DMCA anti-circumvention rules, see Electronic Frontier Foundation, Unintended Consequences: Seven Years under the DMCA (as updated Apr. 2006), available at http://www.eff.org/IP/DMCA/DMCA_unintended_v4.pdf [hereinafter Unintended Consequences].

113 See, e.g., National Research Council, The Digital Dilemma: Intellectual Property in the Information Age 171–76 (2001) [hereinafter Digital Dilemma] (raising objections to the complexity and narrowness of the DMCA encryption research exception). Under the *Reimerdes* decision, a journal publisher could arguably be held liable for violating the DMCA anti-circumvention laws even if the author of an encryption research article it planned to publish qualified for the DMCA exception because the publisher was not itself an encryption researcher. *Reimerdes*, 111 F. Supp. 2d at 320. See Pamela Samuelson, 'Anti-Circumvention Rules: Threat to Science', 293 *Science* 2028 (2001).

Regulating acts of circumvention and public interest uses of technically protected works

The most troubling part of the legislative history of the DMCA anti-circumvention rules was the manner in which Congress dealt with the threat that TPMs posed for the public's ability to engage in fair and other non-infringing uses of copyrighted works protected by TPMs. As we shall see at p. 284, the EU implemented the WCT anti-circumvention norm by making a normative (if incomplete) commitment to ensuring that copyright exceptions and limitations on the scope of exclusive rights must be made as available when copyrighted works are protected by TPMs as when they are not.[114] No similar commitment is apparent in the DMCA rules, although there is ample, if somewhat equivocal, evidence that Congress had tried to assure itself through various measures that it was preserving opportunities for fair and other privileged uses of technically protected digital content.[115]

The initial threat that the White Paper posed to fair and other public interest uses of technically protected copyrighted works was somewhat indirect. The White Paper had not attempted to regulate the act of circumvention, but its proposal to ban circumvention technologies affected public interest uses insofar as circumvention tools were necessary to engage in such uses of content wrapped in TPMs.[116] From the standpoint of copyright owners, however, circumvention technologies that enabled fair or other public interest uses of technically protected works were dangerous because they were too likely to enable infringements. A broad ban on circumvention technologies was, they argued, necessary to protect against massive infringements.

It was not until 1997 that the Clinton Administration proposed a ban on the act of circumventing TPMs used by copyright owners to protect their works.[117] The bill distinguished between two types of TPMs: those used to control access to copyrighted works and those used to protect 'a right of a copyright owner' in a work protected by copyright law.[118] Its sponsors did not

---

[114] See *infra* p. 281 (discussing limits that have hampered the effectiveness of Article 6(4) in achieving this objective).

[115] See e.g., 17 USC. § 1201(c)(1), discussed *infra* nn. 124–125 and 251–257 and accompanying text.

[116] See e.g., Julie E. Cohen (1998), 'Copyright and the Jurisprudence of Self-Help', 13 *Berkeley Tech. L.J.* 1089. Yet, perhaps building a circumvention tool for public interest purposes could be defended as authorized by the law, even if not by the copyright owner. Id. at 1142 n.200. If so, it might have been outside the White Paper's anti-circumvention ban, which recognized both sources of authority as relevant to the scope of the ban.

[117] See H.R. 2281, 105th Cong. (1997).

[118] The distinction between the two types of TPMs is evident in the bifurcation of the anti-tool rules. See id., § 3. The DMCA, as enacted, has retained this distinction. See 17 USC. § 1201(a)(2), (b)(1).

explain why the bill distinguished between these two types of TPMs, nor why it proposed totally banning circumvention of access controls, but not of other TPMs.

A coalition of organizations, including libraries, educational institutions, and other non-profit organizations raised concerns about the direct impact that such a ban would have on fair and other non-infringing uses of copyrighted works in digital form, on access to public domain materials, and on user privacy interests.[119] These concerns did not, however, arouse Congressional interest as much as concerns about overbroad ISP liability. This relative indifference may be explained in part perhaps because the lobbying clout of these nonprofits was minute in comparison with the heft of the copyright, telecom, and technology industries that lobbied about ISP liability. Furthermore, deployment of TPMs to protect copyrighted works was in its early stages, so concerns about impediments to fair and other privileged uses may have seemed speculative.[120]

Yet, if one knows where to look, there is considerable evidence of Congressional concern about enabling public interest uses of technically protected content. By regulating circumvention of access controls, but not of rights controls,[121] Congress decided, albeit implicitly, that circumvention for fair use and other public interest purposes should remain lawful. Congress also created three special public interest exceptions, including one for libraries, archives, and educational institutions to bypass TPMs to make a good faith effort to decide whether to buy the content protected by the TPM if circumvention was necessary to achieve this objective;[122] one that aims to protect user privacy interests implicated when content is protected by TPM; and one that buttresses parental control over minors.[123]

---

[119] See WIPO Copyright Treaties Implementation Act and On-Line Copyright Liability Limitation Act: Hearing on H.R. 2281 and H.R. 2180, Before the Subcomm. on Courts and Intellectual Property of the House Comm. on the Judiciary, 105th Cong. (1997) (testimony of Robert Oakley; testimony of M.R.C. Greenwood).

[120] The important role of the House Commerce Committee in inserting some balance in the anti-circumvention rules is related in Samuelson, *supra* n. 14, at 541–43.

[121] 17 USC. § 1201(a)(1)(A). See Ginsburg, *supra* n. 14, at 6 (noting that section 1201 'does not prohibit the act of circumventing a rights control'). Ginsburg believes that the decision not to regulate circumvention of rights controls was intended to leave room for fair uses of technically protected works. Id. at 10.

[122] 17 USC. § 1201(d).

[123] Id. at § 1201(h), (i). These provisions are, however, a puzzlingly narrow response to concerns expressed about the anti-circumvention ban. See e.g., Samuelson, *supra* n. 14, at 537–53 (explaining the undue narrowness of s. 1201's exceptions); David Nimmer (1999), 'Puzzles of the Digital Millennium Copyright Act', 46 *J. Copyright Soc'y* 401 (1999), available at http://ssrn.com/abstract=208876.

A more general indication of Congressional concern about the impact of s. 1201 on fair and other privileged uses can arguably be found in s. 1201(c)(1), which states that '[n]othing in this section shall affect rights, remedies, limitations, or defences to copyright infringement, including fair use, under this title.'[124] Some members of Congress who spoke about the anti-circumvention rules during the legislative debate over the DMCA seemed genuinely to believe this provision constituted a 'savings clause' to enable fair and other privileged uses of technically protected copyrighted works.[125]

Finally, Congress established a triennial rulemaking process under which the Librarian of Congress (LOC) is directed to examine 'the impact that the prohibition on the circumvention of technological measures applied to copyrighted works has on criticism, comment, news reporting, teaching, scholarship, or research.'[126] The Librarian is authorized to create new exceptions from the ban on circumvention to enable public interest uses of copyrighted works when users of certain classes of copyrighted works show they 'are, or are likely to be . . . adversely affected' by the use of TPMs.[127]

Much contested is whether these provisions of the anti-circumvention rules meaningfully contribute to an adequate balance of public and private interests in the DMCA. The first decision to have considered this question was *Universal City Studios, Inc. v Reimerdes*,[128] in which Judge Lewis Kaplan concluded that Congress had considered, and decided against, allowing circumventions for fair use or other privileged purposes. 'If Congress had meant the fair use defence to apply to [anti-circumvention] actions, it would have said so. The decision not to make fair use a defence to a claim under Section 1201(a) was quite deliberate.'[129]

In affirming an injunction against posting or linking to DeCSS, software designed to bypass the Content Scramble System (CSS) protecting DVD movies, the Second Circuit rejected the argument that s. 1201(c)(1) was a 'fair use savings' clause. The panel declared that this interpretation 'is not only outside the range of plausible readings of the provision, but is also clearly refuted by the statute's legislative history.'[130]

---

124 17 USC. § 1201(c)(1).

125 See e.g., 144 Cong. Rec. H7093 (daily ed. Aug. 4, 1998) (statement of Rep. Bliley) (indicating that the Commerce Committee understood the DMCA legislation to enable consumers to 'exercise their historical fair use rights').

126 17 USC. § 1201(a)(1)(C).

127 Id.

128 111 F. Supp. 2d 294 (S.D.N.Y. 2000).

129 Id. at 322.

130 *Universal City Studios, Inc. v Corley*, 273 F.3d 429, 443 (2d Cir. 2001). But see *Chamberlain Group, Inc. v Skylink Techs., Inc.*, 381 F.3d 1178, 1200 (Fed. Cir. 2004) (regarding s. 1201(c)(1) as a fair use savings clause).

Both the trial court and the Second Circuit considered the triennial rulemaking and the narrowly drawn public interest exceptions to s. 1201 as adequately accommodating fair use and other public interests pertaining to technically protected works.[131] Judge Kaplan characterized the argument that purchasers of DVD movies have the right to circumvent CSS so long as they do not infringe copyrights in DVD movies as 'pure sophistry' and as 'a corruption of the first sale doctrine.'[132] According to Judge Kaplan, the DMCA anti-circumvention laws 'fundamentally altered the landscape of copyright' as to technology provider liability.[133]

Seemingly without realizing it,[134] Judge Kaplan arguably also closed off another possible public interest safety valve in the DMCA by construing DeCSS as a tool for circumventing access controls. If CSS is indeed an access control, then bypassing it would violate s. 1201(a)(1)(A). Insofar as TPMs, such as CSS, are deemed 'access controls' within the meaning of s. 1201, the public interest circumventions that the DMCA was supposed to accommodate by not regulating circumvention of non-access-control TPMs have arguably been foreclosed. Copyright owners have apparently recognized that they may be able to defeat some public interest limitations on the scope of the anti-circumvention rules by adopting persistent access controls as their TPMs of choice.[135]

Given the hostility that *Reimerdes* and *Corley* displayed toward fair use as a limitation on the scope of s. 1201, the next most plausible candidate for an accommodation of public interest uses of digital content protected by TPMs would seem to be the LOC rulemaking procedure. However, this procedure is not a sufficient safety valve for several reasons.

First, it only occurs every three years, and any exceptions created only last for three years.[136] Secondly, it is largely focused on exempting classes of works rather than classes of uses, although classes of uses are more relevant when assessing public interest uses.[137] Thirdly, proposals for exemptions can only be made during the rulemaking process, and a heavy burden of proof has been put

---

131 *Reimerdes*, 111 F. Supp. 2d at 323; *Corley*, 273 F.3d at 443.

132 *Reimerdes*, 111 F. Supp. 2d at 317 n.137.

133 Id. at 324.

134 In discussing circumvention for fair use purposes, Judge Kaplan seemed to accept that technically sophisticated persons would be able to circumvent CSS to make fair uses of DVD movies without violating the DMCA rules. Id. at 388. Yet, his conclusion that CSS is an access control is inconsistent with his conclusion that technical sophisticates could make fair uses of DVD movies.

135 See e.g., R. Anthony Reese (2003), 'Will Merging Access Controls and Rights Controls Undermine the Structure of Anti-Circumvention Law?', 18 *Berkeley Tech. L.J.* 619 (2003).

136 17 USC. § 1201(a)(1)(C)–(D).

137 Id.

on the proponent of any particular new exception to show adverse effects on privileged uses.[138] This contrasts sharply with the EU, which seems to place burdens on its member states and on copyright owners to ensure that privileged uses can be exercised, even when works are technically protected.[139]

Fourthly, s. 1201 does not authorize the LOC to create exceptions to the tool rules, only to the act of circumvention rule.[140] Without some way to obtain appropriate tools, circumvention privileges may not be meaningful. Fifthly, the LOC has generally construed its rulemaking authority in a narrow manner.[141] For these reasons, we agree with the Electronic Frontier Foundation, a prominent civil liberties group, that 'the DMCA triennial rulemaking is fundamentally unable to protect the interests of today's digital media consumers.'[142]

In the latest rulemaking,[143] the LOC moved beyond the exemption of 'particular class[es] of works'[144] and proposed an exemption focused on a

---

[138] See 17 USC. § 1201(a)(1)(C); Electronic Frontier Foundation, 'DMCA Triennial Rulemaking: Failing the Digital Consumer' 3 (2005) [hereinafter EFF on Rulemaking], available at http://www.eff.org/IP/DMCA/copyrightoffice/DMCA_rulemaking_broken.pdf (explaining why ordinary consumers without copyright counsel are unlikely to be able to meet the onerous burden of proof established by the Copyright Office, but '[e]ven with expert assistance, the burdens imposed by the Copyright Office on participants often prove nearly insurmountable'). By focusing the inquiry on proof of adverse effects on non-infringing uses of classes of works, the DMCA makes it difficult to focus on particular uses, a more relevant criterion for fair use analysis. See Bill D. Herman and Oscar Gandy (2006), 'Catch 1201: A Legislative History and Content Analysis of the DMCA Exemption Proceedings', 24 *Cardozo Arts & Ent. L.J.* 121.

[139] See *infra* 'The unfulfilled normative commitment underlying Article 6(4)' at p. 282.

[140] See 17 USC. § 1201(a)(1)(D); EFF on Rulemaking, *supra* n. 121, at 2 ('[A]verage consumers denied access to circumvention tools are not able to make use of the 6 exemptions that have been granted.'). One of us has argued that there should be an implied right to implement a tool to enable a privileged party to make a privileged use of technically protected content. Samuelson, *supra* n. 14, at 554.

[141] See e.g., Diane Leenheer Zimmerman (2001), 'Adrift in the Digital Millennium Copyright Act: The Sequel', 26 *U. Dayton L. Rev.* 279, 283–84. See also ALA, DMCA Section 1201 – The Anti-Circumvention rule (as updated Dec. 22, 2005), (characterizing the LOC exceptions as 'narrow'); EFF on Rulemaking, *supra* n. 121, at 7 (pointing out that the Copyright Office has given a narrower interpretation of fair use in the course of its rulemakings than courts and commentators have done).

[142] Id. at 1. See also id. at 8 (offering suggestions about how the LOC rulemaking could be improved); Aaron Perzanowski (2007), 'Evolving Standards & The Future of The DMCA Anticircumvention Rulemaking', 10 *J. Internet L.* 1, 20–21 (April 2007) (discussing shortcomings of the DMCA rulemaking process).

[143] 37 C.F.R. § 201.40(b)(1) (2007).

[144] See 17 USC. § 1201(a)(1)(B)–(C).

particular type of use by a particular type of user. It created an exception so that media or film study professors could make compilations of clips from CSS-protected movies for use in teaching classes.[145] Much as the LOC deserves credit for this innovative interpretation of its s. 1201 authority, this exemption seems to leave in the lurch everyone else who might want to make fair use clips of CSS-protected movies.[146] Many other fair use clips of technically protected content can easily be imagined, but only those who participate in a triennial rulemaking have a chance of having their fair use interests accommodated through the rulemaking process.

The LOC rulemaking procedure 'is a kind of safety valve' for the DMCA anti-circumvention rules, but as Professor Ginsburg has recently concluded, 'it may not let off enough steam.'[147] Too many public interest uses of copyrighted works are being blocked by TPMs.[148] The checks and balances that Congress arguably embedded in the DMCA have not achieved the necessary balance.

A better balance among competing interests can be attained within the framework of the DMCA anti-circumvention rules.[149] Among the more modest measures, courts could decide that persistent access controls, such as CSS, are not the kinds of 'access controls' that s. 1201(a) actually regulates, which would open up considerably more room for fair use circumventions.[150] They could also find in s. 1201(c)(1) a statutory basis for excusing fair use circumventions.[151] They could, moreover, regulate abuses of s. 1201 and abusive uses of TPMs through the anti-circumvention misuse doctrine first proposed by Professor Burk.[152] Courts could additionally interpret the DMCA

---

145 See 37 C.F.R. § 201.40. For a discussion of the latest rulemaking, see, for example, Ginsburg, *supra* n. 14, at 12–17. Ginsburg notes that the film teacher exception 'departs significantly from prior rule-makings.' Id. at 12–13.

146 For example, an evidence professor might want to bypass CSS in order to take clips from movies about trials to show his class how to (and not to) make objections, while a psychology professor might want to make fair use clips of movies to demonstrate how mentally ill people are depicted. We are hopeful that a judge with a broad view of 17 USC. § 1201(c)(1) might analogize these and similar fair use circumventions to the exemption granted by the LOC, but there is as yet no precedent for doing so.

147 Ginsburg, *supra* n. 14, at 16.

148 See e.g., Armstrong, *supra* n. 14, at 68; Benkler, *supra* n. 14, at 420–27; Lipton, *supra* n. 14, at 124–36; Perzanowski, *supra* n. 142, at 17–18.

149 Professors Burk and Cohen have proposed requiring deployers of TPMs to make unlocking technologies available to enable fair uses by third party escrow agents. Burk and Cohen, *supra* n. 14, at 65–67. Professor Lipton has proposed that the Copyright Office establish an administrative procedure to assist prospective fair users of TPM content. Lipton, *supra* n. 14, at 124.

150 See e.g., Reese, *supra* n. 135, at 663–64.

151 See e.g., Ginsburg, *supra* n. 14, at 21–22; Samuelson, *supra* n. 14, at 539–45.

152 Dan L. Burk (2003), 'Anticircumvention Misuse', 50 *UCLA L. Rev.* 1095.

anti-circumvention rules as inapplicable to any technology that does not pose serious risks of enabling copyright infringement.[153]

The stronger measure to achieve balance in the DMCA anti-circumvention regulations that we propose is the reverse notice and takedown regime discussed in the next section. It would not only permit circumvention to enable public interest uses of technically protected digital content, but it could provide a mechanism to help those who lack the technical expertise to perform public interest circumventions by themselves. In an appropriate case, prospective fair users, after unsuccessfully seeking voluntary cooperation from relevant copyright owners, could seek a declaratory judgment that circumvention for specific public interest purposes should be permitted. Courts in such cases could order copyright owners to cooperate with facilitating such circumventions, including, as necessary, providing the key to unlock the TPM that was inhibiting a particular privileged use to the prospective user or designating a circumvention service to facilitate this action.

SETTING THE STAGE FOR A REVERSE NOTICE AND TAKEDOWN REGIME

The idea for a reverse notice and takedown regime emerged as we reflected upon two groups of cases that have recently challenged the outer limits of protection for copyrighted works in the digital environment. Both have elicited considerable attention and controversy,[154] although most commentaries have not considered the two groups of cases in conjunction with one another. We, however, find in these sets of cases not only a deep symmetry, but the theoretical underpinnings for judicial evolution of a reverse notice and takedown regime that would permit and enable circumventions of technically protected copyrighted content for public interest purposes.

The first group of cases – *Napster*,[155] *Aimster*,[156] and *Grokster*[157] – considered whether online service providers and related software toolmakers who

---

153 The Federal Circuit opened up this possibility by its far-sighted decision in *Chamberlain Group, Inc. v Skylink Technologies., Inc.*, 318 F.3d 1178 (Fed. Cir. 2004), discussed at length *infra* nn. 241–258 and accompanying text.

154 See e.g., Matthew D. Brown et al. (2005), 'Secondary Liability for Inducing Infringement After *MGM v. Grokster*: Infringement Prevention and Product Design', 9 *J. Internet L.* 21 (Dec. 2005); Stacey Dogan (2001), 'Is Napster a VCR? The Implications of Sony for Napster and Other Internet Technologies', 52 *Hastings L.J.* 939; Mark A. Lemley and R. Anthony Reese (2004), 'Reducing Digital Copyright Infringement without Restricting Innovation', 56 *Stan. L. Rev.* 1345; Lipton, *supra* n. 14.

155 *A&M Records, Inc. v Napster Inc.*, 239 F.3d 1004 (9th Cir. 2001).

156 *In re* Aimster Copyright Litigation, 334 F.3d 643 (7th Cir. 2003).

157 *Metro-Goldwyn-Mayer Studios Inc. v Grokster Ltd.*, 545 US 913 (2005).

facilitated P2P file sharing of copyrighted sound recordings by a multitude of individual direct infringers should be held indirectly liable for their users' infringing acts. (We will call these the 'dissemination technology cases.') Entertainment industry plaintiffs in these cases believed that the scale of infringements enabled by these technologies was so vast that courts would be willing to move away from the *Sony* safe harbour for technologies with substantial non-infringing uses in favour of a 'primary use' test for technology/service developer liability under copyright law.[158]

As in the legislative debate that produced the DMCA, the entertainment industry dismissed as unimportant expressions of concern about the public's interest in access to these technologies and services for non-infringing purposes if the entertainment industry gained greater control over technology development.[159] Notwithstanding the many arguments and amicus briefs that the industry marshalled in favour of the primary use test,[160] the Supreme Court maintained a balanced approach to technology/service developer liability in *Grokster*. It preserved the *Sony* safe harbour for technology developers except as to those who actively induce copyright infringement.[161] As in *Sony*, the Court was attentive to the interests of the public in access to dual-use technologies for non-infringing purposes.[162]

In the second group of cases – *Chamberlain*,[163] *Lexmark*,[164] and

---

158 See Brief for Motion Picture Studio and Recording Company Petitioners, Metro-Goldwyn-Mayer Studios v. Grokster Ltd., 545 US 913 (2005) (No. 04-480), available at http://www.eff.org/IP/P2P/MGM_v_Grokster/04-480_Petitioners_brief.pdf [hereinafter MGM Brief]. Recall that the Court had rejected, albeit only just barely so, a primary use test for indirect liability for copyright infringement in the *Sony* case. See *supra* n. 73 and accompanying text. Section 1201 adopts a variant on the primary use test for circumvention technology liability. While in theory a 'primary purpose or design' test, as in the DMCA, is more rigorous than the 'primary use' test for which Universal argued in *Sony*, we are skeptical about how different they would be in practice, given that when a technology is primarily used for an illicit purpose, a challenger of that technology will almost certainly argue that the technology must have been designed to facilitate these illicit uses and that any testimony about beneficial purposes for the design are self-serving misrepresentations to avoid liability. See IP Professor Amicus Brief, *supra* n. 81, at 559–61.

159 See e.g., MGM Brief, *supra* n. 158, 18–20.

160 The many amicus briefs filed in support of MGM's appeal are available at http://www.eff.org/IP/P2P/MGM_v_Grokster/.

161 *Grokster*, 545 US at 937.

162 Id. at 920 ('Given [their] benefits in security, cost, and efficiency, peer to peer networks are employed to store and distribute electronic files by universities, governmental agencies, corporations, and libraries among others.').

163 *Chamberlain Group, Inc. v Skylink Techs*., Inc., 381 F.3d 1178 (Fed. Cir. 2004).

164 *Lexmark Int'l, Inc. v Static Control Components, Inc*., 387 F.3d 522 (6th Cir. 2004).

StorageTek[165] – makers of technologies claimed that by embedding software access controls inside their products, they had obtained the right to control the market for replacement parts or repair services. (We will call these the 'lock-out technology' cases.) The courts ultimately decided these cases by permitting third-party suppliers of parts or services to bypass the lock-out codes and provide competing parts or services, notwithstanding the amplified rights of copyright owners under the anti-circumvention provisions of the DMCA.[166] Judges in the lock-out cases could not accept the unbalanced interpretation of s. 1201 that the plaintiffs had constructed on the foundation laid by *Reimerdes* and *Corley*.

Both groups of cases focus attention on the extent to which recent legislative efforts to bolster the protection of copyright owners operating in the digital environment have unduly narrowed or sacrificed the interests of users, follow-on improvers, competitors, and the public at large that were core components of pre-digital traditional copyright law. In practical terms, however, the two groups of cases affect the public interest at diametrically opposite ends of the spectrum of protected rights.

This section will show that the dissemination technology cases have implications for public interest users who want to access copyrighted works for unauthorized but non-infringing purposes when the works in question have been surrounded by TPMs designed to prevent unauthorized uses. The dissemination technology cases also have implications for the right of public interest users to access technologies that enable lawful uses. These cases recognize both the legitimacy of user access to equipment that enables non-infringing uses and the need for incentives to persuade manufacturers to invest in and create innovative technology, such as P2P file-sharing software, that can enhance non-infringing uses of copyrighted works.[167] By articulating a theory that took the 'bad' technology developers out of the picture, as the Supreme Court did with its active inducement rule in *Grokster*, the Court created a climate in which public interest uses could more freshly be assessed both generally and as they pertain to circumvention of TPMs.

The lock-out technology cases contribute further to this fresh approach by rejecting the plaintiffs' anti-competitive s. 1201 claims as unsound and by importing balancing principles from copyright and patent law as essential to the proper interpretation of s. 1201. Among other things, the courts in *Chamberlain* and *StorageTek* recognized the need to guard the public's interest in making fair and other non-infringing uses of technically protected

---

165 *Storage Tech. Corp. v Custom Hardware Eng'g & Consulting, Inc.*, 421 F.3d 1307 (Fed. Cir. 2005).

166 Digital Millennium Copyright Act, 17 USC. §§ 1201-05 (2000).

167 See e.g., Lemley and Reese, *supra* n. 154.

content. The lock-out cases, in our view, set the stage for judicial development of the reverse notice and takedown procedure we endorse in this chapter.

The Dissemination Technology Cases: *Napster*, *Aimster*, and *Grokster*

In approaching the dissemination technology cases and the controversies they have provoked, we offer some preliminary observations. First, there are very few privileged public interest uses directly at stake when consumers use P2P file-sharing technologies to download entire musical works and sound recordings without payment to authors, artists, and recording studios. Unless one believes that copyrights are an inherently illegitimate form of property, one cannot readily defend the limitless free-riding on copyrighted works that P2P file sharing has engendered in terms of traditional exceptions to copyright protection.[168]

One may lament the demise of any equivalent of the first sale doctrine in the online environment,[169] and one may castigate record companies for clinging too long to outdated business models, without viewing the downloaders as principled defenders of the public interest. Had the DMCA not so shamelessly sacrificed the public interest provisions of copyright law on the altar of TPMs,[170] few copyright law professors would express so much alarm about the cases expanding third-party liability for contributory and vicarious infringement.[171]

What alarms the critics is precisely the potential capacity of the dissemination technology cases, if mishandled by the courts, to exacerbate the imbalance found in the DMCA's anti-circumvention rules and thereby to further reduce the bona fide and legitimate rights of users, improvers, competitors, and the public at large. From this perspective, every expansion of third-party

---

168 Some have argued that the public interest might better have been served by a liability rule than a property rule in response to the P2P file-sharing phenomenon, that is, by grant of a compulsory license to allow file sharing of copyrighted works for noncommercial purposes. See e.g., William W. Fisher III (2004), *Promises to Keep: Technology, Law and the Future of Entertainment*; Neil Weinstock Netanel (2003), 'Impose a Noncommercial Use Levy to Allow Free Peer-to-Peer File Sharing', 17 *Harvard J. L. & Tech.* 1; see generally J. H. Reichman (2000), 'Of Green Tulips and Legal Kudzu: Repackaging Rights in Subpatentable Innovation, 53 *Vand. L. Rev.* 1743 (theory of compensatory liability regime). This would have ensured that revenues would flow back to the composers, performers, and producers of sound recordings while also ensuring that the works were widely distributed.

169 17 USC. §§ 106(3), 109 (2000).

170 See e.g., Litman, *supra* n. 26, at 122–45.

171 See e.g., IP Professor Amicus Brief, *supra* n. 81, at 556–57 (expressing concern about expansion of technology developer liability rules).

liability in this group of cases could potentially further inhibit the already limited range of public interest exceptions to copyright protection. Perhaps worst of all, it could further undermine the incentives to invest in technologies needed for the sharing of information goods for legitimate and important public-good purposes.[172]

The validity of these concerns must, however, be tested against the actual holdings in these cases. Napster, Aimster, and Grokster operated online services that supplied P2P technologies to enable users of their software to search for digital files of commercially distributed copyrighted works on other users' computers, connect directly to the other users' computers in order to make copies of the desired files, and transfer the copies to the requesting users' computers.[173] The principal defence of these P2P developers against charges of secondary liability for copyright infringement was that they qualified for the *Sony* safe harbour for technologies with substantial non-infringing uses,[174] although Napster also raised two DMCA ISP safe harbour defences.[175]

Napster's *Sony* defence characterized the downloading of MP3 files authorized by new artists, the sampling of songs users planned to buy if they liked them, and the archival copying of sound recordings users already owned as substantial non-infringing uses of its technology.[176] Because of the massive amounts of infringement taking place through use of these P2P services, the entertainment industry plaintiffs argued that the *Sony* safe harbour should not be available for services, or alternatively, that it should only be available if the primary use of the challenged technology was non-infringing, as in *Sony*.[177] Another reason to sue this P2P service was that 'it was easier and

---

172 See Lemley and Reese, *supra* n. 154, at 1354–56 (discussing problems of 'dual-use' technologies that can be used in both non-infringing and infringing capacities).

173 *A&M Records, Inc. v Napster Inc.*, 239 F.3d 1004, 1011 (9th Cir. 2001). Napster differed from Aimster and Grokster in that its servers hosted indices through which users could directly search for specific files they wanted to download. Id. at 1012.

174 See e.g., Raymond Shih Ray Ku (2002), 'The Creative Destruction of Copyright: Napster and the New Economics of Digital Technology', 69 *U. Chi. L. Rev.* 263.

175 *A&M Records, Inc. v Napster, Inc.*, 114 F. Supp. 2d 896, 919 n.4 (N.D. Cal. 2000); *A&M Records, Inc. v Napster, Inc.*, 2000 WL 573136, at *3 (N.D. Cal. 2000) [hereinafter Napster II].

176 *Napster*, 114 F. Supp. 2d at 916.

177 Id. at 916 and n. 20. The primary use of the Betamax machine was to make copies of television programs for time-shifting purposes, a use that the Court held was fair. *Sony Corp. of Am. v. Universal City Studios, Inc.*, 464 US 417, 423–24 (1984).

more effective to shut down Napster than to sue the millions of people who illegally traded files on Napster.'[178]

Napster was hardly a neutral ISP providing a vehicle for innocent transmissions of honest exchanges of information or opinions. Yet, it nonetheless claimed immunity under the s. 512(a) safe harbour for Internet transmissions initiated by others[179] and the s. 512(d) safe harbour for information locating tools.[180] The courts in *Napster* rejected its statutory safe harbour defences.[181] Although Napster's network was capable of some non-infringing uses, the fact remained that, as the Ninth Circuit observed, Napster knew or should have known that massive infringements were underway, and its business success depended on encouraging these infringements.[182] In hindsight, Napster's claim to shelter under the *Sony* safe harbour was undermined by its active inducement of infringement, as the Supreme Court later phrased it in *Grokster*.[183]

The court in *Napster* seemed self-consciously to draw parallels between contributory infringement and the safeguards established for ISPs under s. 512 by suggesting that a system operator could avoid liability by purging infringing materials when it knew or should have known about them.[184] Obviously,

---

[178] Lemley and Reese, *supra* n. 137, at 1349. Lichtman and Landes argue that suing third parties instead of the actual direct infringers can be efficient when the former, although only indirectly responsible, are 'typically in a good position to either prevent copyright infringement or pay for the harm it causes.' See Lichtman and Landes, *supra* n. 86, at 409.

[179] *Napster II*, at *6–*8 (ruling on Napster's s. 512(a) defense).

[180] *Napster*, 114 F. Supp. 2d at 919 n. 24. Napster argued that absent notice from the copyright holder, it had no way of knowing which transfers were infringing transfers. Brief for Defendant-Appellant Napster, Inc. at 52, *A&M Records, Inc. v Napster, Inc.* 114 F. Supp. 2d 896 (N.D. Cal. 2000) (Nos. 00-16401 and 00-16403), available at http://www.eff.org/IP/P2P/Napster/brief0818.pdf.

[181] *Napster II*, *supra* n. 158, at *6–*8 (rejecting a s. 512(a) defence); *Napster*, 114 F. Supp. 2d at 919 n. 4.

[182] *Napster*, 239 F.3d at 1020 n. 5.

[183] See *Metro-Goldwyn-Mayer Studios Inc. v Grokster Ltd.*, 545 US 913, 936–38 (2005).

[184] The Ninth Circuit Court of Appeals stated that 'if a computer system operator learns of specific infringing material available on his system and fails to purge such material from the system, the operator knows of and contributes to direct infringement.' *Napster*, 239 F.3d at 1021 (quoting *Religious Tech. Ctr. (RTC) v Netcom On-Line Commc'n Servs., Inc.*, 907 F. Supp. 1361, 1374 (N.D. Cal. 1995)). The Ninth Circuit invoked *Sony*, where the Supreme Court held that if liability had to be imposed, 'it must rest on the fact that they have sold equipment *with constructive knowledge* of the fact that their customers may use that equipment to make unauthorized copies of copyrighted material.' Id. at 1020 (quoting *Sony Corp. of Am. v Universal City Studios, Inc.*, 464 US 417, 439 (1984) (emphasis added)). Although the Supreme Court in *Sony*

a true contributory infringer, such as Napster, had no interest in this safeguard.[185]

Perhaps the most interesting aspect of the *Napster* case was the district court's characterization of Napster's system as a potential barrier to entry for honest purveyors of downloaded music operating under a fee-based system.[186] Here, indeed, is a positive nexus to *Sony*,[187] because the Supreme Court's refusal to ban manufacture of VTRs owing to their substantial non-infringing uses removed an inchoate barrier to entry into the movie rental and cassette business.[188] This result became an unforeseen bonanza for film studios that made considerable revenues by selling movies to rental companies and to consumers. In contrast, the district court correctly perceived the opposite effect in the *Napster* case, and the growth of fee-based providers via iTunes and other systems in the aftermath of Napster's closure would seem to vindicate that thesis.[189]

Aimster, like Napster, made loose, self-serving assertions about the capability of the relevant software system for non-infringing uses, but this was disingenuous coming from someone whose business knowingly depended on the highest possible volume of infringing uses.[190] By co-opting the instant messaging networks of other ISPs to enable file sharers to find each other and search each other's autonomous files, Aimster's contributory acts were more remote and indirect than Napster's.[191] But Aimster's business objectives depended largely on the volume of its infringing uses; its main business activity was to facilitate these same infringing uses; and it structured its computer architecture so as not to know anything about the specific acts of infringement it did its best to facilitate.[192] Club Aimster, furthermore, gave users access to the top 40 songs on the charts for a mere $4.95 a month.[193]

---

did not clarify what could qualify as constructive knowledge, the Court in *Napster* found that the company had materially contributed to the direct infringement committed by end users, since it had provided them with 'the site and the facilities' without which copyright violations could not have been committed. *Napster*, 239 F.3d at 1022–23.

185 Id.

186 *Napster*, 239 F.3d at 1016.

187 See *Sony Corp. of Am. v Universal City Studios, Inc.*, 464 US 417 (1984).

188 See e.g., Lardner, *supra* n. 69, at 297–313.

189 See e.g., IFPI, Digital Music Report 2007, at 4 (2007), available at http://www.ifpi.org/content/library/digital-music-report-2007.pdf ('Digital music sales are estimated to have almost doubled in value worldwide in 2006, reaching an estimated trade value of around US $2 billion').

190 *In re* Aimster Copyright Litigation, 334 F.3d 643, 651 (7th Cir. 2003).

191 Id. at 646.

192 Id. at 650.

193 Id. at 651–52.

Although the Seventh Circuit's *Aimster* decision expressed some concern about not unduly impeding substantial non-infringing uses under *Sony*, it also toyed with imposing potentially burdensome obligations on technology developers to build in infringement-inhibiting technological measures.[194] The force of this speculation has been greatly weakened by the doctrine of 'actively inducing infringement,' on which the Supreme Court finally settled in *Grokster*.[195] In hindsight, it seems that the Seventh Circuit in *Aimster* was really groping its way toward the doctrine of active inducement later recognized in *Grokster*.

In *Grokster*, the software system at issue provided a range of means by which users could search through the pools of shared files while connecting directly with each other, and without reference to any central index hosted by defendants.[196] Neither Grokster nor its co-defendant Streamcast 'operated the network over which the users of their software connected and exchanged files, and the [district] court emphasized the decentralized nature of those networks,' in the sense that 'no information is transmitted to or through any computers owned or controlled by the software makers.'[197] The lower court also recognized that the software was capable of substantial non-infringing uses, including the authorized dissemination of copyrighted works and dissemination of unprotected works.[198] For the district court, and later the Ninth Circuit, the distance of the software providers from the sites of infringement and their lack of active knowledge of specific infringements was sufficient to shelter them from contributory liability under the *Sony* exception, given the potential non-infringing uses to which the software could be put.[199]

For the Supreme Court, however, Grokster and Streamcast had forfeited the safe harbour established in *Sony* for technologies with substantial non-infringing uses, which the Court had drawn from patent law. In *Grokster*, the Court

194 See id. at 648.

195 See *Metro-Goldwyn-Mayer Studios Inc. v Grokster Ltd.*, 545 US 913, 948–49 (2005) (Ginsburg, J., concurring).

196 See id. at 920–22.

197 Lemley and Reese, *supra* n. 154, at 1364. In particular, the Ninth Circuit, quoting the District Court, explained: '[E]ven if the Software Distributors 'closed their doors and deactivated all computers within their control, users of their products could continue sharing files with little or no interruption." See *Metro-Goldwyn-Mayer Studios Inc. v Grokster Ltd.,* 380 F. 3d 1154, 1164 (9th Cir. 2004) (quoting *Metro-Goldwyn-Mayer Studios Inc. v Grokster Ltd.*, 259 F. Supp. 2d 1029, 1041 (C.D. Cal. 2003)).

198 See *Grokster*, 545 US at 935.

199 *Grokster*, 259 F. Supp. 2d at 1036 ('[T]he existence of substantial non-infringing uses turns not only on a product's current uses, but also on potential future non-infringing uses.'); *Grokster*, 380 F.3d at 1161 ('[I]f the product at issue is capable of substantial or commercially significant non-infringing uses, then the copyright owner must demonstrate that the defendant had reasonable knowledge of specific infringing files and failed to act on that knowledge to prevent infringement.')

drew upon another complementary patent law doctrine that disallowed the safe harbour if the defendant had actively induced copyright infringement.[200] Using this approach, neither the relative degrees of remoteness or of the material contribution in the three cases, nor the relative weights of some potential non-infringing uses – allegedly rising to a possible 10 percent of all uses in *Grokster* – could vindicate a *Sony* defence if the underlying intent of the operation was to actively induce copyright infringement.[201]

While some contend that this resolution will unduly chill innovation in dual-use technologies,[202] we have a more optimistic assessment of what *Grokster* accomplished. The *Grokster* decision rejected several proposals to limit the scope of the *Sony* safe harbour. It did not, for instance, exclude services, as such, from the *Sony* safe harbour. It did not adopt any particular standard of intolerable infringing uses. Moreover, it did not adopt a 'primary use' test for judging the lawfulness of dual-use technologies.[203] The Court preserved the safe harbour for technologies with substantial non-infringing uses and focused instead on evidence of actions that demonstrated active and intentional promotion of infringement, which disqualified the defendants from the shelter of copyright's variant on patent law's staple article of commerce limitation.[204]

The extent to which suppliers of dual-use technologies may still benefit from a *Sony* safe harbour remains to be worked out in future cases, and care must be taken not to impair or undervalue actual non-infringing uses where they occur in a good faith context. Over time, however, it has become clear that the recording industry cannot cling to obsolete business models that oblige consumers to purchase music they do not want, and that this industry cannot attain control over P2P technology. Rather, as the district court in *Napster* correctly foresaw, shutting down firms such as Napster effectively

200 See Grokster, 545 US at 935.

201 In *Sony,* the Supreme Court explained that the application of the staple article of commerce doctrine required Betamax products to be capable of *commercially significant* non-infringing uses, meaning that VCRs should be capable of at least one potential legitimate use employed in a numerically significant manner. See *Sony Corp. of Am. v Universal City Studios, Inc.*, 464 US 417, 442–43 (1984). The ultimate outcome of the case was deeply influenced by the Court's finding that unauthorized time-shifting was indeed a legitimate fair use.

202 See e.g., Rob Hof, 'Larry Lessig: Grokster Decision Will Chill Innovation', *Bus. Week Online*, 28 June 2005; Fred von Lohmann, 'Remedying Grokster', *Law.com*, 25 July 2005, http://www.law.com/jsp/article.jsp?id=1122023112436.

203 Pamela Samuelson (2005), 'Legally Speaking: Did MGM Really Win the Grokster Case?', 48 *Comm. of the ACM* 19 (October 2005) (pointing out that the Court rejected virtually all of MGM's proposed tests for liability).

204 Id.

removed barriers to the entry of fee-based music distribution systems,[205] such as Apple's iTunes service. This arguably helped to support the formation of a new business model that may benefit consumers and competition in the long run.

As to the future prospects for non-infringing users of dual-use technologies in general, we cannot accurately evaluate them through the lens of cases dealing with bad faith active inducers of infringement. Moreover, when we try to envision such cases through a cleaner lens, the real barriers to entry will not lie so much in the weakness of the *Sony* safe harbour as in the potentially troublesome intersection between ss. 512 and 1201 of the DMCA.[206]

Implications for Public Interest Uses of Technically Protected Content

Our concern with dual-use technologies that impede non-infringing uses acquires considerably more traction the moment we try to envision the real life obstacles likely to be encountered by legally privileged non-infringing user groups who, by definition, advance some public interest consonant with, rather than antagonistic to, the goals of copyright protection. Here we are concerned with gaining access to copyrighted works in the digital environment in order to extract unprotectable subject matter, such as ideas and disparate facts; to make fair uses of protectable expressions, including research uses; and to exploit codified exceptions to, or limitations on, the bundle of exclusive rights.[207] Also of concern is access to works whose copyrights have expired but which cannot readily be located in public domain copies outside a given digitally controlled network.[208]

Facilitating public interest user groups under section 512

By focusing on user groups whose typically non-profit activities are thought to advance the public interest in education, research, science, and technological progress, we immediately dispel the atmosphere of mistrust arising from

---

205 See *A&M Records, Inc. v Napster Inc.*, 239 F.3d 1004, 1016 (9th Cir. 2001).

206 17 USC. §§ 512, 1201 (2000).

207 17 USC. §§ 102(a), 107–122 (2000).

208 See e.g., Jonathan Band (2005), 'The Google Print Library Project: A Copyright Analysis', *J. of Internet Banking and Com.* (December 2005) (discussing projects to digitize public domain and copyrighted works in major library collections). In theory, anti-circumvention liability should not lie for public interest users who bypass TPMs to gain access to public domain works. However, if publishers use the same TPM to protect copyrighted and public domain works, then any tool that would bypass this TPM will arguably be illegal under s. 1201 because of the copyrighted material also being protected by it.

Napster, Aimster and *Grokster*, and allow courts to think positively about the need to balance public and private interests, as they traditionally sought to do in the pre-digital era.[209] Only when defendants begin to appear in a good faith posture can we really discern what is at stake when the courts make appropriate judgments about the public's interest in access to technologies capable of substantial non-infringing uses.

Of course, P2P systems such as Napster, Aimster and Grokster could not long survive in such an atmosphere because they depend, directly or indirectly, on benefits derived from infringing uses. Private foundations, public entities, and public-private partnerships have already found good reasons to establish P2P file-sharing networks to promote access to information goods for non-infringing public interest purposes. For example, Creative Commons has established such networks for specific subject matter groupings,[210] and scientific efforts to link databases in virtual archives through P2P technologies[211] are growing in number.[212] Science Commons, an affiliate of Creative Commons, has unveiled plans to vigorously employ such technologies in a number of major projects.[213]

These initiatives are likely to increasingly rely on P2P technologies to enable participants to access and share privately held materials, whether copyrighted or not, that have been voluntarily made available to advance the goals of the different user communities in question. Because such communities are,

---

209 *Cf.* WCT, *supra* n. 1, Preamble ('The contracting parties, . . . [r]ecognizing the need to maintain a balance between the rights of authors and the larger public interest, particularly education, research and access to information, as reflected in the Berne Convention . . . . ') We do not mean to suggest that educators, researchers, and the like are the only parties who should be eligible to make public interest uses of technically protected copyrighted works. Many commercial firms engage in fair and other privileged uses, and they too should qualify for the reverse notice and takedown regime. We focus on the nonprofit public interest users in order to make the more general case for the need for the reverse notice regime, as these users are generally perceived in a favourable light in copyright discourse.

210 See Creative Commons, http://www.creativecommons.org.

211 See generally J. H. Reichman and Paul F. Uhlir (2003), 'A Contractually Reconstructed Research Commons for Scientific Data in a Highly Protectionist Intellectual Property Environment', 66 *Law & Contemp. Probs*. 315; Nat'l Research Council, The Role of Scientific and Technical Data and Information in the Public Domain (J. M. Esanu and Paul F. Uhlir, eds. 2003).

212 See e.g., Peter Dawyndt et al. (2006), 'Contributions of Bioinformatics and Intellectual Property Rights in Sharing Biological Information', 188 *Int'l Soc. Sci. J.* 249; Harlan Onsrud and James Campbell (2007), 'Big Opportunities in Access to Small Science Data', *Data Sci. J.* See also Science Commons, http://science.creativecommons.org

213 See id.; see also Abby Seff (2007), 'Will John Wilbanks Launch the Next Scientific Revolution?', *Popular Science* (July 2007).

as a rule, loosely organized and administered, they cannot and should not be charged with the duties of policing the contents of materials made available to the community for copyright infringement. Fortunately, so long as such groups take pains to position their networks within the penumbra of s. 512 of the DMCA, they can obtain all the sharing advantages of P2P systems while largely immunizing themselves from liability for copyright infringement by virtue of the 'notice and takedown' procedures that this provision sets up.[214]

Moreover, s. 512 procedures allow systems managers to vet any infringement claims lodged against participating contributors and to refuse to comply with a takedown request if they choose to back their member's claim of privileged use against an outsider's claim of infringement.[215] Even in a worst case scenario, where the outsider's infringement claim ultimately prevails in a court of law, the public interest goals of the user community should encourage courts in this situation to narrowly tailor injunctions so as to avoid inhibiting any legitimate non-infringing uses.[216]

The 'notice and takedown' modalities of s. 512 thus make it possible to keep P2P networks running for non-profit public interest purposes. Moreover, the 'clean hands' legitimacy of the enterprise should at least ensure that no injunction otherwise affecting some infringing uses of the technology in question would shut down or impede such public interest initiatives. Nor is there anything in the Supreme Court's *Grokster* decision that creates an insuperable barrier to entry for launching these initiatives.[217]

Yet, once a public interest P2P file-sharing network is up and running, problems may arise insofar as the technology allows community members to link to external non-member ISPs where copyrighted works have been deposited on conditions that restrict use or reuse of the material available there. A risk of conflict exists between the search potential of the software to enable non-infringing uses of posted material and the obligations of the service provider to respect the dictates of the copyright owners it hosts on its site. However, assuming that the service provider was covered by s. 512 of the DMCA, this conflict could normally be resolved by 'notice and takedown' provisions with which we are familiar.

---

214 17 USC. § 512 (2000).

215 Id. at § 512(g).

216 Public interest uses of protected works might also be facilitated if courts made more use of the Court's suggestion about the appropriateness of damage awards instead of injunctions in close fair use cases. See *Campbell v Acuff-Rose Music, Inc.*, 510 US 569, 578 n.10 (1994).

217 Indeed, the opening section of the *Grokster* decision speaks in positive terms about P2P technologies. *Metro-Goldwyn-Mayer Studios Inc. v Grokster Ltd.*, 545 US 913, 920–21 (2005).

Under s. 512, all of the standard copyright exceptions and defences are preserved even after the 'notice and takedown' machinery superimposed upon them has been triggered. If the information locating tool triggers an objection from the copyright owner, the searcher can respond by asserting the non-infringing uses (for example, fair uses) that he intends to make of the protected work in question. If the copyright owner acquiesces, the problem is solved. If not, the putative fair user can seek a declaratory judgment to remove the obstacle and vindicate the non-infringing use.

Clearly, these legal modalities would benefit from expeditious administrative procedures to promptly resolve such disputes at low cost, with deferred removal to courts only for specific issues that merited a full dress trial.[218] Our point is that, so long as we are dealing with traditional copyright defences, s. 512 of the DMCA poses no serious barriers to entry for our putative public interest initiative.

How public interest uses may be frustrated by section 1201

Serious problems may arise, however, when copyright owners surround information products available on their websites with technological fences specifically designed to thwart, for example, the search and sharing capabilities of the non-infringing, would-be public interest users.[219] TPM fences may initially prevent searchers from gaining access for the purpose of browsing contents in order to identify material of interest.[220] The same fences may then direct would-be non-infringing users to an electronic gateway, where electronic contracts of adhesion will condition entry on a waiver of all the users' rights that our putative searchers might otherwise put forward to justify access to and use of the information product in question.[221] The electronic fence will

---

218 See e.g., Lemley and Reese, *supra* n. 154, at 1410–25.

219 Firms that want to use TPMs to protect public domain works can, of course, take the precaution of attaching to any bulky ineligible matter, such as a noncreative database, some copyrightable fig leaf component, such as an explanatory introduction, in order to bring the collective work as a whole within s. 102(a) of the Copyright Act and trigger the additional protections of s. 1201 of the DMCA. For implications for science, see Reichman an Uhlir (2003), *supra* n. 211, at 376–79.

220 The DMCA provides an exemption from s. 1201(a)(1)(A) for nonprofit libraries, archives, and educational institutions to bypass access controls 'solely in order to make a good faith determination of whether to acquire a copy of that work.' 17 USC. § 1201(d). This exemption would not, however, apply if the purpose of the circumvention was to index the work or to extract unprotectable facts, ideas, or public domain materials from the technically protected work.

221 See J. H. Reichman & Jonathan A. Franklin (1999), 'Privately Legislated Intellectual Property Rights: Reconciling Freedom of Contract with Public Good Uses of Information', 147 *U. Penn L. Rev.* 875. See also Burk, *supra* n. 152 (discussing anti-circumvention misuse).

thus separate access from use. Insofar as s. 1201(c) permits circumvention for privileged purposes,[222] this will arguably only kick in after lawful access has been gained. Yet, by then, user rights may have been abrogated by contract, and it may already be too late to hack through the electronic fence prohibited by s. 1201.[223]

Ironically, this scenario inverts the situation found in cases such as *Napster*, *Aimster*, and *Grokster* where facilitators of mass infringements sought to hide behind potential non-infringing uses. Here, instead, bona fide non-infringing users risk being thwarted by copyright owners who use access control TPMs to disable privileged uses.

By using TPMs, copyright owners arguably gain the power to opt out of those parts of the copyright system they dislike. They cannot only design TPMs to circumvent public interest uses, but can claim shelter behind s. 1201 for doing so. Because some cases have construed s. 1201 as abrogating fair use and other public interest exceptions as grounds for circumventing TPMs to extract non-infringing material, the public interest goals of the non-infringing user may be absolutely defeated by the TPM.[224] The DMCA does not explicitly allow circumvention for legally permissible purposes, although this would have been consistent with the WCT and seems to have been the intent of some in Congress.

From this perspective, s. 1201 arguably functions as a form of 'active inducement' to avoid the public interest exceptions embodied in the Copyright Act. Copyright owners employ TPMs and s. 1201 protections in order to thwart infringing uses of their works. However, TPMs may protect against all unauthorized uses, both infringing and non-infringing. Although it is technically difficult to differentiate between these two classes of uses prospectively, firms could do more to facilitate some public interest uses of technically protected content if they chose to do so. There is as yet no incentive for copyright owners or TPM vendors to fine tune TPMs to enable non-infringing uses.[225]

Thus, unless there is a way for s. 1201 to be construed to recognize the legitimacy of access to enable non-infringing uses, the statute could become a

---

[222] See *supra* nn. 121–127 and accompanying text for a discussion of s. 1201 and privileged uses.

[223] 17 USC. § 1201 (2000).

[224] See Ginsburg, *supra* n. 14.

[225] One interesting experiment in designing TPMs with fair use in mind is the open source digital rights management technology that Sun Microsystems is developing for digital content that would enable many fair uses. See Gerard Fernando et al., 'Project DReaM, An Architectural Overview' (September 2005), http://www.openmediacommons.org/collateral/DReaM-Overview.pdf.

one-way ratchet for attaining complete enclosure of digital content.[226] At the very least, it establishes a potential barrier to entry for some meritorious public interest initiatives of the kind envisioned above, and it tends to chill investment in developing viable dual-use technologies that could promote more efficient non-infringing uses.[227]

The *Reimerdes* decision has unfortunately provided considerable ammunition for the gutting of the public interest balance in copyright law by setting forth a framework for analyzing s. 1201 claims that, if followed in subsequent cases, excludes consideration of virtually all public interest concerns. Under Judge Kaplan's interpretation of s. 1201, anti-circumvention liability arises: (1) if a copyright owner has adopted a TPM to control access to its copyrighted works (even if they are persistent access controls such as CSS); and (2) if an unauthorized person has developed a technology that bypasses this TPM (relying, if necessary, on an inference that if the defendant's technology bypasses the TPM, it must have been primarily designed or produced to do so).[228] Under *Reimerdes*, it is irrelevant whether copyright infringement has occurred (or was even possible) as a result of the availability of the circumvention tool. Nor does it matter whether the tool might enable consumers to tinker with a copyrighted work he or she has purchased.[229]

Harm to the copyright owner's interests is presumed from the fact of the violation.[230] In Judge Kaplan's view, Congress deliberately decided against permitting circumvention or making circumvention tools to enable fair or other public interest uses of technically protected digital content, and s. 1201(c) provided no shelter for public interest uses once copyright owners have deployed technical locks on their content.[231]

The Lock-out Technology Cases: *Chamberlain*, *Lexmark*, and *StorageTek*

Although Congress seems to have thought the DMCA anti-circumvention rules would protect copyright owners from massive infringements,[232] it did

226 *Cf.* James Boyle (2003), The Second Enclosure Movement, 66 *L. & Contem. Probs*. 33.

227 See Lemley and Reese, *supra* n. 154, at 1390.

228 *Universal City Studios, Inc. v Reimerdes*, 111 F. Supp. 2d 294, 317–19 (S.D.N.Y. 2000). See also *Universal City Studios, Inc. v Reimerdes*, 82 F. Supp. 2d 211, 217 (S.D.N.Y. 2000).

229 *Reimerdes*, 111 F. Supp. 2d at 314–16, 317 n. 137.

230 *Reimerdes*, 82 F. Supp. 2d at 215.

231 *Reimerdes*, 111 F. Supp. 2d at 322–24.

232 See S. Rep. No. 105–190, at 8 (1998) (expressing concern about massive piracy as a reason for adopting anti-circumvention rules).

not take long for some technology developers to realize that these rules, as interpreted in *Reimerdes*, were susceptible to use as a tool for defeating competition in the market for uncopyrightable products and services.[233] Technology developers Lexmark, Chamberlain, and Storage Technology Corp. ('StorageTek') relied on *Reimerdes* in claiming that the DMCA's anti-circumvention rules conferred on them the right to control access, through digital lock-out codes, to software embedded in their products so as to prevent competitors from supplying after-market replacement parts or services.[234]

The lock-out technology cases

Lexmark, a manufacturer of printers and toner cartridges, claimed that the authentication protocol (or digital handshake) component of copyrighted computer programs installed on chips in its printers and toner cartridges was an access control, the bypassing of which violated s. 1201(a)(1)(A).[235] Because Static Control made chips designed and produced to bypass this access control, Lexmark charged it with violating s. 1201(a)(2).[236] Static Control's customers were manufacturers of toner cartridges designed to work in Lexmark printers. The trial court, relying heavily on *Reimerdes*, issued a preliminary injunction against Static Control's manufacture of these chips.[237]

The Sixth Circuit eventually reversed, seemingly on the ground that the DMCA does not apply to digital fences limiting access to functional aspects of the printers.[238] The court's reasoning on the anti-circumvention claim is,

---

233 See e.g., Pamela Samuelson and Suzanne Scotchmer (2002), 'The Law and Economics of Reverse Engineering', 111 *Yale L.J.* 1575, 1642–49 (predicting technology developer misuses of the DMCA rules).

234 *Lexmark Int'l, Inc. v Static Control Components, Inc.*, 387 F.3d 522 (6th Cir. 2004); *Chamberlain Group, Inc. v Skylink Techs., Inc.*, 381 F.3d 1178 (Fed. Cir. 2004); *Storage Tech. Corp. v Custom Hardware, Eng'g & Consulting, Inc.*, 421 F.3d 1307 (Fed. Cir. 2005).

235 *Lexmark*, 387 F.3d at 528–32. Static Control successfully challenged the validity of the copyright in the toner cartridge software because it was a short program with limited functionality and copying was necessary in order to make compatible cartridges capable of running on Lexmark machines. Id. at 535–42.

236 Id. at 531.

237 *Lexmark Int'l, Inc. v Static Control Components, Inc.*, 253 F. Supp. 2d 943 (E.D. Ky. 2003).

238 The court observed:

> In the essential setting where the DMCA applies, the copyright protection operates on two planes: in the literal code governing the work and in the visual or audio manifestation generated by the code's execution. For example, the encoded data on CDs translates into music and on DVDs into motion pictures, while the program commands in software for video games or computers translate into some other

unfortunately, neither very coherent nor persuasive.[239] A concurring judge would more forthrightly have invoked the misuse doctrine, so as to 'make clear that in the future companies like Lexmark cannot use the DMCA in conjunction with copyright law to create monopolies of manufactured goods for themselves just by tweaking the facts of [a] case.'[240]

Shortly after issuance of the preliminary injunction in *Lexmark*, a similar attempt was made to use the anti-circumvention rules to foreclose competition in the market for electronic garage-door opening (GDO) devices.[241] Skylink made a universal GDO that bypassed the digitized 'lock-out' (access control) components of programs Chamberlain had installed in its GDOs and transmitters. Chamberlain argued that the 'plain language' of the DMCA and precedents such as *Reimerdes* and the lower court decision in *Lexmark* provided compelling support for its claim against Skylink.[242] The Federal Circuit strongly disagreed and upheld the lower court's grant of summary judgment to Skylink.

The *Chamberlain* decision is remarkable in several respects. A fundamental premise underlying the Federal Circuit's interpretation of s. 1201 was its perception that Congress had intended the DMCA anti-circumvention rules to be balanced:

> The most significant and consistent theme running throughout the entire legislative history of the anti-circumvention and anti-trafficking provisions of the DMCA . . . is that Congress attempted to balance competing interests, and 'endeavoured to specify, with as much clarity as possible, how the right against anti-circumvention would be qualified to maintain balance between the interests of content creators and information users.' H.R. Rep. No. 105–551, at 26 (1998). The Report of the House

---

> visual and audio manifestation. . . . The copyrightable expression in the Printer Engine Program, by contrast, operates on only one plane: in the literal elements of the program, its source and object code. Unlike the code underlying video games or DVDs, 'using' or executing the Printer Engine Program does not in turn create any protected expression. Instead, the program's output is purely functional.

Lexmark, 387 F.3d at 548.

239 Id. at 545–51. The court, for example, questioned whether the Lexmark authentication sequence was an access control within s. 1201 by observing that purchase of a Lexmark printer allowed access to the program. Id. at 549–50. Because it was possible to access the toner cartridge program if one bought a printer and toner cartridge, the court questioned whether the sequence was an effective access control measure. Id.

240 Id. at 551.

241 *Chamberlain Group, Inc. v Skylink Techs.*, Inc., 292 F. Supp. 2d 1040 (N. D. Ill. 2003), aff'd, 381 F.3d 1178 (Fed. Cir. 2004).

242 *Chamberlain Group, Inc. v Skylink Techs., Inc.*, 381 F.3d 1178, 1186, 1192 (Fed. Cir. 2004).

> Commerce Committee concluded that § 1201 'fully respects and extends into the digital environment the bedrock principle of "balance" in American intellectual property law for the benefit of both copyright owners and users'.[243]

It consequently rejected the notion that the DMCA had created a new exclusive right in copyright owners to control access to their works.[244] Section 1201 should instead be viewed as providing copyright owners with a new cause of action when circumvention of access controls threatened their ability to enforce their exclusive rights under copyright law.

In its search for a more balanced interpretation of the DMCA, the court considered at length linkages between the anti-circumvention rules and rights conferred by copyright law:

> Statutory structure and legislative history both make clear that § 1201 applies only to circumventions reasonably related to [copyright] protected rights. Defendants who traffic in devices that circumvent access controls in ways that facilitate infringement may be subject to liability under § 1201(a)(2). . . . [D]efendants whose circumvention devices do not facilitate infringement are not subject to § 1201 liability.[245]

Without proof of a nexus between the availability of an allegedly unlawful circumvention tool and the existence, or grave threat, of copyright infringement, s. 1201 liability should not be imposed.[246] Thus, it was relevant that:

> Chamberlain has not alleged that Skylink's Model 39 infringes its copyrights, nor has it alleged that the Model 39 contributes to third-party infringement of its copyrights. . . . Chamberlain urges us to conclude that no necessary connection exists between access and copyrights. Congress could not have intended such a broad reading of the DMCA.[247]

To the extent that *Reimerdes* said otherwise, the Federal Circuit disagreed.

Under Chamberlain's interpretation of the DMCA, 'the owners of a work protected *both* by copyright *and* a technological measure that effectively controls access to that work . . . would possess *unlimited* rights to hold circumventors liable under § 1201(a) *merely for accessing that work* even if

---

243 Id. at 1195.

244 Id. at 1192–93. The Federal Circuit has thus rejected the views of some commentators that s. 1201, in effect, created an exclusive right of access. See e.g., Jane C. Ginsburg, 'Copyright Legislation for the "Digital Millennium",' 23 *Colum. J. L. & Arts* 137, 140–43 (1999).

245 *Chamberlain*, 381 F.3d at 1195.

246 Id. at 1195–97.

247 Id. at 1197.

that access enabled only rights that the Copyright Act grants to the public.'[248] The Federal Circuit found this construction of the DMCA 'problematic for a number of reasons.'[249]

For one thing, Congress's exercise of its constitutional authority must be rational; yet, as construed by Chamberlain, s. 1201(a) 'borders on the irrational.'[250] For another, its interpretation of s. 1201(a) 'would flatly contradict § 1201(c)(1) – a simultaneously enacted provision of the same statute.'[251] It was consequently necessary to adopt 'an alternative construction that leads to no such contradiction.'[252]

Construing s.1201(a) as though it was concerned only with control over access, and not with rights protected by copyright law, would be 'both absurd and disastrous.'[253] It would 'allow any manufacturer of any product to add a single copyrighted sentence or software fragment to its product, wrap the copyrighted material in a trivial "encryption" scheme, and thereby gain the right to restrict consumers' rights to use its products in conjunction with competing products.'[254] This would 'allow virtually any company to attempt to leverage its sales into aftermarket monopolies,' even though this would be unlawful under the antitrust laws and the copyright misuse doctrine.[255]

At least as problematic to the Federal Circuit were the implications of Chamberlain's interpretation of s. 1201 for the rights of consumers to make fair uses:

> Chamberlain's proposed construction would allow copyright owners to prohibit exclusively fair uses even in the absence of any feared foul use. It would therefore allow any copyright owners through a combination of contractual terms and technological measures, to repeal the fair use doctrine with respect to an individual copyrighted work – or even selected copies of that copyrighted work. Again, this implication contradicts § 1201(c)(1) directly. . . . Consumers who purchase a product have the inherent legal right to use that copy of the software. What the law authorizes, Chamberlain cannot revoke.[256]

---

248 Id. at 1200.

249 Id.

250 Id.

251 Id. 'A provision that prohibited access without regard to the rest of the Copyright Act would clearly affect rights and limitations, if not remedies and defenses.' Id.

252 Id.

253 Id. at 1201.

254 Id. For analogous concerns about the need for courts to carefully manage boundaries between different modes of intellectual property protection, see *Bonito Boats, Inc. v Thunder Craft Boats, Inc.*, 489 US 141 (1989), which struck down Florida anti-plug mold law as contrary to patent law and policy.

255 *Chamberlain,* 381 F.3d at 1201.

256 Id. at 1202.

Contrary to Chamberlain's contention, which relied on dicta from *Reimerdes*, 'the DMCA emphatically did not "fundamentally alter" the legal landscape governing the reasonable expectations of consumers or competitors; did not "fundamentally alter" the ways that courts analyze industry practices; and did not render the pre-DMCA history of the GDO industry irrelevant.'[257] The Federal Circuit consequently rejected Chamberlain's interpretation of s. 1201 'in its entirety'.[258]

The Federal Circuit had a second opportunity to consider the scope of the anti-circumvention rules in *StorageTek*.[259] StorageTek manufactures automated tape cartridge libraries for mass data storage. When StorageTek sells its tape libraries to customers, it licenses customers to use the functional code for managing the tape libraries but not the code to carry out maintenance functions.[260] Custom Hardware Engineering ('CHE') is an independent business that repairs data libraries manufactured by StorageTek. To enable it to carry out these repairs, CHE developed a program that bypassed a password protection scheme in the StorageTek maintenance code so that it could effectively intercept and interpret error messages generated by that program. Processing the error code information enabled CHE to diagnose and repair data libraries for StorageTek's customers. StorageTek claimed that CHE had violated the DMCA anti-circumvention rules.[261]

Relying on its analysis in *Chamberlain*, the Federal Circuit found no DMCA violation: 'To the extent that [the defendant's] activities do not constitute copyright infringement or facilitate copyright infringement, StorageTek is foreclosed from maintaining an action under the DMCA. That result follows because the DMCA must be read in the context of the Copyright Act, which balances the rights of the copyright owner against the public's interest in having appropriate access to the work.'[262] Even if activation of the maintenance code might violate the firm's contractual rights with customers, this unauthorized activation of the code could not violate the DMCA because the contractual rights 'are not the rights protected by copyright law.'[263] Without proof of a nexus between the

---

257 Id. at 1194.

258 Id.

259 *Storage Tech. Corp. v Custom Hardware, Eng'g & Consulting, Inc.*, 421 F.3d 1307 (Fed. Cir. 2005).

260 Id. at 1309–10.

261 StorageTek also claimed copyright infringement. A majority of the Federal Circuit decided that the 17 USC. § 117 safe harbor for computer maintenance services protected CHE's activities. *Storage Tech. Corp.*, 421 F.3d at 1311–18.

262 Id. at 1318. However, the *StorageTek* decision opens the disquieting possibility that a better-drafted contract could exclude the provision of competing repair services by express terms that this court would uphold. Id. at 1316–17.

263 Id. at 1319.

rights protected by copyright law and the circumvention of the TPM, no violation of the DMCA anti-circumvention rules could occur.[264]

Broader implications of the lock-out technology cases

While this trio of cases – *Lexmark*, *Chamberlain* and *StorageTek* – reached the right results, they failed to consider a fundamental postulate of US intellectual property law, namely, that the exclusive rights that copyright law confers cannot be used to defeat competitive uses of non-copyrightable functional products or features that are suitable for regulation under the more pro-competitive mandate of the patent laws.[265] This proposition, established by the Supreme Court in the 1880 landmark case of *Baker v Selden* and extended by *Baker*'s progeny, stands for the necessity of maintaining a clear line of demarcation between industrial and artistic property laws.[266] Properly understood, *Baker v Selden* authorizes intermediate copying of even an entire copyrightable work in order to extract the non-copyrightable functional elements, so long as the competitor's ultimate production avoids any unnecessary taking of protected expression.[267]

Unfortunately, some commentators have obscured the pristine meaning of *Baker v Selden*,[268] which Professor Kaplan, among others, clearly understood.[269] There has been a regrettable tendency to treat *Baker* as merely

---

[264] Id.

[265] *Baker v Selden*, 101 US 99 (1880). See e.g., *Sega Enters. Ltd. v Accolade, Inc.*, 977 F.2d 1510 (9th Cir. 1993) (affirming the lawfulness of reverse engineering of copyrighted software to get access to interface information which was beyond the scope of copyright protection); *Atari Games Corp. v Nintendo of Am., Inc.*, 975 F.2d 832 (Fed. Cir. 1993) (accord).

[266] See generally J. H. Reichman (1989), 'Computer Programs as Applied Scientific Know-How: Implications of Copyright Protection for Commercialized University Research', 42 *Vand. L. Rev.* 639, 649 n. 288 (analysing historical meaning of *Baker v Selden* and criticizing commentators' misinterpretations, especially that of Melville Nimmer's treatise); Pamela Samuelson (2007), 'Why Copyright Law Does Not Protect Processes and Systems', 85 *Tex. L. Rev.* 1921, 1944–61 (demonstrating that Nimmer's interpretation of Baker is unsound).

[267] See Pamela Samuelson, 'Baker v. Selden: Sharpening the Distinction Between Authorship and Invention', in *Intellectual Property Stories* 181, 181–92 (Rochelle Cooper Dreyfuss and Jane C. Ginsburg, eds. 2004) (discussing *Baker*'s repudiation of copyright protection for useful arts and its implications for the lawfulness of reverse engineering uncopyrightable technologies).

[268] See e.g., Melville B. Nimmer and David Nimmer, *Nimmer on Copyright* §§ 2.03, 2.18 (2006) (interpreting *Baker* narrowly).

[269] See Benjamin Kaplan, *An Unhurried View of Copyright* 63–66 (1966). See also Reichman, *supra* n. 249, at 649 n. 288; Samuelson, *supra* n. 249, at 1953–61; Lloyd L. Weinreb (1998), 'Copyright for Functional Expression', 111 *Harv. L. Rev.* 1149, 1175.

endorsing a form of fair use in cases involving functional works[270] rather than as an independent and fundamental, perhaps even constitutionally based, subject matter requirement of the federal intellectual property system.[271] *Baker v Selden*, properly understood, establishes fundamental limits on the ability of copyright owners to exercise control over the development of technologies because this would bypass the strictures of the patent law.[272] Because of this, the DMCA cannot override *Baker*, and its fundamental policy prescriptions cannot be frustrated by the provisions of that Act.[273] There is, moreover, no legislative history suggesting that Congress intended to override *Baker* and its progeny in adopting the DMCA anti-circumvention rules.

The Federal Circuit deserves considerable praise for expressly recognizing that balance is a bedrock principle of intellectual property law and for developing a framework for interpreting s. 1201 that enables courts to develop a balanced approach to interpretation of the DMCA's anti-circumvention rules insofar as copyright owners try to use them to block fair and other non-infringing uses of technically protected copyrighted works. Just as the court in *Netcom* rejected the White Paper's unbalanced and overly broad interpretation

---

270 *Sega Enters. Ltd. v Accolade, Inc.*, 977 F.2d 1510 (9th Cir. 1993); *Atari Games Corp. v Nintendo of Am., Inc.*, 975 F.2d 832 (Fed. Cir. 1993).

271 US Const. Art. I, § 8, cl. 8 (giving Congress power to 'promote the progress of science and useful arts, by securing to authors and inventors exclusive rights for limited times for their *respective* writings and discoveries' (emphasis added)). See also J.H. Reichman, 'Legal Hybrids Between the Patent and Copyright Paradigms', 94 *Colum. L. Rev.* 2432 (1994) (discussing the fundamental premises of patent and copyright regimes).

272 Insofar as *Sony* held that technologies lacking in substantial non-infringing uses can be regulated by copyright law, even if technologies with substantial non-infringing uses cannot be, we regard *Sony* as consistent with *Baker*'s fundamental precepts.

273 We are concerned about whether federal appellate courts will vindicate the pristine meaning of *Baker v Selden* or even perceive its critical importance for satisfactorily resolving this class of cases on more than ad hoc, tentative grounds. We are also concerned about the Federal Circuit's tendency to defer in some cases to so-called 'contractual' terms (regardless of the lack of meaningful assent by the 'licensee') of mass-marketed products, which undermines our confidence in the staying power of that court as a check on abuses of public interest limitations on intellectual property rights. See e.g., *Monsanto Co. v McFarling*, 363 F.3d 1331 (Fed. Cir. 2004) (enforcing 'license' on a bag of seeds sold to a farmer). Courts dealing with *Lexmark* or *Chamberlain*-like DMCA claims may find it useful to consider Professor Burk's intriguing theories of 'anticircumvention misuse.' Burk, *supra* n. 135. This would avert the risk posed if the DMCA anti-circumvention rules allowed every product sold on the general products market to obtain 150 years of copyright protection behind digitized electronic fences that have nothing to do with the protection of literary and artistic works.

of the reproduction right,[274] courts interpreting s.1201 should reject *Reimerdes*' unbalanced and overly broad interpretation of s. 1201 in favour of the framework set forth in *Chamberlain* and *StorageTek*, which we believe is far more consistent with the letter and spirit of the WCT and with Congressional intent in enacting the anti-circumvention rules.

The Reverse Notice and Takedown Framework

Building on the insights of *Chamberlain* and *StorageTek*, courts faced with public interest challenges to the DMCA anti-circumvention rules should follow *Netcom*'s lead by developing a notice and takedown approach to balancing the interests of copyright owners and the public. A reverse notice and takedown procedure to enable privileged uses of technically protected works is consistent with s. 1201. It would lower the barrier to entry for public interest users and reconcile the tensions between s. 1201(a) and 1201(c).

The basic concept

Under our proposal, any confrontation between the user community's efforts to make non-infringing uses of material available to the public on a website and the copyright owners' technological fencing under s. 1201 could elicit a demand from the user group for a right to a limited bypassing of TPMs for legitimate purposes. For example, they might assert a need to index the material in question and extract specified components, in order to complete a specified non-infringing project. Copyright owners could be given 14 days either to object to the limited circumvention or to allow it by silence, without prejudice. In case of denial, the user group would be entitled to seek a declaratory judgment to vindicate its claim to an entitlement to circumvent a TPM for the purpose of engaging in the specified non-infringing use.

To become fully operational, this proposal would benefit from standardized procedures concerning the form in which notice should be given to copyright owners for 'reverse notice and takedown' demands. It would also require courts to allow those providing needed decryption skills and technology to benefit from the same privileged use exception that a *demandeur* had ultimately vindicated either in court or by silent acquiescence of the copyright owner. Above all, such a regime would particularly benefit from the kind of expeditious, low-cost administrative tribunals proposed in other contexts.[275]

These long-term considerations should not, however, obscure the feasibility or desirability of immediately instituting ad hoc case-by-case judicially

274 See *supra* n. 33 and accompanying text.

275 See e.g., Lipton, *supra* n. 14, at 149–55.

devised reverse notice and takedown procedures to promote the formation of a jurisprudence of permissible non-infringing uses of technically protected content to complement and supplement the jurisprudence of infringing uses discussed above.[276] *Netcom* has shown that courts in the US can evolve balanced solutions in response to digital copyright problems. Reverse notice and takedown procedures could attenuate the tension between s. 1201(a) of the DMCA, which on its face seems oblivious to fair use and other permissible uses of technically protected content, and s. 1201(c), which seeks to preserve public interest uses. The exact contours for attaining this goal need to be worked out over time.

Section 1201(a) might seem to imply that it is not lawful to develop self-help decryption devices to crack the technological fence and remove unprotected or unprotectable matter. But bona fide non-infringing users should be able to petition for the right to have a tool to extract specified matter for specified non-infringing uses. If these proposals are documented by supporting evidence, they could trigger recourse to s. 1201(c) in order to prevent s. 1201 from perversely thwarting legislatively and judicially sanctioned permitted uses.

Resort to a reverse notice and takedown procedure of this kind would help make the DMCA into an instrument that promotes adequate protection of copyrighted works without creating barriers to entry that thwart new technologies for sharing unprotected matter. It could facilitate licensing to non-profit entities on reasonable terms and conditions, and it could help to frustrate growing tendencies to put public domain matter off limits by encasing it in impenetrable electronic fences. It could also attenuate the systematic use of digitized, electronic prior restraints on speech, which are likely to eventually provoke constitutional challenges.[277] Indeed, an extension of the reverse notice and takedown model could present would-be users of public domain material with a workable choice between sustaining the costs of securing and implementing judicially approved circumvention or purchasing the public domain matter from the vendor at reasonable prices for the sake of convenience.

Illustrative applications

Below are four examples of situations in which courts might find the proposed reverse notice and takedown procedure useful:[278]

---

[276] After all, the 'notice and take down' provisions of s. 512 of the DMCA emerged from a negotiated compromise derived from the teachings of prior case law on contributory infringement in the digital environment. See *supra* nn. 36–57 and accompanying text.

[277] *Cf.* Benkler, *supra* n. 14, at 414–29 (challenging the constitutionality of the DMCA anti-circumvention rules); Ginsburg, *supra* n. 14, at 21 (anticipating such challenges).

[278] These examples largely reflect the scope for the proposed reverse notice and

(1) Some years ago, the American Civil Liberties Union challenged the constitutionality of a law requiring public libraries to install filtering software if they take funds to promote Internet access to patrons. The filters were meant to protect minors from accessing indecent or otherwise harmful materials. However, such software under- and over-blocks content, and it impedes access to materials which, though harmful to minors, may qualify as constitutionally protected speech for adults.[279] When the Supreme Court ultimately ruled against the constitutional challenge, it recognized the under- and over-blocking problem, and held that over-blocking interfered with the legitimate interests of adults in accessing some blocked materials.[280]

The challenge for libraries since that decision has been to decide whether to install filters, and if installed, which filtering software to choose. Libraries may want to conduct a comparative assessment of the efficacy of software filtering programs, but filtering software will likely use TPMs to block access to the list of sites that the software blocks. Because makers of filtering software are likely to consider block-lists as proprietary trade secrets, they are unlikely to agree to bypassing the TPMs. Library staff may also lack sufficient expertise to bypass the TPMs to make such an assessment.[281]

---

takedown procedure under US law. As we explain at p. 281, we believe that the reverse notice and takedown procedure would also be an appropriate and desirable means for EU member states to implement their obligations under the Copyright Directive. But the precise scope of those obligations is a matter that different member states have read differently. See *infra* text accompanying nn. 309–310. For other examples of public interest uses that have been or may be thwarted or chilled by the DMCA, see e.g., Benkler, *supra* n. 14, at 388–89; Ginsburg, *supra* n. 14, at 20; Lipton, *supra* n. 14, at 113–15; Sadd, *supra* n. 14, at 321–22; Samuelson, *supra* n. 14, at 544–45, 548–49, 553. See also Electronic Frontier Foundation, *Unintended Consequences: Seven Years under the DMCA* (as updated April 2006) available at http://www.eff.org/IP/DMCA/DMCA_unintended_v4.pdf.

[279] *United States v Am. Library Ass'n*, 539 US 194 (2003).

[280] Justices Kennedy and Breyer thought that the interests of adults in access to a wider array of materials was adequately addressed by provisions of the Congressional legislation that allowed libraries to unblock sites for patrons wishing to view blocked but nonetheless lawful content. Id. at 214–15 (Kennedy, J., concurring); id. at 215–20 (Breyer, J., concurring). Unblocking may, however, involve circumvention of a TPM, which could run afoul of s. 1201(a)(1)(A).

[281] See Pamela Samuelson (2007), 'Principles for Resolving Conflicts Between Trade Secrets and the First Amendment', 58 *Hastings L.J.* 777, 790–91 (discussing an effort to reverse engineer a TPM to get access to block-list information for filtering technologies, such as those widely used by libraries, that was thwarted by threats of DMCA anti-circumvention liability).

It is in the public interest for libraries to have access to this information. Under a reverse notice and takedown procedure, a court could order the software filtering firms to take down the TPMs so that the comparative analysis could take place. The software filter developer could petition the court to condition the takedown on the libraries' willingness not to reveal the trade secret block-lists. We have confidence that courts could fashion appropriate relief that balanced the interests of the libraries in being able to communicate findings with other librarians and the interests of the software developers in keeping the list data secret.

(2) A linguistics professor might want to develop a compilation of clips from movies to show that the word 'redskins' in Western movies has been systematically used in a derogatory fashion.[282] If this professor is not a technically sophisticated person, he or she may not be able to bypass CSS in order to make these clips from DVD movies. If the professor requests access to unprotected forms of these movies to engage in the stated fair uses and this request is ignored or denied by the motion picture studio copyright owners, the linguistics professor should be able to ask a court to order the studios to provide the appropriate access to the movies or to authorize the takedown by a circumvention service on their behalf.[283]

(3) The Computer History Museum is among the entities that might want to undertake a project to preserve computer programs written during the 1960s to early 1980s.[284] Some software developers have employed TPMs to control access to the programs; many programs are, moreover, stored in now-obsolete formats and/or on obsolete storage media that have effectively become TPMs. A Computer History Museum researcher

---

282 See Samuelson, *supra* n. 14, at 540 (giving this example). Public interest users should not, in our judgment, have to undertake extra expense and effort to search for possible alternative formats for the works of which they want to make fair use when a technically protected format is near at hand. In this respect, we join the EFF's criticism of the Copyright Office for its unwillingness to consider the inconvenience and expense of such efforts as a factor favouring permitting fair use exemptions for such users. See EFF on Rulemaking, *supra* n. 138, at 4–5.

283 See e.g., Ginsburg, *supra* n. 14, at 17 (suggesting that judges could authorize circumvention services to facilitate fair uses of works protected by TPMs).

284 It is not entirely clear whether computer programs in machine-executable forms would have been protectable under the Copyright Act of 1909, although the US Copyright Office began accepting registration of computer programs as copyrightable works in the mid-1960s. See Copyright Office Circular 31D (January 1965), reprinted in Duncan M. Davidson, 'Protecting Computer Software: A Comprehensive Analysis', 1983 *Ariz. St. L.J.* 611, 652 n. 72. Obviously, bypassing a TPM protecting access to programs written in this period would not give rise to s. 1201 liability if the programs were not copyrightable, but the risk for a preservationist in circumventing these old TPMs would nevertheless be real, given the registrations accepted then.

would have to bypass the TPMs to preserve this historical material and store it in updated formats. Rather than waiting three years for the next LOC rulemaking,[285] Computer History Museum personnel should be able to ask a court to issue a reverse notice and takedown order insofar as copyright owners of the software did not agree or could not be found to give consent to bypassing the TPM.[286]

(4) Security researchers are often interested in reverse engineering TPMs, such as those used to protect commercially distributed sound recordings, for purposes such as determining if the TPMs might cause software to be installed on users' computers that would cause the computers to be vulnerable to security attacks or that might surreptitiously monitor and report back on users' behaviours.[287] Undertaking such research would almost certainly involve bypassing the TPM and making tools to do so. Given the narrowness of the encryption research or computer security testing exceptions to s. 1201, this activity would probably not qualify for a statutory safe harbour.[288] Yet, the work would nevertheless be in the

285 17 USC. § 1201(a)(1)(C). There is currently a partial exemption for libraries and archives to bypass a TPM to preserve digital content stored in obsolete formats, but this may not apply to museums and it certainly does not authorize the making of tools in order to engage in such circumventions. See Perzanowski, *supra* n. 142, at 16 (discussing the narrowness of the exception for obsolete formats).

286 Difficulties in locating copyright owners have prevented many creative and educational reuses of copyrighted works, especially many older ones. The US Copyright Office has proposed allowing reuses of so-called 'orphan works' to proceed if the reusers have made reasonably diligent efforts to seek permissions. *See* US Copyright Office, *Report on Orphan Works* 8 (2006). A similar problem may arise with TPMs. With the possibility of up to $2500 of statutory damages per circumvention at stake for violation of s. 1201, see 17 USC. § 1203(c)(3), there is a risk that public interest users, such as archivists, would be deterred from preservation activities. With a reverse notice and takedown procedure, the archivist could be assured that he or she would incur no liability for this circumvention as long as he or she did not infringe copyrights in the works.

287 See e.g., Deirdre Mulligan and Aaron Perzanowski (2007), 'The Magnificence of the Disaster: Reconstructing the Sony BMG Rootkit Incident', 22 *Berkeley Tech. L.J.* 1157. Another public interest issue posed not only by the Sony BMG rootkit incident but more generally is that right holders do not always give notice that they have deployed TPMs in mass-marketed digital content. Without notice of TPMs, it becomes possible to inadvertently violate ss. 1201(a)(1)(A) and 1201(a)(2) if one reverse engineers a purchased copy of digital content.

288 If, for example, the TPM does not use encryption, but some other technique, the encryption research exception would, strictly speaking, not apply. See 17 USC. § 1201(g). The computer security testing exception only applies if one is testing a computer network for security flaws. Id. at § 1201(j). The unduly narrow nature of these exceptions is discussed in: National Research Council, *The Digital Dilemma: Intellectual Property in the Information Age* 171–76 (2001).

public interest, even if the right holder in the sound recording did not approve of this activity.

Security researchers ought to be able to engage in such reverse engineering and to disclose the results of their research at scientific conferences.[289] In keeping with the reverse notice and takedown regime, a court could determine that research-related activities of this sort are lawful under a proper interpretation of s. 1201.

Other considerations

Although it would be more cost-effective to have a streamlined administrative process for considering reverse notice and takedown requests,[290] a judicially

---

[289] See e.g., Joseph P. Liu (2003), 'The DMCA and the Regulation of Scientific Research', 18 *Berkeley Tech. L.J.* 501, 528–37 (arguing for flexibility in the anti-circumvention regulations as applied to scientific research). It is worth pointing out that security researchers are unlikely to be interested in getting access to the digital content protected by the TPM; they are primarily interested in the TPM itself and how it might interact with the content. As long as such researchers do not engage in or knowingly facilitate copyright infringement, their activities should not violate the DMCA. A reverse notice and takedown regime could be adapted to facilitate such research.

[290] See e.g., Lipton, *supra* n. 14, at 155 ('Administrative approaches tend to be more flexible and less formal in their procedures than judicial processes and are generally less costly than judicial hearings.'). We recognize that our proposal has at least two disadvantages. First, few prospective privileged users may have the resources to seek judicial support for reverse notice and takedown challenges to technically protected content, and second, the prospective privileged users will have to identify themselves to the copyright owner rather than making spontaneous fair or other non-infringing uses without informing the relevant copyright owners. See Burk and Cohen, *supra* n. 14, at 59–61 ('[A] preauthorization requirement would be costly and would chill spontaneous uses. . . . [A]pplication to a third party is likely to compromise the sort of anonymity that users presently enjoy. . . . Spontaneous uses likely would disappear altogether. . . . [U]nder this system, fair use might become the sole provenance of well-capitalized firms with the resources to engage in the process.').

The first problem may be mitigated by the rise of public interest organizations (including nonprofit organizations such as the Electronic Frontier Foundation and high technology clinics such as those in operation at American University, Boalt Hall, Stanford, and USC Law Schools) with the capacity to represent prospective fair users. Moreover, in time, an administrative process might be set up to resolve these challenges, as Lipton proposes, supra n. 14, at 149–55.

As to the second problem, a comparative approach is necessary. Realistically, the fair use infrastructure that Burk and Cohen propose is less likely to be achievable than the reverse notice and takedown procedure we propose. So while their proposal is more socially optimal than ours in that copyright owners would not have to know the identity of the prospective fair user, ours is more socially optimal in that courts can actually make it happen. Moreover, a reverse notice and takedown procedure might, in time, lead to something akin to the fair use infrastructure they envision, if copyright developed case-by-case evolution is, in our judgment, preferable to a statutorily mandated administrative process. The case-by-case approach is more dynamic, flexible, and responsive to the fine details of each situation. It is, moreover, likely to lead to a normative framework for dealing with such requests. We fear that a statutorily created administrative process at this point would remain vulnerable to political economy problems akin to those that brought about the unbalanced DMCA anti-circumvention rules in 1998.

Once the courts develop normative baselines for dealing with reverse notice and takedown requests, however, an administrative process could evolve over time to apply and refine this normative framework. This development could also induce copyright owners to engage in private initiatives consistent with this framework, such as designating circumvention services to which putative public interest users might apply to obtain circumvention for non-infringing purposes.[291]

We believe that courts will be able to discern when putative public interest users are not acting in good faith when making reverse notice and takedown requests. Courts can also put in place safeguards to ensure that the reverse notice and takedown regime does not bring about the increased infringements that the DMCA was enacted to avoid (for example, by ordering copyright owners to make use of trusted circumvention services rather than ordering takedowns of the TPMs that might lead to massive infringements).

Whether courts in the United States will, in practice, defend good faith public interest communities against technologically induced inhibitors of non-infringing uses with the same zeal they have thus far used in guarding against online inducers of infringement in *Napster*, *Aimster*, and *Grokster* remains to be seen. Certainly, the logic with which the courts have justified limitations on regulation of dual-use technologies resonates with similar concerns to vindicate non-infringing uses of technically protected content and to remove barriers now thwarting development of appropriate technologies to achieve this goal. A judicially engrafted reverse notice and takedown solution could provide a minimalist bridging device to achieve this balance. *Chamberlain* and *StorageTek* provide a conceptual framework for an interpretation of s. 1201 out of which the reverse notice and takedown approach we propose could develop through common law adjudication.

owners found it more efficient to designate a service to deal with public good circumvention claims instead of having to respond to them on a regular basis.

[291] Indeed, this may be a way to accomplish the 'fair use infrastructure' that Burk and Cohen envisioned some years ago. See Burk and Cohen, *supra* n. 14.

REVERSE NOTICE AND TAKEDOWN AS A MODE OF IMPLEMENTING ARTICLE 6(4) OF THE EU COPYRIGHT DIRECTIVE

As noted earlier, the reverse notice and takedown approach is eminently consistent with the WCT, which expressly reserved legally permitted uses from the scope of the obligatory anti-circumvention measures.[292] In countries that adopted the treaty verbatim, such as Japan, there can be no domestic or international objections to any effort to introduce the reverse takedown and notice approach. Because of the civil law traditions prevalent in the EU, it would not be feasible for member states to adopt the reverse notice and take-down regime through common law litigation. So it is fortunate that the EU Copyright Directive has provided a general (if incomplete) framework for member states to achieve a balanced solution by providing legal reinforcement of TPMs used by copyright owners to protect their works while at the same time enabling public interest uses of technically protected content.

Indeed, Art. 6(4) of the EU Copyright Directive *requires* member states to adopt mechanisms that preserve the ability of users to take advantage of certain exceptions and limitations guaranteed by copyright law notwithstanding the application of TPMs.[293] The proposed reverse notice and takedown procedure is one way in which member states could fulfil that obligation.[294] Moreover, such a procedure would effectuate the basic normative commitment to the continued availability of exceptions to exclusive rights expressed in Art. 6(4).[295] In fact, it does so more fully than current member state implementation of the Article (which has arguably been confined by textual limits on the scope of Art. 6(4)) itself.[296]

---

292 WCT, *supra* n. 1, Art. 11, which states:

> Contracting Parties shall provide adequate legal protection and effective legal remedies against the circumvention of effective technological measures that are used by authors in connection with the exercise of their rights under this Treaty or the Berne Convention and that restrict acts, in respect of their works, which are not authorized by the authors concerned or *permitted by law*.

Id. (emphasis added).

293 See Copyright Directive, *supra* n. 10, Art. 6(4).

294 See *infra* 'Application of reverse notice and takedown under Article 6(4)' at p. 288.

295 See *infra* 'The unfulfilled normative commitment underlying Article 6(4)' at p. 282.

296 See *infra* text accompanying nn. 294–297. For a summary and analysis of member state implementation, see Guido Westkamp, 'The Implementation of Directive

In this section, we explain the basic contours of Art. 6(4) of the Directive, and how adoption of the reverse notice and takedown procedure would implement member states' obligations under that provision. This discussion also allows us to elaborate further on some aspects of the proposal already mentioned in this chapter.

The Unfulfilled Normative Commitment Underlying Article 6(4)

The EU Copyright Directive starts from the general normative position that exceptions and limitations that would have been available absent the application of TPMs should remain available notwithstanding the application of such measures.[297] Unlike the DMCA, the Copyright Directive does not contain a list of exemptions from the circumvention prohibitions.[298]

However, the EU legislators were aware of the risk that TPMs might become an absolute prohibition restricting users from engaging in acts permitted under

2001/29/EC in the Member States' (Feb. 2007), in *Copyright Directive Implementation Study*, *supra* n. 11.

[297] See Copyright Directive, *supra* n. 10, Art. 6(4). Of course, this is not the only normative commitment embodied in the Directive. The Commission also sought to create a climate in which copyright owners would pursue new business models for online distribution of content. Reconciliation of these competing policy objectives may explain, although not coherently, the different constrictions on Art. 6(4). See *infra* text accompanying nn. 311–314.

[298] Recitals 48 and 51 of the Directive suggest the possibility of exemptions for cryptography research and public security. See id., recitals 48, 51. See also Richard Li-Dar Wang, 'DMCA Anti-Circumvention Provisions in a Different Light: Perspectives from Transnational Observation of Five Jurisdictions', 34 *AIPLA Q.J.* 217, 237 (2006). Because the Directive lacks any specific exemptions, it is seen by some as rejecting any right of 'self-help.' However, some member states have implemented rights of self-help to circumvent TPM under strict conditions. See Copyright Directive Implementation Study, *supra* n. 11, at 106 (describing Norwegian and Danish implementation).

Moreover, there is nothing in the Directive to suggest that the 'appropriate measures' called for by Article 6(4) might not include immunity from liability after the right holder had failed to make available the means of benefiting from an exception or limitation. See id. at 108–109 (noting the Directive's preference for voluntary arrangements by right holders, but suggesting that the broad language of 'appropriate measures' leaves much room for member states to adopt different approaches); cf. Christophe Geiger, 'The New French Law on Copyright and Neighbouring Rights of 1 August 2006 – An Adaptation to the Needs of the Information Society?', 38 *IIC* 401, 421–23 (2007) (noting the dangers of deferring entirely to right holder arrangements and arguing that 'the only measure that would truly have been "appropriate" within the meaning of Article 6(4)' would have been a prohibition on right holders applying TPM to deprive the public of the benefit of exceptions with a 'pronounced social function').

traditional copyright law.[299] Concern about that prospect found expression in Art. 6(4).[300] The first paragraph of Art. 6(4) provides that:

> Notwithstanding [the prohibitions against acts of circumvention and circumvention devices], in the absence of voluntary measures taken by right holders, including agreements between right holders and other parties concerned, member states shall take appropriate measures to ensure that right holders make available to the beneficiary of an exception or limitation provided for in national law in accordance with [various articles in the Directive listing permissible exceptions to copyright, such as copyright in connection with teaching], the means of benefiting from that exception or limitation . . . . [where that beneficiary has legal access to the work].[301]

The Directive thus seems to take the position that a technological adaptation, namely, the application of TPMs, should not alter the balance that existed under default rules of copyright law with respect to the enjoyment of exceptions and limitations.[302] We call this principle 'prescriptive parallelism,' to convey the notion that the traditional copyright balance of rights and exceptions should be preserved in the digital environment.[303]

Article 6(4) is only one dimension of parallelism in the EU Directive. It also contains a provision that anticipates a reduction in private copying levies under national copyright laws, potentially to zero, where copyright owners have applied TPMs to works and thus secured by technology what they formerly obtained through legally sanctioned levy schemes.[304] Copyright

---

299 See Lionel Bently and Brad Sherman, *Intellectual Property Law* 309–11 (2nd edn 2004) (noting fears expressed).

300 See Bernt Hugenholtz (2000), 'Why the Copyright Directive is Unimportant, and Possibly Invalid', 22 *Eur. Intell. Prop. Rev.* 501 (describing Art. 6(4) as 'a provision that is presumably intended to reconcile the interests of right owners employing technical protection measures with the interests of users wishing to benefit from copyright limitations'); Bently and Sherman, *supra* n. 299, at 310 ('As regards the relationship between the technological measures and exceptions to copyright, article 6(4) of the [Copyright Directive] provides for a strange, barely comprehensible, compromise.').

301 See Copyright Directive, Art. 6(4).

302 Article 5(3)(o) also permits member states to create exceptions or limitations to rights provided for in Arts. 2 and 3 'in certain other cases of minor importance where exceptions or limitations already exist under national law, provided that they only concern analogue uses . . . .' Copyright Directive, Art. 5(3)(o).

303 Compare similar concept expressed in Agreed Statements, *supra* n. 2, statement concerning Art. 10.

304 Article 5(2)(b) of the Copyright Directive permits member states to create exceptions or limitations to the reproduction right 'in respect of reproductions on any medium made by a natural person for private use . . . on condition that the right holders receive fair compensation which takes account of the application or non-application of technological measures referred to in Article 6 to the work for subject matter concerned.' Copyright Directive, Art. 5(2)(b).

owners should not be able to double dip, and should receive the same level of effective protection, whether through law or technology.

We do not want to overstate the principle of prescriptive parallelism underlying the EU Directive. Article 6(4) is a means by which the EU sought to ensure that the balance of copyright law was maintained after the application of technological protection measures.[305] But that goal is pursued against the broader backdrop of a Directive that contemplates adjustments to the legal rights of both copyright owners and users to reflect the availability and application of such measures. For example, one of the principal objectives of the EU Directive was to provide legal protection against circumvention of technological protection measures, which might be conceived as enhanced legal protection for copyright owners in light of enhanced copying capacity.[306]

Moreover, the prescriptive parallelism of Art. 6(4) must also be viewed against the treatment of exceptions by the EU Directive generally. Although the stated objective of the Directive was in part to harmonize the disparate sets of exceptions and limitations available under national copyright laws in the EU, the Directive effected only a very modest amount of harmonization, at least in the short run.[307] Its broad list of exceptions is largely permissive,[308] although there is a mandatory exception for ephemeral copies,[309] and there is a restriction on adoption of further exceptions.[310]

---

[305] See Hugenholtz, *supra* n. 300, at 501.

[306] See Copyright Directive, *supra* n. 10, Art. 6(1)–(2). During the legislative debates, the Commission apparently suggested that *all* exceptions listed in Article 5 should explicitly prevail over contrary TPMs, and Article 6(4) was the compromise provision that reconciled the Commission's position with that adopted by the Council of Ministers (which was more supportive of right holders' freedom to use TPMs). See Copyright Directive Implementation Study, *supra* n. 11, at 104.

[307] See generally Copyright Directive Implementation Study, *supra* n. 11; see also Inst. for Info. Law, Univ. of Amsterdam, *The Recasting of Copyright and Related Rights for the Knowledge Economy* (2006). These studies were commissioned by the European Commission's Internal Market Directorate-General.

[308] See Copyright Directive, Art. 5(2)–(3) (providing that member states *may* provide for certain exceptions or limitations); see also Hugenholtz, *supra* n. 300.

[309] See Copyright Directive, at Art. 5(1). The Directive states:

> [T]emporary acts of reproduction . . . which are transient or incidental and an integral and essential part of the technological process and whose sole purpose is to enable a transmission in the network between third parties by an intermediary, or a lawful use, of a work or other subject matter to be made, and which have no independent economic significance, shall be exempted from the reproduction right.

Id.

[310] See id. at recital 32. But see id., Art. 5(3)(o) (quoted *supra* n. 285). It might be that over time the mere listing of permissible exceptions will cause a convergence as different national legislators begin to work from the same turnkey list, secure in the

More importantly for purposes of this chapter, the failure to *mandate* the adoption of a wide range of exceptions undermines the effectiveness of Art. 6(4) in achieving its general goal of prescriptive parallelism. Article 6(4) only guarantees that technological protection measures should not impede the ability of third parties to take advantage of exceptions or limitations if they are provided in national law.[311] Furthermore, there are a number of other significant textual constraints on the potential effectiveness of Art. 6(4), including its limitation to seven defined exceptions rather than all exceptions or limitations existing in national law,[312] its inapplicability to works made available on-demand,[313] and

---

knowledge that adopting such exceptions will not meet with the objections of the European Commission.

[311] See id. at Art. 6(4).

[312] These include exceptions for copying by libraries and educational institutions, copying for the benefit of persons with a disability, and copying for the purpose of scientific research. There is no coherent explanation, other than raw political compromise, for the inclusion of these exceptions but not others in Art. 6(4). See Copyright Directive Implementation Study, *supra* n. 11, at 110 ('Because this provision was negotiated in the last hours before adoption of the final text of the Directive, there is no public record available to shed light on the legislator's intent. As a result, the list of limitations included in Article 6(4) appears highly arbitrary.'). Indeed, the arbitrariness of the list may simply reflect the broader failure of the Directive to rationalize treatment of exceptions generally. See id.

Moreover, Art. 6(4) does not, for example, include uses that users are entitled to make because a work is in the public domain or because all that is taken is otherwise unprotected by copyright law. It can be argued that the protections of Art. 6 do not apply to public domain material in the first place because right holders are not in a position to authorize uses of such works. As a result, some national legislatures have taken the position that TPMs on public domain works can be circumvented without liability. See Urheberrechtsgesetz [Copyright Act], 12 September 2003, BGBl. I at 1774, Art. 1, §95(a)(2) (F.R.G.). Of course, in practical terms, if right holders package public domain works with some protected works, it is unclear whether this interpretation will be sufficient to save access to such works without more affirmative legislative statement. See Bently and Sherman, *supra* n. 299, at 309.

[313] The mechanisms of Art. 6(4) do not apply where the work is made available on an on-demand basis because the provision is inapplicable where 'the work or other subject matter is made available to the public on agreed contractual terms in such a way that members of the public may access them from a place and at the time individually chosen by them.' The language of this sentence in the directive itself makes the scope of the limitation uncertain and could be tested in a number of ways. See Bently and Sherman, *supra* n. 299, at 311 n. 132 (noting room for dispute regarding the phrase 'agreed contractual terms'); see also Copyright Directive Implementation Study, *supra* n. 11, at 112 (suggesting that confining this limit on Art. 6(4) to negotiated contracts would be consistent with the legislative purpose).

More importantly, the on-demand language surely cannot be read in ways that render the general provision meaningless. See Maciej Barczewski (2005), 'International Framework for Legal Protection of Digital Rights Management Systems', 27 *Eur. Intell. Prop. Rev.* 165, 167 (noting that reading the 'available contractually on-demand' its unclear relationship with the anti-circumvention and interoperability provisions in the Software Directive.[314]

These limitations in the text of the Directive have caused many scholars to doubt the capacity of the provision to achieve its declared objectives.[315] In deference to ordinary canons of interpretation, we are reluctant to read the limits in Art. 6(4) in ways that render the general provision meaningless.[316] However, rather than focus on the details of the limitations of Art. 6(4) as enacted, and perhaps looking forward to the possible revision of the Directive to take into account a recent report commissioned from the University of Amsterdam Institute for Information Law,[317] we will view the conceptual mechanism of Art. 6(4) as a means of ensuring continued viability of privileged uses notwithstanding the application of technological protection measures. More particularly, we will consider the reverse notice and takedown proposal as a vehicle for implementing Art. 6(4) and exploring its possible reform.

Reverse Notice and Takedown as a Mode of Implementing Article 6(4)

The reverse notice and takedown proposal articulated in 'Setting the stage for a reverse notice and takedown regime' at p. 255, essentially consists of two

---

limits in Art. 6(4) in ways that allowed digital lock-up of all works available online would conflict with the directive's aims); see also *infra* text accompanying n. 306. The same interpretive rationale surely should be applied to yet another limit on Art. 6(4), namely, that because the provision only applies where the beneficiary has legal access to a work, it is arguably ineffective against access control measures. See Severine Dusollier (2003), 'Fair Use by Design in the European Copyright Directive of 2001', Comm. of the ACM, April 2003, at 51, 53–54 (2003) [hereinafter *Fair Use by Design*]; Dusollier, *supra* n. 11.

314 Council Directive 91/250/EEC, 1991 O.J. (L 122) 42 (EC) [hereinafter Software Directive]. The anti-circumvention provisions and interoperability exceptions in the Software Directive appear to survive the adoption of Art. 6. See Copyright Directive, *supra* n. 10, recital 50; see also Software Directive, *supra*, Art. 7(1)(c); Bently and Sherman, *supra* n. 299, at 311–312 (discussing UK implementation and noting different treatment of software).

315 See Hugenholtz, *supra* n. 300; Dusollier, *Fair Use by Design*, *supra* n. 313.

316 See Thomas Rieber-Mohn (2006), Harmonising Anti-Circumvention Protection with Copyright Law: The Evolution from WCT to the Norwegian Anti-Circumvention Provisions, 37 IIC 182, 188 (offering an interpretation of which contractual arrangements by right holders would pre-empt member state intervention by reference to the need to give Art. 6(4) some meaning); Barczewski, *supra* n. 313, at 167.

317 See Copyright Directive Implementation Study, *supra* n. 11. That report concluded that 'the principle underlying article 6(4) . . . is worth maintaining' but recommended that the provision be simplified and clarified in a number of ways that ensure its effectuation. See Copyright Directive Implementation Study, *supra* n. 11, at 116.

parts. First, implicitly, all uses privileged under traditional copyright principles should continue to be privileged in an era of digital rights management. The application of TPMs should not alter the balance of rights between copyright owners and users.[318] This is a substantive principle, which might be followed with different modifications in different countries.[319]

Secondly, in order to effectuate this substantive principle, users need a mechanism by which to vindicate their rights and to secure the certainty required to engage in creative activity privileged under traditional copyright principles. Different institutional or procedural means through which to pursue this objective are possible,[320] but we believe the reverse notice and takedown procedure affords a number of distinct advantages, many of which were canvassed in 'Setting the stage for a reverse notice and takedown regime' at p. 255.

As an initial matter, we believe the proposed reverse notice and takedown procedure should be considered as a means of implementing member state obligations under Art. 6(4). This proposal should be studied by countries committed to compliance with the EU regime, which includes not only the member states of the EU, but also countries that commit to such a regime (whether in general terms or in detail) in bilateral trade negotiations.[321] Even

---

318 See e.g., Paolo Spada, *Copia privata ed opera sotto chiave* ['Private Copies and Locked Down Works'], 2002(1) *Rivista Di Diritto Industriale* 591, 597–598 (stating that the system of technological protection measures provided authors by the EC Directive must acknowledge the exceptions to authors' rights, including privileged uses, because 'these are an integral part of the authors' rights system and not merely contingencies of contract or the owners' brute force') (trans. JHR).

319 Even within the traditional copyright system, exceptions are quite different from one country to the next. How each country might want to approach the digital environment is unlikely to be more uniform.

320 For example, Professor Spada believes that the Directive entitles privileged users disadvantaged by TPMs to assert their rights under the Directive in national courts. See Spada, *supra* n. 318, at 598.

321 Compliance with EU law is an obligation not only of all European Union member states, but also of member states of the European Free Trade Area (EFTA), as well as a number of countries pursuing future European Union membership or entering into bilateral trade agreements with the European Union. See Maximiliano Santa Cruz (2007), 'Intellectual Property Provisions in European Union Trade Agreements: Implications for Developing Countries', *Int'l Centre for Trade and Sustainable Development* 2–3. In the past, the bilateral trade agreements negotiated by the EU have contained obligations with respect to intellectual property stated at a very general level, such as compliance with the WIPO Copyright Treaty. See id. at 10. In contrast, the United States has in its bilateral trade agreements sought to secure compliance with more detailed standards that resemble the language of the DMCA rather than the terms of the WCT. See Chander, *supra* n. 18, at 206. However, some observers have detected a shift in the EU approach toward the more aggressive US approach in more recent negotiations. See Santa Cruz, *supra*, at ix–x, 18.

if certain limits apparently embodied in Art. 6(4) turn out to circumscribe its actual scope in EU member states,[322] member state implementation of a narrower provision (for example, with respect only to certain exceptions) might still afford insights as to how the basic structure of the proposed reverse notice and takedown procedure could be enhanced to better ensure that anti-circumvention provisions are consistent with privileged uses.

Moreover, such an exercise might also highlight the ways in which Art. 6(4) could itself be broadened as EU legislators consider a revision of the Directive in light of the recent report by the Institute for Information Law at the University of Amsterdam.[323]

Application of Reverse Notice and Takedown under Article 6(4)

Under Art. 6(4), right holders are required to ensure that beneficiaries of exceptions have the ability to exercise those exceptions notwithstanding the application of technological protection measures to copyrighted works.[324] If right holders do not voluntarily ensure that result, member states are obliged to devise a mechanism to compel it.[325]

Member states have implemented this obligation in a number of different ways.[326] Each of the different forms of implementation offers a model for preserving privileged uses; yet, most are deficient and would benefit from a reverse notice and takedown procedure.[327]

Triggering an entitlement to relief

The reverse notice and takedown procedure would be available to any particular user who wished to engage in a privileged use with respect to even a single work. Thus, the threshold would be substantially lower than the 'adverse effect on classes of work' standard found in the rulemaking authorization contained in the DMCA, even as refined under the 2006 rule-

322 See *supra* text accompanying nn. 311–314.

323 See Copyright Directive Implementation Study, *supra* n. 11, at 132–33 (criticizing limits of Art. 6(4)).

324 See Copyright Directive, *supra* n. 10, Art. 6(4).

325 See id.

326 See generally Westkamp, *supra* n. 296; see also Copyright Directive Implementation Study, *supra* n. 11, at 132 ('In some member states, only individual beneficiaries may claim the application of the limitation, while in other countries, interest groups and third parties also have the right to do so. In yet other member states, administrative bodies may be entitled to force right holders to make the necessary means available to beneficiaries of limitations.').

327 Of course, much of the blame can be laid at the door of the Directive itself. See Copyright Directive Implementation Study, *supra* n. 11, at 132–33.

making.[328] But this more generous approach is fully consistent with Art. 6(4), which would appear to allow analysis of particular uses of particular works by particular users.[329]

One could argue that the unavailability of a single work to be put to a single use might be deemed insufficiently substantial a cost to justify the mechanisms contemplated by Art. 6(4). But this calculus depends in part upon the nature of the mechanism and upon what is contemplated by the member state as an 'appropriate measure' in response to any given inability to exercise an exception granted by copyright law. If the procedure were speedy, and if 'appropriate measure' meant one that permits a single circumvention, then there would be virtually no real cost to a state acting on the basis of a lower trigger threshold.[330]

Because the reverse notice and takedown procedure contemplates the possibility of relief in the form of a limited exemption for a particular user, it would seem perfectly appropriate that the obligation of member states should arise more easily than if broader relief were sought. As the recent refinement by the Librarian of Congress of the notion of 'classes of works' reflects,[331] the sub-categories of privileged uses that emerge from a matrix of affected works, from groups of users, and from a range of uses, are substantial and disparate. Not only must different forms of relief be available, but also different levels of need to actuate permitted uses should trigger such relief.

The fact that relief under the reverse notice and takedown procedure might be appropriate even with respect to a single use of a single work should not preclude the possibility of using the procedure where technological protection measures are having a more pervasive effect. Arguably, the relief available under any state-imposed mechanism should reflect the degree and type of harm caused by the application of technological protection measures. Thus, member states may need to create more intrusive or structural relief for third-party users or competitors if lawful uses of entire classes of works are being impeded.[332]

While this type of analysis parallels that conducted by the Register of Copyrights in the triennial rulemaking to some extent, the reverse notice and

---

328 See Exemption to Prohibition on Circumvention of Copyright Protection Systems for Access Control Technologies, 71 Fed. Reg. 68472 (27 November 2006) (to be codified at 37 C.F.R. §201) [hereinafter 2006 Rulemaking], at 6–7.

329 See Copyright Directive, Art. 6(4) (incorporating by reference exceptions in Art. 5 that involve particular uses for particular purposes including, for example, copying for the purpose of scientific research).

330 See Symposium, 'The Law & Technology of Digital Rights Management', 18 *Berkeley Tech. L.J.* 697, 760, 765 (2003) (remarks of Graeme B. Dinwoodie on Anticircumvention Regulations in the United States and Elsewhere).

331 See 2006 Rulemaking, *supra* n. 328.

332 See Symposium, *supra* n. 330, at 765–66 (remarks of Dinwoodie).

takedown procedure might remedy some of the deficiencies of that procedure. In particular, despite refinement in the 2006 rulemaking of the notion of adverse classes, the Register remains limited in the relief that she can offer, namely, the grant of a temporary exemption to a specified category of works from the application of s. 1201.[333] And that relief does not immunize third parties who, through the distribution of devices, assist in ensuring that privileged uses are made. Moreover, the process occurs only every three years.[334]

Implementation of Art. 6(4) in the UK includes the possibility that the complaint of obstruction to the exercise of privileged uses can be made on behalf of a class of users.[335] This type of claim should be a component of the reverse notice and takedown procedure. It would provide a useful, more flexible, and more dynamic complement to the rulemaking procedure.[336]

Encouraging the proper role for voluntary arrangements

We believe that the reverse notice and takedown proposal should be available to users and competitors even if copyright owners voluntarily make works available by overriding TPMs to some extent. In this respect, the proposal might appear to depart from the strict text of the EU Directive. Under the Directive, the obligation upon member states arises 'in the absence of voluntary measures taken by right holders, including agreements between right holders and other parties concerned.'[337] However, even though the provision contemplates some room for right holders to forestall legal intervention through voluntary arrangements such as contract, this freedom cannot be

---

333 See *supra* text accompanying n. 137.

334 See *supra* text accompanying n. 136.

335 See Copyright and Related Rights Regulations, 2003, SI 2003/2498, Art. 24, § 296ZE(2) (UK), available at http://www.opsi.gov.uk/si/si2003/20032498.htm ('person being a representative of a class of persons prevented from carrying out a permitted act'); see also Unterlassungsklagengesetz [UklaG, Injunctions Act], 27 August 2002, BGBl. I at 3422, as amended by Urheberrechtsgesetz [Copyright Act], 10 September 2003, BGBl. I at 1774, Art. 3, § 3a (FRG).

336 If the request could not be made on behalf of a class of users, there might arise the problem whether similarly situated third parties could rely on responses of copyright owners to a request from a user under the reverse notice and takedown procedure. To the extent that the request invokes a 'purpose exception', it is unlikely that copyright owners would make distinctions between users and thus as a practical matter similarly situated third parties could rely on relief granted by copyright owners. To the extent that copyright owners did make distinctions for improper reasons, occasion may arise to invoke Dan Burk's proposed anti-circumvention misuse doctrine. See Burk, *supra* n. 135. With respect to 'identity' exceptions, persons falling within the group of beneficiaries entitled to exercise the exception should be able to take advantage (that is, treat as 'precedential') relief granted to others possessing the same identity.

337 Copyright Directive, *supra* n. 10, Art. 6(4).

unlimited without rendering Art. 6(4) meaningless.[338] In any event, we do not believe that right holders have, in fact, undertaken such voluntary measures thus far, which is why a reverse notice and takedown regime is sorely needed.

The very availability of the reverse notice and takedown procedure may, in fact, facilitate licensing on reasonable terms and conditions and induce other voluntary measures to ensure that exceptions can be exercised; voluntary measures that adequately preserved the ability to exercise those exceptions would obviate the need for member states to take further action against right holders. Whether acting in advance of the threat of later sanctions (under the general language of Art. 6(4)), or under contemporaneous threat (in the case of the reverse notice and takedown procedure implementing that provision), the shadow of legal compulsion might foster private ordering that is more balanced in nature.[339]

The only type of 'voluntary measure' expressly referenced in Art. 6(4) is 'agreements between right holders and other parties concerned'.[340] However, reaching consensus among the vast range of interests now implicated by copyright law may be quite difficult. The process of legislating copyright law, which often approximates a contractual negotiation, has become tortuous and slow. It is unlikely that agreements between copyright owners and users over taking down TPMs will be easy to achieve.

Because many exceptions depend on the type of use, rather than the category of user (i.e., purpose exceptions, not identity exceptions), it may not suffice merely to identify the relevant beneficiaries with whom to negotiate. If the obvious categories of users are singled out as beneficiaries, focusing on identity exceptions, it will privilege traditional 'fair use communities,'[341] which may constrain important sources of creativity. Consensus among collectives often ignores the needs of single users or users within very loosely organized communities, and the reverse notice and takedown proposal will accommodate these potentially important creators.

Agreements are not the only form of voluntary measure through which right holders might forestall the intervention of member states. For example, right holders might apply TPMs in ways that permit privileged uses. Although this outcome might seem ideal in theory, such an approach carries with it technological limitations. Implementing such fact-specific exceptions as the fair

---

[338] See Rieber-Mohn, *supra* n. 299, at 188 (arguing that voluntary measures by right holders must be 'appropriate' in order to avoid member state intervention and must occur within a reasonable period of time).

[339] Some private ordering has clearly occurred in the shadow of Art. 6(4). See Copyright Directive Implementation Study, *supra* n. 11, at 107.

[340] See id.

[341] See also Ginsburg, *supra* n. 14.

use doctrine or other privileged uses in computer code will prove immensely difficult.[342] Thus, this cannot be the sole mechanism through which to ensure privileged uses.

Moreover, such arrangements raise broader normative concerns. Relying on copyright owners accurately to map technology to legal rules delegates immense power to those owners both in the interpretation of the default rules and in assessing the adequacy of the technology used to guarantee permitted uses.[343] Even if the copyright owners accurately interpreted and implemented existing permitted uses, technological features would remain inherently backward-looking.[344] One of the advantages claimed for the fair use doctrine is its capacity to adapt efficiently to reflect new technological conditions.[345]

The European Commission viewed legislative intervention as a background threat to provide incentives for voluntary arrangements with copyright owners. Even so, the reverse notice and takedown approach – immediately guaranteeing the right to demand the exercise of privileged uses, regardless of voluntary arrangements – may be preferable. The desired end is the same:

---

[342] See Nic Garnett, 'Automated Rights Management Systems and Copyright Limitations and Exceptions', WIPO Doc. No. SCCR/14/5 (27 April 2006), available at http://www.wipo.int/edocs/mdocs/sccr/en/sccr_14/sccr_14_5.doc.

[343] See Eduardo M. Penalver and Sonia Katyal, *Property Outlaws* (Fordham Law Legal Studies Research Paper No. 90, April 2007), available at http://ssrn.com/-abstract=745324 (discussing 'anti-delegation' architecture of copyright law). To the extent that we wish to rely on the incorporation of privileged uses in the architecture of the technological protection measures, it might be important to enlist the support of unfair competition or consumer protection law in requiring the disclosure by copyright owners of the precise nature and extent of technological protection measures. This objective has been secured in a number of European countries, in part through DRM-specific legislation (e.g., Germany), Urheberrechtsgesetz [Copyright Act], 12 September 2003, BGBl. I at 1774, Art. 1, § 95(d) (F.R.G.), and in part through litigation under general principles of consumer protection (e.g., in France). See Association CLCV / EMI Music France, Tribunal de grande instance [TGI] [ordinary court of original jurisdiction] Nanterre, 6e ch., 24 June 2003 (Fr.), *available at* http://www.legalis.net/jurisprudence-decision.php3?-id_article=34 (fining Sony for failing to disclose TPM). As a result, market forces may play a greater role in ensuring that copyright owners do not abuse the application of technological protection measures in the first place. See also Nika Aldrich, *A System of Logo-Based Disclosure of DRM on Download Products* (29 April 2007), available at http://www.ssrn.com/ abstract=983551.

[344] Of course, the same may be true of agreements reached between copyright owners and users. Thus, any voluntary agreement that is concluded ideally should go beyond the articulation of present substantive rules and contemplate procedural or institutional components that facilitate attention to the spontaneity and dynamism of the ways in which users might wish to engage with copyrighted works.

[345] See H.R. Rep. No. 94-1476, at 66 (1976); see also Pamela Samuelson (1993), 'Fair Use For Computer Programs and Other Copyrightable Works in Digital Form: The Implications of Sony, Galoob and Sega', 1 *J. Intell. Prop. L.* 49.

encouraging private parties to make arrangements that allow valuable and privileged uses.

Ensuring an Effective Ability to Engage in Privileged Uses

One of the principal points of contention in implementing the WCT has been whether national legislation should prohibit both acts of circumvention and devices designed to facilitate circumvention. Creating exceptions to a prohibition on circumventing technological protection measures may be effectively meaningless if third parties with the technological capacity to engage in circumvention are not able to provide privileged users with circumvention tools.

Article 6(4) requires member states to ensure that right holders make available to the beneficiary of an exception or limitation the means of benefiting from that exception or limitation. This may impose a more affirmative obligation on member states to ensure that circumvention tools are available to some degree. Certainly, the forms of relief contemplated by Commission officials under the provision include quite affirmative steps, such as the distribution of the 'unlocking keys' necessary to circumvent the technological protection measures.[346]

If the reverse notice and takedown procedure is to ensure the possibility of privileged uses notwithstanding the application of TPMs, the procedure might offer standing to providers of circumvention tools. Alternatively, third-party service providers might be afforded the right to take advantage of the relief secured by individual users under the procedure. Earlier in this chapter, we thus suggested that courts 'allow those providing needed decryption skills and technologies to benefit from the same privileged use exception that a *demandeur* had ultimately vindicated either in court or by silent acquiescence of the copyright owner.'[347]

Copyright law does not typically permit a third party to defend the legality of their activities on the basis that it is facilitating the exercise of privileged uses by another party (outside the context of secondary liability).[348] Yet,

---

346 See Dusollier, *Fair Use by Design*, Nora Braun (2003), 'The Interface Between the Protection of Technological Protection Measures and the Exercise of Exceptions to Copyright and Related Rights: Comparing the Situation in the United States and the European Community', 25 *Eur. Intell. Prop. Rev.* 496, 502.

347 See *supra* text accompanying n. 275.

348 See *Princeton Univ. Press v Mich. Document Serv.*, 99 F.3d 1381, 1391 (6th Cir. 1996), cert. denied, 520 US 1156 (1997) (quoting William Patry, *Fair Use in Copyright Law* 420 n. 34 (1996)) (arguing that 'the courts have . . . properly rejected attempts by for-profit users to stand in the shoes of their customers making nonprofit or noncommercial uses'). The historical weakness of prohibiting commercially

absent the involvement of such third parties, the rights secured by the reverse notice and takedown procedure may effectively become worthless.[349] In this context, the proposal thus derogates from parallelism with traditional copyright law, but it does so because the technological realities are different. A commercial copy shop might have improved the efficiency of professors producing course packs or students making personal copies, but the copying could have occurred without their help.[350] The same is not true of technological circumvention (otherwise there really would be some doubt about whether the measures were 'effective').

Developing appropriate forms of relief

Of course, one can avoid this debate entirely, at least within the structure of Art. 6(4), by noting that this question is closely tied to the question of relief. To the extent that the relief provided is more structural in nature, such as requiring the modification of the TPMs or the distribution of the work in unprotected format, procedural devices such as expanded standing or third-party beneficiary rules would be unnecessary. Such 'structural' relief does appear consistent with the type of approach contemplated by Commission officials under Art. 6(4), when they suggested that the relief might include the 'distribution of unlocking keys.'[351]

---

oriented third parties from claiming third-party beneficiary status with respect to the assertion of privileged uses forced the British House of Lords, in a leading case involving control of the spare parts market, to adapt a doctrine based in property law that imposed restrictions on the initial seller of the property, rather than find a right personal to the user of the property. Thus, in *British Leyland Motor Co. v Armstrong Patents* [1986] 1 All ER 850 (HL) (UK), the Court held that the owner of copyright in the drawings of an exhaust pipe of a car could not enforce that copyright so as to prevent the sale of unauthorized spare parts because to do so would derogate from the grant of the property right in the car.

This doctrine, though short-lived in UK copyright law because statutory revisions quickly addressed the specific problem of spare parts and rights in the designs of useful articles, highlights the importance of limiting the rights of the right holder rather than conferring personal rights only on individual users. *Cf. Canon Kabushiki Kaisha v Green Cartridge Co.*, [1997] AC 728 (PC) (appeal taken from HK) (per curiam opinion by Lord Hoffman); *Mars UK v Tecknowledge Ltd* [2000] FSR 138 (Ch.) (UK) (opinion of Jacob LJ) (noting effect of demise of the *British Leyland* principle under UK law).

349 See Copyright Directive Implementation Study, *supra* n. 11, at 133.

350 See *Princeton Univ. Press v Mich. Document Serv.*, 99 F.3d 1381 (6th Cir. 1996), cert. denied, 520 US 1156 (1997).

351 See Jorge Reinbothe, 'The Legal Framework for Digital Rights Management', Digital Rights Management Workshop, Brussels, 28 February 2002, at 2, available at http://ec.europa.eu/information_society/eeurope/2005/all_about/digital_rights_man/doc/workshop2002/drm_workshop_brx_rev.doc.

Focusing on the nature of relief available under the reverse notice and takedown procedure might be a cleaner approach than innovating with procedural devices. At p. 255, we suggested that copyright owners receiving the reverse notice and takedown request would either have the responsibility to take down the TPMs that impeded privileged uses or the obligation to contest the use on legally actionable grounds.[352] Compliance with such a request would, of course, effectively grant structural relief, albeit without judicial or administrative intervention. A failure to comply with the reverse notice and takedown request could then provide a user group with standing to seek the right to circumvent for the purposes of specified non-infringing uses.

If the user group was successful, the ability of similarly situated third parties to take advantage of the court's decision would depend upon the nature of the relief granted. In countries that recognize the doctrine of collateral estoppel, third parties could clearly rely on the court's determination as to whether the use in question was privileged. However, spreading the full benefits of the court's ruling might depend upon whether the court simply permitted the requesting party to circumvent, permitted the user group to employ a provider of circumvention services to unlock the TPM, or ordered the copyright owner to modify the TPM.[353]

The significance of the nature of the relief granted in this regard becomes clearer when one examines the deficiencies in one member state's implementation of Art. 6(4). Under the provisions implementing Art. 6(4) in the UK, users who are unable to engage in a privileged use due to the application of TPMs may petition the Secretary of State.[354] The Secretary of State can require the copyright owner to demonstrate a 'voluntary measure or agreement' or face 'directions' that enable the relevant beneficiary to take advantage of the copyright exemption.[355] If the copyright owner fails to follow those directions, it will be found in breach of a duty actionable by the user that complained.[356]

This procedure suffers from several deficiencies. In particular, it requires an application to the Secretary of State every time a user believes its right to engage in a privileged use is being impeded.[357] The reverse notice and take-

---

352 See *supra* 'The basic concept' at p. 274.

353 It might also depend upon any conditions that the court placed on the exercise of the rights granted to the user. See *supra* text accompanying nn. 266–267.

354 Copyright and Related Rights Regulations, 2003, SI 2003/2498, Art. 24, §§ 296ZD(2), 296(2) (UK).

355 See id. at § 296ZE(3).

356 See id. at § 296ZE(6).

357 Other national laws employ different institutions to determine the claims of the users. For example, under Greek law, the matter is referred to mediators and, absent consent to the mediators' conclusion, to the Court of Appeal. But these institutions are

down procedure may also suffer from a similar problem if applications must be made on a case-by-case approach and the relief contemplated simply authorizes a particular user to circumvent a particular technological protection measure and no more. However, this direct approach should prove much simpler than a formal referral to an administrative body, and practice under the proposal – as supplemented by judicial decisions, when necessary – should facilitate reliance on the mechanism over time, especially in common law jurisdictions.

If the 'directions' from the Secretary of State required the copyright owner to modify the TPM, as a Recital of the Directive hints, one form of 'appropriate measure' might be one that would have an across-the-board effect.[358] If the relief that a user could request under the reverse notice and takedown procedure could likewise take this form, a similar *erga omnes* effect could be achieved.[359]

The possibility of structural relief is important in ameliorating another weakness of the UK procedure (which might also, to some extent, be levelled at the reverse notice and takedown proposal). Requiring application by the beneficiary of the exemption fails to give adequate weight to those instances where creative acts covered by a privileged use are spontaneous in nature.[360] Copyright exemptions traditionally operated on the premise that the

still assessing whether a technological protection measure is impeding any particular privileged use, not whether an act of circumvention (or a device) will ex post be excused from liability because of that fact. See Law 3057/2002 (Official Gazette A/239/10 October 2002), Art. 81, Implementation of the Directive 2001/29/EC of the European Parliament and of the Council of 22 May 2001 on the Harmonization of Certain Aspects of Copyright and Related Rights in the Information Society and Other Provisions, available at http://portal.unesco.org/culture/en/file_download.php/3368a2bd0fffab9a5310a8e00abfb926Greek_law+.pdf (Greece). See generally Copyright Directive Implementation Study, *supra* n. 11, at 67–68 (summarizing institutional choices made).

[358] See Copyright Directive, recital 51 (providing example of 'modifying an implemented technological measure').

[359] The recital expressly mentions 'other means' of ensuring the ability to engage in privileged uses. One of the responsible Commission officials suggested at the time the Directive was adopted that these means might include 'handing out locking keys'. See Reinbothe, *supra* n. 351, at 2. Certainly, the language of 'right holders making available to the beneficiary' seems to suggest affirmative conduct, beyond merely enacting an exemption to allow the beneficiary to engage in an act of circumvention (though that would also be a possible measure).

[360] Requiring an application to a government official in order to engage in creative activity also devalues the importance of privacy or anonymity as an aspect of the creative environment. See *supra* n. 290 (admitting this defect). In the notice and takedown procedure established by s. 512, the copyrighted works at issue are created prior to the joining of dispute. Thus, the procedure does not interfere with the spontaneity of creative acts, or the potential importance of anonymity in the creative process.

user would engage in the contested act and the legitimacy of that act would later be determined by application of the allegedly relevant exemption, a practice whose risks might also inhibit actual resort to spontaneous uses. The departure from this traditional assumption is in part simply a product of the application of TPMs, which of themselves establish an inverted default of 'ask first, act later'. Nevertheless, requiring individualized applications in order to engage in privileged uses does not help.

Here again, if structural relief could be requested by a user seeking to engage in privileged uses, the costs of such a procedure and the repressive effect of having to seek permission would more often become a one-time occurrence. This supports the suggestion above that the reverse notice and takedown procedure should permit the *demandeur* to seek broader relief than merely obtaining immunity to circumvent.

While such structural relief as requiring the modification or elimination of technological protection measures may, at first blush, seem quite radical, it is fully consistent with Art. 6(4), which contemplates that copyright owners have an affirmative role to play in ensuring the preservation of the balance of rights between owners and users of works.[361] To be sure, the relief that would be secured through the mechanisms implementing Art. 6(4) is not detailed in the Directive, and some commentators have argued that it cannot require the copyright owner to reveal the digital lock.[362] But a per se rule foreclosing such relief is inconsistent with the open-ended nature of the Directive, and indeed with statements by Commission officials after its adoption.[363]

Whether such relief could undermine the efforts of copyright owners to protect against even infringing uses[364] would depend upon the terms under which such disclosure was made. For example, if a handover of the digital lock were conditioned on the manner in which the information was used or disclosed, it might enable the privileged uses without undermining the copyright owner's legitimate rights to protect against infringement. This possibil-

---

361 See Copyright Directive Implementation Study, *supra* n. 11, at 68–69 (noting affirmative nature of obligations).

362 See Braun, *supra* n. 346, at 502 (arguing that 'handing over the 'key' to circumvent the technological measure to users is inappropriate and would endanger the whole system of technological measures').

363 See Reinbothe, *supra* n. 351, at 2; Bently and Sherman, *supra* n. 299, at 311.

364 Some might argue that our entire proposal will cause more infringement. But every time you legitimate any dual-use technology, there is a risk of infringement. On the other hand, if you lock up all works in technological fences, there is a risk of fewer public interest uses. For the reasons explained in 'Checks and balances in the ISP safe harbours and anti-circumvention rules' at p. 234, we think that the balance between these two risks needs to be better calibrated, and can be done so without jeopardizing the ability to enforce copyrights effectively against bad actors.

ity should make the reverse notice and takedown procedure attractive to industry. To the extent that the information is disclosed to third parties who will facilitate the privileged use by a particular *demandeur*, the provision of circumvention services as opposed to the manufacture of devices is less likely to implicate the copyright owners' nightmare scenario.

Likewise, under the original Australian implementation of the WCT, the statute allowed circumvention devices to be supplied to a beneficiary of an exception for a permitted use if the person making the privileged use provided the supplier with a signed declaration to that effect.[365] In any event, allowing a circumvention service provider to assist a particular user should be less problematic.[366]

No predetermined single form of relief should be established. One size will likely not fit all, given the wide range of uses that should be privileged. Yet, there may be circumstances when, under defined conditions, even the disclosure of the digital lock might be appropriate. One of the benefits of the fair use doctrine has been its flexibility and its ability to adapt to changing circumstances. The capacity of technology to effectuate a balance of rights, and what that balance should be, may well be very different in five years time. Bodies established under Article 6(4) in the European Union, and courts in the United States under a reverse notice and takedown procedure, should remain free to develop appropriate means to ensure the continued ability to engage in privileged uses.

Broader Perspectives and the Role of the Commission

The reverse notice and takedown procedure is precisely the type of conceptual approach that is mandated, albeit in a narrow form, by Art. 6(4). A member state could implement the reverse notice and takedown procedure as a means of fulfilling the obligations imposed by Art. 6(4). As a result of the Directive's inadequate harmonization of exceptions and the opaque language of Art. 6(4) itself, it is unclear how many privileged uses are protected by Art. 6(4).[367] Some countries have implemented Art. 6(4) without clear reference to specific

---

365 See Jeffrey Cunard et al., WIPO Standing Comm. on Copyright and Related Rights, 'Current Developments in the Field of Digital Rights Management', WIPO Doc. No. SCCR/10/2 (1 August 2003), available at http://www.wipo.int/documents/en/meetings/2003/sccr/pdf/sccr_10_2.pdf.

366 See Ginsburg, *supra* n. 11, at 17.

367 See Copyright Directive Implementation Study, *supra* n. 11, at 169 (suggesting revision of Art. 6(4) to 'give protected status to those limitations that . . . reflect the fundamental rights and freedoms enshrined in the European Convention on Human Rights, [and] those that have a noticeable impact on the Internal Market or concern the rights of European consumers').

limitations; others have explicitly singled out specific limitations as preserved by Art. 6(4) despite the application of TPMs.

The most that can be said with any confidence is that implementation in member states has been inconsistent.[368] But, even absent any further harmonization of different national choices, each member state could adopt the reverse notice and takedown procedure as a mechanism to preserve the precise range of privileged uses that the member state reads as permitted by the Directive.[369]

Even if the Commission might not look favourably on any effort to expand the general norm of Art. 6(4) beyond the narrow context in which the Directive currently requires it, this would not preclude other countries from introducing a reverse notice and takedown procedure. To the extent that the US or the EU might seek to repress such efforts through bilateral trade negotiations, Art. 6(4) shows that acting within the regime of DRM to protect uses privileged by traditional copyright law is fully consistent with the WCT. If the EU can limit copyright owners' control as to some undefined exceptions, why could another country not do so with respect to all exceptions traditionally protected by copyright law and consistent with international copyright obligations?

Moreover, even within the EU, the Commission's recently solicited review of the copyright *acquis* might provide an opening for some reform of existing law, including the expansion of the general principle contained in Art. 6(4). The reverse notice and takedown procedure discussed in this Article should be given serious attention during the Commission's review. At least, a Policy Statement from the Commission acknowledging the ability of member states to build upon the underlying norm of Art. 6(4), even beyond a strict reading of the text, might provide room for important procedural innovations in ways that truly effectuate the values not only of the Directive but of the WCT that it claims to implement.

CONCLUSION

By the end of the multilateral negotiations held at Geneva in 1996, the intense struggle among stakeholders representing content providers, the telecommu-

[368] See Marcella Favale, 'Technological Protection Measures and Copyright Exceptions in EU27: Towards the Harmonization', at 10 August 2007, http://www.law.-depaul.edu/institutes_centers/ciplit/ipsc/paper/Marcella_Favale Paper.pdf, at 22 (draft paper presented at Intellectual Property Scholars Conference) ('Every country that decided to single out only some exceptions, picked from the list a different selection from that [in Art. 6(4)] of the Directive, and from that of the other countries.').

[369] See *supra* n. 319 and accompanying text (making this point).

nications industry, online service providers, and the educational and scientific communities produced a workable compromise in the WCT. The importance of preserving access to the copyrighted culture protected in cyberspace under the new Treaty was expressly recognized in at least three important places:

(1) The broad preambular recognition of 'the need to maintain a balance between the rights of authors and the larger public interest, particularly education, research and access to information;'[370]
(2) The further express recognition, in Article 11, that the international standard for reinforcing TPMs was not meant to entitle authors to 'restrict acts, in respect of their works, which are . . . permitted by law;'[371]
(3 And the express understanding in the Agreed Statement concerning Article 10, which permitted contracting parties 'to carry forward and appropriately extend into the digital environment' existing limitations and exceptions in their national laws and 'to devise new exceptions and limitations that are appropriate to the digital network environment'.[372]

This historic compromise made it possible to establish a balanced legal infrastructure for worldwide networked communications of copyrighted works in the digital environment.

Unfortunately, at the national implementation phase, the balance struck at Geneva gave way, in the US, to the one-sided provisions of the DMCA and, in the EU to the only slightly less unbalanced approach of the EU Directive. While the DMCA formally acknowledged the need to preserve privileged uses in s. 1201(c), ss. 1201(a) and (b) have arguably separated access from privileged use and made it difficult, and under some interpretations impossible, to raise questions of privileged use once TPMs control access to copyrighted works. The EU Copyright Directive took an equally tough approach to restricting access through TPMs. Although the Directive generally invoked a need to respect exceptions and limitations in local law, it simultaneously limited the scope of the provision enabling such privileged uses.

The end result on both sides of the Atlantic has been the emergence of a distorted, unbalanced copyright regime in cyberspace with a growing chorus of complaints from educational, scientific, and other public interest users, among others, and a growing revolt against the legal restraints on legitimate uses of the copyrighted culture in some quarters. The abusive possibilities inherent in the DMCA's access control provisions became dramatically visible in the recent lock-out cases, where TPMs were used to perpetuate the kind of

370 WCT, *supra* n. 1, Preamble.
371 Id., Art. 11.
372 Agreed Statements, *supra* n. 2, statement concerning Art. 10.

'fraud on the patent law' that the Supreme Court had struck down in its 1880 decision in *Baker v Selden*.[373]

Moreover, these extreme distortions of basic copyright principles mask the much greater daily pressures that the DMCA puts upon the public interest user community, which depends upon easy and continuous access to ideas, facts and other inputs to knowledge that copyright laws have never been allowed to protect. Unless these distortions are remedied, a copyright system that was designed to promote progress by expanding the outputs of literary and artistic works could end by choking off access to essential inputs to the production of knowledge as a global public good in the digital environment.

Our proposal for a reverse notice and takedown procedure – designed to reduce the tensions between access protection measures and privileged uses – attempts to rebalance the copyright equation in cyberspace before the damaging effects of overprotection give rise to systematic failure or breakdown. Among its many advantages in the US is the fact that it can be judicially developed and applied on a case-by-case basis, with low transaction costs and relatively few risks to either side. It allows bona fide public interest users to continue their work without undue interference from TPMs and with the support of the content-providing industries themselves, who may verify the legitimate uses being enabled and contest uses that seem to stretch the boundaries of legally defined privilege. It builds on workable procedures that have already proved their usefulness in the context of ISP liability, while enabling pinpoint litigation on borderline issues that all sides will want clarified. There is good reason to believe that industry itself might prefer a gradualist mechanism of this kind to more intrusive legislative measures with unknown future consequences.

If judicial experimentation with a reverse notice and takedown procedure proved unsuccessful for reasons we cannot foresee, it could be judicially abandoned as easily as it had been adopted. If, instead, it proved effective, the end results could eventually be codified both in the US and abroad on the basis of the experience gained in the meantime. In that event, our proposal would have helped copyright law to regain its traditional balance in the digital environment while implementing the true spirit of the historic compromise originally embodied in the WIPO Copyright Treaty of 1996.

---

[373] 101 US 99 (1880).

Index